Realism's Empire

Realism's Empire

Empiricism and Enchantment in the
Nineteenth-Century Novel

Geoffrey Baker

The Ohio State University Press
Columbus

Copyright © 2009 by The Ohio State University.
All rights reserved.

Library of Congress Cataloging-in-Publication Data
Baker, Geoffrey, 1973–
    Realism's empire : empiricism and enchantment in the nineteenth-century novel / Geoffrey Baker.
       p. cm.
    Includes bibliographical references and index.
    ISBN-13: 978-0-8142-1098-7 (cloth : alk. paper)
    ISBN-10: 0-8142-1098-8 (cloth : alk. paper)
    ISBN-13: 978-0-8142-9196-2 (cd-rom)
    1. Realism in literature. 2. English literature—19th century—History and criticism. 3. French literature—19th century—History and criticism. 4. German literature—19th century—History and criticism. 5. Balzac, Honoré de, 1799–1850—Criticism and interpretation. 6. Trollope, Anthony, 1815–1882—Criticism and interpretation. 7. Fontane, Theodor, 1819–1898—Criticism and interpretation. I. Title.
    PN3340.B35 2009
    809'.912—dc22
                            2009007632

This book is available in the following editions:
Cloth (ISBN 978-0-8142-1098-7)
CD-ROM (ISBN 978-0-8142-9196-2)
Paper (ISBN: 978-0-8142-5610-7)
Cover design by Laurence Nozik.
Type set in ITC Century.

CONTENTS

Preface and Acknowledgments   vii

INTRODUCTION
Empire and Remapping Realism

(a) Space, Form, Content: The Fate of Distance   1
(b) Imperial Knowledge, Colonial Knowledge: The Fate of Difference   9
(c) The Problem with Progress: The Fate of Fiction   13
(d) Précis of Chapters   20

PART I.
Balzac and the Problem of Empiricism

CHAPTER 1. Empiricism and Empire: *La Peau de chagrin*   27
(a) The Orientalist Paradox and the Object(s) of Empire   29
(b) Seeing as Knowing: Realism and the Matter of Disenchantment   36

Chapter 2. Marginal Realism in *Le Père Goriot*   47
(a) The World Without: The Mandarin and the Subject(s) of Empire   48
(b) The World Below: Vautrin on Being Seen and Known   53
(c) "À nous deux!": An Ethics of Disenchantment   60

Chapter 3. Realism, Romance, and *La Fille aux yeux d'or*   65
(a) The World in Paris: Paquita Valdès and the Ubiquity of the Foreign   66
(b) Unmapping Paris: The Space of Enchantment   70
(c) On Seeing and Not Seeing: A Sense of Disenchantment   78

PART II.
Trollope and the Problem of Integration

Chapter 4. Economies of Romance and History in *Phineas Finn* — 87
(a) "The Colonies Next Door": Irishness as a Realist Fact — 89
(b) The *Bildung* of Phineas Finn: Irishness as a Realist Problem — 94
(c) Unrealist History: On Pretending Not to Know — 101

Chapter 5. Mapping and Unmapping *Phineas Finn* and *Phineas Redux* — 109
(a) The Space of Disenchantment — 110
(b) Loughlinter, London, and the Space of Reenchantment — 117
(c) On Not Knowing: Detection, Empiricism, and the Verdict on the Evidence — 124

Chapter 6. Global London and *The Way We Live Now* — 131
(a) Business as Unusual: Foreignness, Crime, Commerce — 132
(b) "Metropolitan Danger": Melmotte and the (Other) Americans — 136
(c) Unrealist City: The New Mobility and the Way We Lived Then — 143

PART III.
Fontane and the Problem of Familiarity

Chapter 7. "Berlin wird Weltstadt": Nation, City, and World in *Cécile* — 155
(a) Nation and World in Fontane's Early Fiction — 157
(b) Region, Romance, and the Rails — 163
(c) Business as Usual: Berlin and the Banality of the Foreign — 167

Chapter 8. The Imaginative Geography of *Effi Briest* — 175
(a) Unreal Realism: Imperial Knowledge and Space — 177
(b) Secularization and the Place of Enchantment — 182
(c) Dueling Epistemologies and the Chinese Ghost — 188
(d) Effi's End: Disenchanting Enchantment — 193

Conclusion: The Limits of "Realism" — 205
(a) Realism and Romance, Reconsidered — 205
(b) Epilogue — 209

Works Cited — 215
Index — 233

PREFACE AND ACKNOWLEDGMENTS

> If one wished to put it drastically, one could say that your study is located at the crossroads of magic and positivism. That spot is bewitched.
> —Theodor Adorno, letter to Walter Benjamin

This book is premised on the observation that pivotal works by some prominent European novelists in the nineteenth century are structured around figures imported from the margins of their world. The new and central positioning of the foreign within the domestic occasions a variety of consequences for the narrative, its construction of space, and its reflection and production of a particular historical moment. Honoré de Balzac's Magic Skin in *La Peau de chagrin* (1831); the Chinese Mandarin of *Le Père Goriot* (1835); the colonial woman of *La Fille aux yeux d'or* (1835); Anthony Trollope's various Irish Members in *Phineas Finn* (1869) and *Phineas Redux* (1874); the provocative foreigners of *The Way We Live Now* (1875); Theodor Fontane's itinerant Scot in *Cécile* (1887); and the Chinese ghost that Fontane called the center of his masterpiece, *Effi Briest* (1895), all originate or represent origins well outside of Balzac's Paris, Trollope's London, and Fontane's Berlin. Once they inhabit the domestic space of these novels, though—a fact which in itself testifies to an important cultural shift and a new mobility—they have profound effects on both space and the novel. This is a study of those effects, their historical contexts, and their possible consequences for our understanding of realism.

A brief examination of the history of foreign incursions into European space in prose fiction and nonfiction must quickly acknowledge that such entries are far from unique to the nineteenth century. In what many allege to be the first western novel,[1] Cervantes's *Don Quijote de la Mancha*

---

1. For just a few contrasting recent views on this, see, for example, Michael McKeon's *The Origins of the English Novel* (273–94), which begins its discussion of novels with the *Quijote*,

(1605/1615), Spain is already posited as a site of Mediterranean mixture; characters from Spain and North Africa come and go freely or against their will in a manner that reflects the close and contentious historical relationship between those regions. What happens in the nineteenth century differs in important ways, however. Even if novels of that period owe some of their most deep-seated narrative strategies and generic allegiances to Cervantes and to the larger history of the genre, the importation of foreign figures in these later works emphasizes the astonishing and new complexity that novelists of the period saw in the world they tried to record. The distinctiveness of such figures in the works of Balzac, Trollope, Fontane, and others can best be understood when placed in the general historical and cultural context of imperialism, especially at the appearance of what has become known as globalization. Recent scholarly attention to and theorizations of imperial space have failed to fully account for its vexed reproduction in the form of prose fiction—substantial disagreements between major critics like Franco Moretti and Edward Said only emphasize this—and the attendant complications are usually glossed over in the history of the novel as a genre. Part of what makes the use of foreign figures in narratives of the nineteenth century so particular is that it corresponds to the onset of an era of literary realism in which writers like Balzac, Trollope, and Fontane all implicated their works. Because understandings of realism are central not just to the authors in question and to their narrative projects but also to some of the most prominent theorists of empire and novelistic space (e.g., Edward Said), it is vital that we reevaluate the relationship between literary realism and the tension between empiricism and enchantment inherent in nineteenth-century understandings of the imperial project. Yet, while commonly accepted ideas of realism can abet the analysis of the novels discussed below, the texts themselves often challenge the most conventional definitions of literary realism as a narrative mode or literary-historical era. In works that explicitly and implicitly debate, perform, or sponsor aims judged by many critics to be "realist" ones, Balzac, Trollope, and Fontane tether the concerns of their narrative form to the historical shifts which their novels witness: the disenchantment of the world through scientific explanation and imperial exploration; the mixture of disparate people and things wrought by the broad pursuits of science and empire; and the construction of the city as a prime site for the portrayal and complication of such mixture. As these shifts all create significant problems

---

slightly revising Ian Watt, who treats Cervantes' novel rather as a "myth" alongside *Faust* and *Don Juan* and views Defoe's *Robinson Crusoe* (1719) as the first of its genre (Watt 85). Margaret Doody, at the other end of the spectrum, begins with what she calls "The Ancient Novel" and traces the genre back to Chariton, Xenophon, Heliodorus, and Petronius, around and just after the beginning of the Common Era (Doody 13–172).

for the very novels depicting them, Balzac, Trollope, and Fontane simultaneously articulate the possibilities and try the limitations of a nascent narrative mode that ultimately pervades the fictions of the nineteenth century.

~

THE COMPLETION of this project would have been impossible without the generous and continuing support, advice, and inspiration of my dissertation committee: William Collins Donahue, Marie Josephine Diamond, Uri Eisenzweig, and Bruce Robbins. Bill Donahue was a true mentor, continually providing invaluable topical expertise, encouragement when needed, and skepticism when required. Josephine Diamond likewise offered her consistent support and expansive knowledge, not just as a reader of my dissertation but a former chair of the Program in Comparative Literature at Rutgers. Other program chairs and acting chairs—Janet Walker, Richard Serrano, and Elin Diamond—made it not just possible but enjoyable to finish this project. In conversations or in classes, my interest in realism and empire was further piqued and encouraged by Richard Duerden, George Levine, John McClure, Judith Ryan, Richard Serrano, Scott Sprenger, James Swenson, Janet Walker, Steven F. Walker, and Tim Watson, who all had a hand in shaping this argument, often without knowing it. Two generous grants from the German Academic Exchange Service (DAAD) were indispensable in improving my German and beginning the research on this project in Berlin, in the spring of 2002, and a Faculty Development Award from the California State University at Chico allowed me the time needed to finish preparing the manuscript in 2008. A very different version of chapter 1 was published in the *Yearbook of Comparative and General Literature*, and portions of other chapters benefited from feedback from audiences and fellow presenters at the American Comparative Literature Association, German Studies Association, the German Department at Duke University, and the Humanities Center at CSU—Chico. I thank my supportive colleagues at CSU—Chico, and, finally, I am grateful to The Ohio State University Press, and especially Sandy Crooms, Eugene O'Connor, and Malcolm Litchfield, for giving my work a home and easing me through the final stages of the process.

This book is dedicated to my family, for their never-ending support; to my fearless and patient teachers in the California public schools, from Gladys Blalock in sixth grade to Doris Lang in twelfth; and to the memory of Douglas Lee Kratz.

INTRODUCTION

EMPIRE AND REMAPPING REALISM

(a) Space, Form, Content: The Fate of Distance

> And now—no emotion, my boy!—there are no great distances nowadays on our little earth.
>
> —Gustav Freytag, *Soll und Haben* (244)

At the close of Montaigne's "Des cannibales," published in his *Essais* in 1581, the New World arrives in the Old one. Three Native Americans, the narrator tells us, "were at Rouen, at the time that King Charles IX was there. The King spoke to them for a long time; they were shown our fashion, our pomp, the style of a proper city. After that, somebody asked them their opinion" (1.263).[1] The natives respond with commonsensical critiques of royalism and social inequality in Europe, bold addenda to the text's earlier denigration of Catholicism and corruption. This ending is marked partly by humor, but it serves more importantly to concretize, as critiques supposedly launched on French soil, the essay's more allusive and trans-Atlantic earlier comparisons of society in Europe and in the Americas. Contrast, with this image of Montaigne's, the remarkable closing pages of Daniel Defoe's novel, *Robinson Crusoe* (1719). Having returned to Europe with the novel's title character, the island native Friday takes center stage in an apparently gratuitous episode which the narrator introduces thus: "Never was a fight managed so hardily, and in such a surprizing manner, as that which followed between Friday and the bear, which gave us all (though at first we were surprized and afraid for

---

1. For all quotations not originally in English, page numbers refer to the original-language editions cited. Where other translations have been consulted, they have usually been substantially modified but are also listed in the works cited.

him) the greatest diversion imaginable" (287). Montaigne's and Defoe's texts are similarly built on the cultural difference between the domestic and the foreign, but they employ this difference to radically incongruous ends: Montaigne to the critique of French culture and its excesses, and Defoe to the "greatest diversion imaginable," an episode that is out of place in both the structure and tone of *Robinson Crusoe*.

The difference here is as important as the parity. Montesquieu, one of Defoe's contemporaries, later meshes the two aims of diversion and critique, using humor derived from radical cultural difference to leaven a broadside at his own society in the *Lettres persanes* (1721), a series of letters offering comical but critical Persian perspectives on France. Tracing the development within the French tradition offers a view of how this device changes over the next century, up to the beginning of Balzac's career as a novelist. As the eighteenth century progresses toward the apex of Enlightenment in form of the *Encyclopédie* (1751–80) a pattern appears to emerge in a slow reduction of humor and a continual amplification of the text's design as social critique. Madame de Graffigny's *Lettres d'une Péruvienne* (1747), modeled on Montesquieu's epistolary work, performs a similar critique while adopting a much more serious tone, as does Voltaire's *L'Ingénu* (1767), one of his least comical shorter prose works. Like Montaigne's essay, *L'Ingénu* brings a Native American to France, but Voltaire's version of this crossing begins to address the difficulties of assimilation, placing equal emphasis on the character of the immigrant and the culture in which that immigrant settles. By the time Claire de Duras writes *Ourika* (1826), in which a Senegalese woman struggles unsuccessfully to find acceptance in a Parisian culture that pretends to cherish ideals of enlightened racial tolerance, the narrative fate of the foreigner in Europe appears essentially tragic. These earlier works rely consistently on an imaginable and preservable distance between the Old World and the New World, a distance both geographical and cultural. Geared as these texts are toward a symbolic instrumentalization of the foreigner within a larger ideological attack on Europe, the portrayal of the foreign arrivals to Europe often positions them as possessors of virtue and commonsensical reason that are lacking in the cultures of their colonizers. As the condition of possibility for the value of foreignness on which the critiques rely, distance—relations of space—remains uncontested in these works. The nineteenth-century works by Balzac, Trollope, and Fontane discussed below can also be situated within this tradition, in the sense that they likewise deploy foreign figures and characters. However, because their deployment adopts a fundamentally different narrative form, and because it seems motivated by narrative needs that vary from author to author, it must be seen as a momentous shift within that tradition. This tradition itself is not the primary aim of this study, but it reveals the thematic terrain on which the authors examined chose to engage their changing world. Through an investigation of the relationship between the use of foreign figures in the nineteenth-century novel and the effect of these figures on the novels' articulation of space (and especially urban space), diminishing distance, and the authors' particular method of realism, we can begin to sketch the impact this shift has on the form of the novel.

The nineteenth-century evocations of the foreigner-in-Europe motif begin in the metropolis, which had already begun, in the years leading up to Balzac's first novels, enjoying a certain privileged position in the construction of narrative. In Franco Moretti's *Atlas of the European Novel 1800–1900*, for example, a handy map represents graphically the location of major "narrative complications" in six Jane Austen novels. The largest concentration of these "complications" is in London, where, according to Moretti, all but one of the novels sees its course change sharply. This should perhaps be surprising, given the associations that usually spring to mind when one considers the typical locale of an Austen novel; London is not her primary domain. Moretti himself, though, is *not* surprised by the density of complication in London, ascribing it quickly to the idea that it is "the busiest city in the world" (18). Because this is Moretti's introduction to what will become a critique of Edward Said's reading of the narrative space of Austen's *Mansfield Park*, it merits a closer look. If Said and Moretti are both grappling with the relationship of national domestic center and colonial periphery to the structure and narrative demands of the nineteenth-century novel in and beyond Austen, then the idea of the city is crucial here, in ways that Said's important contributions never elevate to the level of a central concern. The city can be said to serve as, simultaneously, the locus of a domesticity and reason that counter the novels' "irrational" colonial energies, and as the site where these energies infiltrate and come to complicate even nonurban novels like those of Austen. The opposition between Said's and Moretti's differing approaches to the ordering of novelistic space provides valuable context for one of the elemental issues in my argument: the avowal, within certain novels of the nineteenth century, of the disappearance of regions of mystery and romance due to cartographical and general scientific advancements. Pivotal moments in the work of Balzac, Trollope, and Fontane illustrate the crucial role that remappings or unmappings of narrative space play in the development and complication of novels that have been implicated in (or that implicate themselves in) the project of literary realism.

As attempts to organize space coherently, realist narrative and the activity of empire-building can be partnered, to a degree. Said certainly sees them as close relatives, since they both arise from what he calls "imaginative geography," the capacity to envision the commanding and ordering of raw space

(*Orientalism* 71). In both *Orientalism* and *Culture and Imperialism*, Said is careful to situate physical space as the base around which all other concerns organize: "Underlying social spaces are territories, lands, geographical domains, the actual geographical underpinnings of the imperial, and also the cultural contest. To think about distant places, to colonize them, to populate or depopulate them: all of this occurs on, about, or because of land" (*Culture* 78). This "*geographical* notation, the theoretical mapping and charting of territory that underlies Western fiction, historical writing, and philosophical discourse," thus opens the possibility of the physical act of colonization (58; emphasis in original). It comprises the accumulation of imperial potential, the paradigm formation required for the shift to late capitalism. One ultimate result of this process—a consequence crucial to the novels of the period—is the production of what Said calls a "hierarchy of spaces" that situates the "metropolitan center" at the nucleus of a constellation of less domestic, less controlled territories whose force in this structure serves to provide "stability and prosperity at home." Under the aegis of its centrality, the word "home" accrues "extremely potent resonances" in relation to the foreign that counters it (58–59). These are already weighty claims for the importance of a geographical inclination and the schism between home and away, but Said articulates far weightier ones, ultimately tethering the geographical to the epistemological. "The geographical sense," he argues, "makes projections—imaginary, cartographic, military, economic, historical, or in a general sense cultural. It also makes possible the construction of knowledge" (78). Such confidence in the absolute authority of space for the production of culture creates a decidedly unequal relationship between space and the literary text. Moretti, in an effective but reductive phrase, characterizes this sort of inequality as a belief that "space acts upon style," that space determines style (*Atlas* 43). Despite Moretti's curt assessment, though, Said's particular attention to map-making is important here.

Because it expresses and concretizes acquired knowledge, cartography acts as an agent of disenchantment, a process that will become an immediate and obvious concern to writers of fiction. Benedict Anderson's *Imagined Communities* specifically addresses the potentially secularizing and demystifying consequences of the cartographical project in an important but largely unnoticed leitmotif. Along with the census and the museum—which inform my reading of Balzac's *Peau de chagrin* and, briefly, of Fontane's *Effi Briest*—maps were, Anderson claims, powerful tools toward hegemonic legitimation within imperial culture (164).[2] However, as a constituted form of knowledge, they have the related and perhaps unintended effect of evis-

---

2. The year after Anderson's book appeared, Susan Stewart's *On Longing* further developed this idea of the museum as a "mode of control and containment" (160).

cerating or displacing other forms of knowledge. As the world found itself mapped, all its darker and unknown corners reduced to grid and number, "Cairo and Mecca were beginning to be visualized in a strange new way, no longer simply as sites in a sacred Muslim geography, but also as dots on paper sheets which included dots for Paris, Moscow, Manila and Caracas, . . . these indifferently profane and sacred dots" (170–71). Anderson sees this loss of one "style of continuity"—the master narrative of religion—as the birthplace of another: the master narrative of nationalism (11). Anderson's theory of the birth of the nation from the death of religion is provocative here, because it relates interestingly to two other genealogical pronouncements: Moretti's story, in *Atlas of the European Novel 1800–1900*, of the birth of the nation-state as it is negotiated and concretized by novelists, by their willful drawing and redrawing of boundaries both cultural and ethnographical; and Lukács's earlier account of the birth of the novel as a substitute or glue for the now "broken" "circle whose closed nature was the transcendental essence of" the lives of the ancients (*Theory of the Novel* 33).[3] Lukács posits the novel as both result of and potential remedy for the modern discontinuity represented by the broken circle. His essay imagines a key if not foundational role, within the history of the novel, for the process of desacralization to which Anderson directs our attention, and thus, if we pair these two thinkers, a commensurate role for the imperial pursuits that Anderson finds partly culpable of such desacralization.

To state the problem only in this way, though, is to miss half of imperialism. If, by partnering Anderson and Lukács, one can situate empire at the source of the demystification that necessitates the rise of the novel, one must also see it as the enabler of adventure narratives like *Robinson Crusoe* and of the mystery at work in the imported foreigners of Balzac, Trollope, and Fontane, whose novels often envision foreign figures as romantic potential. Fiction invokes the unstable relationship between colony and imperial center—even at the most bureaucratized level of this relationship—as a narrative possibility. Moretti suggests this in the course of his disagreement with Said over Austen's *Mansfield Park*. Said claims, in *Culture and Imperialism*, that Austen's structure of the novel and the crucial role that the Bertrams' colonial plantation plays in it, demonstrate or reproduce in novelistic form the national domestic center's absolute, factual economic need for the colonies: "What sustains this life [at Mansfield Park] materially is the Bertram estate in Antigua. . . . [N]o matter how isolated and insulated the English place

---

3.. Peter Brooks will later speculate, like Lukács, that "[t]he emergence of narrative plot as a dominant mode of ordering and explanation may belong to the large process of secularization . . . which marks a falling-away from those revealed plots . . . that appeared to subsume transitory human time to the timeless" (*Reading* 6).

(e.g., Mansfield Park), it requires overseas sustenance.... The Bertrams could not have been possible without the slave trade, sugar, and the colonial planter class" (85, 89, 94).[4] Moretti's objections to this are both historical and narratological. On historical grounds, he explicitly doubts that the English economic need for the colonies was as dire as Said claims, and he adduces a number of historical analyses of British imperialism to support this doubt. On narratological grounds, Moretti offers another reason for Austen's use of Antigua in *Mansfield Park*, one that encapsulates the idea of the demands of narrative: tension, complication. In order to allow for some chaos at Mansfield Park, without which we have no novel, Sir Bertram's watchful presence must be sent far, far away. According to Moretti, Sir Bertram "goes, not because he needs the money, but because Austen needs him out of the way" (26). In other words, it is the English novel, and not the English economy, that absolutely needs the colonies in *Mansfield Park*.[5] By repositioning narrative articulations of space at the center of national imaginings of it, as *Atlas of the European Novel* does, Moretti ultimately claims that Austen creates her novels' England. Or, to warp his earlier pronouncement: The novel acts upon space. Henri Mitterand has similarly claimed that novelistic space is "a topology that imposes its own laws on real cartography" (*L'Illusion réaliste* 8). Yet between the novel that acts on space and the space that acts on the novel, there exists a more complex arrangement endemic to the enterprise of literary realism—a type of novel which, in its efforts *realistically to record or reflect a certain space* (space acting upon style), finds its mere recording of space challenged by its need to accede to the demands of the narrative and to *complicate that fixed space* (style acting upon space). "Crooked paths" rather than straight ones, writes Viktor Shklovsky in his *Theory of Prose*, "are called into being by specific conditions—by the demands of the plot" (36).

This tension between *style* and *space* can be recast as one more familiar to the long tradition of aesthetics, the tension between narrative *form*, the manner and structure of narration, and narrative *content*, the object of narration. It animates the novels analyzed here, just as it silently anchors the disagreement between Moretti and Said. Despite their differences, however, Moretti, Said and Anderson are all invested in the question of how Western imperial projections come to construct the world outside, be it by cartographical or cultural imposition. This question has crucial resonance within

---

4. These multiple ellipses in the quotes from Said mirror Moretti's quoting of Said's text.
5. Austen's novel is not the first to use a trip to the colonies to generate domestic fiction. In Sarah Scott's 1762 novel, *A Description of Millenium Hall*, the narrator George Ellison writes that his entire journey through western England—which makes possible his visit to Millenium Hall and thus the novel describing it—is the product of a doctor's prescribed remedy for "the ill effects of my long abode in the hot and unwholesome climate of Jamaica, where, while I increased my fortune, I gradually impaired my constitution" (54).

the unfolding of a novel, whether because geography and national socioeconomic necessity can dictate the course of the novel (Said) or because the novel's formal need for complication dictates its geographical projections, the space that it treats as content (Moretti). Neither Said nor Moretti considers in particular the role that secularization or disenchantment—the sudden perceived limitation of the possibilities for narrative complication—may play in addressing the question of the novel's complex relationship with its own space. John McClure's book on what he calls *Late Imperial Romance* is extremely useful to that end, though. McClure writes that British novelists at the turn of the twentieth century—he refers specifically to H. Rider Haggard, Virginia Woolf, Arthur Conan Doyle, and Joseph Conrad—were so troubled by the disappearance of mysterious, story-engendering places occasioned by the complete mapping of the world, that they sought to either unmap the mapped and known world or find fictional potential in new, siteless geopolitical phenomena, like espionage.[6]

> Thus in 1894, almost a decade after the onset of the scramble for Africa, H. Rider Haggard complains that "soon the ancient mystery of Africa will have vanished" and wonders where "will the romance writers of future generations find a safe and secret place, unknown to the pestilent accuracy of the geographer, to lay their plots?" In Haggard's paradigmatic version of what is to become an oft-repeated tale, the key terms are "Africa," "mystery," "romance," and "geographer." The first three are aligned, of course, against the fourth: the geographer, apt representative of rationalizing forces, threatens to map Africa and rob it of its mystery, leaving "romance writers" without a setting for their stories. Eighteen years later in another imperial romance, Arthur Conan Doyle combines the same elements in a strikingly similar lament. Now that "the big blank spaces in the map are all being filled in," a character declares in *The Lost World* (1912), "there's no room for romance anywhere." And just three years later, in Virginia Woolf's first novel, *The Voyage Out* (1915), we find a character condemning imperial entrepreneurs for "robbing a whole continent of mystery." (11)

McClure records this preoccupation with the fate of the imagination as cul-

---

6. Lenin, in *Imperialism: The Highest Stage of Capitalism*, envisions a different yet equally claustrophobic possibility brought on by the complete mapping and colonization of the world, one that will be acted out in the form of the Cold War beginning with World War II:

> As there are no unoccupied territories—that is, territories that do not belong to any state—in Asia and America, ... we must say that the characteristic feature of this period is the final partition of the globe—not in the sense that a *new* partition is impossible—on the contrary, new partitions are possible and inevitable—but in the sense that the colonial policy of the capitalist countries has *completed* the seizure of the unoccupied territories on our planet. For the first time the world is completely divided up, so that in the future *only* redivision is possible; territories can only pass from one "owner" to another, instead of passing as unowned territory to an "owner." (76)

minating in the waning moments of the nineteenth century, the moment at which the completion of the global cartographical project finally "eradicat[es] the last elsewhere," but it is in fact a much older concern. Goethe could, in 1804, already quote Wilhelm von Humboldt's complaint that archaeological advances were being made only "at the cost of the imagination" [auf Kosten der Phantasie] (12.109). Later in the nineteenth century, George Eliot's characters make similar laments in *Middlemarch* (1871–72), complaining, for example, that "There should be some unknown regions preserved as hunting-grounds for the poetic imagination" (75). As we shall see, these worries over the fate of the imagination are inextricable from the development of realism in the authors discussed in this project.

Such sentiments might be surprising from the architect of Berlin's public museums and from the pages of English realism, but the tension at work here—between exploration and the imagination—is reproduced repeatedly in realist novels well before the turn of the twentieth century. Fredric Jameson's *The Political Unconscious* accounts for it in a chapter on Balzac, and McClure's *Late Imperial Romance* is, in many ways, a long answer to Jameson's question of how romance can be understood to have survived the processes of disenchantment and secularization. Jameson has more fundamental generic categories in mind, though. Leading into a discussion of Balzac and Dreiser, he proposes that

> the problem raised by the persistence of romance as a mode is that of substitutions, adaptations, and appropriations, and raises the question of what, under wholly altered historical circumstances, can have been found to replace the raw materials of magic and Otherness which medieval romance found ready to hand in its socioeconomic environment. A history of romance as a mode becomes possible, in other words, when we explore the substitute codes and raw materials, which, in the increasingly secularized and rationalized world that emerges from the collapse of feudalism, are pressed into service to replace the older magical categories of Otherness which have now become so many dead languages. (130–31)[7]

With Jameson's question and with McClure's observations in mind, one can reconsider the relationship between the novel and geography, and in so doing offer three theses. This book will address the manner in which, first, certain nineteenth-century novels rely on an imported colonial figure

---

7. Moretti poses a different question of substitutions in a footnote to *Atlas of the European Novel*: "Did the novel replace devotional literature because it was a *fundamentally secular form*—or because it was *religion under a new guise?*" (169 n30; emphasis in original)

to generate or organize their fiction (the "complications" to which Moretti alludes, the "substitute codes" for romance, in Jameson's wording). Second, in an affront to any established disenchantment or routine expressed by the novel, this peripheral figure occasions a remapping or unmapping of mapped and ordered urban space. And, third, the city becomes an indispensable component of this analysis, by virtue of both its centrality within an imperial infrastructure and its centrality within the narrative structure of many purportedly realist novels. ("Realism," Peter Brooks claims in *Realist Vision*, "is nothing if not urban" [131].) Finally, following Said's equating of space and knowledge, if these novels by Balzac, Trollope, and Fontane are partial contestations of cartography, they must also, by extension, be legible as epistemological testings, perhaps even as duels between different styles of knowledge.

(b) Imperial Knowledge, Colonial Knowledge: The Fate of Difference

> I left the temple and stood in the blinding sunlight feeling quite benumbed by what I had seen. My European mentality boggled at the experience.
> —Heinrich Harrer, *Seven Years in Tibet*

> [A]s the nationalist B.G. Tilak was later to recall, people "were dazzled at first by the discipline of the British. Railways, Telegraph, Roads, Schools bewildered the people."
> —Eric Hobsbawm, *The Age of Capital*

The notion of a duel within these novels presupposes a decidedly binarizing paradigm, one that is actually invested in the production of conflict. In his introduction to *Late Imperial Romance*, McClure points out that this conflict arises in the context of a spatial opposition: "most imperial adventure fiction translates the basic imperial division of the world (metropolis and colonies or potential colonies) into a familiar romance division, with the West represented as a zone of relative order, security and secularity, the non-Western world as a zone of magic, mystery, and disorder" (8). It is important, though, that this division holds true as well for domestic realist fiction in the age of imperialism. Jane Eyre, for example, at the youthful outset of the novel named for her, confesses in 1847 that she thought Swift's *Gulliver's Travels* to be fact rather than fiction and that, "as to the elves, having sought them in vain among foxglove leaves and bells, under mushrooms and beneath the ground-ivy mantling old wall-nooks, I had at length made up my mind to the sad truth that they were all gone out of England to some savage country, where the woods were wilder and thicker, and the population more scant" (21). Jane's "sad truth" is that England has been disenchanted, and romance is now the property of other regions.[8] If the particular valences between East and West are not as blatant in realist fiction as they are in romance adventures—that scholarship on realism as a mode has largely ignored them attests to their relative subtlety—it is because realist fiction only rarely makes obvious forays into those zones of "the non-Western world" that are coded as locational opposites to Western order and domesticity. The division and its symbolic power still pertain, though, and the imported foreign figure represents a convenient shorthand for the partition and its lingering tensions; the authors can thus recall or summon the idea of geographical division without abandoning the typical domestic setting of the novel. Jameson writes of the "smuggling" of "magic and providential mystery" that is meant to counter the effects of "rationalization" and provide a sort of "symbolic appeasement" (*Political Unconscious* 134). The divide between domestic and foreign is often, but not always, cast simply as a divide between imperial and colonial in the novels by Balzac, Trollope, and Fontane to be analyzed here. It expresses itself also as an epistemological tension, a competition between what the text envisions as two radically different forms of knowledge. This tension is perfectly suited to realist fiction, which is itself a narrative mode premised on questions of knowledge and the representation of truth, according to George Levine: "Whatever else [realism] means, it always implies an attempt to use language to get beyond language, to discover some non-verbal truth out there. The history of English realism obviously depended in large measure on changing notions of what *is* 'out there,' of how best to 'represent' it, and of whether, after all, representation is possible or the 'out there' knowable" (*Realistic Imagination* 6).[9] Novels that bring the "out there" into the "in here" foreground and amplify the contrasting epistemologies represented by the two terms.

---

8. Eliot, in *Adam Bede* (1859), scripts a similarly rustic moment of disenchantment: "It was a wood of beeches and limes, with here and there a light silver-stemmed birch—just the sort of wood most haunted by the nymphs: you see their white sunlit limbs gleaming athwart the boughs, or peeping from behind the smooth-sweeping outline of a tall lime; you hear their soft liquid laughter—but if you look with a too curious sacrilegious eye, they vanish behind the silvery beeches, they make you believe that their voice was only a running brooklet, perhaps they metamorphose themselves into a tawny squirrel that scampers away and mocks you from the topmost bough" (130).

9. Note that Levine stresses an *attempt* to get beyond language. Levine demonstrates that the authors of realist novels were not at all duped by their own narrative mode; they try to get beyond language but are not naïve enough to think it always possible. Raymond Tallis's *In Defence of Realism* addresses this stereotype, along with numerous others, in an insightful treatment of "Misconceptions About Realism" (195–98).

Alongside McClure's notion of the basic division of the imperial world into zones of order (the imperial center) and zones of disorder (the colonies, the uncharted), many critics and historians have mapped differing epistemologies as a split between East and West or between colonizer and colonized. These debates have remained absent from scholarship on realism, though, and, because they question or complicate some of the fundamental assumptions underlying our views of literary realism, their absence has only aided realism's long-standing reputation as a ploddingly monological mode whose basic assumptions always go unquestioned. Empirical science, one of the central influences on realism, is in this debate consistently allied with the forces of Western empire. Partha Chatterjee, for example, sees in imperial culture and in anticolonial nationalism a division between

> two domains—the material and the spiritual. The material is the domain of the "outside," of the economy and of statecraft, of science and technology, a domain where the West had proved its superiority and the East had succumbed. In this domain, then, Western superiority had to be acknowledged and its accomplishments carefully studied and replicated. The spiritual, on the other hand, is an "inner" domain bearing the "essential" marks of cultural identity. (6)

It is in this "inner" domain, Chatterjee claims, the domain of the "spiritual," that the East can gain leverage against the West.[10] Said also explicitly links science with the Western impulse toward imperialism in *Orientalism:* "The greatest names are, of course, Linnaeus and Buffon, but the intellectual process by which bodily (and soon moral, intellectual, and spiritual) extension—the typical materiality of an object—could be transformed from mere spectacle to the precise measurement of characteristic elements was very widespread" (119). Buffon will be acknowledged as a major influence by Balzac's *Comédie humaine*, which mentions him no less than five times in its famous general preface. Said's picture of a scientific and rational imperialism becomes complicated if not self-contradictory later, however, when he allies empire with religious fanaticism in a passage whose inner tensions will guide most of the chapters in this book. Ashis Nandy, like Chatterjee, most specifically scripts the differences as a contest between styles of knowledge.[11]

---

10. Recent scholarship on nineteenth-century Europe's interest in the occult strengthens the notion of a duel between empirical and spiritual epistemologies. As Richard Noakes has pointed out, "Victorian investigators of Spiritualism believed" that such "erratic phenomena" could ultimately "be reduced to natural laws" (24). By 1908, Frank Podmore could write a book called *The Naturalisation of the Supernatural*. Some go so far as to map this duel (as Chatterjee and others do) onto the geographical divisions of imperialism. See Luckhurst and Viswanathan.

11. See also Azim, who writes that "The secular nature of British education in India split the colonial terrain further along lines of secular (colonial) or religious (native) education" (14). As

"Resistance," Nandy asserts, "takes many forms in the savage world. It may take the form of a full-blooded rejection of the modern world's deepest faith, scientific rationality" ("Shamans" 269). Resistance and the combat implied by it are central as well to the dueling "philosophies of knowledge" that Nandy describes in "The Savage Freud" (96). Nandy points to Freud's own observation, in a letter to Lou Andreas-Salomé, that certain of his first Indian readers conceived of him as an Englishman, neatly capturing the manner in which the invasion of a new science or form of knowledge (psychoanalysis) became quickly conflated with a more familiar imperial invasion (101–2).

Science and the empirical epistemology in general are opposed to the epistemology of the oppressed in the colonial equation, as many critics have expressed it. However, certain narrative avatars of scientism in the nineteenth century are even more specifically adduced as uniquely useful to imperialism, and are, not coincidentally, intimately related to the creation of realist narrative. Ranajit Guha, in an essay on the narrative strategies of colonial power, refers to "historiography...as a form of *colonialist knowledge*" where it is bound up with policy (70; emphasis in original). This assumption is already at work in 1811, when William Playfair publishes his study of *British Family Antiquity: Containing the Baronetage of Ireland* and dismisses all accounts of events in Irish history "previous to the era of authentic history, which began with the invasion of Henry II" (quoted in Gilmartin 30). History, in this context, does not exist in any credible form until the colonialists arrive, and one could state more strongly Guha's declaration of historiography as colonialist knowledge; proper history, for Playfair in 1811, simply belongs to Britain.[12] Playfair's idea of two histories at odds with each other complements Guha's expression of history as a battleground: "every struggle for power by the historically ascendant classes in any epoch involves a bid to acquire a tradition" (77). Nandy, too, articulates the notion of resisting the narrative of history within the colonial cultures to which he refers as, by turns, "savage" and "ahistorical": "The old classification between the historical and ahistorical societies may not have broken down, but all large ahistorical societies now have sizeable sections of population which have become, through a process of over-correction, entirely captive to the historical mode" ("Shamans" 263). Whether in Guha's idea of historiography,

---

Nandy points out, Kaylan Chatterjee extends this idea of a duel to the domain of literary study, when he treats Lukács's dismissal, in 1922, of Rabindranath Tagore's *The Home and the World* (1915). Lukács objects to what he perceives as a Ghandist "religiosity," and Nandy draws from this critique a collision between secular literary hermeneutics and texts inflected with religion; see "Lukacs's Choice" (Nandy, *Illegitimacy of Nationalism* 15–19).

12. In a chapter on "The Concept of Archaism in Anthropology" in *Structural Anthropology*, Lévi-Strauss observes a similar dynamic in one of two problematic criteria anthropologists use to categorize societies as "primitive": "the history of these peoples is completely unknown *to us*, and on account of the lack or paucity of oral traditions and archaeological remains, it is forever beyond our reach" (103; emphasis mine).

Playfair's idea of "authentic history," or Eric Hobsbawm's mention of "unhistorical" or "semi-historical" cultures in *The Age of Capital*'s chapter on "Building Nations" (85), history as a type of knowledge becomes a means of categorizing nations.

The preoccupation with history here is important in a discussion of realism, for the increasing prominence of historiography in the eighteenth and nineteenth centuries is often read alongside the rise of realist narrative, by critics as diverse as Erich Auerbach, who refers to the "historism" of Balzac; Lukács; Ian Watt; and Peter Brooks, who writes of "the nineteenth century's ... foregrounding of the historical narrative as par excellence the necessary mode of explanation and understanding" (*Reading* 6–7). Historical consciousness is, furthermore, repeatedly tethered to secular consciousness, a point that Said's closing remarks in *The World, the Text, and the Critic* make abundantly clear, as he explicitly equates "a sense of history" with "a purely secular view of reality" (290–91). Bearing in mind the realist novel's debt to historiography and history's supposed secularism, one must recall as well Guha's and Dipesh Chakrabarty's warnings on the limitations of purely secular historiography. Guha, for example, points out that Western historiography "fails to comprehend ... the religious element in rebel consciousness" when writing about Indian uprisings against the British (83), while Chakrabarty sees such failure as a symptom of more general methodological shortcomings, which the next chapter discusses in more depth. Following Guha's and Chakrabarty's pronouncements, attention to what seems unsecular or unrealist in realist narratives forces us to reappraise the relationship between secularism and realism. The novels of Balzac, Trollope, and Fontane on which this project focuses have all been said to employ realist narrative strategies or to belong, simply put, to a body of work or a literary-historical epoch termed "realist." Yet these novels also rely on energies or epistemologies irreducible to the historiographical and empirical allegiances of realism as most critics—and most realist novels themselves—have understood and constructed it.

(c) The Problem with Progress: The Fate of Fiction

The form of the novel is closely linked to the process of demystification, not merely in Lukács's understanding of demystification as the condition necessary for the rise of the novel, but in an ongoing way, throughout the history of the genre, as Michael McKeon has argued. This becomes clear when one focuses on negotiations of space in the novel, which are especially dynamic in the works treated in this project. In elaborating on the idea of the development of homogeneous, disenchanted, grid-like space, Jameson writes that

> [t]he emergence of this kind of space will probably not involve problems of figuration so acute as those we will confront in the later stages of capitalism, since here, for the moment, we witness that familiar process long generally associated with the Enlightenment, namely, the desacralization of the world, the decoding and secularization of the older forms of the sacred or the transcendent, the slow colonization of use value by exchange value, the "realistic" demystification of the older kinds of transcendent narratives in novels like *Don Quixote*, . . . and so on. ("Cognitive Mapping" 349)

The "familiar" Enlightenment desacralization to which he refers is much more complex in the novels treated below, in which it is cast more often against a willful reenchantment.[13] In other words, there is a measure of resistance to this "slow colonization." Jameson first raises the issue of disenchantment earlier, in *The Political Unconscious*'s chapter on realism in Balzac discussed briefly above. He reiterates what "any number of 'definitions' of realism assert": "that processing operation variously called narrative mimesis or realistic representation has as its historic function the systematic undermining and demystification, the secular 'decoding,' of those preexisting inherited traditional or sacred narrative paradigms which are its initial givens" (152). One must measure these arguments against Jameson's notion of a "longing for magic and providential mystery," which might ruthlessly complicate a narrative mode such as realism, whose very aims are, according to Jameson, incompatible with such energies. The conflict between rational demystification and the irrational longing for mystery that Jameson sees in narrative matches the paradox that Said recognizes in *Orientalism*. In a paragraph meant to delineate the book's title term, Said unites within his definition of "Orientalism" both *realism*—which he describes as a mercilessly normative, empirical, and disciplinary discourse—and *paranoia*, which he opposes to such normativity, empiricism, and history (72).[14]

To envision realism alongside or even in collusion with its opposite, as Said and Jameson appear to do, is to problematize most scholarship on real-

---

13. I use the idea of reenchantment here differently than Payne does in his book, *The Reenchantment of Nineteenth-Century Fiction: Dickens, Thackeray, George Eliot and Serialization*. While Payne convincingly teases out a "discourse of benevolence and self-sacrifice from a lost Christian culture" (147) in the writings, behavior, and serialization of the three authors he treats, I deploy the term in a manner less restricted to religious tradition and more in line with an aesthetic ancestry of magic, mystery, and romance. This can include, but not be restricted to, religion.

14. Homi Bhabha, in his reading of this passage, repeats the link between "colonial power" and "realism," claiming that the former's "system of representation, a regime of truth, . . . is structurally similar to realism" (*Location* 71).

ism. Since at least Hippolyte Taine, realism as a narrative mode has commonly been viewed as an agent or reflection of scientific positivism and positivist historiography. Eric Downing has pointed out, in a recent study of German realist fiction, that even prominent Germanists such as Robert Holub and Russell Berman have lately constructed realism as "a heavily normed discourse, or style, that purports to universal, transparent, natural, and ahistorical status, and that simultaneously and necessarily excludes or represses both self-consciousness and otherness" (11–12). Katherine Kearns also captures these criticisms well, when she writes that "Realism" is "often charged with blindsiding social, political, and epistemological complexities, with throwing its considerable materialistic weight against all that would challenge or suborn the status quo" (7). Early in the history of the term,[15] realism's supposedly direct reference to external reality was looked on favorably as a fulfillment of art's truest mimetic aims, and unfavorably as a pandering to reality that abandoned the Renaissance and neoclassical injunction to improve the world in art, following the aesthetics of Sir Philip Sidney or Boileau, for example. The positive association of realism with an admirable mimetic project—with an attempt to, in Levine's phrasing, "get beyond words" to some truth or reality—is surely behind the claims of certain modernist critics and writers who proudly described works of modernism as "realist" or "realistic," even where the version of "reality" and the strategies for representing it are markedly different from those of nineteenth-century authors. Thus can Auerbach speak in *Mimesis* of Virginia Woolf's realism just a few years after Woolf herself all but labels James Joyce a realist in her essay, "Modern Fiction." Lukács, fearful of the modernist trend toward a broader application and muddying of the term *realism*, attempts to reinstall a barrier in 1957, in his *The Meaning of Contemporary Realism*[16]: We are faced, Lukács claims, with "the dilemma of the choice between an aesthetically appealing, but decadent modernism, and a fruitful critical realism. It is the choice between Franz Kafka and Thomas Mann" (92). For Lukács, then, if his choice of Kafka and Mann as the exemplary dichotomy is any indication, realism opposes modernism because it is constituted by a reality immediately familiar and recognizable as such. This is clearly not the "reality" that is meaningless outside of quotation marks, to

15. Mortimer gives a useful and brief version: "*Realism* is a historical term. It became a widespread critical concept in France only in the late 1840s and 1850s and was sanctioned in 1856 when a journal of that name appeared, Duranty's *Le Réalisme*, or in 1857 when Champfleury's essays in defense of the concept were published, with the same title" (3). Marshall Brown reaches further back, examining the genealogy of the word "real" in aesthetic and philosophical discourse in the mid- to late-eighteenth century (226) and ultimately measuring it against Hegelian *Wirklichkeit* and its impact on Auerbach's influential conception of the representation of reality.

16. The essay's German title is *Wider den mißverstandenen Realismus*, or *Against Misunderstood Realism*, which was somewhat defanged in English. Theodor Adorno takes issue with many of Lukács's points in Adorno's "Extorted Reconciliation," and especially contests his claims about the choice between Mann and Kafka.

which Vladimir Nabokov refers later in the century in his postscript to *Lolita* (314). The consequences of this sort of split can be seen more broadly in the modernist caricature of realism as a naïve faith in its own referentiality to a knowable reality. The novels of Samuel Beckett, for example, repeatedly lampoon this trust as a troubling dishonesty on the part of writers who gesture toward external realities as context or condition for their narratives.[17] Even critics who would defend realist narrative against accusations of referential naïveté have nonetheless demeaned it as "régressive" because of its attempt to construct a "referential fullness" [plénitude référentielle] within itself, an idea sponsored by both Roland Barthes, in the celebrated "L'effet de réel," and Pierre Macherey, in his chapter on Balzac's *Les Paysans* in *A Theory of Literary Production* (Barthes 90). Acknowledging that there are already instances of aggressive anti-realism in the later nineteenth century (Nietzsche, for example), the more strident and enduring critiques are born in the modernist moment and piqued further by poststructuralist recontextualizations of the idea of representation itself.

Realism escapes these attacks—and becomes much more complex—when one reads it, not merely as the disciplinary narrative that it partly is, but also as the counternarrative that unfolds simultaneously. In responses to critiques of realism by both modernist and poststructuralist critics, George Levine and Marshall Brown in 1981 offer more nuanced and capacious conceptions of realist narrative as a site of struggle. Their posture provides a framework in which to reconsider the novels discussed in this book. These novels are explicitly implicated in the realist endeavor by both their narrators and their authors, but they are also works within which the value of realism can be and is contested. This contest is often initiated through the introduction of foreign figures. Partially a sign of its time, Levine's study openly casts itself as a response to "the antireferential bias of our criticism and to the method of radical deconstruction that has become a commonplace" (*Realistic Imagination* 3).[18] Against the stereotype of a monological realism, Levine asserts instead that "realism posits 'mixed' conditions" (4). Brown's essay strives, similarly, to give "a flexible historical picture" (233) of realist narrative and of definitions of realism. Robert Holub derides Brown's "flexibility"

---

17. Raymond Tallis (112) cites Beckett's *Molloy* (1951). The novel's second part begins with the lines "It is midnight. The rain is beating on the windows," a realist assertion of place and time severely undercut—even mocked—by the novel's final lines: "I went back into the house and wrote, 'It is midnight. The rain is beating on the windows.' It was not midnight. It was not raining" (Beckett 92; 176). Beckett's explicit attacks against a prime novel of European realism (Fontane's *Effi Briest*) in the play, *La dernière bande* (*Krapp's Last Tape*, 1958) have long been noted by scholars, largely for their comic value. See Turner (234).

18. Furst, too, offers a more nuanced picture: "The realist novel must be taken at one and the same time as a record (more or less faithful, as the case may be) of a past social situation *and* as a texture made of verbal signs" (*All Is True* 24). Kearns, like Furst, espouses a more complex view of realism from *within* a deconstructive stance, holding that realism cannot be monological, because everything written is already of (at least) two minds.

as "amorphousness" in his 1991 monograph on German realism, but the flexibility is, for Brown, precisely the point (14). Brown explains realist narrative as a product of "interplay" between "Jakobson's metonymic or sequential order" and "metaphorical or substitutional order" (231); as "the ordered or hierarchical intersection of contrasting codes" (233); and as "a structure of ordered negations perceived within the text quite independently of any relationship between the text and what is assumed to be its 'world'" (237). The emphasis is on realism's internal struggles—struggles made explicit by all three of the authors studied here.

The present project, though, will endeavor to read an interplay between the strategies of realist narrative and the material that realist narrative describes and which, as we shall see, frequently challenges those strategies. Brown makes a useful distinction between "realisms of form" and "realisms of content" that is crucial here, because it maps readily onto Moretti's distinction between *style* and *space* so important to the novels discussed below (233).[19] Yet Brown's distinction is no less important generally, because literary realism has always been theorized through discussions of either the form or the content of the work, or, less frequently if at all, of both. Balzac's own appeal to natural history, for example, constructs a formal and structural ancestry for the strategies he hopes to develop in the *Comédie humaine*; his preoccupation with physical material and his painstaking description of it, on the other hand, have led some critics to see that material content (be it a social milieu writ large or a single room in a small Paris *pension*) as the real force of his realism.[20] However, the divorce between the text and its world implied by this arrangement clashes, to some degree, with the stated missions of Balzac, Trollope, and Fontane, and with the discernible preoccupations of their works. All three of these authors can be said to adhere, in *both* the form *and* the content of the novels analyzed below, to an abiding interest in and debate over two developments related to the imperialist epistemology that Nandy, Chatterjee, Guha, and Said describe: historiography and empiricism. Some critics have linked these two terms as interrelated developments,[21] but no deliberate link between them is necessary for one to appreciate the extent to which historiography and empiricism are equally essential in the fiction of Balzac, Trollope, and Fontane, and in the long tradition of scholarship on realist fiction.

---

19. Howells would likely abolish this distinction, claiming rather that true realism is a realism of both form and content: "Realism is nothing more than the truthful treatment of material," he writes, in a formulation that simultaneously highlights *material* (content) and the manner of its *treatment* (form) (38). See also Kearns, who claims that "Realism premises that observable realities can be and should be articulated novelistically through verisimilitude" (86).

20. Or of any realism. Bill Brown refers to a general "mimetic physicality of realism" (166).

21. See Hayden White's *Figural Realism* (43) and McKeon (42–43, 68, 420–21).

To say that empiricism and historiography operate, in the nineteenth-century novel, at the levels of both content and form is to make a few specific claims in each case. First, it is to claim that, taking the example of historiography, these writers structure their novels (the level of *form*) according to conventions of historical narration, causal connection, and temporality. Trollope's *The Way We Live Now* begins to challenge these conventions under extreme pressure from the shrinking of its world (*content* thus complicates *form*). Second, the novels simultaneously appeal, at the level of *content* and often in a strikingly explicit manner, to accepted historical or social reality outside of their narrative. This dual use of history, as both form and content, is not necessarily unique to the nineteenth century. Indeed, reliance on history as a *source* for narrative (history as *content*), and a view of historiography as a *strategy* (*form*) for arriving at or articulating truth, are at least as old as the modern novel. *Don Quijote*'s narrator speaks of "truth, whose mother is history, rival of time, storehouse of great deeds, witness of the past, example and lesson to the present, warning to the future" [la verdad, cuya madre es la historia, émula del tiempo, depósito de las acciones, testigo de lo pasado, ejemplo y aviso de lo presente, advertencia de lo por venir] (1.95). The notion of history as *depósito de las acciones* hints simultaneously at the levels of *content* and *form*, for in addition to "deeds," isolated historical episodes, the word *acciones* also denotes the plots of literary works. History is, therefore, not just as external source for content or isolated episode (*deed*) but also an organizer of larger structure (*plot*). Balzac, Fontane, and—perhaps most explicitly—Trollope all lean on history in both the form and content of their works: in the form, because their narratives follow the historiographical rules of causal connection; and in the content, because they rely on external historical reality as backdrop for their plots, as the familiar, material frame of reference, what Richard Altick has called the "presence of the present" (the Parliamentary interests of Trollope's novels, for example). These authors also foreground empiricism and the knowledge of the senses, albeit in different ways and to different ends. The deployment of empiricism in their novels goes beyond what one critic has seen as realistic *détaillisme* (Dubois 88), and it surpasses the preoccupation with material things and places, or attempts at cartographical verity, to which so many critics have called attention. Rather, like historiography, empiricism also becomes an element of narrative form simultaneously deployed by and disputed within the novels treated below. Ian Watt, in *The Rise of the Novel*, goes so far as to pinpoint empiricism as the single starting point for realism: "Modern realism, of course, begins from the position that truth can be discovered by the individual through his senses" (12). When Balzac's narrator in *La Peau de chagrin*, for example, proceeds by revealing only what is externally observable before making deductions or hypotheses based on what is observable, the novel is adopting the form of empirical science. Balzac deploys that mode of narration everywhere in *La Comédie humaine*.

Historiography and empiricism organize the fiction of Balzac, Trollope, and Fontane, and the particular confluence of the two in the novels treated below constitutes an important moment of literary-historical development. These preoccupations are not the sole property of the nineteenth century, but they are most central there. Indeed, Marshall Brown points out that such "elements of realism can undoubtedly be found in the literature of all ages, though it seems undeniable that their frequency and prominence increased in the nineteenth century" (233). Critical though he is of Brown, even Holub concedes this point, the notion of a certain "era" of realism grounded on the sudden historical prominence of realist strategies (174). Fundamentally, the two forces of historiography and empiricism, taken together, articulate another narrative (or collective fantasy), that of progress: the history of science, one might say, or the workings of science within history. That much is already implied in Max Weber's claim, "Scientific work is chained to the course of progress" (137). Weber makes this statement in the very essay, "Science as a Vocation," in which he famously articulates the costs of that progress as "disenchantment" [Entzauberung], the eradication of mystery through knowledge. If the narrative of progress—or, as Chakrabarty would have it, the "metanarrative of progress"—is so "deeply embedded in our institutional lives however much we may develop . . . an attitude of incredulity toward such metanarratives," this notion of progress is no less a cornerstone of the novels to be analyzed below, several of which are directly interested in the lives of institutions (Chakrabarty 88).[22] Though coded differently by each author and by each novel, progress is both foregrounded and feared in these texts through the use of the imported foreign figure and the specific significance of each importation. Balzac's novels of the early 1830s tend to script the advances of science and empire as an explicit dissolution of mystery or romance, challenged by the marginal characters and objects that become central to the texts. Trollope demonstrates, over the course of his six Palliser novels and the contemporaneous *The Way We Live Now*, the difficulties for narrative in light of this disenchantment and the assault of progress on tradition. Progress is linked, for a distressed Trollope, to the increasingly easy communication of England with the outside world, the communication that facilitates in the first place the arrival of the foreign in the space of the domestic. Fontane, too, relies on the technological tropes of simplified communication, both verbal (in the image of a character in *Cécile* who is employed laying

22. Hobsbawm refers to the "secular ideology of progress" (*Age of Capital* 271).

telegraph wires all over the world) and physical (in the image of *Effi Briest*'s port town as a node of global commerce and exchange), as emblem of the struggle between historical advancement and mystery.

One can return here to Moretti's concept of novels that build nations, where this introduction began, for the nation is itself partially a product of the collective fantasy or narrative of progress. Homi Bhabha has claimed that the narrative of the nation is an attempt to "mediate between the teleology of progress" and the "'timeless' discourse of irrationality" ("DisseminiNation" 294). The same is certainly true of realist novels, even when studies of realist novels have failed to notice the extent to which the relationship with the irrational is in fact one of mediation rather than simple exclusion. The irrationality of which Bhabha speaks is, however, neither timeless nor nationless in the novels treated below. It is, rather, constructed precisely through its historical and extranational associations. As such, it is content to challenge the form of realism.

(d) Précis of Chapters

The rise of the museum embodies a slow merger of empiricism and historiography. In chapter 1, this merger provides a means of reading the introduction, into Balzac's novelistic output and main metropolitan setting, of a foreign figure, the titular *Peau de chagrin*. A famous scene early in the novel, in which the protagonist browses a collection of antiquities in a shop before bringing them into a historical coherence, has been read by some critics as an example of the fantastic (e.g., Tzvetan Todorov) and by others (e.g., Henri Mitterand) as a nascent realism. The novel fosters a duel between these two modes, though, between a rigidly empirical narrative method and an object—the Middle Eastern talisman found in the shop—that cannot be explained by empirical science and that lies outside the necessities and causalities of history. *La Peau de chagrin* finally allegorizes a disenchantment that is explicitly linked to science; the talisman dwindles to nothing and, in the final scene, Balzac's narrator reckons the costs of technology.

Chapter 2 places the imperial contexts of *La Peau de chagrin*—largely ignored by critics—into sharper relief, introducing the manner in which empire and questions of colonial violence come to structure Balzac's *Le Père Goriot*. Both novels lean on references to the colonies, but *Goriot*'s allegory of the Mandarin, when read against the domestic machinations on which it passes judgment, links exoticism, colonial violence, and money. The criminal Vautrin and his embodiment of a global criminal underworld appear to open the city as a site of mystery; however, he only serves, finally, to underline the text's ambivalence toward vestiges of romantic thought and action, which are consistently undercut by the language of rationalization. The Mandarin represents the notion, introduced in *La Peau de chagrin*, that domestic gains come at the expense of colonial others, but it also highlights the dubious position of the foreign in the novel.

Paris is embedded in a global imperial geography in *Le Père Goriot*, but *La Fille aux yeux d'or* makes this arrangement even more immediate. It seems, in the latter novel, that the entire world comes to Paris, and chapter 3 investigates the narrative consequences of this diminished distance. The city is methodically unmapped, rendered foreign and mysterious in order to meet the demands of a disenchanted, romance-hungry Parisian. Against prevailing readings of this text, which have inevitably divorced the anthropological tones of the first portion from the more comfortably narrative tones of the second portion, I argue that the two halves function together in an attempted description of Paris and progress. France's capital becomes, through the imported colonial figures in Balzac's early novels, both the specific site and paradigm of disenchantment and the site of timid resistance to this process.

Chapter 4 charts the shifting and problematic mobilizations of foreignness—specifically, Irishness—in Trollope's *Phineas Finn*. In this second of the six Palliser novels, Trollope draws his title hero from Ireland, which he explicitly equates with romance and even refers to as "the colonies next door." This novel and its sequel are aberrant in the English tradition because Trollope situates the Irish in them so centrally, and the novels begin to confront a problem of realistic representation. Forced to grapple with vestiges of romance in an otherwise realist text, *Phineas Finn* codes and recodes the value and location of Irishness in a clumsy effort to balance romance and the real. Trollope's Pallisers share with Balzac's early fiction a concern over the fate of romance even as they attempt to meticulously record the political and colonial history of the time.

The challenges that *Phineas Finn* cannot quite meet are hyperbolized in the perennially underappreciated *Phineas Redux*. Chapter 5 examines the manner in which the quandary over how to represent "romantic" foreigners within a realist novel begins to alter Trollope's conception of space. The Palliser novels also weigh disenchantment within this conflict, from *Phineas Finn*'s demystification of Scott's romantic territories to the reenchantment of these same territories in its sequel, which is marked finally by a startling urban chaos and stylistic slippage. *Phineas Redux* introduces foreign energies into the English capital—murderous Scots, Continental rogues—and this tension occasions, by the end of the novel, an epistemological crisis explicitly wedded to a crisis of fiction. As *Phineas Redux* ends, Trollope begins the work of placing the city in a global geography that will ultimately be expressed in terms of the burgeoning global market in *The Way We Live Now*.

Chapter 6 examines the continued, ambivalent portrayal of foreign figures as simultaneous signifiers of the romantic and the rational in *The Way We Live Now*, with specific focus on the Americans. The railway speculator Augustus Melmotte, the novel's most enduring and villainous character, is a quasi-Gothic figure borrowed from Goethe, Charles Maturin, and Balzac. Though Melmotte is too often—and mistakenly—read as Jewish, *The Way We Live Now*'s uncertainty as to his origins is important, and Trollope uses him to anchor a stark portrait of global commerce and the dangerous interconnectedness of distant places. As in Balzac's *La Fille aux yeux d'or*, the outside world becomes increasingly present in London, and Trollope's narrative retreats to the countryside, the novel's last bastion of Englishness and stability. The demands of Trollope's portrayal of the shrinking world ruthlessly complicate his normal, staid pattern of narrative exposition, as the city and world he depicts become irrevocably compact.

Chapter 7 begins by acknowledging some of the complexities that attend any analysis of imperialism in the context of Germany, which differs significantly from that of other European national traditions in which colonial undertakings occurred earlier and were more entrenched. Fontane's fiction begins by constructing a German metropolis that can then be inserted into a global geography, and, when seen in this light, his novels build toward a crucial moment in *Cécile* when a character declares Berlin a *Weltstadt* or *World-City*. *Cécile* foregrounds the differences between the urban and rural at a time when those differences, as one character remarks, are seen to steadily decrease. Despite this, the novel marks Berlin off as a site of struggle between disenchantment and the desire for romance, through the character of Gordon, a Scot who emblematizes simultaneously the processes of globalization through technology and the possibility for romance and narrative complication.

Cécile sets the stage, in a sense, for Fontane's masterpiece, *Effi Briest*, through a damaging depiction of (quasi-)adultery that clashes with Fontane's earlier, more optimistic portrayal of it in *L'Adultera* (1882), and through an attention to the shrinking world. This shrinking—the reduction of unknown regions to tourist sites and ordered maps—and the linked issue of disenchantment are keys to understanding what Fontane called the "pivot" [Drehpunkt] of *Effi Briest:* the novel's Chinese ghost. Scholarly attention to the ghost reflects the limitations of common understandings of "realism," which can readily account for the ethnicity of the ghost but is at a loss in the face of its supposed supernatural property. Moreover, the spatial situating of adultery, for which the ghost stands as partial symbol, complicates its potential as a romantic alternative. Finally, pronouncements on imperialist organization of space by Said, Gayatri Spivak, and Raymond Williams enable a discussion of Fontane's arrangement of zones of order and zones of romance, where this introduction began. Marginal areas become portals for the reintroduction of enchantment into a secularized domestic space organized by metropolitan Berlin. On these attempted reenchantments, though, Fontane remains ambivalent. The world's mysterious places have been quotidianized, the novel asserts. The figure of the Chinese ghost foregrounds the duel between romance and the real, and its movements and shifting status circumscribe a simultaneous longing for enchantment and a final acknowledgment of its impossibility.

Part I

Balzac and the Problem of Empiricism

CHAPTER ONE

EMPIRICISM AND EMPIRE
La Peau de chagrin

> Museums which emerged during the nineteenth century, especially ethnographic and natural history museums, were formed by collections brought to the West from the rest of the world.
> —Eilean Hooper-Greenhill, *Museums and the Interpretation of Visual Culture*

> Without empire, I would go so far as saying, there is no European novel as we know it, and indeed if we study the impulses giving rise to it, we shall see the far from accidental convergence between the patterns of narrative authority constitutive of the novel on the one hand, and, on the other, a complex ideological configuration underlying the tendency to imperialism.
> —Edward Said, *Culture and Imperialism*

A passage in Edward Said's *Orientalism* contains a brief but complicated definition of the book's primary topic:

> Philosophically, then, the kind of language, thought, and vision that I have been calling Orientalism very generally is a form of radical realism; anyone employing Orientalism, which is the habit for dealing with questions, objects, qualities, and regions deemed Oriental, will designate, name, point to, fix what he is talking or thinking about with a word or phrase, which then is considered either to have acquired, or more simply to be, reality. Rhetorically speaking, Orientalism is absolutely anatomical and enumerative: to use its vocabulary is to engage in the particularizing and dividing of things Oriental into manageable parts. Psychologically, Orientalism is a form of paranoia, knowledge of another kind, say, from ordinary historical knowledge. These are a few of the results, I think, of imaginative geography and of the dramatic boundaries it draws. (72)

There is a paradox here in the idea that Orientalism is driven by impulses both secular, empirical, enumerative *and* nonsecular, nonhistorical, paranoid. This paradox is, of course, not lost on Said. More importantly, though, the conflicting energies in this definition aptly frame the two linked historical developments on which this chapter focuses: the crystallization of an empirical epistemology, emblematized by the rise of the museum; and the contemporaneous birth of realist narrative. They also recall the indispensable role that imperialism and its understanding of space played in both these births, which were registered in the shifting role of, attention to, and collection of material things.

Several scholars have already begun the work of theorizing collecting's and collections' relation to narrative. Mieke Bal builds usefully on the "subjective presence in narratives," which serves to "focalise" what is narrated and is, Bal argues, analogous to the selection and organization inherent in the act of collecting (98). While Bal has used the idea of collecting to interrogate "very characteristic feature[s] of narrative" such as chronology (101), James Clifford has, in a quite different way, used literary theory (Bakhtin's, for example) in order to question or reformulate accepted anthropological stances on collecting (236). The present effort cannot attempt to engage the ties between objects and narrative on so large or general a scope. Instead, I will put Said's paradoxical Orientalism to a reading of the transformation of the private collection (and especially the *cabinet de curiosités* and the *Wunderkammer*) into the public museum at the outset of the nineteenth century, with all of the shifts that attended or contributed to this transformation: rarity, for example, cedes ground to representativeness, and the anachronic anecdote loses its place to organic history. This reassessment of the museum's history is essential to a reading of Honoré de Balzac's 1831 novel, *La Peau de chagrin* (translated variously as *The Magic Skin*, *The Wild Ass's Skin*, or *The Fateful Skin*), which is named after the near-Eastern talisman that the protagonist, Raphaël de Valentin, purchases in an antique shop in Paris. Beginning with the narrator's longwinded descriptions of the shop's vast and varied collection, the novel wears both its exoticism and its materialism on its sleeve. However, rather than independently reify the two Orientalisms articulated in the quote by Said above, *La Peau de chagrin* instead puts them into explicit conflict with each other, pitting empiricism against enchantment. In so doing, Balzac's novel registers many of the same epistemological and cultural shifts visible in the changing role of collected objects in early-nineteenth-century Europe. Moreover, the importance of the collection in the nineteenth-century novel extends beyond Balzac, as later chapters demonstrate, and it testifies to the growing importance of and perceived relationship between history and empiricism. Finally, moving beyond the novel's mere reflection of social realities, Balzac's simultaneous awareness and wariness of these cultural shifts offer a new context for understanding the rise of realism, a concern all at once central to the idea of the museum, the development of Balzac's narrative style, and Said's notion of Orientalism.

(a) The Orientalist Paradox and the Object(s) of Empire

A brief examination of Said's paradoxical Orientalism—which is both empirical and paranoid, both enumerative and imaginative—highlights the importance of its constitutive tension. Shortly after the definition of Orientalism cited above, Said emboldens his terms, claiming that "these two aspects of Orientalism are not incongruent, since by use of them both Europe could advance securely and unmetaphorically upon the Orient" (73). This is modest, even guarded language (note the cautious double negative of "not incongruent"), but the chary tone is probably warranted by the tendency, in debates over imperialism and its complex epistemological foundations, to see in empire *either* a violent manifestation of relentless secularization *or* an outgrowth or variety of religion itself, as Said more often seems to see it. Patrick Brantlinger, too, in *Rule of Darkness*, sees affinities between imperialism and occult religious practices popular during the age of empire. Other theorists of imperialism and anti-imperialism have, by contrast, related the colonial drive not to religious impulses but rather to the sort of secular/scientific motivations that Said also describes, and I discussed a number of these thinkers above, in the introduction. Shifting these motivations to the plane of actual policy, historian Bernard Cohn enumerates the "'investigative modalities' devised by the British to collect the facts" in India, among these "the procedures by which appropriate knowledge is gathered, its ordering and classification, and then how it is transformed into usable forms such as published reports, statistical returns, histories, gazetteers, legal codes, and encyclopedias" (5). Horkheimer and Adorno's *Dialectic of Enlightenment* and Benedict Anderson's *Imagined Communities* explicitly make these modalities players in the rise of capitalism. Horkheimer and Adorno write that "The program of the Enlightenment"—which is to them, one recalls, not simply a historical period but rather a transhistorical epistemology and the logical engine of capitalism—"was the disenchantment [Entzauberung] of the world; the dissolution of myths and the substitution of knowledge [Wissen] for fancy [Einbildung]" (9). Similarly, when Anderson writes of how "Cairo and Mecca were beginning to be visualized in a strange new way, no longer simply as sites in a sacred Muslim geography, but also as dots on paper sheets which included dots for Paris, Moscow, Manila and Caracas," he sees in the rise of the imperial market a challenge to the force that informs Said's second, nonsecular Orientalism (Anderson 170–71).

Said may not have dwelt on the paradox that he adduces between empire's two epistemologies, but others have emboldened the tension and even scripted it as a duel. Ashis Nandy, for example, has asserted shamanism, "the repressed self of the society," as an alternative to drily empirical Western thought, because the former can "articulate some possibilities . . . which the 'sane,' the 'mature' and the 'rational' cannot self-consciously express or seriously pursue" ("Shamans" 266). Dipesh Chakrabarty amplifies Nandy's claims through his strikingly similar complaint that historiography's ardent secularism sets troubling "limits to the ways the past can be narrated" (Chakrabarty 89). Chakrabarty does not mention Said anywhere in his *Provincializing Europe,* but the book is a clear engagement with the "secular criticism" Said sponsors in *The World, the Text, and the Critic,* which bluntly equates "a secular attitude" to "a sense of history" (290). This is but a cursory reinvocation of a debate aired more fully in the introduction, above, but it frames an investigation of the unstable terrain of the collection of objects at the outset of the nineteenth century. What is ultimately at stake between the secularists and the antisecularists, between the models of empiricism and those of enchantment, is the same thing that organizes, especially in the 1820s and 1830s, the codification of the museum: the narration of the past and the best means of accomplishing it. Not coincidentally, the novel and the rise of realism are equally invested in this problem.

A glance at the changing status of collections at the turn of the nineteenth century in Europe reveals a moment of fundamental renegotiation that evinced itself in four major and related ways. Cobbling together episodes from the many and varied attempts to account for these renegotiations can be illuminating. First, Henning Bock's descriptions of sixteenth-century *Kunstkammer* and their slow metamorphosis into the public museums of nineteenth-century Berlin reenact the growing importance of public access to collections in post-Revolutionary Europe (113).[1] Bock largely credits Wilhelm von Humboldt with this important change in the German context, but Humboldt's ambivalence toward the overall project of collecting casts an interesting shadow. Krzysztof Pomian's discussion of the earliest printed catalogs of objects for sale testifies to a drift from private, noble holdings toward commercial interests in valued objects (*Collectors* 39). This commercial interest then tapers off as the collective public becomes a proprietor and the trade in collections of artifacts wanes palpably in the 1820s, thanks to the

---

1. For a more sustained investigation of the aftermath of the Revolution and its effect on collecting, see Wrigley. For a useful discussion of differences in audience in the organization of collections, see Jordanova.

growth of the market for art ("De la collection" 22). Similarly, following the establishment of the Archives Nationales in France in 1794, the administration of collections becomes an increasingly public project.

Second—and, according to Pomian, completely related—the content-emphasis of a collection becomes less invested in the presentation of rarity (the *curiosités* and the *Wunder* of the older collections) and more interested in the value of the general, the representative. In his book-length study of *Collectors and Curiosities*, Pomian sees curiosity—interest in rarity—itself as an opponent of rational science. Tony Bennett's history of the museum builds on Pomian's narrative of epistemological crisis, moving it past the historical scope of Pomian's book and into the nineteenth century. According to Bennett, Pomian's work tethers the *cabinet de curiosités* to a "pre-scientific rationality in its commitment to a view of nature's infinite variability and diversity" (Bennett 39):

> [T]he cabinet of curiosities, in its design and in its social relations, reflects its role as a storehouse of a knowledge that is, at once, rare and exclusive, intelligible only to those with the time, inclination and cultural training to be able to decipher the relationship in which each object stands to the whole.
>
> The initial challenge to the principles of curiosity, Pomian argues, came from the changing focus of natural history displays which, through the eighteenth century, came increasingly to accord priority of attention to the normal, the commonplace and the close-at-hand at the expense of the exceptional and the exotic. (41)[2]

Bennett picks up here where Pomian must leave off, and the former's attention to the early part of the nineteenth century bears most directly on the collection's development into the museum and the museum's relationship to realist narrative, which one can see at work in Balzac's novel.

Third, internal divisions within collections begin to express exterior geographical or cultural divisions. Pomian reminds us that, "in 1826, the Département des Sculptures antiques du Louvre is split into two divisions, one of which brings together *Greek, Roman and Medieval Monuments* and the other *Egyptian and Oriental Antiquities*" ("De la collection" 24). This new distinction is symptomatic of a new cartographical role adopted by the museum collection, which Eilean Hooper-Greenhill has compared to "the drawing of a map" (*Museums* 18). Like maps, she argues in a manner

---

2. The literary corollaries to this focus on the representative are many, but one might think quickly of Annette von Droste-Hülshoff's novella, *Die Judenbuche* (*The Jew's Beech Tree*, 1842), whose subtitle deceptively labels it a *Sittengemälde* or general "painting of customs" in the same way that Flaubert will subtitle *Madame Bovary* (1857) *Mœurs de Province* or "provincial mores" and George Eliot subtitles *Middlemarch* (1871–72) *Study of Provincial Life*.

reminiscent of Anderson's *Imagined Communities*, museums "created cultural unities from disperse experiences": "A major function of museums during the modernist period was the mapping of the world through the collection of artifacts." Hooper-Greenhill's dates for this "modernist period"—1820 to 1975—are intriguing (16). They correspond roughly, on the early end, to Jean-Baptiste-Joseph Fourier's *Description de l'Égypte* (1809), which Said uses as a beginning in *Orientalism:* "For my purposes here," Said writes, "the keynote of the relationship was set for the Near East and Europe by the Napoleonic invasion of Egypt in 1798.... [T]he Napoleonic expedition, with its great collective monument of erudition, the *Description de l'Égypte*, provided a scene or setting for Orientalism" (42–43). If 1809 marks a decisive starting point for this historiographic and ethnographic process, Franco Moretti has made very similar claims for the literary evocations of it. In *Atlas of the European Novel 1800–1900*, he reads a cluster of novels written between 1803 and 1818 precisely as Hooper-Greenhill reads the museum—as the encapsulation, mapping, and reinforcement of geographical divides. As my discussion of Balzac's novelistic cartography below will emphasize, Moretti's opposition to Said on this point is important, especially in his attempt to understand the lingering hierarchy of domestic and colonial space that Said begins to deconstruct in Austen's *Mansfield Park*.

Finally, this newly introduced East/West schism in the Louvre's collection mirrors the overall development, within the world of collections and the collections of the world, toward the order and coherence which organize the museological project precisely at the advent of literary realism. Susan Crane has recounted Goethe's visits to major Rhine- and Main-region collections of art and antiquities in a manner that highlights, albeit anecdotally, an increasing focus on ordered collections as against what Goethe called a "chaos of ruins" (qtd. in Crane, "Curious Cabinets" 77). In 1813, Goethe expressed his disappointment at the disorder that reigned in the collection of Ferdinand Franz Wallraf, a professor in Bonn who assembled his possessions, according to Goethe, "without any methodical sensibility or love of order" (76). Two years later, on the other hand, Goethe praised collector Franz Pick, Wallraf's apparent opposite in collecting practices. In Goethe's words, Pick

> has conscientiously collected each and every antique thing that came into his hands, which would be enough of a service, but he has served an even greater purpose in that he has earnestly and wittily, sensitively and cleverly brought order to a chaos of ruins, enlivened them and made them useful and enjoyable.... One looks through the collection with ever changing interests, which each time necessarily take a historical direction. (77)

Goethe's admiration of the collection-as-history here is crucial and prefigures later, explicitly history-minded exhibitions. Crane reminds us that E. H. Toelken, the director of Berlin's royal antiquities collection, in 1835 excluded objects empty of contextual, historical value. "The new museums" of this time, Crane writes, "wanted to represent history through selected historical objects, whose historical value was not determined by sheer age or uniqueness" (75). The material object—carefully "selected"—thus becomes the vessel of historical meaning.

Somewhere in between Goethe's cries for order in 1813 and 1815, and Toelken's 1835 demands for historicized objects, a collector in Balzac's Paris would come to his own similar conclusion on collecting. Stephen Bann and Bennett have both rhapsodized this important moment as an "epistemological break" (Bann 71), but it has a special significance in the scope of this chapter, because the transformation Bann and Bennett find so compelling happens to bookend, historically speaking, *La Peau de chagrin*'s 1831 publication, in which Balzac's narrative performs an identical metamorphosis. Bann and Bennett refer to the collection of Alexandre Du Sommerard, eventual curator of Paris's Musée de Cluny. Balzac was more than aware of Du Sommerard, which makes all the more interesting the thematic links between Balzac's novels and the idea of collecting. Balzac refers to Du Sommerard briefly in 1842, the year of Du Sommerard's death, in *La Muse du département* (*Comédie humaine* 4.646), and in 1847's *Le Cousin Pons* (7.491). *Splendeurs et misères des courtisanes*—finished in 1847 but begun well before that, in 1835—reveals an earlier and somewhat deeper fascination with the collector, specifically mentioning items "acquired . . . from Du Sommerard" (6.618). Before his move to "the late Gothic town-house of the Abbots of Cluny," Bann recounts, Du Sommerard's collection of antiques was a model of disorder (69). *L'Antiquaire*, an 1825 painting by the artist Charles Caius Renoux (1795–1846), depicts Du Sommerard in the midst of his chaotic collection "of objects crammed into a small space, with armour and fire-arms invading the carpet." All of this changed with his move to Cluny, according to Bann, who draws from contemporary journalistic evaluations of Du Sommerard's improved display: "Du Sommerard's collection, as displayed in the Hôtel de Cluny from the early 1830s, was not only a striking spectacle. It was a new experience" (70). Bann attributes the transformation of this collection to "a discernible shift in the character of historical discourse," a concern to which Du Sommerard's own correspondence attests (78). Calling Sir Walter Scott "the great Scottish painter," Du Sommerard praises the writer's efforts to rekindle interest in the medieval period and argues that "the same means, a methodical collection of the brilliant remains [dépouilles] of our ancestors, would contribute a lively interest to the reading of our chronicles" (qtd. in Bann 67).³ Du Sommerard's word *dépouilles* and the idea of remains figure repeatedly in Balzac's *Peau de chagrin*, but even more arresting is Du Sommerard's claiming of narrative as a model for the museum.

The language mirrors Goethe's in its praise of method and history, but the objects here are still servants of or visual aids to history. In this sense, Du Sommerard does not go as far as Friedrich Kruse had just a few years prior. In 1822, Kruse, "one of the founders of the Thuringen-Saxon historical association for the study of national antiquity, quoted a fellow co-founder approvingly: 'antiquity does not give us history, collecting does'" (qtd. in Crane, "Story, History" 188).⁴ Du Sommerard's reverence for his version of history introduced order to his collection, but he left it up to the chroniclers like Scott to shoulder the narrative. Balzac's own narrated collection, in *La Peau de chagrin*, can be only partially accounted for in the space between the chaotic Du Sommerard collection of 1825 and the immaculately curated one of the 1830s, because this later assemblage restricted itself to one historical period. What Du Sommerard's collections lack—namely, narrative—was already being bestowed upon objects by Kruse and another important figure who identified himself by his production—namely, natural history—rather than by his objects of study. When Baron Georges Cuvier's stagist theories of a natural history derived from the fossil record are added to Du Sommerard's ordered Parisian collection, the collision of organized antiques and the historicizing extrapolations of a narrative voice approximates what seems to happen in the antiquities shop at the outset of Balzac's *Peau de chagrin*, which subjects the material content to a coherent narrative form.⁵

3.. Russell Berman quotes Georg Forster, the cartographer on Cook's second circumnavigation in 1773, who similarly frets over an abundance of isolated pieces of knowledge with no organizing narrative: "facts were collected in all parts of the world, and yet knowledge was not increased. They [the learned in Europe] received a confused heap of disjointed limbs, which no art could reunite into a whole; and the rage of hunting after facts soon rendered them incapable of forming and resolving a single proposition" (qtd. in *Enlightenment or Empire* 43).

4. James Clifford might disagree, claiming that "collecting presuppose[s] a story" (236). This may hold true for private collecting—in which, say, the collector targets certain items for acquisition, knowing beforehand what is and is not available to her or him—but it cannot be true of archaeological finds or of the sort of history-construction Kruse has in mind, where the field of found objects is uncertain and remains uncertain until the object's relationship to other objects is determined.

5. Foucault highlights the importance of this epistemological shift in *The Order of Things*, as he tracks the idea of *visibility* and *vision* in developments in taxonomy and the rise of natural history collections (132–38). The result is, Foucault concludes, *history* under a "renewed name" (138). Mitchell leans on Foucault in his discussion of the role of Cuvier and others during the period of Romanticism, drawing useful distinctions between fossils and totems that he then maps onto an epistemological difference between fossilism's "modernized natural history" and totemism's "*primitive* natural history" (178; emphasis in original). Also responding to Foucault, Bill Brown traces a relationship between increasingly "narrative exhibitionary genre[s]" in American ethnographic museums at the end of the nineteenth century and the use of things in contemporary narratives, especially Sarah Orne Jewett's *The Country of the Pointed Firs* (1896). The transformation of collections he constructs refers more to "the so-called life-group exhibits" (92) than the injection of historical narrative into nonhuman object exhibits that we see in Europe in the earlier period I am discussing, yet there are some key similarities; Brown refers to an increasingly "materialist epistemology" (83), for example, and quotes Curtis Hinsley on the

However, the developments of knowledge that participate in this transition do not come without certain costs; even direct participants in this process felt this. A brief assessment of these perceived losses demonstrates how the birth of the museum and the death of the collection of curiosities are inseparable from the paradox of Said's with which we began, and from the related debate surrounding the function of empiricism and enchantment in the imperial project. Hooper-Greenhill's claim that "Museums which emerged during the nineteenth century, especially ethnographic and natural history museums, were formed by collections brought to the West from the rest of the world," can be even more strongly stated (*Museums* 18).[6] As Paula Findlen reminds us, the natural history *museums* were not the only beneficiaries of "the new material abundance that flowed into European cities from all corners of the world"; rather, all of "early modern natural history" was the "product" of these objects acquired by the empire (301).[7] Yet where science advanced, the imagination retreated. The process of what sociologist Max Weber would in 1918 label *Entzauberung*—"disenchantment," the eradication of mystery through reason and scientific progress (139)—had begun to make itself felt. The museum represents a major part of this process, because it is premised on the most empirical of epistemologies; by presenting the object itself, the museum's sole purpose is, precisely, to leave nothing to the imagination, leading one scholar bluntly to call the museum "a way of seeing" (Alpers 27). Wilhelm von Humboldt, despite his crucial role in opening collections to the public in Berlin, was already conscious of the damage being done by such progress by 1804, when Goethe quotes his lament that archaeological knowledge was being won only "at the cost of the imagina-

---

museums' move from the "exceptional" to "the everyday, the mundane" (87).

6. See Gould for an early discussion of the immediate relevance of imperial expansion and the plundering of artifacts in the creation of the Louvre.

7. The idea of colonial objects and subjects flowing back into the centers of the imperium recalls Makdisi's reading of Wordsworth's *Prelude*, with its "powerful overseas presence" of "peoples and commodities brought from the farthest reaches of the colonial system to London" (30). Makdisi points out that Wordsworth's description of urban heterogeneity "inverts the space of London, turning it inside out (like the mirror in Plato's cave) so that the entire external world and the imperial connections that have made it into a world all but ruled by Britain, can all be seen at once. The space of London itself turns into the space of empire; so that one need go no further than London to see much of the entire planet" (31). Adding to Makdisi's reading, I would note that the condensation occurs in Wordsworth's lines partly as a museological natural history collection:

At leisure let us *view*, from day to day,
As they present themselves, the *spectacles*
Within doors, troops of wild beasts, birds and beasts
Of every nature, from all climes convened;
And, next to these, those mimic sights that ape
The absolute presence of reality,
Expressing, as in mirror, sea and land,
And what earth is, and what she hath to show. (quoted in Makdisi 31; emphases mine)

Wordsworth describes imperialism here in terms of the museum's epistemology of optics and presence.

tion" (12.109). This sentiment is loudly echoed in an 1831 introduction to *La Peau de chagrin*.

(b) Seeing as Knowing: Realism and the Matter of Disenchantment

> The negative standard to which natural history is opposed is very often the credulous mystifications of "romance"...
> —Michael McKeon, *Origins of the English Novel*

The dyad of empiricism and enchantment, when mapped onto the shifting status and purpose of the collection of objects in nineteenth-century Europe, becomes troubled, and Balzac's *La Peau de chagrin* makes this trouble a central theme. That this theme is no small, peripheral concern in the novel is amplified by the passionate language of its second preface, which frames the opposition in terms of competing narrative methodologies. At the head of a collection called *Philosophical Novels and Stories* (*Romans et contes philosophiques*), of which *La Peau de chagrin* was to be the prize piece, Balzac's friend Philarète Chasles sees precisely this problem: "Where is the marvelous? What has faith become? Analysis consumes society by explaining it [ronge la société en l'expliquant]: the more the world ages, the more difficult [pénible] a task narration is" (10.1186).[8] The essay goes on to claim the marriage of empirical observation and active imagination as Balzac's greatest early achievement. It should probably be noted here, as Pierre Citron has done elsewhere, that there is reason to believe that Balzac penned this introduction himself, only to have Chasles sign off on it (10.1185). In the same month, Sainte-Beuve also described *La Peau de chagrin* as a bizarre mix of the scientific and the spiritual, calling it "*fetid* and *putrid*, spiritual, rotten, illuminated, sparkling and marvelous in its way of seizing the tiniest things and making them shine, of stringing together imperceptible pearls and making them ring out in a clatter of atoms" (1.263; emphases his). Marcel Proust would later claim that Sainte-Beuve had "misunderstood" Balzac (194), but Proust, like Chasles and Sainte-Beuve, cannot avoid marveling at the *Comédie humaine*'s provocative mélange of the senses and the imagination, "this medium-sized reality, too chimerical for life, too down-to-earth [terre à terre] for literature" (202). Balzac's grappling with these two modes

---

8. Sprenger's discussion of Balzac's unique anthropology in *Louis Lambert* (1832), a novelistic contemporary of *La Peau de chagrin*, is the only other work, to my knowledge, that addresses this important dilemma in Balzac: "Writing within an historical context in which faith was being overtaken by doubt, and where divine love and grace were being supplanted by skepticism and rational analysis, where collective social values were giving way to individualism, the questions to be raised, declares Balzac, are these: 'What form will the religious feeling assume? What will be its new expression?'" (6).

underwrites, one could argue, much of his work, but *La Peau de chagrin* makes the duel between them its fulcrum.

The strange cohabitation—within a near-Eastern talisman found in an antique shop—of the material and the spiritual in the novel asserts itself from the outset. Raphaël de Valentin, a young student in Paris, gambles away his last napoleon, then wanders along the Seine entertaining thoughts of suicide. He enters an antique shop run by an ancient man and two assistants, and exits later in possession of a donkey skin with the alleged power to grant wishes in exchange for years off of the wisher's life. Raphaël, putting his new powers to constructive use, wishes for an orgiastic feast and, in the second of the novel's four parts—although most critics see only three, largely ignoring the epilogue[9]—this feast takes place while Raphaël narrates his romantic woes, his unrequited love for a woman called Fœdora, to his friend Émile. This second part ends with the announcement that Raphaël has inherited a fortune from a long-lost Irish uncle in Calcutta, just as Raphaël's faithful friend Pauline will later become wealthy when her father returns from the Indies a beneficiary of the colonial project. (A treatment of both these windfalls introduces the next chapter.) Part Three sees Raphaël safely ensconced in a mansion, hermetically sealed off from anything that could provoke desire in him and thus, through the alleged machinations of the Magic Skin, reduce his life. He throws the skin away only to see it brought back to him, and he finally parades it past a series of scientists, each of whom attempts in turn, and unsuccessfully, to explain the Skin through his own branch of empirical science. Despondent, Raphaël goes to a spa town, wins a duel, returns to Paris, and dies, the trusty Pauline weeping over his body.

So, what does one make of the Magic Skin and of an early novel by a writer seen by some critics[10] as the first novelist of realism? Answers have varied wildly, but two of the most prominent examples illustrate clearly the complex relationship between even the most opposed readings of *La Peau de chagrin*. For example, Tzvetan Todorov begins his famous book on *The Fantastic* with *La Peau de chagrin* and even discusses it in some depth, but Henri Mitterand also uses it as his starting point, in a book on realism. The opposition in these two critics' readings—between the realist enumerative and the fantastic imaginative—recalls the paradox of Said's that is unable to cleanly separate empiricism from enchantment. In very different ways,

---

9. Brooks is just one example of this omission: "*La Peau de chagrin* falls into three sections" (*Reading* 48).

10. Balzac's realism is, of course, still a matter of lively debate. Dargan's "Balzac's General Method" gives a useful history of the disagreements. See also Doody 274–300, who perhaps unfairly calls *La Peau de chagrin* a "holiday from realism" (296); Fernandez, "La "Méthode de Balzac" and *Balzac*; Lukács, who claims that Balzac "overcame" romanticism but then went on to further it (*Studies* 64); Macherey 258–98; and Taine, who first and most extensively tethers aesthetic realism to scientific positivism.

both Todorov and Mitterand are reading the same material, colonial object, and they both start in the antiquities shop where the object is found. Here, at unavoidable length, is the most famous passage in this episode—the narration of the collection, which is itself perhaps the most famous part of the novel. This is largely the same chunk of text in which Mitterand and Todorov are so interested:

> A crowd of sorrowing faces, gracious and terrible, obscure and clear, far and near, gathered in numbers, in myriads, in whole generations. Egypt, rigid and mysterious, arose from her sands in the form of a mummy swathed in black bandages; then the Pharaohs swallowed up nations, that they might build themselves a tomb; and he beheld Moses and the Hebrews and the desert, and a solemn antique world. Fresh and smooth, a marble statue spoke to him from a twisted column of the pleasure-loving myths of Greece and Ionia. Ah! who would not have smiled with him to see, against the earthen red background, the brown-faced maiden dancing with gleeful reverence before the god Priapus, wrought in the fine clay of an Etruscan vase? The Latin queen caressed her chimera. The whims of Imperial Rome were there in life, the bath was disclosed, the toilette of a languid Julia, dreaming, waiting for her Tibullus. Strong with the might of Arabic talismans, the head of Cicero evoked memories of a free Rome, and unrolled before him the scrolls of Titus Livius. The young man beheld *Senatus Populusque Romanus*; consuls, lictors, togas with purple fringes; the fighting in the Forum, the angry people, passed in review before him like the cloudy faces of a dream. [Mitterand stops citing here.] Then Christian Rome dominated these images. A painter had laid heaven open; he beheld the Virgin Mary wrapped in a golden cloud among the angels, shining more brightly than the sun, receiving the prayers of sufferers, on whom this second Eve Regenerate smiles pityingly. At the touch of a mosaic, made of various lavas from Vesuvius and Etna, his fancy fled to the hot tawny south of Italy. He was present at Borgia's orgies, he roved among the Abruzzi, sought for Italian love intrigues, grew ardent over pale faces and dark, almond-shaped eyes. He shivered over midnight adventures, cut short by the cool thrust of a jealous blade, as he saw a mediaeval dagger with a hilt wrought like lace, and spots of rust like splashes of blood upon it. India and its religions took the shape of the idol with his peaked cap of fantastic form, with little bells, clad in silk and gold. Close by, a mat, as pretty as the bayadere who once lay upon it, still gave out a faint scent of sandal wood. His soul was awakened by a goggle-eyed Chinese monster, with mouth awry and twisted limbs, the invention of a people who, grown weary of an ever-unified beauty, find an indescribable pleasure in the fecundity of ugliness. A salt-cellar from Benvenuto Cellini's workshop carried him back to the Renaissance at its height, to the time when there was no restraint on art or morals, when torture was the sport of

sovereigns; and from their councils, churchmen with courtesans' arms about them issued decrees of chastity for simple priests. On a cameo he saw the conquests of Alexander, the massacres of Pizarro in a matchbox, and religious wars disorderly, fanatical, and cruel, in the shadows of a helmet. Joyous pictures of chivalry were called up by a suit of Milanese armor, brightly polished and richly wrought; a paladin's eyes seemed to sparkle yet under the visor. (10.70–71)

Balzac's enumeration and description of these objects culminates in the arrival of the Magic Skin. The text quickly marks the shop off as a locus of enchantment, as Raphaël is said to "leave real life, climb by degrees toward an ideal world," but this enchantment is contained within material objects and will finally be subsumed within scientific discourse (10.70). First described as a "chaos of antiquities" [chaos d'antiquités]—a phrase that recalls Goethe's assessment of Wallraf's chaotic collection as well as the idea of cosmological beginnings—the rational gazes of Raphaël and the narrator serve to organize chaos into material history, to give form to the store's inchoate content (10.69). Once this process has begun, the individual artifacts in the room become recognizable points in a distinctly occidental historiography: Egyptian mummies reference the Hebrew Exodus, whence we move to Greece and Rome, witness the advent of Christianity fading into the Italian Renaissance, at which point Europe encounters the Orient, and India and China enter the picture. Images of violent empire ensue, first through Alexander and then Pizarro. Finally, moving into the later sixteenth and seventeenth centuries, the anatomist and collector Frederik Ruysch (1638–1731) collides with artists like Jean Goujon (ca. 1510–ca. 1565) and images of newly acquired territories like Tahiti and Illinois (10.72). A number of critics have ignored the manner in which Raphaël and Balzac's narrator organize the chaos merely by perusing *in a certain sequence* the objects presented. Nicole Cazauran sees the store having "neither order nor reason" (93), Mitterand writes of "the incoherence of the scene [tableau]" (28), Leo Bersani opines that "continuous historical time" is "undermined by a mass of unrelated objects from different periods and different places" (71), and Samuel Weber claims that "the tableau is as confused as the casino is clear" (35). David Bell specifically warns against the idea of order in the shop, writing instead of a "semantics of disorder" (*Circumstances* 187).[11] In effect,

---

11. Millott and Watson are the few to acknowledge the manner in which order is brought to the shop, but Millott's reading of the scene stresses a poetic rather than historical coherence (87). Watson justifiably dismisses Bell's assumption of disorder and sees instead a "grouping . . . of heterogeneous elements into large conceptual categories" in the store (122). The actual descriptions of the collection undercut this idea in favor of a chronological narrative, though. Similarly, Orlando notes that "each object is metonymically or antonomastically evocative: a part capable on its own of furnishing the imagination with the relative historical and geographical whole" of the culture to which that object belongs, without grasping the larger historical coherence created (185). Arlette

though, the antiques create a roughly chronological history of civilization as seen through Western eyes. The one glaring anachronism here is, importantly, Alexander's imperial expansion, which is grouped alongside Pizarro's "massacres"; in placing these thematically similar events together, out of sequence, Balzac highlights the theme of (imperial) violence rather than its mere historical place. The narrator will, shortly thereafter, laud paleontologist Cuvier, whose stagist interpretations of the fossil record are accurately reconstructed in the stagist, material-based history offered by the antiquities in *La Peau de chagrin*.

The emphasis on collected material here is only part of a broader empiricism being contested within the novel, and the fascinating owner of the antique shop merits a closer look. He is, on a superficial level, both the purveyor of the collection and the one who offers to Raphaël the titular object that will dictate the course of the novel. Moreover, as the shopkeeper tells his own history, he awakens Balzac's readers to the duel of ideas they are to witness. In a lengthy speech in which he opposes *pouvoir* (to be able) and *vouloir* (to want), *voir* (to see) and *savoir* (to know), the merchant reveals that he has traveled the world, wanted everything, experienced everything, seen everything, and known everything (10.85–87). Critics have focused on the opposition of *pouvoir* and *vouloir*, largely because they come up more frequently in the speech, and probably also because it is revealed later in the novel that Raphaël is the author of a treatise on the will (*volonté*). The shopkeeper, however, scorns these concerns: "What is madness, if not an excess of desire or power?" (10.87). And if *voir* and *savoir* are not dealt with as extensively within the shopkeeper's harangue, it is because they are more important questions within the overall novel's wrestling with an empirical—and especially optical—epistemology. "Is not to see, to know?" [Voir, n'est-ce pas savoir?], the old man asks Raphaël (10.86). This fundamental question of vision and knowledge drives *La Peau de chagrin* even if Raphaël is not yet aware of it: "I want to live with excess!" he cries, seizing the Magic Skin, choosing *vouloir* and *pouvoir* over *voir* and *savoir* (10.87). "Is not to see, to know?" though, is the same question answered by the development of the museum as a tool for or repository of knowledge. The shop's owner finishes his lecture by degrading vision and interrogating the empirical predilection he adduces earlier. His proposition that vision is knowledge presupposes both a sensory epistemology and the notion that *savoir* is an unquestioned good, which Balzac's novel will relentlessly problematize and finally question outright.

Michel also sees a dehistoricized thematic coherence: "Raphaël read the death of civilizations through the bric-à-brac of the antiquities store" (157). Levin mentions that the "chaos" is "somehow organized" but does not elaborate (185).

There is another level, though, to Balzac's simultaneous deployment and wariness of scientific models and the urge for clarity. The mode of natural history most closely associated with Cuvier—who is lauded by *La Peau de chagrin* as well as by Balzac's master preface to the *Comédie humaine*—wielded its narrative powers in the interest of explanation, as a means of linking diachronic events or objects causally. The relevance for typical understandings of realist narrative is clear: if a causal explanation trusts the possible and prizes the probable,[12] the sort of aesthetic probability often termed *vraisemblance* can be understood as a causally acceptable set of narrative moments, what Dargan calls "harmony" and "accumulation" in his essay on Balzac's realism (1), a notion echoed more recently in Dällenbach's idea of the "regularity and insistence" of Balzac's descriptions (28). Buchanan has discussed the Enlightenment roots of this variety of historiography, and she points to its adoption by antiquarians in the early nineteenth century as a means of vindicating a hobby being slowly supplanted by art collection (171). Many authors make merely superficial metaphorical reference to scientific practice, Buchanan declares, in their efforts "to link antiquarianism with the associations brought to mind by science," and one could include Scott's 1816 novel, *The Antiquary* (172). Other authors, however, lean on scientific imagery in what amounts to "a statement of methodological intent," and, although Buchanan does not elaborate on this group, one would have to number Balzac among them. Indeed, a number of Balzac's admirers have envisioned him as the sort of explainer that Cuvier aspired to be; Proust's pithy comment is useful here, that Balzac's "style does not suggest, does not reflect [reflète]: it explains" (207). Such appreciations complicate Martin Kemp's argument, in *The Science of Art: Optical Themes in Western Art*, that *explanation* has been the property of science as against art's penchant for *illusion*. Pamela H. Smith and Paula Findlen counter that "both groups [i.e., scientists and artists] were engaged in a struggle to make sensory knowledge of nature authoritative" (14). Balzac's *Peau de chagrin* contributes to this exchange by contextualizing the moment at which the artist begins to shamelessly envision herself or himself as a scientist or natural historian, the moment at which the artist attempts to explain *and* entertain—or to reveal the fruits of empirical observation and the active imagination, to return to the language of Chasles's introduction to the novel.

Coherence is the immediate consequence of *La Peau de chagrin*'s catalogue of the merchant's antique collection, as the quasi-mystical ecstasy of exotic and ancient things is apparently brought under the historian's umbrella. This scene merely serves as precursor to a more sustained duel

12. Knoepflmacher on George Eliot: "Her 'realism,' she now recognized, merely demanded a close faithfulness to probability, not a rejection of the 'ideal or eclectic'" (32–33).

between history and mystery, however. Raphaël, hesitating, "remained in the philosophical doubt recommended by Descartes, and was thus, in spite of himself, under the power of those inexplicable hallucinations whose mysteries are condemned by our pride or that our impotent science strives in vain to analyze" (10.77). This is strong language, but Balzac's narrator overturns it moments later, depicting reason's disenchantment as even stronger. The narrator rationalizes away Raphaël's reaction through a variety of biologizing and psychologizing sluices:

> If he let himself be momentarily dominated by a belief worthy of children listening to their nurses' tales, one must attribute this error to the veil stretched over his life and his understanding by his meditations, to the exhaustion of his irritated nerves, to the violent drama whose scenes had just heaped on him all the horrid pleasures contained in a piece of opium. This vision had taken place in Paris, on the Quai Voltaire, in the nineteenth century, times and places where magic should be impossible. (10.79)

This sort of moment is repeated later in the century. The butler Gabriel Betteredge in Wilkie Collins's *Moonstone* (1868), for example, protests another character's idea of "a conspiracy of living rogues, set loose on us by the vengeance of a dead man" (33). "Whoever heard the like of it," Betteredge asks, "in the nineteenth century, mind; in an age of progress, and in a country which rejoices in the blessings of the British constitution?" As in *La Peau de chagrin*, magic's impossibility is explained by the narrative present and the characteristics of the narrative's domestic space. Raphaël's reasoned dismissal turns to history in order to conclude with the observation that Napoleon had had similarly emotional effects on people, and that those effects were certainly not magical. The notion of shame at the belief in the supernatural ("a belief worthy of children") is, as we shall see later, also an important concern in the fiction of Trollope and Fontane. Balzac, however, does not dwell on it as Fontane's Innstetten does in *Effi Briest*; instead, Raphaël awakens from his reveries, "bec[omes] a man again, recognize[s] in the old man a creature of flesh, quite alive, in no way phantasmagorical, and live[s] again in the real world." At this point, the narrative has been tempted by and resisted mystery, and the talisman is imported into the text.

The elderly shopkeeper offers the Magic Skin to Raphaël as a means of curing his woes, but Balzac goes to great lengths to make it clear that this object is something entirely other. It is interesting that, in the writing of the novel, geographical and cultural specificity seems to have been far less important to Balzac's envisioning the Skin than the mere fact of its Eastern origin. In early drafts of *La Peau de chagrin*, the talisman was said to be engraved in Sanskrit. The lengthy Arabic citation engraved on the Skin and reproduced by the text of the novel today was a later addition, one that Balzac borrowed from an Orientalist friend in Vienna; the Arabic text went prominently into the novel, but Balzac forgot to change, in subsequent editions, the word "sanscrit" to "arabe" (10.84). Scholars have long since noted this carelessness for its own sake—Alois Richard Nykl was the first, in 1919—but clearly it reveals as well that the crucial thing for Balzac was simply that the Skin come from *an* outside. If one wishes to push the angle of imperialism in the novel, then the shift to from Sanskrit to Arabic strengthens the case by dint of France's interests in the Middle East at the time. The narrator further separates the talisman from the Western tradition by contrasting Eastern fables with figures like the Sphinx and the Griffin, "whose existence is in some way mythologically admitted" (10.83). Balzac waffled, in the various editions of *La Peau de chagrin* that were published in the 1830s, between referring to these canonical figures as "mythologically" or "scientifically" admitted, just as he would later strike the adjective "orientale" in favor of "talismanique" (10.1250). Such slippage suggests a notion of science as the property of the West—one recalls similar views amongst postcolonial critics—as much as it hints at an elision of things Oriental and things supernatural.

The status of the Magic Skin remains in question throughout the novel: Is it a natural object or a supernatural phenomenon? The glow that seems to emanate from it is quickly explained away "mathematically" by Raphaël, before he has even taken it out of the shop (10.82). When he tries to scrape the Arabic writing off of the talisman and is unable to do so, he also accounts for this strange fact scientifically, by claiming that "the industry of the Orient has some secrets that are truly unique to it" (10.83). He says this in a worried tone, though, his certainty in science shaken, and with good cause, for, before he has gotten far from the shop, his first wish—for a dinner feast—seems to have been granted. Other fulfilled wishes follow in the forms of wealth, and then victory in a duel, yet in the granting of this first wish Raphaël sees a "natural" stringing-together of events rather than "the accomplishment of his wishes," and he is not the only one to betray skepticism (10.92). Todorov maintains that

> None of Raphaël's desires is realized in an unlikely fashion. The banquet he requests had already been arranged by his friends; the money comes to him in the form of a legacy; the death of his adversary in a duel can be explained by the fear Raphaël's own calm provokes [he is only calm, of course, because he is already convinced of his own impending doom]; lastly, Raphaël's own death is due, apparently, to phthisis and not to supernatural causes. Only the skin's extraordinary properties openly confirm the intervention of the marvelous. (68)

Todorov asserts here what the novel bears out as well: that there is nothing in the events of *La Peau de chagrin* that does not conform to an empirical notion of what is possible and can be explained through natural causes, an observation that could potentially drain the magic out of both Balzac's novel and the text inscribed in Arabic on the talisman.

The material, however, does maintain its mystery. *La Peau de chagrin* uses its central, Oriental object to claim a path between the epistemology of enumerative empiricism that constructs the collection, and the epistemology of imaginative mysticism that describes a talisman outside of history. The passage of Todorov's cited above can be read as a partial concession to the material base of the fantastic that Todorov wants to see in Balzac. But Mitterand—the scholar of realism—makes a similar concession in the other direction, labeling Balzac's particular realism in *La Peau de chagrin* a "fantastique des choses" (11). The critical unease here and elsewhere[13] is apt in assessments of a novel that exhibits its own ambivalence between materialist comfort and what cannot be contained by material science. Balzac, too, hedges his bets. The physicist and chemist, after failing to fit the Skin within their materialist paradigms, simply exile it and return to business as usual: "They were taken with laughter, and dined as people who see, in a miracle, nothing more than a phenomenon" (10.252). Physical science, for all the plaudits it wins earlier in the novel, becomes offset by a loss. *La Peau de chagrin* continues to behave as if everything has its clear, explicable material cause until, finally, even a satisfactory explanation for the shrinking of the Magic Skin will be offered, and in a manner that trivializes the issue terrifically, when a scientist calls the shrinking of skin a "fact inexplicable and yet natural, that, since the beginning of the world, has been the despair of medicine and of beautiful women" (275). The scientists tire of the object precisely once they judge it both "inexplicable" and "natural." In so doing, they manage to simultaneously preserve their naturalism and situate the Skin outside of material science's concerns with what can be explained.

For Balzac, as for Wilhelm von Humboldt, the reliance on science does not come without a price. In the mostly ignored epilogue to *La Peau de chagrin*, the novel acknowledges the costs by painting the twin epistemologies in Said's paradox as forces blatantly inimical to each other. In one of the final images of this epilogue, Raphaël's faithful Pauline is said to stand guard over his family's tomb on a river island, where she "seemed to prevent a steamboat from passing, . . . wanted to protect her country against modern

---

13. Consider, for example, Cailliet, who doesn't even mention *La Peau de chagrin* in his monograph on Balzac's magical motifs; and Lukács (*Balzac*), who, in the words of a somewhat skeptical Bisztray, "willingly accepts the irrational element of *La Peau de chagrin*" (65).

invasions" (294).[14] The body of the novel bears witness to a collision, within the talisman and its role in *La Peau de chagrin*, between the enchantments of the exotic and supernatural, and the disenchanting forces of science that are first embedded in the text by the reaction to the antique shop's collection. The novel's epilogue gives us the most loyal and sympathetic character, Pauline, fighting a losing battle against a process already well underway, but what is at stake is much closer to home. It is important that this image closes the novel. *La Peau de chagrin* is often relentlessly realist, well within the sort of empirical, "self-abnegating," objective narrative epistemology George Levine has discussed (*Dying to Know* 3).[15] Pauline's defense of the countryside against the onslaughts of science and technology weighs in against the same realist narrative mode whose roots were entangled with contemporaneous advances of science and whose form Balzac was still negotiating.

La Peau de chagrin is, of course, not the only novel of the nineteenth century to ground itself on collections or collectible objects, a narrative obsession that Balzac termed "bricabracologie." In addition to Scott's *The Antiquary*, Balzac's own *Cabinet des antiques* (1837–39), Charles Dickens's *The Old Curiosity Shop* (1841), and Theodor Fontane's *Vor dem Sturm* (*Before the Storm*, 1878), all employ the sort of pat references to antiquarianism that Buchanan derides as superficial rather than methodological. Objects and the idea of collecting serve, in these novels, largely to illustrate a character, and Dickens's text even exhibits a certain dread of things: "We are so much in the habit of allowing impressions to be made upon us by external objects, which should be produced by reflection alone," the narrator of *The Old Curiosity Shop* claims (19). As Henry James pointed out, however, Balzac had a

---

14. This image of Pauline perhaps calls to mind other images of defense against modern invasions, from Joseph Conrad's *Heart of Darkness* (1902) and the "wild and gorgeous apparition of a woman" who faces down Marlowe's steamer (55–56), to Tayeb Salih's short story, "The Doum Tree of Wad Hamid." In Salih's story, the tree is contrasted with technology and associated instead with the supernatural and with local tradition. It grows "in a patch of rocky ground by the river, standing above it like a sentinel" (14). The story's ending resists the suggestion that "there's plenty of room for all these things: the doum tree, the tomb, the water-pump, and the steamer's stopping place" (19). Flaubert lampoons the duel between modernity and tradition in a painting by Pellerin in *L'Éducation sentimentale*: "It showed the Republic, or Progress, or Civilization, in the form of Christ driving a locomotive through a virgin forest" (2.330).

15. Balzac's narrator prizes, from the outset, an objective, journalistic style, claiming that its unadorned sentences have more of the sublime in them than any poetry, dramas, or novels (65). And the verb *dépouiller*—to flay or skin, along with its cousin, *dépouilles*, or *remains*—appears so many times in *La Peau de chagrin* that one wonders whether Balzac isn't literally anticipating Émile Zola's autopsy-like narrative project in *Thérèse Raquin* (1867). Taine anticipates this comparison already in 1865—one might even suggest that he anticipates Zola's preface to *Thérèse Raquin* itself—when he refers to Balzac's style as a "dissection": "au lieu de peindre, il disséquait" (*Nouveaux essais* 80). The Danish critic Herman Bang likewise noted Balzac's influence on and proximity to Naturalism, claiming that those who used to read *La Comédie humaine* now read *Les Rougon-Macquart* (118), and calling Balzac "a Darwinist who didn't know Darwin" (120).

"mighty passion for *things*—for material objects" (48). *La Peau de chagrin* is one of a small number of works—including, perhaps, Wilkie Collins's *The Moonstone* (1868), Conrad Ferdinand Meyer's *Das Amulett* (1873), and Eça de Queiroz' *A Relíquia* (1887)—whose attention to a specific object acquires a structural momentum and importance of its own. Balzac deploys the idea of the collection and an uncollectible object in a narrative that becomes an interrogation of the epistemological changes that altered the role of collections and objects and oversaw the rise of realism.[16]

One sees this narrative tendency toward scientific organization and material observation by focusing on the pivotal moment in the antiquities shop and the one central antique that drives the whole novel. Balzac's interest in science crops up repeatedly in the 1830s—in *La Recherche de l'Absolu* (1834), *Louis Lambert* (1832), and the invention of cheaper paper in *Les Illusions perdues* (1837–42)—and his related interest in collections yields *Le Cabinet des antiques* and the memorable collection of *Le Cousin Pons*. The collection in *La Peau de chagrin*, however, unites these two interests, brings the farthest corners of the world into Paris and allows a Parisian gaze to order and enumerate them, and an empirical epistemology to be troubled by them. Vincent Pecora has argued that Balzac creates a sort of "ethnographic museum" before the widespread existence of such museums (149), but Balzac's collection and the birth of the museum appear as complementary developments. Moreover, the debt owed to empire by the museum, ethnography, and natural history, throws into relief the important Eastern origin of the title object that cannot be incorporated into what Cohn calls the "museological" imperialist modality. Such modalities only draw half the picture of empire. The Orient is, to Said's Orientalist, not just the stuff of museums, but the raw material of dreams and nightmares. *La Peau de chagrin*'s empirical method is clear, its sympathies less so. In what must thus be an unfair fight between empiricism and enchantment, Balzac's novel forces the two halves of this paradox to confront each other in the negotiation of a narrative mode, and then betrays its own disenchantment at the result.

---

16. As the nineteenth century nears its end, collections retain their narratological importance, but the milieu is altered: the museum/cabinet becomes the department store, the collector the consumer. This is the logical result of: the private collection's movement into public space; the continued shift, within collections, from rarity to representativeness (now mass-producedness); and the evolving emphasis on order. Zola's *Au Bonheur des Dames* (1882) shows how the divisions between East and West are reproduced as classifications of product quality and exchange value, and the spatial arrangement of the department store's collection testifies to a paralyzing desire rather than a narrative possibility. If the department store's use in narrative is the heir to earlier novelistic depictions of collections, it should not surprise us that Zola's prose in *Au Bonheur des Dames* often seems to ape Balzac's description of the collection in *La Peau de chagrin*. Saisselin genders this transformation, with specific reference to Zola and Dreiser, in his chapter "Enter Woman: The Department Store as Cultural Space" (Saisselin 33–49).

CHAPTER TWO

MARGINAL REALISM IN
LE PÈRE GORIOT

> "Ah!" he sighed. "If I had but the pen of Balzac! I would depict this scene."
>
> —Agatha Christie, *Murder on the Orient Express*

An exchange between Vautrin and Madame Vauquer roughly halfway through *Le Père Goriot* (1835) mobilizes an important uncertainty, which the text couches in metaphors of materialism and antiquarianism. It is the same uncertainty that pervades Balzac's elaboration of the epistemological duel in *La Peau de chagrin*, and so it will serve here as a bridge between that earlier novel's dependence on a foreign, physical object to embody a crisis of knowledge, and *Le Père Goriot*'s situation of this crisis and of its larger implications within the world. Vautrin jokingly begins,

> "If we start weeping, there'll be an explosion; but I'll gather up the debris with an antiquarian's care."
> "There's a man who knows the language of true French gallantry [galanterie française]!" said the widow, bending over to speak in Madame Couture's ear. (3.207)

Because the reception of *Goriot* has insistently read Vautrin as a Romantic and even Revolutionary figure, it may surprise us that he could even pretend to the sort of orderly care of the antiquarian. Madame Vauquer's take on Vautrin's attractive gallantry, on the other hand, sits quite comfortably with the reading most scholars have made of him as a charming, disarming rebel. This critical consistency has precluded a hard look at the manner in which Vautrin, rather than simply act as foil to the character of Père Goriot or of

Madame de Beauséant, also represents a facet of what Dean de la Motte has called "the bureaucracy created under Napoleon and usually associated with the mechanized, scientific approach to administration" (55–56). The character of Vautrin will be central to this chapter, because he incorporates themes already voiced tentatively in *La Peau de chagrin*—the potential for enormous financial gain in the colonies, for example—and because, more importantly, he anchors the entirety of *Le Père Goriot*. Vautrin's absence from the novel would eviscerate Rastignac's moral dilemma and the manner in which this dilemma complicates the text's portrayal of social class, and would obscure the local import of Rastignac's global allegory of the murder of a Chinese Mandarin, which transports this moral dilemma into the broader, increasingly knowable world. Balzac and Rastignac both make the ties between the hypothetical victim and the avowed criminal explicit, and, from outside and underneath Paris, the Mandarin and Vautrin together structure *Le Père Goriot*.

This chapter will begin by tracing the shared narrative strategies and thematic game of *La Peau de chagrin* and *Le Père Goriot* in order to demonstrate the increasing importance of the world outside Paris as determiner of fates within Paris, the increasing narrative reliance of the domestic on the exotic. The almost superficial significance of the colonies in *La Peau de chagrin* acquires legitimate weight in *Goriot*. A close examination of the relationship between the allegory of the Mandarin and the potential facilitators of social mobility in the novel highlights the increasing complexity of the relationship between the city and the world, the domestic and the exotic, disenchantment and the possibility of its renegotiation. The allegory relates most obviously to Vautrin and his planned violence against Taillefer, as numerous critics have pointed out. However, Vautrin's machinations and their hints at colonial violence cannot be cleanly separated from the figures of Goriot and Beauséant. More significantly, Balzac's rendering of Vautrin's character betrays a constant overlapping of the same two energies that animate *La Peau de chagrin*, one coded as romantic and one coded as disenchanting. *Le Père Goriot*'s fundamental ambivalence toward the outcome of this duel gives a more concrete narrative form to the epistemological crisis engendered earlier by *La Peau de chagrin*.

(a) The World Without: The Mandarin and the Subject(s) of Empire

Goriot builds on several important developments in Balzacian narrative that were discussed at length in the last chapter: a narrative mode motivated by an empirical epistemology that often proceeds by observed facts and deduces their significance, for example; and the imperial penumbra of the plot, which is at best subtle in *La Peau de chagrin* but a necessary component of any reading of Vautrin and the Mandarin. Furthermore, *Goriot* shares thematic ground with Balzac's *L'Histoire des Treize* (1833–35) and especially with *La Fille aux yeux d'or* (1835), which was conceived in 1830, well before *Goriot* was begun, and finished while Balzac was making final revisions to *Goriot*. Both are novels of Paris—indeed, their intransigent urbanism distinguishes them from a partly provincial work like *Illusions perdues*—and both consider and attempt to alter the fate of fiction in a milieu Balzac saw as disenchanted, these "times and places where magic should be impossible," as the narrator of *La Peau de chagrin* puts it (10.79). Still, it is tempting to buy into a general critical tendency to oppose *La Peau de chagrin* and *Le Père Goriot*. As the story goes, one is fantastic, the other realistic; one Romantic, the other Realist; one philosophical, the other historical. Only a handful of critics have dared link the two works, largely in an attempt to position the earlier one as an evolutionary stepping stone in the novelist's career. Arlette Michel points to *La Peau*'s "foundational value" in Balzac's depictions of Paris (114). André Vanoncini positions the novel as "the product of a transitional phase in Balzacian creation between the inspiration of the youthful novels . . . and the entry into the age of reason that will culminate in the great realist works, like *Eugénie Grandet, Père Goriot*" (73). Maurice Bardèche's authoritative account of Balzac's work up to and including *Goriot* (a goal which asserts, in itself, the perceived importance of this text) aims to treat the "return of characters at the moment at which it was invented by Balzac, that is, by studying *Le Père Goriot*" (284). The characters whose return so impresses Bardèche all appear first, although he does not point this out, in *La Peau de chagrin*: Rastignac, Taillefer, Raphaël. It is Hugo von Hofmannsthal, however, who touches on what might be the most significant point of contact between *Goriot* and *La Peau*, when he sees in both novels an attempted erasure of the authorial voice, claiming, "You say '*Peau de chagrin*' and don't recall a poet's [Dichter] achievement; you think of old Goriot and his daughters and don't think about what the author's [Verfasser] name is" (382). What von Hofmannsthal indirectly praises here is the same narrative empiricism on which the last chapter focused; the author is removed enough that we recall only the objects and the people. On a fundamental narrative level, the realist care evinced by *Goriot*'s painstaking attention to milieu, character, and objectivity descends from *La Peau de chagrin*. Consider the manner in which, for example, *La Peau*'s narrator repeatedly gives us observed facts and possible explanations of them. Rather than simply tell the reader that Raphaël was innocent, Raphaël's observed behavior is said to "indicate an innocent soul" while his "physiognomy expressed a resignation" (10.58; 10.61).[1] One must compare this to the initial descriptions of Victorine Taillefer in *Goriot*, whose "eyes of grey mixed with black expressed a softness, a resignation" (3.59), and of Vautrin, whose face "offered signs of hardness" (3.61). The narrator of *La Peau de chagrin* goes so far at times to avoid straying from the observable that, when inner feelings simply must be described, as in the second section, he has a character do it in dialogue.

La Peau de chagrin shares with *Goriot* more than its narrative mode. Balzac's imperial allusions in the former are muffled, their function largely cosmetic and hardly fundamental. (Thus have they largely escaped critical attention.) Apart from the colonial shadings of the Magic Skin itself, Raphaël and Pauline are both made wealthy by colonial commercial interests. This is the announcement to which Raphaël awakens, after the all-night orgy:

> Well, sir, you are the sole heir of the Major O'Flaharty, deceased in August of 1828, at Calcutta.
>
> It's an *incalcuttable* fortune!, cried the critic.
>
> The Major having bequeathed several amounts to public institutions in his will, the French Government sent in a claim for the remainder to the East India Company, the notary continued. (10.208)

The pun *incalcuttable*, which links incalculability with the foreign locale of Calcutta, is obviously an important one, and it foreshadows Vautrin's penchant for *calculation*. If one chooses to believe in the powers of the Magic Skin, this sudden fortune fulfills Raphaël's second wish. The revelation is curious for several reasons, beginning with the distinctly Irish surname of Raphaël's benefactor, who is identified as Raphaël's uncle in an early draft of the novel, a detail that survives only in an editing error (cf. 10.1314) later in the final version of the text, where a character proposes a toast to "son [Raphael's] oncle, le major Martin O'Flaharty," despite the narrator's never having specified the relationship (10.209). It is also significant that the same event to which Raphaël owes his good fortune—the government's seizing of the assets of the Compagnie des Indes—will prove to have been the ruin of the Rastignac family in *Le Père Goriot*. Eugène de Rastignac tells M. de Restaud, "my great-uncle, a vice-admiral, lost everything in the King's service. The revolutionary government refused to recognize us as creditors [n'a pas voulu admettre nos créances] when it liquidated the Compagnie des Indes" (3.99). The juxtaposition taints Raphaël's inheritance, sanctioned as it is by the Revolution, as much as it assures Balzac's readers of the legitimacy

---

1. These deductions surpass the "physiognomical thought" that Rivers discusses.

of Rastignac's upward mobility, which *Le Père Goriot* thus presents as a restoration on a smaller scale.

From similar geographical distances, the story of Pauline's inheritance in *La Peau de chagrin* brings closure to an adventure whose beginning emerges earlier in the text, during Raphaël's extended monologue:

> One evening Pauline told me her story with touching simplicity. Her father had been a major in the horse grenadiers of the Imperial Guard. He had been taken prisoner by the Cossacks, at the crossing of the Beresina; and when Napoleon later on proposed an exchange, the Russian authorities made search for him in Siberia in vain; according to the other prisoners, he had escaped with a view of going to the Indies [avec le projet d'aller aux Indes], and since then Mme. Gaudin, my landlady [Pauline's mother], had been unable to obtain any news of her husband. (10.140)

Nor does the reader hear further news, until Pauline and Raphaël are reunited later, at which point she tells him, "My father has returned. I am a rich heiress" (10.229). Precisely whence he is returned is made clear a few pages later, when Pauline states more specifically, "He has returned from the Indies" [Il est revenu[2] des Indes] (10.232). Such unexpected homecomings factor, of course, in some of Balzac's other texts, most famously in *Le Colonel Chabert* (1836) but more matter-of-factly and with similarly colonial tones in *Eugénie Grandet* (1833), with Charles Grandet's return from the Indies; or in the later *Modeste Mignon* (1844), where, in the space of about two paragraphs in the third chapter, Dumay goes to America and returns rich. (Jane Eyre's sudden inheritance from her uncle abroad also comes to mind.) The colonies in general and the Indies in particular are thus important and neglected elements of both *La Peau de chagrin* and *Le Père Goriot*. Their centrality to the latter novel, though, moves beyond the facilitation of the plot and into its very possibility, for without the ruination of the Rastignac family during the liquidation of the Compagnie des Indes, there is no story of Eugène's desire to rise, and thus no novel.

Though not a specifically French colonial image in any strict historical sense, the introduction of the Chinese Mandarin into *Le Père Goriot*'s Paris is given imperial resonance, just as it is also linked specifically to Vautrin's plot against Taillefer. Rastignac "wandered about [flâna] nearly all day, his thoughts racing feverishly in a way familiar to any young man suffering from excessive expectations. Vautrin's arguments [raisonnements] had brought him to reflect on social life, just at the moment when he ran into his friend

---

2. Note the coincidence of Pauline's word for "returned," which bears connotations of finance.

Bianchon in the Luxembourg Gardens" (3.164). Rastignac asks Bianchon whether he remembers a certain passage from Rousseau (the editors of the Pléiade point out that it is actually from Chateaubriand): "Do you recall the passage where he asks what the reader would do if he could become rich by killing some old Mandarin in China without stirring from Paris, simply by willing it so?"[3] Bianchon claims he would not, but Rastignac continues to push him, raising examples from Rastignac's own situation, including the need of money for women. Bianchon's final refusal of hypothetical murder is illuminating but rarely explored in depth. He answers Rastignac thus:

> But you are asking the question that everyone has to face when they start out in life, and you are trying to cut the Gordian knot with a sword. You have to be Alexander, my dear fellow, to behave like that, otherwise you end up in gaol. For my part I am content with the modest living [la petite existence] I shall make in the provinces, where I shall quite simply [tout bêtement] take over from my father. A man's desires can just as easily be satisfied in the smallest of circles as within an immense circumference. Napoleon didn't dine twice a day, and couldn't take any more mistresses than a medical student doing his house training at the Capucins. Our happiness, my friend, will always lie between the soles of our feet and the crown of our head. Whether it costs a million francs a year or a hundred louis our basic perception of it is just the same within us. So I conclude that the Chinaman lives. (3.165)

The passage merits close attention, because it accomplishes several related things at once in *Le Père Goriot* and because Trollope's *The Way We Live Now* mimics it intriguingly (see chapter 6). First, Bianchon casts the shadow of empire over the entire dilemma by referring to Alexander and Napoleon. Without pointing to these emperors, Ginzburg's important essay, "To Kill a Chinese Mandarin," still situates the dilemma similarly and powerfully by referring to a reprise of the allegory in the later *Modeste Mignon*. The poet Canalis addresses Dumay: "At this moment, the most important [utile] Mandarin in China is breathing his last and the empire is going into mourning, and does that make you sad? In India, the English are killing thousands of

---

3. This allegory was first probed in depth by Ronaï. The Pléiade editors point to a far earlier incarnation of this dilemma in one of Balzac's youthful novels, *Annette et le criminel (Argow le pirate)*, where the question is the same but the context altered: "You, over there, if you could kill, with a look, a man in New Holland who is at death's door, and do it without a soul knowing, and if this little half-crime brought you a brilliant fortune, tell the truth now, wouldn't you already be in *your* hotel, in *your* carriage? You'd be saying, 'My horses, my land, and my credit!' You wouldn't hesitate to repeat, 'A gentleman like myself . . . !'" (*Comédie humaine* 3.1280). The fact that Balzac shifts the allegory from "Nouvelle-Hollande" to China might pique the curiosity of Ginzburg, who asks, "But why China?," a question neither he nor anybody else ever really answers (162). Certainly Balzac's documented knowledge of China could have been put to use in the novels, were the specific geographical location important. On his knowledge of China, see Robb (38) and Dali, who treats its significance in the *Comédie humaine* after 1842.

people like ourselves [qui nous valent], at this very moment the most ravishing woman is being burned alive; but have you enjoyed your cup of coffee any less?" (1.593). Clearly, Balzac either saw or came to see in the fate of the allegorical Mandarin an embodiment of imperial violence. Ginzburg finds new resonance for this old allegory (whose roots stretch back to Aristotle) in Balzac's period, "with the emergence of a global economic system," a view bolstered by reflecting on the provenance of coffee—a reminder here that the daily comforts of Europeans are underwritten by the suffering of others elsewhere (166). Second, alongside his portrayal of the allegory in grand imperial terms, Bianchon's entire speech finds virtue in smallness, in the same comforts of domestic compromise that Bruce Robbins sees in his reading of Dickens's *Great Expectations*, which draws on Ginzburg and the Mandarin and compares Magwitch to Vautrin (*Upward Mobility* 76). Bianchon is "content with the modest living I shall make in the provinces, where I shall quite simply take over from my father" (3.165). This allure of the rural and its function within a shifting imperial geography returns in Trollope's *The Way We Live Now* and Fontane's *Effi Briest*, but one final note on Bianchon's language leads into an exploration of the central figure of Vautrin. Bianchon speaks, self-deprecatingly, of succeeding his father in the medical practice, "tout bêtement" [stupidly]. The implication is a changing of the guard that occurs without any sort of thought or calculation. In this, as in many other things, Bianchon's refusal of intelligence and greatness and of the violence that greatness requires, according to the allegory, is simultaneously a critique of the entire Paris that Balzac draws in the novel through Rastignac's several mentors: Vautrin most importantly, but also Madame de Beauséant and Goriot. Vautrin's alliance with reason and calculation goes unremarked by critics, who have consistently read him as a revolutionary and romantic figure. He is this, of course. But Balzac also paints him with the same brush of rationalization that colors the portraits of Goriot and Beauséant. In this dual role, Vautrin encapsulates a narrative vacillation between enchantment and enlightened disenchantment.

(b) The World Below: Vautrin on Being Seen and Known

>The Hindoo characters followed; and the English translation appeared at the end, expressed in these mysterious words:
>
>"In the name of the Regent of the Night, whose seat is on the Antelope, whose arms embrace the four corners of the earth.
>
>"Brothers, turn your faces to the south, and come to me in the street of many noises, which leads down to the muddy river.

> "The reason is this.
>
> "My own eyes have seen it."
>
> There the letter ended, without either date or signature. I handed it back to Mr Murthwaite, and owned that this curious specimen of Hindoo correspondence rather puzzled me.
>
> —Wilkie Collins, *The Moonstone*

Vautrin's function within the structure of the allegory of the Mandarin is unquestionable, even if some critics attempt to separate the criminal from the allegory. David Ellison, for example, examines "two of the novel's characters, Bianchon and Vautrin, both of whom present Rastignac with moral problems to solve and lessons to be learned" (76). These "moral problems" are actually one problem told twice, however, and Balzac's narrative makes this clear. Recalling Rastignac's introduction of the Mandarin in the passage cited above, it is "Vautrin's arguments" which force the young man to "reflect on social life," and this reflection that, apparently, elicits the allegory. For Rastignac, the relationship is clear: Vautrin must be read through the allegory, and the allegory must be read through Vautrin. The challenge that this presents to scholarship on *Père Goriot* resides in the uncomfortable disequilibrium between Vautrin as a romantic figure and Vautrin as murderer of the romantic potential that inheres in the foreignness of the Chinese Mandarin. The romance of this distance is amplified in the passage, cited above, from the later *Modeste Mignon*. After weighing both sides of Vautrin's character, it becomes clear that he is best seen as an embodiment of the same epistemological duel at work in the Magic Skin of *La Peau de chagrin*; Balzac's depiction of Vautrin as romantic anti-hero from the underworld is consistently complicated by the novel's approach to both the underworld and romance. The Parisian coldness and calculation that Chasles (if not, by name, Balzac) loathes in his preface to *La Peau de chagrin* and that the narrator of *La Fille aux yeux d'or* savages one year later, show a disenchantedly rational side of Vautrin. They also link him in spirit to both Madame de Beauséant and Goriot, despite critics' occasional need to oppose Vautrin to both of these characters. Moreover, the taint of imperialism subtly voiced by Bianchon's refusal of murder persists.

Vautrin's embodiment of what James Reid refers to as "an invisible criminal underworld" ("Reading" 68)—the glimpse Vautrin provides Balzac's readers of such a world—conveniently contains elements of enchantment within a metaphorics of space. As I mentioned in the introduction, John McClure has asserted that this sort of fictional flight into the unmappable underworld of global crime and espionage is a hallmark of postmodern fiction's attempt to reenchant a demystified world (e.g., Don DeLillo or Thomas Pynchon). Such strategies against *Entzauberung* might have been inherited from Kipling or Conrad (e.g., *Under Western Eyes*, *The Secret Agent*). Kipling's short story, "The Mutiny of the Mavericks" (1891), opens with an image of global reach and criminal connectivity: "When three obscure gentlemen in San Francisco argued on insufficient premises they condemned a fellow-creature to a most unpleasant death in a far country, which had nothing whatever to do with the United States" (70). But Balzac's employment of shadowy organizations like Vautrin's *Société des Dix mille* or Ferragus's *Treize* clearly performs the same function. In an article enumerating "fantastical aspects of Paris in the realist novels of Balzac," Geneviève Poncin-Bar would add to the category of the fantastic "the entire subterranean Paris whose presence Balzac tests intensely, monstrous bedrock that he uncovers [qu'il fait ressurgir]" (239). Questions will arise later as to whether the underworldly subplot in *Goriot* can fairly be categorized as fantastic, but Poncin-Bar's assessment of it initially seems to be borne out by characters themselves in the novel: Poiret's immediate and terrified reaction at the mere mention of the society's name is telling, for example (3.190). Furthermore, the newness and foreignness of organized criminality is emphasized by the detective Gondureau, who must translate for Michonneau and Poiret the "forceful expressions in thieves' language" [énergiques expressions du langage des voleurs], the slang and wholly unfamiliar uses of *sorbonne* and *tronche* (209). One recalls the opening salvo of Eugène Sue's popular *Les Mystères de Paris* (1842–43), also a lesson in strange, criminal vocabularies that alerts readers to their entry into an entirely different manner of conceiving the world: "A *tapis-franc*, in the slang of thievery and murder, means a smoking-house or inn of the very lowest class. A discharged convict, who in this foul language is called an *ogre*, or a woman of the same class who is called an *ogresse*, commonly keeps a tavern of this kind, haunted by the refuse of the Parisian population: liberated galley slaves, sharpers, robbers, and assassins congregate there" (31; his emphases). The underworld is not just a place; it is an alien paradigm and a separate language.

The strangeness of the underworld combines complexly, in the figure of Vautrin, with a sense of its geographical uncontainability and transcultural ubiquity. I have already suggested that, in Bianchon's rendering of his verdict on the dilemma of the Mandarin, the imperial allusions he makes and that Balzac later emboldens in *Modeste Mignon* serve to contextualize the crime in global terms. The actual murder of Frédéric Taillefer is commanded by Vautrin but committed by an Italian colonel, Franchessini (whom Rastignac later sees at Madame de Beauséant's ball, at the novel's end, and mistakes for Vautrin [3.266]). Yet Vautrin's international aspirations extend beyond European assassinations and become literally colonial when he reveals to

Rastignac his plans to depart for America:

> You see, I have an idea. My idea is to go off and live like a patriarch in the middle of some big estate, a hundred thousand acres for example, in the United States, in the South. I want to become a planter out there, own slaves, earn a cool few million from the sale of my cattle, tobacco, and timber, living like a king.... I need two hundred thousand francs, because I want two hundred niggers to satisfy my taste for the patriarchal life. Niggers, do you see? They are children, but fully grown, and you can do what you like with them without some inquisitive Royal Prosecutor coming along to ask you questions [vous en demander compte]. With this black capital, I would have three or four million in ten years. (3.141)

Foreign soil—and not just colonial French soil—will be necessary if Vautrin is to own his slaves, since the Revolutionary government had already abolished slavery (in France in 1791, and in French colonies in 1794). This passage reiterates the relationship that *Le Père Goriot* patiently constructs between violent crime and personal profit, and, in this context and by dint of its recalling the allegory of the Mandarin, Vautrin's plan again summons the idea of colonial abuses into the local murder underway. This is followed immediately by Vautrin's intricate laying out of his plans for Taillefer's assassination, for Rastignac's marriage of Victorine and consequent access to her inheritance, from which Vautrin will exact his small commission. The conversation horrifies Rastignac, but not as much as it ought to; soon afterward, as he ponders the exchange, "A voice cried out to him: 'Eight hundred thousand francs!'" (3.163). The crying voice is an inner one. That final amount, though, was never spoken by Vautrin, who gave Rastignac only the raw numbers (3.142); Rastignac has, all on his own, done the required math to arrive at his projected portion of the profits. And, on the next page, he turns to China to frame the dilemma he will put to Bianchon.

The fixation on profits—in short, the number-crunching—suggests an aspect of Vautrin's character that forcibly problematizes attempts to read, in the criminal-underworld implications of his role in *Le Père Goriot*, figures of enchanted or romantic potential. To be sure, superficial textual traces of romance are palpable in his character, as critics have repeatedly noted. Madame Vauquer's judgment, from the passage cited in the first paragraph of this chapter, that Vautrin is a symbol, if ironically twisted, of "la galanterie française," is just one example (3.207). He is referred to—and by the narrator at times, no less—as a "démon" (3.184), a Mephistophelian "tempter" (3.185), a "Turc" (3.204), and an "infernal poem in which were painted every human sentiment, except for one: repentance" (3.219). Such descriptions have easily lent themselves to the one-sided reading most critics make of this complex figure. James Smith Allen claims that "Vautrin embodies the spirit of revolt in nineteenth-century France" (109). According to Alfred Glauser, Vautrin "is the metaphor of the spirit that knows the secrets of evil and good, and ends up an incarnation of that beauty that is founded on an undeniable, satanic magic" (585). Vito Carofiglio sees him as "anarchical student of Rousseau, 'révolté' and luciferean" (155), while, according to Alexander Fischler, Vautrin is a "dark angel" (844). Finally, Catherine Savage declares, in what becomes a moral condemnation of *Le Père Goriot*'s alleged values, that Vautrin "is a romantic outlaw who has chosen the underside of society in which to achieve individual conquest" and that he thus provides, for Balzac's novel, "the values of individualistic, anarchical Romanticism" (104). Savage's and Carofiglio's apparent conflation here of the literary and the political invites a closer look at how these values—romanticism, revolution—function within Balzac's own novelistic sphere.

A number of Romantics were, of course, Revolutionaries, in France and elsewhere. Yet even if literary historians tend to partner the two terms, it should not surprise us that Balzac would keep romance and revolution separate, even see them as enemies. In so doing, he echoes contemporary conservatives like Edmund Burke, whose *Reflections on the Revolution in France* (1790) refer to the upstart classes as "mechanical, merely instrumental" (42). Burke sees in the new, spirit-numbing Revolutionary bureaucracy proof that "the age of chivalry is gone.—That of sophisters, oeconomists, and calculators, has succeeded; and the glory of Europe is extinguished forever" (76). De la Motte's argument, briefly adduced above, will bear lengthier treatment here, for it reminds us that Balzac, too, equated Napoleonism not with romance and enchantment but rather with its rationalization:

> Balzac, who would go on to write *Physiologie de l'employé* ("Physiology of the Bureaucrat" [1841]), itself to be incorporated into a later version of La Femme supérieure entitled *Les Employés (The Bureaucrats)*, is one of the earliest and most penetrating critics of the bureaucracy created under Napoleon and usually associated with the mechanized, scientific approach to administration synonymous with modern life. (55–56)[4]

In Flaubert's *L'Éducation sentimentale*, Deslauriers repeats this sentiment, ranting that, "When I think that you have to fill in anything up to twenty-eight forms just to keep a boat on the river, I feel like going off to live among

---

4. Suck argues convincingly for a distinction between pre-Revolutionary *raison* and post-Revolutionary rationalization, which is inextricable from "the sphere of commodity circulation" (34).

the cannibals [anthropophages]. The Government is eating us alive [nous dévore]!" (2.170). Deslauriers' language even recalls that of Chasles's preface to *La Peau de chagrin*, and the idea that the scientific mindset is eating away at (*ronge*) society. Vautrin is certainly romantic—at least superficially so, via the sorts of pat references and coded phrases enumerated above—yet one must keep this surface romanticism separate from his revolutionary import, which owes itself to the frequent comparisons of him to Napoleon, and to his own frequent invocations of Rousseau, whom James Swenson has persuasively read as one of the first authors of the Revolution.

It may be going too far to position Vautrin as the sort of *employé* to which de la Motte refers and about which Balzac wrote at length and out of spite. Yet a careful discovery of the hyperrational side of Vautrin illustrates to what extent one cannot simply envision him as an otherworldly, underworldly figure. Even the possible enchantments of criminality have been subsumed, in *Goriot*, within a continual disenchantment. Where the narrator refers to Vautrin as a "démon," Vautrin presents himself in the most reasonable light, telling Rastignac, "I want it to be not passion, not despair, but reason that sets you [qui vous détermine] to come to me" (3.183). This stands in stark contrast to the modest ideals of Bianchon, who will simply and unreflectingly ("tout bêtement," one recalls) follow in the footsteps of his father's provincial practice, thereby refusing to kill the Mandarin, refusing to rise. The rational side of Vautrin fits in, too, with the narrator's description of him in terms of the same technology that disenchants the ending of *La Peau de chagrin*. In an image that will be repeated more forcefully in *La Fille aux yeux d'or*, we are told that Vautrin's "face presented a phenomenon that can only be compared to that of the motor [chaudière], full of that steam capable of moving mountains" (3.218). And where the narrator, one page later, colors Vautrin as a "tempter," with its obviously Faustian tones, Vautrin admonishes Rastignac to think and find objectivity: "Two or three more reflections on high politics, and you will see the world as it is" (3.185), a moment of deference to the optical epistemology that is both central to Balzac's articulation of disenchantment and a widely assumed principle of literary realism. (Peter Brooks, for example: "My understanding of realism turns crucially on its visuality" [*Realist Vision* 71].) Elsewhere, Vautrin opines against randomness and chance, stating that, "When of two living men one must disappear [in a duel], one would have to be an imbecile to leave oneself over to chance [pour s'en remettre au hasard]" (3.136). These are not the words of a heady, unthinking romantic hero, and so the narrator is correct to refer to Vautrin as "this ferocious logician" [ce féroce logicien], in a phrase that seems to capture both halves of this character (3.178). Bearing this in mind, then, and recalling his penchant for number-crunching and plans for speculation, Vautrin may be

Chapter Two: *Marginal Realism in* Le Père Goriot ~ 59

most revealingly pigeonholed by Lukács and Bardèche; the former proclaims that Vautrin fulfills "the turn from ideal to reality [Wirklichkeit]" (*Balzac* 60), while the latter sees in *Le Père Goriot*'s criminal not a descendant or avatar of Mephistopheles but rather a forebear of Balzac's later character Gobseck (Bardèche 288). Karl Marx's *Capital*, of course, offers Gobseck as the prime example of unethical and unchecked accumulation (735).

The double-depiction of Vautrin as alternately romantic and revolutionary—recalling that, for Balzac, the revolution is an exercise in disenchantment—must complicate the criminal subculture that the novel would have him represent. As I have suggested, this subculture is marked off in *Le Père Goriot* as a new body of knowledge and style of being, requiring its own vocabulary and organization. The insistent portrayal of Vautrin's rational side, though, tarnishes the underworld's potential mystery, shows it to be, in fact, quite worldly. In an essay on realism and the detective novel, Isabelle Husson-Casta makes a remark that may help frame, in a larger context, the sort of claim I am making here about the complexity of the criminal underworld in terms of disenchantment:

> Detective fiction will be arranged from the following materials—a degraded romanticism, a carefully [prudemment] stereotyped realism, symbolistic flourishes—into a playful and at times casual condensation: the hyper-realism of cartographic or toponymic detail, contrasts with the larger project of detective fiction [le projet policier global], which is inevitably idealist, as it presupposes the resolution of enigmas and the restored coherence of a world subject to [en proie à] the Law. (114)

It would not be wholly inappropriate to suggest that we read *Goriot* as a detective novel. In the opening pages, the narrator, referring to Rastignac, claims that, "without his curious observations, and his skill at producing himself in the salons of Paris, this tale could not have been colored in those truthful hues which, without any doubt, it owes to his shrewdness, as well as to his interest in penetrating the mysteries of a shocking situation" (3.56). The mystery, of course, is that of Goriot's hidden relationship to his daughters, and Rastignac, playing the detective, does get to the bottom of it. Husson-Casta's assessment of the novel's obsession with "the resolution of enigmas" and restoration of coherence is entirely apposite in the case of Vautrin. It would be a mistake, though, to term this drive for resolution—the assumption that things can be explained "coherently"—a sort of "idealism" that is *opposed* to realism, because it is also a hallmark of scientific inquiry, empirical explanation, and thus disenchantment. In an almost comical way, Vautrin himself acknowledges that the empirical will be his downfall in his flight from the law. Throughout the novel, he sings the refrain,

> I've roamed the world for many a year
> And I've been seen in many lands . . .
> [J'ai longtemps parcouru le monde,
> Et l'on m'a vu de toute part . . .] (3.82, e.g.)

The last time he sings this refrain before he is captured, though, he cuts the last line off:

> I've roamed the world for many a year
> And I've been seen . . .
> [J'ai longtemps parcouru le monde,
> Et l'on m'a vu . . .] (3.200)

He has been seen, not everywhere this time—not "de toute part"—just seen, and that suffices. The "invisible criminal underworld" that Reid mentions is finally entirely visible and, ultimately, policeable. In this especially, *Le Père Goriot* belies Lukács's contention that "Vautrin's function in Balzac's *Human Comedy* is the same as that of Mephistopheles and Lucifer in Goethe's and Byron's mystery plays" (*Studies in European Realism* 61). Unlike Mephistopheles and Lucifer, the Parisian criminal of Balzac's imagining stands on solid ground and inhabits a social system that can hold him to account. Vautrin, of course, escapes to reappear in *Illusions perdues* and *Splendeurs et misères des courtisanes*, but *Le Père Goriot* ends with his law-enforced removal from the text. Vautrin's parting words issue a challenge to empiricism and detection, as D.A. Miller has asserted: "[T]he moment when 'explanations are in order' may rightly give rise to the desire to withhold them (like Balzac's Vautrin, whose last words to the police as they open his closet and seize his effects are 'Vous ne saurez rien')" (vii). Yet the mobility and unmappability that Vautrin represents are endangered as much by his plot-ordained capture as by his character's earlier, repeated turns to the vocabulary of reason and calculation.

(c) "À nous deux!": An Ethics of Disenchantment

Vautrin is not alone in exercising this vocabulary in the novel, and the disenchanting side of him bleeds into Balzac's depictions of two other key characters, illuminating the entire world of *Le Père Goriot* as a disenchanted one. Madame de Beauséant and Père Goriot have often been positioned opposite Vautrin: Beauséant as a more ethical mentor in Rastignac's struggle for upward mobility and access to society, and Goriot as a more appropriate father figure to Rastignac. "Through both his name and his attributes," Fischler argues, "Vautrin is also diametrically opposed to Mme de Beauséant, Rastignac's other Mentor, for *se vautrer* is the exact antithesis of *beauséer*" (844). What the nominal opposition suggests, though, Balzac's narrator will not corroborate; the text expresses an ambivalence in the construction of Beauséant similar to the one it shows in the construction of Vautrin. It is true that Rastignac invokes, early on, the fairy-godmother motif, telling her, "If you knew the situation of my family, . . . you would want to play the part of one of those fairy godmothers who enjoyed clearing away the obstacles facing their godsons" (3.108). This benign role, though, is not one that Beauséant accepts, and she instead instructs Rastignac in much the same terms Vautrin uses: "The more coldly calculating you are," she tells him, "the further you'll go" [Plus froidement vous calculerez, plus avant vous irez] (3.116). Of Mme de Nucingen, Beauséant tells Rastignac, "Use her" [Servez-vous d'elle], an exhortation to exploitation that mirrors Vautrin's wish for slaves. Where Rastignac is reluctant to enlist himself in Vautrin's most diabolical plot against Taillefer, though, he volunteers his services to Beauséant, when she asks him, hypothetically, "Would you kill someone for my sake?" Eugène responds, "Twice over" (3.109). Madame de Beauséant's methods of mentorship share with Vautrin's an emphasis on calculation and exploitation, and a propensity—even if it remains only hypothetical—for violence, and Rastignac himself notes this similarity (3.146).

Beauséant's echoing of Vautrin demonstrates persuasively that the rationalization lamented in Chasles's preface is actually pervasive in Paris, from top to bottom. That Goriot himself also lapses into the vocabulary of Vautrin is even more important, for, as the tragic title figure in the novel, Goriot is often rendered by critics as an endlessly giving and eternally unselfish father. Balzac's own notebooks, in the first mention of *Le Père Goriot*'s subject, refer to "a good man . . . having ruined himself [s'étant dépouillé] for his daughters . . . dying like a dog" (3.5). It must be remembered, though, that he is also a businessman, a war profiteer for whom the aristocracy has nothing but contempt: the Duchess of Langeais refers to him as "this Loriot, who sold wheat to the choppers of heads" (3.114). The scenes depicting Rastignac's vacillation between the poles of Vautrin and Goriot set these two characters against each other as opposites, and this is amplified by the anger Goriot shows when hearing of Rastignac's interest in Victorine Taillefer. Interest in Victorine means interest in Vautrin's plot; Goriot's quick and angry reaction to the rumors, and Rastignac's equally swift denunciation of them and declaration of his love for Goriot's daughter, seem to further position Goriot as the foil of Vautrin, as his competitor for narrative space.[5] Yet at this same moment, Goriot shows a total lack of regard for the life of another, of Taillefer, whose death in the impending duel is certain and whom Rastignac wants to warn:

> "Taillefer's son fights tomorrow, and I've heard that he'll be killed."
> "What's that got to do with you?" [Qu'est-ce que cela vous fait?], said Goriot. (3.199)

It is perfectly appropriate that the next voice we hear is Vautrin's. By the end of the novel, Goriot's repeated wishes to return to Odessa and make more money to support his daughters bear only a faint resemblance to Vautrin's plans for America and slavery, but Goriot's repeated cries for vengeance against his sons-in-law speak a darker language: "Kill them! Death to Restaud, death to the Alsatian" (3.278). Finally, the shadow of the Revolution touches both Vautrin and Goriot. Just as Vautrin's association with the Revolution complicates him, it does the same for the calculating merchant, or, as Sandy Petrey points out, "a commoner enriched by the Revolution" (92). Goriot's occasional resemblance to Vautrin forces a harder look at the novel's ending, where Balzac links them in spectacular—and spectacularly inconclusive—fashion.

Anthony Pugh praises *Le Père Goriot*'s finale in Père Lachaise as a "structurally perfect ending" partially because it allows the reader to "witness stage by stage the decline into compromise with society" (30–32). Yet this ending cannot be reduced to an uncomplicated sponsorship of compromise. Rastignac's final incitement to duel—his "grandiose words: 'It's between the two of us now!'" [mots grandioses : « À nous deux maintenant! »]—pulls together yet again the figures of Vautrin and Goriot, who have both uttered these words before (3.290). Vautrin first uses the phrase "À nous deux!" during the conversation with Rastignac in which the former first mentions his dream of owning slaves (3.137). Goriot uses it, too, though, and also in conversation with Rastignac, during a diatribe against his son-in-law Restaud in which he imagines calling him out to duel: "À nous deux!" (3.247). Even critics who point out that Rastignac's final cry from the cemetery owes itself *both* to Goriot *and* to Vautrin, fail to observe that it also must conjure the memory of the dead Taillefer (e.g. Petrey 111–12). Taillefer is the concrete avatar of

---

5. Woloch has argued, in his insightful reading of the novel, that Goriot competes with Rastignac—and not with Vautrin—for primacy in the narrative, if our focus is on whom the novel constructs as major and minor characters (246). Within Rastignac's own story, though, the opponent to Goriot's plot is that of Vautrin, and Rastiganac must choose between them.

the abstract Mandarin, the local exemplar of the global allegory, the one who must die in order for Raphaël to rise, according to *Le Père Goriot*'s narrative logic. Ginzburg alludes to the economy of this relationship and the history of its slow progression into the realm of the global market, but the novel makes its zero-sum nature a true leitmotif, opposing Taillefer and Rastignac in subtle but important ways. Vautrin structures the opposition around money; Taillefer's death means his money will become Rastignac's, should Rastignac agree to Vautrin's plan. Quietly, repeated images bolster the contrast: whereas Taillefer "has fought in a duel. He's been wounded in the forehead [il a reçu un coup d'épée dans le front]," for example, for Rastignac "success is written on [his] handsome forehead [beau front]" (3.211; 3.229). Vautrin's forehead, meanwhile, stores his numbers: "'Here's where I keep my account books!' he said, hitting himself in the forehead" (3.220). Rastignac's challenge to Paris signals his affirmation of the zero-sum game, the ontology of the duel, in which, as in Rastignac's summation of Vautrin's version of Paris, it is "every man for himself" [chacun pour soi] (3.150). Or, as the narrator continues Rastignac's inner monologue: In Paris, "He would, as on a battlefield, have to kill in order not to be killed, cheat in order not to be cheated; where he would have to leave his conscience at the barricade" (3.151).

The ending is "structurally perfect" for another reason, though. In accepting the zero-sum perspective of the duel, the "À nous deux!," Rastignac is also rejecting a different possibility. This rejected possibility is likewise marked off in the text by repeated uses of "à nous deux," and it is thus contrasted explicitly to the duel. If "à nous deux" has become, at the end of *Le Père Goriot*, a challenge, it is first used as an incitement to good works from outside of Paris, from the fallen, provincial Rastignac family. In her letter to Eugène in Paris, his sister Laure recounts how their other sister Agathe "was sweet. She said, 'Let's send him the three hundred and fifty francs from us both [à nous deux]!'" (3.128). Later, Rastignac adopts this formulation and its charitable ethos in his care of the dying Goriot, telling Bianchon, "My good Bianchon, ... we'll take care of him, the two of us [à nous deux]" (3.258). There are two versions of the number two: the beneficent and the maleficent, the two that help each other help a third, and the two that will reduce themselves to one. Rastignac's vacillation between Laure's (provincial) and Vautrin's (urban) versions of the number two accompanies the duel framed by the moral dilemma of the Mandarin, repeating the language of this dilemma and, in so doing, highlighting further the centrality of this Eastern image to the novel's story of Rastignac's formation in the West.

Balzac uses the allegory of the Mandarin to both center Rastignac's moral dilemma within the novel and anchor it within the increasingly knowable world outside the Paris of the novel. Ginzburg reminds us that the "turning inward" of the dilemma "takes place across a geographical space—the distance from France to China—infinitely wider than the Mediterranean world Aristotle wrote of" (162). "Infinitely wider," yes, but also infinitely more imaginable, traversable, and able to be envisioned within a "global economic system" (166) and its increasing mobility of people. Sociologist Saskia Sassen has analyzed the effects of this increased mobility in her writings on what she calls the "global city," an idea that will become useful later in this project, as it helps to account for Balzac's, Trollope's and Fontane's particular depictions of imperial centers. Balzac later, in *La Fille aux yeux d'or*, displaces the ideas of both enchantment (whether in the form of the distant, foreign exotic or the domestic underground) and the destruction of it from the allegorical sphere where, in the Paris of *Le Père Goriot*, these ideas frame everything. Ginzburg is right to embed this dilemma within a brief nod to worldly space, just as countless critics of *Goriot* have continually attended to the novel's articulation and production of urban and Parisian space.[6] These critics, as the following chapter demonstrates, have endlessly invoked Balzac's *milieux* as testaments to realism, coordinates of mimetic precision. In a consideration of the fate of enchantment in *Goriot*, though, the Mandarin performs, along with Vautrin, a complex function. A careful rereading of Vautrin complicates some of the more simplistic critical renderings of him as a romantic revolutionary, for there is in him just as much calculation as there is excitement, as much of the careful antiquarian as there is of the smooth-talking gallant. The extra-Parisian influence of the Chinese Mandarin is inextricable from Vautrin and the moral dilemma he forces on Rastignac. This figure, along with the sub-Parisian murmurings of the criminal underworld Vautrin represents more explicitly, encapsulates the same novelistic energies that the Magic Skin embodies in *La Peau de chagrin*: the desperate narrative indecision between the criminally mysterious and its opposite, between what cannot or should not be known and its very cancellation.

---

6. See Bell's "Balzac and the Modern City"; Guichardet's "Un jeu de l'oie maléfique"; Pimentel-Anduiza; Pold; and Reid, most of whom are discussed in the following chapter, in an examination of the unmapping protocols of *La Fille aux yeux d'or*. Mozet's book is also useful in this context, because of its attention to the spatial push and pull between Paris and Provinces. For a comparative look at the Paris of the realist novelists, see Warning's chapter, "Der Chronotopos Paris bei den ‚Realisten'" (269–312).

CHAPTER THREE

REALISM, ROMANCE, AND
LA FILLE AUX YEUX D'OR

> The city of the realists is detailed and mapped.
> —Peter Brooks, *Realist Vision*

The relationship between otherness and the construction of space in Balzac's *La Fille aux yeux d'or* offers a means of reframing the question of disenchantment. The link between enchantment and space is not surprising when one recalls the manner in which the question of enchantment seems to require that of empire, and the manner in which the question of empire requires, as Said has argued, that of space. For Said, as I demonstrated in the introduction, physical space is the base around which all other concerns organize, and, although he writes in *Culture and Imperialism* on the grander scale of "territories, lands, geographical domains," his ideas also pose useful questions in the tighter confines of the urban (78). The last chapter showed that Vautrin's character is poised somewhere between rationalization and romance in *Le Père Goriot*; this ambivalence accompanies an aborted reenchantment of known Parisian space, an incomplete attempt to envision uncontrollable elements in the capital's own backyard. Moreover, because an understanding of Vautrin is inseparable from an understanding of the Chinese Mandarin, Vautrin and the Mandarin serve, in a sense, to fix Paris within a global geography. Balzac's apparent unwillingness to give us Vautrin as a fully and uncomplicatedly romantic figure finds a different home in the character of Henri de Marsay in *La Fille aux yeux d'or*, the final third of *L'Histoire des Treize*. The strategy by which *Goriot* is structured by elements from outside and underneath, is less subtle in the story of Paquita Valdès and her two lovers, as the novelistic work of opening Paris to the wider world finds more excessive and destructive form.

This analysis of the world and the city in *La Fille aux yeux d'or* grounds itself in a primary challenge to any exegesis of the novel, namely the apparent stylistic and thematic imbalance between the first fifth and the rest of the text. If part of the task of critical reading is to explore possible coherence in a work—or barring that, to explore the purpose of incoherence—then any examination of *La Fille aux yeux d'or* must, by necessity, ask the question of how these two parts can possibly function together. There is immense critical unease over the textual rupture, but the text's two parts do function together if the novel's central concern is Paris. Otherness is negotiated spatially in the Paris of *La Fille aux yeux d'or*, and the otherness of Paquita Valdès in particular presides over blatant moments of what John McClure has called "unmapping"; familiar, rationalized Paris is reenchanted at the fundamental level of space and one's intimate understanding of it. The novel's disordering of Paris and the effects of this process on the cynicism and rationalization of Henri de Marsay recall the dueling narrative modes of the text's two sections: the bitter social anthropology at the outset and the foregrounding of the exotic and romantic thereafter. Olivier Bonard has claimed that *La Fille aux yeux d'or* is "a new stage in the evolution... that leads [Balzac's] style and his vision toward the great novels" (155). This chapter suggests that, by construing Paquita's otherness as against urban and domestic order, part of the novel's importance rests on its explicit exemplification of the more subtle epistemological and narrative tensions that organize *La Peau de chagrin* and *Le Père Goriot*. *La Fille aux yeux d'or* is, on this level, a text about a disenchanted metropolis seeking an enchantment of which it remains wary, and which it finally destroys.

(a) The World in Paris: Paquita Valdès and the Ubiquity of the Foreign

The apparently remarkable pairing of what critics have insisted on seeing as two distinct portions of text in *La Fille aux yeux d'or* has had a complex effect on the reception of the novel. This confusion is most evident in the widespread terminological slippage. Critics have referred to the novel's first portion as an "essai" (Bordas 340), "introduction" (Tintner 243), "préface" (Dubois 177) or "prologue" (Heathcote 109; Kadish 270; Massol-Bedoin 32; Soelberg 459), and to the second portion as a "roman" (Bordas 340), "récit" (Massol-Bedoin 32), "histoire" (Soelberg 459) or "story" (Tintner 243). Then there are Jean-Yves Debreuille, who splits the work into two "demi-romans" (151), and those who ignore the first portion completely. A few critics have dealt with the parts together and essayed to explain their coherence: Frølich by focusing on the theme of fire, Diamond by attending to textual excesses and the focus on speculation in the two parts, and Shoshana Felman by linking the class concerns of the first portion to the gender concerns of the second. Soelberg's explanation is that both the "prologue" and the "histoire" counsel the reader, "Distrust language: *see!*" (465), a nod to an optical epistemology that this chapter will revisit later. Perhaps because it is simply too obvious, the idea that the first portion's focus on Paris might forecast a novel about Paris has not gained as much traction. Since my concerns here revolve simultaneously around exploring a possible structural coherence in *La Fille aux yeux d'or* and reading the novel's articulation of Parisian space, the very Parisian preoccupations of the so-called prologue will weigh in as a thematic center for the entire text. Yet, if this novel is, ultimately, a novel about Paris, it approaches this object in a complex manner that is best understood in the context of otherness and disenchantment.

Otherness and foreignness have already been important to the discussion of *La Peau de chagrin* and *Le Père Goriot*. Seen broadly, the foreign is a pervasive element in Balzac's œuvre, even if it refers most often to European foreignness. Martine Gärtner has examined Germany's influence on certain of Balzac's novels and his narrative style, for example, and Victor Leathers has catalogued the appearances of Spain and Spanish characters in the *Comédie humaine*. Fernand Baldensperger's exhaustive account of what he calls Balzac's *Orientations étrangères* extends its range beyond Europe; yet, because of a debilitatingly strict correlation of the foreign and the oriental, Baldensperger's analysis passes over the foreignness of characters who are either *not* referred to as oriental or *not* explicitly visible as representations of the oriental.[1] One of the most remarkable aspects of *La Fille aux yeux d'or* is that, to an astonishing extent, the entire text is determined within Paris by characters who come from elsewhere (Paquita Valdès) or who are clearly attached to an elsewhere, by their birth or blood (Henri de Marsay), for example. Trollope's *The Way We Live Now* and Fontane's *Cécile* will perform the same urban consolidation of distant places by importing characters from elsewhere. *La Fille aux yeux d'or* differs in that it draws together, within certain characters, numerous distant cultures into a sort of controlled constellation of otherness that approaches but is not yet an internationalism or cosmopolitanism. This finally provides a stark counterpoint to the apparent focus on Paris that opens the novel and the attention to Parisian space that dominates it. A brief look at precisely how Balzac's narrative accomplishes this drawing-together underscores the reduction of global distance and rear-

1. Jourda falls prey to a different error, essentially cataloguing instances of any foreignness—be it Danish, English, or African—as similarly exotic.

ticulation of global space—at the level of character—that complicates Paris in *La Fille aux yeux d'or*.

He may not know it, but Henri de Marsay is the son of a French mother and an English father, "the natural son of Lord Dudley and the famous Marquise de Vordac" (5.1054). Balzac's narrative uses this hidden knowledge—the identity of de Marsay's "father, whose name it is doubtful he knew" (5.1056)—to score some ironic comic points, as when de Marsay claims, in ignorance of his own half-Englishness, "We are taking so many things from the English these days that we could become hypocrites and prudes like they are" (5.1071). Despite de Marsay's joking, however, *La Fille aux yeux d'or* does not rely on the *cultural* cleft between England and the continent to any great extent, as Thackeray and Collins will later do; consider the half-English and half-French Becky Sharp of *Vanity Fair* (1847–48), whose villainy is repeatedly linked to her French half, or Franklin Blake in *The Moonstone*, whose continental education is said to evince itself in Germanic philosophizing and Romanic flares of temper. It is more interesting to note here what the movements of Lord Dudley, his lovers, and his "masterpieces" (as the narrator wryly refers to his scattered children and the "relations that he creates for them everywhere") say about the increasing irrelevance of global distances in the aftermath of and as a partial result of the Revolution. De Marsay's unknown half-sister, Euphémie, is the daughter of lord Dudley and a "dame espagnole," and she is raised in Cuba and returned to Madrid, but comes finally to Paris (5.1058). The distance between Paris and Cuba is, one might argue, required by the novel's desire to emphasize the late reunion of a half-brother and half-sister who do not know each other until the very end. (It is a recognition gambit of which even Heliodorus would be proud.) Balzac resolves the plot structure by anchoring it to a historical event and deferring first to geographical distance and then to its diminution. This tendency announces, well before the fact, the bundle of various geographical origins, races, and cultures brought into Paris by Paquita and her retinue.

No concept of hybridity can accurately capture the chaotic interminglings of *La Fille aux yeux d'or*, in which various alterities are often conjoined within single characters and, broadening the perspective, within groups of associated characters. Paquita's entourage is the best example of this. Surrounding her in Paris, in the apartment owned by her father, are her manservant Christemio and her mother. The African figure of the servant/bodyguard Christemio, "a mulatto by whom Talma would have been inspired to play Othello, if he had met him" (5.1075), is marked off by the narrator as the epitome of colonized peoples, as "a man whom every imagination, from those that shiver in Greenland to those that sweat in New England, will paint by the phrase: *this was an unfortunate man*" (5.1076). The text explicitly positions Christemio in the colonies before situating him in Paris and finally waffling on his actual otherness by comparing his misery to that of Parisians. These disturbances are bolstered when Paquita's mother is introduced by Paquita herself as "a slave purchased in Georgia for her rare beauty" (5.1081). The Asian-ness of Georgia could certainly have been a matter for debate, but Balzac's narrator will situate it thus when describing Paquita later, and Georgia brings further complexity to the picture of Paquita's origins and what they signify in Paris. Paquita is, the narrator points out, a "beautiful creature tied to the houris of Asia by her mother, to Europe by her education, to the tropics by her birth" (5.1093). Add to these details the mysterious letters that Paquita receives from London, and she becomes a nexus of geographical instability, a novelistic embodiment of the world's arrival in and confounding of Paris. I have already mentioned Balzac's conflation of the "oriental" and the "foreign," and Baldensperger's chief example of this tendency is the depiction of Paquita in *La Fille aux yeux d'or* (10). The narrative indecision here recalls the ambivalence in *La Peau de chagrin*'s depiction of the Magic Skin as engraved alternately in Sanskrit and Arabic, a testament to the idea that general foreignness and not any cultural specificity may have mattered most to Balzac. What is accidental in the regional incertitude of *La Peau de chagrin*, though, is apparently methodical in *La Fille aux yeux d'or*, where great care is taken to highlight the many sources of Paquita Valdès. Sharpley-Whiting asserts that "the situating of Paquita is somewhat frustrated by a fluid Balzacian cartography that traverses countries (France, Spain, Cuba, England, and Georgia) and cultures" (44), but the frustration itself is important; the difficulty in situating Paquita is the main point. Moreover, if Paquita represents a site of cultural mixture and cartographical confusion that has come to rest in Paris, she opens up a connection between the text's two parts which critics have not considered. Paris, too, is marked off by the narrator as a site of mixture, in terms alternately colonial and commercial, when the prologue describes the "commerçants" of Paris, the "petty bourgeoisie . . . that spreads its hands over the Orient, takes from there shawls disdained by the Turks and the Russians; harvests from as far away as the Indies" (5.1045). The capital of the nineteenth century appears as the world's center, "the head of the globe, a brain bursting with genius that leads human civilization" (5.1051). This suggests a point of contact between the narrator's descriptions of Paquita, who literally represents much of the outside world, and the space of Paris in relation to the outside world, hinted at in the first pages.

Yet neither the introduction to nor the narrative of Paquita and Henri is primarily concerned with this outside world. The focus here is Paris and what happens to it when distances between periphery and center decrease, and when traffic between the domestic and the exotic becomes almost mundane, commercialized, rationalized. *La Fille aux yeux d'or* recognizes this problem early and tests the possibility of reversing the process. If Paris represents, as the narrator suggests it does, "Nécessité," then the presence of Paquita offers the possibility of contingency,[2] of indeterminacy, perhaps what Sharpley-Whiting calls "fluidity" when speaking of Balzac's cartography. Indeed, the fluidity here, in the introduction and origins of Paquita and the depictions of Paris's reach into the world, is analogous to a larger, more fundamental enactment of cartographical uncertainty. Having based its notion of alterity on ideas of distance and space, *La Fille aux yeux d'or* uses Paquita and uses Henri's attempts to access her in order to unmap the metropolis, ushering in elements of mystery that the novel's bitter preface assures us have been effaced by the rationalizing powers of post-Revolutionary global commerce. The narrative consequences of the unmapping reveal a text finally at odds with its own efforts at reenchantment and uncomfortable with the increased profile of the world within the metropolitan center. Trollope echoes this discomfort in the face of the foreign throughout the 1860s and 1870s, while Fontane's Berlin novels phrase the dilemma differently, pondering instead the possibility that the rationalized metropolis is beyond saving, even by the enchanted exotic.

(b) Unmapping Paris: The Space of Enchantment

> I thought of the eyes of a researcher who doesn't want to discover anything but wants, rather, to make something unknown, to pace off and enlarge the realm of the unknown.
>
> —Peter Handke, *Repetition*

> Andy Horowitz, one of McCandless's friends on the Woodson High cross-country team, had mused that Chris "was born into the wrong century. He was looking for more adventure and freedom than today's society gives people." In coming to Alaska, McCandless yearned to wander uncharted country, to find a blank spot on the map. In 1992, however, there were no more blank spots on the map—not in Alaska, not anywhere. But Chris, with his idiosyncratic logic, came up with an elegant solution to this dilemma: He simply got rid of the map. In his own mind, if nowhere else, the *terra* would thereby remain *incognita*.
>
> —Jon Krakauer, *Into the Wild*

---

2. Warning's chapter, "Chaos und Kosmos: Kontingenzbewältigung in der Comédie Humaine," holds that Balzac's overall project seeks to minimize chance (35–76). Chance might seem problematic in a realist project, but I am suggesting here a more sustained tension between necessity and contingency, just as there is a more sustained tension between disenchantment and romance than traditional understandings of realism allow.

The prolific critical attention to Balzac's painstaking recreation of nineteenth-century Paris, from Friedrich Engels and Lukács to Jeannine Guichardet and Christopher Prendergast, has often focused on his mimetic exactitude and its perfect relevance to typical understandings of literary realism as mimetic exactitude. Guichardet and Prendergast especially have addressed Balzac's vision of Paris as city but largely divorced it from the imperial apparatus of which Balzac makes it an integral part. *La Fille aux yeux d'or* specifically inserts Paris within a global network of empire and commerce, and its position in this framework both enables and enriches the production and disturbance of Parisian space in the novel. If Franco Moretti is right to claim, in *Atlas of the European Novel*, that the need for the colonies in the western European novel has more to do with narrative necessity than with historical-economical veracity, then *La Fille aux yeux d'or* presents a new possible perspective on the nearness of the colonies to the metropolitan center.

Scholars have, however, been primarily preoccupied with elaborating Paris in isolation (or, in the case of Nicole Mozet, Paris in relation to the provinces), and Guichardet, Prendergast and David F. Bell have written at length on the ordering of Parisian space in Balzac's texts. Guichardet leans on the idea of Balzac as an archeologist, bringing coherent narrative to scattered aspects of the city, as if ordering ancient ruins. The cataloguing of Paris commences in earnest quite early, as Prendergast points out in *Paris and the Nineteenth Century*. He quotes Maxime du Camp who, already with a hint of disenchantment, wrote "in the later part of the century . . . that never before had the city been so minutely described, monitored, surveyed, classified, generally 'cleaned' up taxonomically as well as practically: 'It [Paris] is registered, catalogued, numbered, surveilled, lit [éclairé], cleaned, directed, cared for, administered, arrested, judged, imprisoned, interred'" (2). The vocabulary here is telling, and especially in the context of Balzac's novels; du Camp's choice of words repeatedly hints at a dark story of bureaucratization ("enregistré," "administré"), legal intervention ("arrêté," "jugé"), and the reduction of mystery ("éclairé"), all of which have served to imprison and bury Paris. Prendergast later mentions Parisian planner Georges-Eugène Haussmann in the mid 1840s and the lament of a disciplined and managed city from which all surprise had been stripped; and Alfred de Vigny, who, in 1844, calls public transportation a "silent and cold calculation" (quoted on 10–11). Balzac articulates these same sentiments earlier in the century, and they anchor my reading here of this important stage in the *Comédie humaine*.

Balzac's Paris in the 1830s is, like that of Haussmann and Vigny, a city being modernized, for better and worse. In *Real Time: Accelerating Narrative from Balzac to Zola*, Bell argues that technological advances and population growth in the nineteenth century fundamentally altered western European culture's perception of space, time, and, by extension, distance. He postulates that "there was a growing sense of speed—in both the movement of people and the conveying of messages—before the extensive development of the railroad in the 1840s and 1850s in France" (1).[3] As an investor in transportation projects in the 1830s, Balzac knew railways, and he registered the acceleration of life (Robb 139). Biographer Graham Robb writes that, "in the seemingly quiet residential areas of Paris, Balzac estimates the speed of interesting rumour at about 9 m.p.h. When the Duc de Berry was assassinated on the steps of the Opéra in 1820, the news spread to the heart of the Île Saint-Louis in ten minutes" (52). Reading a passage from Dickens's *Oliver Twist* (1837), Bell introduces the idea that punctuality and regularity in public transport (here stagecoach lines) had become expected and even demanded before train schedules were normalized.[4] Bell points out that the criminal Sikes, after committing murder in London, is dogged by "the pursuit organized by the quick dissemination of information about the crime and about Sikes himself" (3). The scene as read does indeed demonstrate that fast transport was becoming a commonplace, but it also says something important—and new—about the city that complicates Bell's case for the increasing connectedness and organization of urban space. Sikes returns to London, Bell writes, because there "he believes he has a better chance to hide than he does in any village along the stagecoach line." (Similarly, Mr. Bennet in Austen's *Pride and Prejudice* [1813] concludes that Lydia and Wickham must be in London, because, he asks, "where else can they be so well concealed?" [227].) Turning to Balzac's Vautrin, then, Bell renders the mysterious neighbor of Goriot and Rastignac instead as a master cartographer who has "thoroughly explored" and theorized the connection both between and within the city and the pension (72). If the previous chapter has demonstrated the dual nature of Vautrin between rationalization and mystery, though, a careful reading of *La Fille aux yeux d'or* can similarly complicate the idea of a relentlessly ordered Paris. The familiar city, in this novel, does not stay familiar.

The novel's first portion repeatedly gestures toward disenchantment in Paris and often does so within the context of a materialism or empiricism that recalls the collection of curiosities in *La Peau de chagrin*. "À Paris," the

---

3. As Bell himself points out, his point here feels analogous to David Harvey's notion of compressed postmodern space and time. While the specifics are clearly different, this is another point—along with McClure's on "unmapping"—at which the nineteenth-century novel first explores terrain that has been seen by critics as unique to postmodern writing. See Bell 8–9.

4. This observation is problematic. In Anthony Trollope's *The Duke's Children* (1880), for example, we learn that punctuality was precisely *not* expected by public transport; Lord Gerald, having missed his train by counting on its departing late, complains, "Who on earth would have thought that they'd have been so punctual? They never are punctual on the Great Eastern" (140).

narrator complains, "no sentiment can resist the burst of things," and even basic passions like "l'amour" and "la haine" have been debased (5.1040). The narrator's discussion of the Parisian worker, "le prolétaire," describes "an existence where thought and movement combine less for the purpose of throwing joy in than for the purpose of *regularizing* the action of sorrow" (5.1042; emphasis mine). The business world is depicted similarly, in the disenchanted vocabulary of weights and measures: "At each moment, the man of money weighs the living, the man of contracts weighs the dead, the man of the law weighs conscience. Obligated to speak unceasingly, everybody replaces the idea with the word, sentiment with the sentence, and their soul becomes a larynx" (5.1047). The reduction of ideas and feelings to embodied language, of the soul to a physical organ, provides a stark and concrete image of *Entzauberung*. These images are not, however, restricted to the opening, pseudo-anthropological salvoes of the novel. Later, as Henri and his sidekick Paul de Manerville converse in Paul's apartment, discussing Henri's progress in his pursuit of Paquita, a pleasantly surprised Henri remarks, "I've ended up finding in this Paris an intrigue accompanied by serious circumstances, major perils" (5.1077). Henri incorrectly goes on to claim, though, that the romance is done: "Now that I know that this beautiful girl, this masterpiece of nature is mine, the adventure has lost its spice" (5.1078). In positioning himself as the conqueror of a woman who represents what is "de la nature," Henri invokes again his being an agent of the very disenchantment that the book's introduction adduces. Henri's arrival in *La Fille aux yeux d'or* highlights this persuasively.

Here, as in *Le Père Goriot*, where Rastignac puts to Bianchon the dilemma of the Mandarin, public gardens (in *Goriot*, the Luxembourg Gardens, in *La Fille aux yeux d'or*, the Tuileries) are a site for the introduction of narrative complication with distinctly violent and colonial undertones. The scene begins with a transition from the narrator's generalizing diatribe against Paris into a narrowing of focus on Henri:

> Quod erat demonstrandum, that which was to be demonstrated, if one may be permitted to apply scholastic formulae to the science of manners [la science des mœurs].
>
> Upon one of those fine spring mornings, when the leaves, although unfolded, are not yet green, when the sun begins to gild the roofs, and the sky is blue, when the population of Paris issues from its cells to swarm along the boulevards, glides like a serpent of a thousand coils through the Rue de la Paix towards the Tuileries, saluting the hymeneal magnificence which the country puts on; on one of these joyous days, then, a young man as beautiful as the day itself, dressed with taste, easy of manner—to let out the secret he was a love-child, the natural

son of Lord Dudley and the famous Marquise de Vordac—was walking in the great avenue of the Tuileries. (5.1054)

Bordas has argued that this transitional moment is a "quite visible" "suture point" between introduction and narrative (340) but that what dominates finally is "the permanent instability of a hesitation between two récits, two styles, two meanings" (344). This stylistic hesitation frames an epistemological duel to be treated later in more depth, but the passage cited above should show that Balzac's narrator is precisely not pushing two unrelated bodies of text together; rather, he is slowly inserting a specific character into the Parisian world he has just laboriously created during the introduction, as a means of testing his hypotheses about Paris. The idea that this transition is a slow and careful one is bolstered when one recalls the narrator's early contention that "To the youthful beauty of English blood they [the young people of Paris] unite the firmness of southern traits, the French spirit" (5.1053). In this blend of English and French, the narrative is already preparing us before the fact for the introduction of the half-French, half-English Henri. Despite the syntactic break ushered in by the "Or" that commences the first sentence of the story of Henri, this is a gradual shift from hypotheses to case study, and there is even an occasional return, during the narrative, to the anthropological tone of the introduction (see 5.1059–61). Importantly, the testing of these hypotheses on the disenchantment of Paris will require the introduction of an Other, Henri's exotic love interest.

Like Vautrin, Henri enters the story as a paradoxical figure, simultaneously an agent of disenchantment and a cutting romantic figure, an "Adonis" (5.1054). Disenchantment here takes the distinct shape of pedagogically methodical secularization, and its importance to Henri's character and to his pursuit of Paquita must not be underestimated. In perfect keeping with Balzac's tendency to distinguish between religious faith and the social institution of religion, Henri's formation comes at the hands of an abbé who schools the youngster in worldliness rather than otherworldliness.

> He taught the child in three years what he might have learned at college in ten. Then the great man, by name the Abbé de Maronis, completed the education of his pupil by making him study civilization under all its aspects: he nourished him on his experience [expérience], led him little into churches, which at that time were closed; introduced him sometimes behind the scenes of theatres, more often into the houses of courtesans; he dismantled [démonta] human emotions for him one by one; taught him politics in the drawing-rooms, where they simmered at the time, enumerated to him the machinery of government, and

endeavored out of attraction towards a fine nature, deserted, yet rich in promise, to virilely replace a mother. (5.1055)

Henri is molded, therefore, into precisely the sort of Parisian critiqued in the book's opening pages. Beset by "ennui" at the ease of his romantic conquests, Henri approaches Paquita as a chance for adventure and romance (5.1070). The narrator explains that Paquita is an inspiration to the imagination, that she represents "the most luminous ideas, those expressed about women by oriental poetry" (5.1066). A romantic target so at odds with the dry and unimaginative picture of Paris that Balzac gives us earlier in the novel ought to fulfill Henri's desires for enchantment and excitement, but Paquita does not, apparently: "Despite the fact that Paquita Valdès presented him with the marvelous collection of perfections that he had not yet fully enjoyed, the pull of passion was almost nothing in him" (5.1070). After Henri believes he has won Paquita's affections, the narrator tells us that "he had come, like rulers, to implore of chance some obstacle to conquer, some enterprise that demanded the deployment of his inactive moral and physical forces." Henri's disenchantment demands the contingency that the narrator has already connected to the Orient, as against the necessity of Paris.

The narrator provides a series of literary intertexts that underscore Balzac's negotiation of a narrative mode adequate to the task of capturing both the disenchantment of Paris and the urge for a reenchantment that will be situated in terms of imperial space. The first of these are references to Richardson and Beaumarchais that highlight the uniqueness that Balzac is claiming for *La Fille aux yeux d'or*. Due to Henri's ennui, the narrator claims, "to render to him the emotions of a true love, he needed, as did Lovelace, a Clarissa Harlowe," a woman whose conquest requires prolonged, heroic struggle. The narrator goes on to equate Henri's friend Laurent with Beaumarchais's Figaro, but only to highlight the elements of Henri's and Paquita's story that are new: "Thus, the living play [la pièce vivante] was more deeply knotted by chance [nouée par le hasard[5]] than it had ever been by any dramatic author" (5.1071). By "la pièce vivante," Balzac's narrator means *La Fille aux yeux d'or*, and this is his preemptive claim to the veracity of the plot, which Balzac would later, in his "Postface de la première édition," defend as "true in most of its details" before going on to write that "the most poetic circumstance, which makes the crux [nœud] of the story, that of the resemblance of the

---

5. The word is *nouée*, one with clear narratological implications (*dénouement*, e.g.); Balzac is clearly thinking here of emplotment, and defensively pitting the strangeness of his "real" (*vivante*) plot against the less strange dramatic ones. The word *nœud*, or *knot*, used in the following quote given, again shows a relationship between this later passage's vocabulary and the vocabulary used in the passage that Balzac is defending.

two main characters, is exact" (5.1111). All that Balzac the writer—"un copiste"—will acknowledge as innovation is that he has dictated the novelistic structure of the true events, combining them in a new way; he blames a disenchanted society for his need to do this, just as the narrator links Henri's own disenchantment to his thirst for *Clarissa*-like pursuit. "By leveling every condition, by explaining everything [en éclairant tout]," Balzac claims, modern society has made it incumbent on the writer to innovate, altering not the truth of events or content but rather the narrative manner—the form—of their discovery. *La Fille aux yeux d'or*, though, leading into the next literary reference that impacts the treatment of enchantment, space and otherness (a mention of Ann Radcliffe), will still seek more modest, subtle means of reenchantment.

The narrator's reference to Radcliffe occurs within a lengthy description of Henri's initial journey (for so it is portrayed, despite the fact that it is merely a carriage ride within Paris) to Paquita, one of several specific moments of urban unmapping in the novel:

> At the hour mentioned Henri was on the boulevard, saw the carriage, and gave the password to a man who looked to him like the mulatto. Hearing the word, the man opened the door and quickly let down the step. Henri was so rapidly carried through Paris, and his thoughts left him so little capacity to pay attention to the streets through which he passed, that he did not know where the carriage stopped. The mulatto let him into a house, the staircase of which was quite close to the entrance. This staircase was dark, as was also the landing upon which Henri was obliged to wait while the mulatto was opening the door of a damp apartment, nauseating, unlit, the chambers of which, barely illuminated by the candle which his guide found in the ante-chamber, seemed to him empty and ill-furnished, like those of a house whose inhabitants are away. He recognized the sensation which he had experienced from the reading of one of those novels of Ann Radcliffe, in which the hero traverses the cold, sombre, and uninhabited rooms of some sad and deserted place. (5.1078)

Massol-Bedoin has insisted that the enigma "poses itself very quickly in spatial terms, and the initial question *Who?* is displaced, very rapidly, by the question *Where?*" (38). Secrecy is, according to her reading of it, constructed spatially in *La Fille aux yeux d'or*, although she does not elaborate on the narrative means toward this. Speed here, the speed of the carriage through the streets of Paris, renders these streets mysterious and incomprehensible to Henri. Rather than confirm the easy connectedness and rationalization of urban space, Balzac's narrator uses diminished distance as an instance of mystery. Henri's journey takes him into a different narrative space and time, and hints at a different sort of narrative altogether, the Gothic. Franco Moretti assures us in *Atlas of the European Novel* that "space acts upon style"—that the space being represented enables narrative but also limits it (43). Discussing *Illusions perdues*, he takes his point further and asserts that "without a certain kind of space, a certain kind of story is simply impossible" (100). Henri's first journey in *La Fille aux yeux d'or* complicates this formulation. The story here and the problem of disenchantment that Balzac's narrator specifically invokes and intends to address both seem to require the production of a certain kind of space, and, more importantly, a certain specific style of narrative associated with that kind of space. This strategy is repeated countless times, as the century progresses, and not least in the work of Trollope and Fontane.

The aim of this carriage-ride passage is to render a familiar Paris foreign. It accomplishes this first by unmapping regions with which de Marsay is intimately familiar and then by presenting us with ex-urban and pre-realist literary corollaries. The passage above is not even the starkest instance of this in *La Fille aux yeux d'or*; later, on de Marsay's second ride in the carriage, he is actually blindfolded by Paquita's Moorish bodyguard. There are similarities to the first carriage ride, but the context and description are radically different, and the text insists on Henri's knowledge of Parisian geography even as his journey undermines it:

> There was one resource still open to a young man who knew Paris as well as Henri. To know whither he was going, he had but to collect himself and count, by the number of gutters crossed, the streets leading from the boulevards by which the carriage passed, so long as it continued straight along. He could thus discover into which lateral street it would turn, either towards the Seine or towards the heights of Montmartre, and guess the name or position of the street in which his guide should bring him to a halt. But the violent emotions which his struggle had caused him, the rage into which his compromised dignity had thrown him, the ideas of vengeance to which he abandoned himself, the suppositions suggested to him by the circumstantial care which this girl had taken in order to bring him to her, all hindered him from the attention, which the blind have, necessary for the concentration of his intelligence and the perfect lucidity of his recollection. The journey lasted half an hour. When the carriage stopped, it was no longer on the street [pavé]. (5.1086–87)

The tension between Henri's knowledge of Paris and its sudden unfamiliarity relates to another complex aspect of the novel's space, one that Massol-Bedoin has highlighted: "A paradoxical place, this Hôtel San Réal: Henri must reconnoiter in full mystery while entering it, and yet it is one of the most situable places in the narrative, the most anchored in a 'realist' topology" (38). Paradoxically, the narrator has carefully led readers out of the urban without leaving Paris. The ensuing jungle imagery that follows through on the departure from the pavement in the above passage becomes overwhelming, as Henri arrives in a garden where he "smelled the flowers and the odor particular to trees and greenery. The silence reigning there was so profound that he could distinguish the noise made by some drops of water falling from the humid leaves" (5.1087). Fontane's narrator in *Effi Briest* similarly relies on the sensory impact of nature—the sound of wind in leaves—to mark a moment of potential enchantment. Beyond Paquita's cosmopolitan provenance in *La Fille aux yeux d'or*, her exoticism and otherness are inseparable from the reenchantment of urban space that occurs en route to her. Content, to twist Moretti's words, seems to act upon both form and space here.

(c) On Seeing and Not Seeing: A Sense of Disenchantment

The smells and sounds of the tropics that inflect the narrator's description of Paquita's residence emphasize the text's empirical sympathies, but vision is the central sense in *La Fille aux yeux d'or*. If the first carriage ride only prepares us for the greater lengths the narrator will go to in the depiction of the second carriage ride, towards a more thorough unmapping of Paris, the unmapping during this second ride is qualitatively different because it addresses this sense. Henri's first journey renders Paris unfamiliar through speed and the too-rapid adjustment of distances; the second renders Paris unfamiliar by robbing him of his eyesight. By addressing the reenchantment of the city in terms of first space and then stunted empirical knowledge, *La Fille aux yeux d'or* opens an epistemological duel that ultimately recalls the foundational questions of *La Peau de chagrin* and of my larger argument here. The two previous chapters have read *La Peau de chagrin* and *Le Père Goriot* as texts invested in but finally ambivalent towards the disenchantment of post-Revolutionary French culture as Balzac saw it, and furthermore as texts anxious to forestall the process of *Entzauberung* but wary of the means and implications of this resistance. The tension between empiricism and enchantment in this equation is an elemental aspect of *La Fille aux yeux d'or* as well, and, seen as such, it can bridge the narrative gap perceived between the novel's supposedly disparate two parts.

What some critics have termed a visible rupture between the first and second portions of *La Fille aux yeux d'or* is, on closer reading, actually built as a far more subtle transition from one narrative style to another. If the narration of Henri's story begins with the paragraph cited above at length ("Or, par une de ces belles matinées de printemps . . ."), and if this beginning signifies a break from the more anthropological posturing of the novel's opening pages, then how can one account for the similarly anthropological tone of the lengthy description of the youth of Paris, which is given well after the commencement of Henri's story? (5.1059–61). This, paired with the sly introduction of Henri's half-French/half-English ancestry mentioned earlier, renders much more complex the relationship between the novel's two major narrative tones. They must be seen as alternating styles rather than cleanly delineated sections. More importantly, within each of these two separate styles, there is another duel going on, one that reproduces the duel between narrative modes as a conflict between two epistemologies at odds with each other: on the one hand an empirical, scientistic epistemology encapsulated here most often by the use of vision; and on the other hand a more fantastic epistemology that sets itself explicitly against and degrades the empirical. In a manner very much like *La Peau de chagrin*, *La Fille aux yeux d'or* structures itself around this conflict.

On the occasion of his third carriage-ride through Paris to visit Paquita, Henri's scientific instincts are, as if counter-intuitively, *emphasized* by his restricted vision. This time, the narrator explains, he "obligingly allowed his eyes to be covered. Then, with that firm will which only truly strong men have the ability to summon, he brought his attention and applied his intelligence towards guessing [deviner] through which streets the carriage was traveling" (5.1097–98). The lengthy passage that follows shows Henri thinking like a scientist or detective, prizing empirical knowledge and causal explanation to an extraordinary degree. Reflecting on the precautions that Paquita's handlers take to ensure the secrecy of their locale—driving him in a carriage, blindfolding him—Henri knows that if he had walked to the hôtel San-Réal "he could have . . . picked off the branch of a bush, examined the nature of the sand that would have attached itself to his boots" (5.1098). Balzac's language here makes Henri emblematic of the desire to explain or demystify through "recherches," to "éclairer." Though his ability to gauge the precise location of the boudoir is impaired, his impulses toward its discovery are clear. In a sharp departure from the frantic first two journeys to Paquita, the unmapping here is paired with a calm reflection on the means of charting the route and the possibilities for explaining it. It continues an empirical sense that figures earlier in Henri's story, as when, for example, Paquita's address is written out within the narration as an actual, complete address, along with the narrator's description of the penmanship, "long, slender characters that announced [qui annonçaient] the hand of a woman" (5.1067).

Paquita stands against the empiricism emblematized by Henri's approach to their relationship and to the mysteries of it, but not as its simple opposite. Indeed, the hybridity which Kadish sees in Paquita's character can be extended to the manner in which she elicits a complex combination of desires for and styles of knowledge. The text is suggestive on this point; for example, an explicit reference to the Girl With the Golden Eyes is followed immediately by a reminder of the important "union so bizarre of the mysterious and the real, of shadows and light, of the horrible and the beautiful, of pleasure and danger, of Heaven and Hell" central to the story (5.1091). The play of extremes here highlights the manner in which Paquita's character will later be said simultaneously to arouse several different varieties of knowledge: "Paquita responded to this mysterious passion so dramatically expressed in Faust, so poetically translated through Manfred, and that pushed Don Juan to excavate [fouiller] the heart of women, hoping to find there this boundless thought which so many ghost-hunters seek, which the learned [les savants] believe they see in science, and which mystics find in God alone" (5.1101). The tension between romance and empiricism in the above passage is palpable. Goethe's *Faust* and Byron's *Manfred*[6] both play with the sort of extremes that Balzac hints at earlier in *La Fille aux yeux d'or*, and both texts are equally concerned with the limits and costs of knowledge. However, even the romantic Don Juan here is conjoined with science, as he is said to excavate, in a very archaeological sense—*fouiller*—the hearts of women. Paquita awakens, according to the narrator, a desire for extremities that sees religious mysticism (Balzac's word) on a par with rational science. Recall Massol-Bedoin's judgment of the paradoxical hôtel San-Réal, which is simultaneously a site "en plein mystère" and "one of the most situable places in the narrative, the most anchored in a 'realist' topology" (38). Paquita is problematic for the world of *La Fille aux yeux d'or*, because she confounds disparate types of knowledge within a text that is already attempting to negotiate between them. The confusion is amplified by Henri's conflicting longing for romance (obstacles in his way) and attempts to methodically displace romance (his analytic efforts and attempts to divine the location of the San-Réal). A return to the novel's introduction, with its anthropological gestures, underscores the same ambivalence at work there.

Akin to the opposing energies—empirical and romantic—at play in the narrated portion of *La Fille aux yeux d'or*, the introduction vacillates between textual strategies easily categorizable as those of science and those

---

6. Its inspiration from Goethe readily acknowledged, Byron's play even structures Manfred's quest as an epistemological duel: Act I begins with the summoning of spirits in Scene I, and ends with the real-life conversation with the Chamois Hunter; Act II begins with the Chamois Hunter, moves toward the conversation with the Witch in Scene II, and ends with the summoning of the Destinies in Scene III. There are constant, clearly foregrounded shifts between this-worldly and other-worldly knowledges in Manfred's quest for information on mortality.

of the wholly unscientific. The careful division of Paris into manageable, describable social parts organizes the introduction, with its turn-by-turn elaboration of the proletariat, the world of business, and the world of leisure, as well as the later addition of the world of Paris's youth. The approach is almost Aristotelian in its depiction, and Linnaean in its classification, of visibly separate categories of being. Yet alongside this scientific, explanatory impulse is a vocabulary inherited from the supernatural, and above all from Dante's *Divine Comedy*; the classifications that Balzac's narrator offers are structured as hierarchized circles of the inferno that is Paris. A moment very early in *La Fille* even conjures the atmosphere of Victor Hugo's poem, "Les Djinns," published just a few years prior in *Les Orientales* (1829): Balzac's "all smokes, all burns, all shines" [tout fume, tout brûle, tout brille] recalls the "All flees/All passes" [Tout fuit,/Tout passe] that concludes Hugo's poem, which is simultaneously charged with supernaturalism and orientalism.[7] Prendergast has noted the stylistic discomfort of Balzac's opening phrasings in *La Fille aux yeux d'or*, claiming that "the fires which consume [Paris] are not just the hell-fires of Dante; the drift of the metaphor is as much secular as theological" (58–59). Prendergast's analysis ultimately situates the secularization of Paris more prominently, in Balzac's Paris, than the very public fretting over that secularization, and Prendergast turns toward an important closing image from the introduction—that of a steamboat—to drive his point home. The image is more complex than his reading allows, and it binds together not just the secularization of the city, but also the energies of exploration that contribute to it and that may, paradoxically, offer possible respite from it.

The image of Paris as a steamboat is the final movement of the introduction before the anthropological summation of sorts that combines the worlds of proletariats, bourgeois, and aristocrats.

> Thus this city can no more be moral, or cordial, or clean, than the engine of those proud leviathans you admire when they cleave the waves! Is not Paris a sublime vessel freighted with intelligence? . . . The barque may roll and pitch; but she cleaves the world, illuminates it [y fait feu] through the hundred mouths of her tribunes, works [laboure] the scientific seas, rides with full sail, cries from the height of her tops, with the voice of her scientists [savants] and artists: "Onward, advance! Follow me!" (5.1052)

The picture here is an undecided one, and the narrator emphasizes, one page later, that "Paris is essentially the land of contrasts" (5.1053). However, Prendergast argues that Balzac here comes

---

7. Like Balzac's novel, Hugo's poem also ends with an erasure: "L'espace/Efface/Le Bruit."

out of the sphere of the organic, the natural, into that of the mechanical and the man-made. At this closing moment, the writing will change metaphorical tack once again. In one of Balzac's more baroque imaginings, the text places us on the high seas: Paris is elaborately compared to a ship and, in the initial moment of the figure, to its engine.... The city as vessel repeats the familiar allegorical motif of the journey, the idea of Paris and its history as an adventurous, discovery-laden voyage. The city as engine, however, has more interesting implications. The engine ('la chaudière motrice') is, of course, a steam-engine, and it is an image that Balzac will use on more than one occasion in the *Comédie humaine* as an analogy for modern society. Science thus returns in the form of technology. (58)

The reading makes its allegiances clear, if the engine motif is "more interesting" than the voyage motif that ought to be inseparable from it. Prendergast goes on to tease the theme of entropy out of the passage, linking it—though not in name—to the disenchantment that Balzac's critique of Parisian culture elevates as a central problem.

The dual nature of Balzac's passage is crucial, however. The steamboat certainly embodies the onslaught of science and progress, but it does so within an almost nostalgic allusion to the romance of exploration and within a more troubling glance at the historical outcomes of this romance: the soldiers on deck are described as "novateurs ou ambitieux" and will finally seek a glory that has been degraded to pleasure ("de la gloire qui est un plaisir") and a love that is only for gold ("des amours qui veulent de l'or"). Pleasure and gold, the two things that *La Fille aux yeux d'or* loathes the most as the symptoms of Parisian malaise, lurk in even the romanticized aspects of the steamboat motif. This appears to signal, at the same time, a progression in Balzac's depiction of the possibilities of enchantment and the imagination—or, more properly put, an increased pessimism towards these possibilities—because it recalls the finale of *La Peau de chagrin*, where Pauline resists the upriver penetration of a steamboat, which the narrator labels an "invasion moderne" (10.294). Even the romantic potential of exploration is coded here, in the steamboat of *La Fille aux yeux d'or*, as a step toward disenchantment, toward the market-driven leanings mentioned earlier when the narrator situates Paris at the heart of global commerce. The introduction thus prepares us for the novel's cold, conclusive dismissal of Paquita and any romantic potential she represents. In a manner redolent of the scientists' dismissal of the Magic Skin in *La Peau de chagrin*, Paul de Manerville's enquiry as to the fate of Paquita after her murder is met by a rejoinder from Henri that brusquely reduces the disturbing and almost inexplicable crime scene in the San-Réal to a vague but clearly physical explanation:

"So, whatever became of our lovely Girl With the Golden Eyes, you great scoundrel [scélérat]?"
   "She died."
   "Of what."
   "Of the chest." [De la poitrine.] (5.1109)

Before this, Henri's exchange with Ferragus has already assured him that "the traces of this fantasy" will be removed. *La Fille aux yeux d'or*'s prolonged ambivalence between the contingencies of enchantment and the necessities of disenchanted Paris appears, at the end, to be at an end.

The removal of The Girl With the Golden Eyes from *The Girl With the Golden Eyes* shares something else with *La Peau de chagrin*'s upriver-bound steamboat: the invasion of the modern as an evisceration of the primitive is depicted in terms of violence against the feminine. The penetrative, invasive steamboat of *La Peau de chagrin* finds its counterpart in Henri's attempts to chart the course he blindly and repeatedly takes toward Paquita's hidden dwelling. If Henri and the city of Paris are painted, in general, with the colors of disenchanting science, technology and calculation (for, like Vautrin, Henri is said to "calculate" [5.1094]), women are offered up in the novel as their opposite. This chapter has attempted to weigh the foreign elements brought into the story via Paquita and her entourage, and their significance within and final banishment from the novel. Janke Drent has disclosed Balzac's likely source for the character and story of Paquita, and it is important that Balzac's sole addition to the events Drent mentions is the lesbianism of Paquita. However, despite Henri's immediate, visceral reaction to the sudden and unforeshadowed revelation of lesbianism, the narrative is not content to soil his hands with the blood of Paquita, even though he intends to and attempts to kill her. De Marsay's half-sister Euphémie removes Paquita from the text without making it necessary for de Marsay to involve himself in such a crime of passion. Henri is permitted to remain the spectator. Predictably, Euphémie is portrayed during this scene as outside reason and empirical knowledge, deprived of sight. She "did not *see* Henri" [ne *vit* pas Henri] and is too impassioned "to *see* [*apercevoir*] all of Paris, were Paris to form a circus around her" (5.1107; emphases mine).

La Fille aux yeux d'or plays a significant role in the overall dynamic of the duel between disenchantment and its interruption. By beginning to think about this dynamic in terms of the burgeoning global market, Balzac both explicitly registers the advancement of imperialism from exploration to full-blown marketization and implicitly reproduces the process in novelistic form. The results were already hinted at in the discussion of *La Peau de chagrin*, but the thought will bear expansion here. The moral dilemmas inspired by global commerce reappear in Balzac's later works, but the manner in which these dilemmas arise is transformed as the century progresses. Consider the Alhambra or the "Turkish" woman in Flaubert's *Éducation sentimentale* (1869). Paquita's divan is a forebear of these locales, but the mysterious presence of a hidden, oriental chamber in the middle of Paris dissolves into commodity in two ways in Flaubert's novel: on the one hand, orientalist kitsch recast as a cheesy nightclub (the Alhambra), which Frédéric Moreau derides as cheap and stupid; on the other hand, orientalist eroticism recast as a brothel on the outskirts of town run by a woman named Zoraïde Turc, whose actual Turkishness is seriously doubted by the narrator. Still later, in Zola's *Au Bonheur des Dames* (1882), the same geographical divisions—between Europe and the outside world—that underwrite Paquita's potential to enchant are reduced to merchandising selling points in department stores. Balzac's *La Peau de chagrin*, *Le Père Goriot*, and *La Fille aux yeux d'or* anticipate these developments. They map the moment of a crisis of knowledge and narrative, yielding Balzac's mode of realism as a negotiation between the extremes of empirical and romantic epistemologies and between the poles of empirical and romantic narrative modes. More importantly, these three novels demonstrate that this crisis is finally unthinkable—at least to Balzac—apart from the concerns of a wide, mysterious world becoming inevitably smaller and increasingly less mysterious.

Part II

Trollope and the Problem of Integration

CHAPTER FOUR

ECONOMIES OF ROMANCE AND HISTORY IN *PHINEAS FINN*

"I have already, through my future mother-in-law, heard of a place that I think will suit: it is to undertake the education of the five daughters of Mrs. Dionysius O'Gall of Bitternutt Lodge, Connaught, Ireland...."
  "It is a long way off, sir ... and then the sea is a barrier—"
  "From what, Jane?"
  "From England."
  —Charlotte Brontë, *Jane Eyre* (1847)

I have shorn my fiction of all romance.
  —Trollope, letter to George Eliot (October 1863)

I am well aware now that English readers no longer like Irish stories. I cannot understand why it should be so, as the Irish character is peculiarly well fitted for romance.
  —Trollope, *An Autobiography* (1877; published posthumously in 1883)

A moment of Trollopian self-consciousness introduces the dilemma that organizes this chapter, which brings the complex forces of colonial identity to bear on the simultaneous shrinking of the world and Trollope's novelistic fretting over problems of romance, realism, and representation. Phineas Finn has just been acquitted of murder, and the narrator writes:

> Our pages have lately been taken up almost exclusively with the troubles of Phineas Finn, and indeed have so far not unfairly represented the feelings and interest of people generally at the time. Not to have talked of Phineas Finn from the middle of May to the middle of July in that year would have exhibited great ignorance or a cynical disposition. But other things went on also. Moons waxed and waned; children were born; marriages were contracted; and the hopes and fears of the little world around did not come to an end because Phineas Finn was not to be hung. (*Phineas Redux* 2.256)

Finn is simultaneously central to the elaboration of larger social concerns ("the feelings and interest of people generally") and yet totally marginal to these concerns, as the narrator further demonstrates by proceeding to elaborate a plot strand that has nothing at all to do with Finn. Similar ambivalence emerges in a glance at the reception of *Phineas Finn* (1869) and *Phineas Redux* (1874), as Jane Elizabeth Dougherty has pointed out, with particular relevance to Finn's foreignness: "Phineas is a successful and sympathetic character, and yet it may well have been a blunder on Trollope's part to make him Irish. Phineas's Irishness is and is not evident in the text; it is both crucial and incidental to Phineas's characterization; the narrative trajectory of the Phineas novels is at once enabled and disabled by the ethnicity of their eponymous hero" (133). It was, of course, Trollope himself who, long after the writing of the two novels, saw Finn's Irishness as an authorial "blunder" (*Autobiography* 318), and Patrick Lonergan claims that this admission has caused literary critics to ignore his ethnicity (147).

Historians have *not* passed over Finn's Irishness without comment, and their contributions have primarily raised the issues of exactly how Irish Trollope's Irish Member is and whether there was a real-life model for the character. Where this debate has surfaced, the question of literary realism (in the guise of historical accuracy) is not far behind, for both Phineas's certain Irishness in the eyes of some and his certain un-Irishness in the eyes of others have been adduced as evidence of a lapse in or partial failure of Trollope's realist project in the Palliser novels. Trollope himself equated Irishness with romance, but this must be complicated by the manner in which Finn's story is said to contribute to a realistic "representation" of general society. This central ambivalence is significant in Trollope's Palliser series, because Phineas Finn, the young Irishman who heads to London to enter Parliament, appears in four of the six novels and lends his name to two of them. A brief examination of the evolving role of the Irish in the English novel of the nineteenth century can clarify the literary-historical significance of *Phineas Finn* and set the stage for a discussion of the relevance of Finn's contested Irishness—linked, in Trollope's mind, to romance—to this curious two-volume *Bildungsroman*. The narrative indecision surrounding Finn's identity is finally inseparable from formal considerations of the *Phineas* novels, which, like the Balzac novels already examined, constantly require a romance of which they are constantly wary. Ensuing chapters will explore the manner in which Trollope's concern with romance and its disappearance manifests itself in spatial terms, as Great Britain is remapped in the *Phineas* novels; and the troubling insertion of the English metropolis into the global marketplace in *The Way We Live Now*.

(a) "The Colonies Next Door": Irishness as a Realist Fact

In his book, *Paddy & Mr. Punch*, historian Roy Foster reminds his readers that, despite what he calls the recent "fashionable preoccupation" with "representation of 'The Other'" in the wake of Foucault, the question of Irish otherness has long been an established historiographical field (171). Foster is quick to mention the influence of two books by another historian, L. Perry Curtis, Jr., whose *Apes and Angels: The Irishman in Victorian Caricature* "began a long-running discussion" when it was first published in 1971. In an addendum to a reprinting of *Apes and Angels*, Curtis has also seen himself as a forerunner of these later scholarly achievements: "Little did I think when I set out all those years ago to investigate the origin and function of the Irish ape-man that the results would one day strike me as analogous to standing in the entrance hall of some huge mansion still under construction, with many unbuilt rooms that would one day be lavishly furnished by Foucault, Said, and a host of other cultural architects, designers, and decorators" (180). The extent to which one can employ postcolonial theory and theories of imperialism to the status of Ireland is still a matter for debate.[1] Andrew Murphy usefully rehearses the problems in the introduction to his book on early modern English literature and Ireland. Yet while Murphy castigates Said and others (especially Terry Eagleton and Richard Kearney) for "fail[ing] finally to engage with the particularity of the Irish situation, . . . preferring instead to assimilate Ireland's colonial experience to a greater global imperial paradigm," he ultimately acknowledges the relevance of such paradigms to an analysis of the Irish situation: "The nature of English intervention in the affairs of Ireland *is* always in some ways colonial. The English always behave in some ways like colonialists, and the Irish are always in some ways perceived as the colonized. But in other ways, the exact nature of the English initiative in Ireland is altogether more ambiguous" (15, 28). Trollope's narrator in *Phineas Finn* will once bluntly refer to Ireland as "the colonies next door" (1.270). The novelistic negotiation and renegotiation of this ambiguity, though, becomes clearer through a general sketch of how the Irish were viewed in nineteenth-century England and a brief glimpse of their use in the nineteenth-century English novel up to the publication of Trollope's *Phineas Finn*.

Petulant nationalism and permanent laziness were the chief stereotypes of the Irish in England in the wake of the United Irishmen's rebellion of 1798

---

[1]. Edward Said, though, has no trouble seeing Ireland as colonial/postcolonial in "Yeats and Decolonization."

and the Act of Union of 1800. A central role for the Famine in Irish emigration to England has long been assumed. Emily Brontë's *Wuthering Heights*, for example, was published in 1847, at the Famine's peak, and Eagleton's *Heathcliff and the Great Hunger* examines the possible effects of the Famine Irish on the novel and its sublimated anti-Irish sentiment. E. P. Thompson's *The Making of the English Working Class*, however, disputes the relevance of the Famine to English contact with the Irish; Thompson asserts instead that the events of 1798 and 1800 (the United Irishmen's Rebellion and the Act of Union, respectively), and not the Famine in 1847, mark the turning point in Irish immigration to England (429). Census statistics support this. As Linda Colley has pointed out, by 1831—well before the Famine's onset—Irish immigrants already constituted 5% of the British labor force and inspired a backlash visible in (ultimately unsuccessful) Protestant resistance to Catholic Emancipation in 1829 (329). The Famine is still important to literary evocations of the Irish, but the most powerful early impressions register the Irish less as victims of history than as a permanent threat to it. The Irish in England were seen, in the words of another historian, as a working-class mass "politically antagonistic to the Establishment," as objects of danger rather than pity (O'Connor 36). This is indeed how they appear, for the most part, in British novels after 1798: in muffled form in Scott, and more loudly in Brontë, Gaskell, Dickens, and Thackeray.

The importance of the rebellion of 1798 cannot be underestimated in any analysis of English attitudes toward the Irish in the early nineteenth century. The uprising precipitated Parliament's passing the Act of Union of 1800, which shackled Ireland firmly to Great Britain until 1926, and it seemed significant enough to Napoleon that he committed several thousand French troops to aid the Irish insurgents. When one recalls Franco Moretti's insistent reading in *The Way of the World* of the nineteenth-century English *Bildungsroman* as a nullification of the democratizing effects of Napoleon's armies—who represented a lawless new order and a subversion of the old one—then this historical alliance between Irish nationalism and the godless continental revolutionaries demonstrates partially why the Irish were perceived as a constant threat to national security. Moretti quips, in *Atlas of the European Novel*, that in nineteenth-century English novels "France is clearly the epicenter of the world's evils" (30). A cartoon from October of 1798, even depicts, mockingly, "The Allied Republics of France and Ireland," an alliance made more disturbing because the French continental aggression had not yet ended, according to Douglas, Harte and O'Hara (11). As Donald MacRaild has noted, "In an age when the ruling élite generally feared the leveling tendencies of the working class, the Irish stood out as either agrarian rebels, nationalist conspirators or industrial militants" (131). The Irish were thus threatening on several fronts, and additional risings in 1803 and 1848 did nothing to diminish this sentiment in England.

Scott is a key writer for Trollope, who valued *Ivanhoe* as one of his favorite novels, and rewritings of Scott permeate the Palliser series.[2] In a more general way here, though, *Waverley* is especially important, because it functions as a prototype for the nineteenth-century English *Bildungsroman* (as both Moretti and Lukács have argued) and because it reveals the subtlety with which fear of Celtic unrest could appear, however romanticized, in a novel. As the author himself writes in *Waverley*'s first chapter, the narrative was begun in 1805, a mere seven years after the United Irishmen uprising of 1798 and two years after its aftershock in 1803. Scott himself was personally affected by the rebellion of 1798,[3] and so it is not too much to admit the possibility that Scott bore 1798 in mind when he commenced writing his account of another Celtic revolt, the one chronicled in *Waverley*. Saree Makdisi has linked *Waverley* to Irish unrest, arguing that, "at a certain political level, the subjugation and colonization of the Highlands represented not only the conquest of a previously wild and unruly revolutionary zone, but also the reclamation of this zone from the cultural influence of Ireland" (79). Scott's narrative makes mention of "Irish officers" in Waverley's rebel army (196) and twice refers to "Fin Macoul" (201), also written as "Finn M'Coul" (214), the leading figure of the Fianna, a group of Ulster warriors in Irish mythology. Essentially, *Waverley* seems as determined to link the Scots and the Irish as Trollope will later be to separate them, and Scott's narrator refers to the Scottish army several times as, less specifically, Gaelic. Associating the Scottish rebels with the Irish almost forces one to remember that the Irish were friendly with Napoleon, and Scott concretizes the comparison when he points out that one of the more renegade Scots fighters first greets Waverley while wearing a French uniform. The Highland armies are rendered as a commingling of Scottish, Irish, and continental energies that would be associated with revolution at the time of Scott's writing, even though the novel is set before the Revolution. The Celtic rebellion in *Waverley* is quelled, but Scott's novel relies on representational subtleties that disappear in later novels' use of the Irish.

2. Faulkner has examined the influence of Scott on Trollope's failed historical romance, *La Vendée* (1850), but Scott's shadow also hangs over Trollope's more conventional realist works, especially *Phineas Finn*.

3. Hoefnagel writes that Lord Downshire, the guardian of Scott's fiancée, caused Scott much consternation when he failed to reply to Scott's request to marry Margaret Charlotte Carpenter, Downshire's charge. Scott became "impatient and assumed that Downshire was making inquiries about him" (149). The real reason for Downshire's delayed response and his subsequent failure to attend the wedding was his required presence in Ireland to quell the rebellion. The uprising chronicled in *Waverley* was still a matter of cultural interest well into the nineteenth century; Sir John Everett Millais, Trollope's illustrator for *Phineas Finn*, painted *The Order of Release 1746* (1852–53), which depicts the release of a kilt-wearing Scottish prisoner by a Redcoat. On Millais and Trollope, see Hall 8–88.

"At a time when portrayals of Irish characters were often negative," Lonergan writes of *Phineas Finn*, "Trollope presented his readers with a realistic and sympathetic Irish politician—and developed his character during one of the most significant periods in Irish history" (147). Not every portrayal of the Irish was negative, to be sure, but even genial characters like the O'Dowds in Thackeray's *Vanity Fair* (1847–48) are overpowered by the roguery both Celtic and continental of the Irish protagonist in the earlier *Barry Lyndon* (1844).[4] The industrial agitators of Gaskell's *North and South* (1854)[5] are Irish, as is the hard-drinking curate Malone in Brontë's *Shirley* (1849). Yet the larger pattern of the Irish in the nineteenth-century English novel is their service as convenient foils to the English protagonist and as unwitting plot-enablers in these protagonists' upward struggle. As David Copperfield begins "Life on my own account," Dickens has him make the acquaintance, in the bottling warehouse of Murdstone and Grinby, of two youths to whom he will feel an incessant aversion: Mick Walker and Mealy Potatoes. "Mick" is of course a common, pejorative appellation for Irishmen, but the reference to "mealy potatoes" is almost shocking, given that *David Copperfield* began its serial publication in 1849, towards the end of the Irish potato famine. David worries that his association with Mick and Mealy will stain him forever, and he is anxious to preserve "a space between" himself and the two boys (157). The vocabulary of difference is even more telling: "Mealy Potatoes *uprose* once, and *rebelled* against my being so distinguished," David claims (159, emphasis mine). The episode at the bottling factory so disgusts David that it drives him to his aunt in Dover, a move that enables everything that happens afterward in the novel. Brontë constructs a similar scenario in *Villette* (1853). The tone is set early on by first-person narrator Lucy's offhand equation of "faithless[ness]" and the "Celtic (not Saxon) character" (73), but the case of Sweeney, the governess whom Lucy replaces, is more vivid:

> Beside a table, on which flared the remnant of a candle guttering to waste in the socket, a coarse woman, heterogeneously clad in a broad-striped showy silk dress and a stuff apron, sat in a chair fast asleep. To complete the picture, and leave no doubt as to the state of matters, a bottle and an empty glass stood at the sleeping beauty's elbow. . . . By some means or other she had acquired, and now held in possession, a wardrobe of rather suspicious splendour. . . . I need hardly explain to the reader that this lady was in effect a native of Ireland. (130–33)

---

   4. Much has been written on Thackeray and his treatment of the Irish in his *Irish Sketch Book* (1843) and in *Barry Lyndon*. See, for example, Brewer, Klotz, and Colby.
   5. *Nice Work* (1988), David Lodge's rewrite of *North and South*, recasts the Irish as Asians. The implication is that, in the 1980s, the Irish are no longer sufficiently "other" for the narrative's needs.

Chapter Four: Economies of Romance and History in Phineas Finn ~ 93

Mrs. Sweeney's Christian name is Hibernice, an obvious play on the Latin for Ireland, Hibernia. Before Lucy has even met her, she is implicated in theft, drunknness, idleness, wastefulness, and coarseness, and she must finally be removed from the school in the presence of "an agent of the police" (133). This episode, like the one in *David Copperfield*, enables the narrative that follows it, for it is Sweeney's vacancy that Lucy fills. Brontë's language—"I need hardly explain to the reader"—is confident in the accuracy of her depiction of an Irishwoman and highlights a culturally accepted pattern of such portraiture.

Trollope inherits such conventions from his contemporaries and forebears. However, unlike all of them but Thackeray, Trollope had spent significant time in Ireland, as a postal inspector, and even begun his writing career there. His commitment to realism, which he admits in his autobiography, may have forbidden him from relying on convenient stereotypes, but this same commitment to realism must be measured against Trollope's belief that "the Irish character is particularly well fitted for romance" (*Autobiography* 156). In 1866, just three years before the publication of *Phineas Finn*, the narrator of Trollope's short story, "Father Giles of Ballymoy," plays on Ireland's romantic associations:

> Ireland is not very well known to all Englishmen, but it is much better known than it was in those days. On this my first visit to Connaught, I own that I was somewhat scared lest I should be made a victim to the wild lawlessness and general savagery of the people; and I fancied, as in the wet, windy gloom of the night, I could see the crowd of natives standing round the doors of the inn, and just discern their naked legs and old battered hats, that Ballymoy was probably one of those places so far removed from civilisation and law, as to be an unsafe residence for an English Protestant. (440)

Candidly acknowledging the common stereotypes of and antipathy toward the Irish—for Trollope both deliberately reproduces and carefully avoids them in *Phineas Finn* and *Phineas Redux*—Trollope envisions the *Phineas* novels at a point of transition in English history, in the development of the English novel, and in the emerging global economy. If I have dwelled at length on the tradition within which and the historical circumstances surrounding which Trollope is writing, it has only been in order to highlight, in this chapter and the two subsequent chapters, the extent to which Trollope does something new at a time of enormous change. Phineas Finn performs the same narrative task as the talisman, the netherworldly criminal, and the objectified colonial woman in the Balzac novels discussed above. As the foreign arrival in London, he forces the novel to grapple with questions of representation that paint a complex picture of the interplay between romance (Trollope's conception of Irishness) and the real (the political histories to which the Palliser novels bear witness) in Trollope's novelistic world, within the dynamic of textually negotiated ethnicity. Finn's rise may be, as one critic has termed it, "anomalous" because he is an Irishman in a realm where Irishmen have not been well received, as several characters point out to him (Dougherty 140). "But in these days," the narrator of *Phineas Finn* remarks in an apparently unnecessary generalization at the outset, "we have got to like red hair" (1.32). This is the ambiguity Murphy mentions, and the novels' expression of it records a commensurate ambivalence toward the need for romance in a shrinking world of duty and compromise.[6]

(b) The *Bildung* of Phineas Finn: Irishness as a Realist Problem

In Dougherty's article on Phineas Finn, whom she terms "Trollope's Irish Hero," she twice remarks that *Phineas Finn* is "ostensibly a Bildungsroman" (136, 143). Trollope meant the novel to be read as a *Bildungsroman* and took great pains to that end. This bears directly on the question of Irishness and Englishness in the *Phineas* novels, because novels in the *Bildungsroman* tradition attempt the smooth socialization of their youthful protagonist. So, determining the place, in English society, of an outsider from Ireland becomes the implicit task of *Phineas Finn*. In contrast to the rebellious and unsocializable heroes of someone like Stendhal, Moretti claims in *The Way of the World*, are the almost unpalatably conservative narratives of the English novels, where the heroes consistently allow themselves to be restrained in their struggle for self-actualization or hierarchy-threatening upward mobility. *The Way of the World* attributes this national difference and the striking "stability of narrative conventions and basic cultural assumptions" in the English *Bildungsroman* partially to the fact that England, unlike the continent, "had never been touched by Napoleon's forces" (181). This generalization is abetted by the absence of Thackeray from Moretti's study, and Trollope also goes unmentioned in *The Way of the World* or *Atlas of the European Novel*, despite his enormous success as a novelist in nineteenth-century England. Reading *Phineas Finn*—and, to a lesser extent in this chapter, *Phineas*

---

6. P. D. Edwards, in *Trollope: His Art and Scope*, writes of Trollope's "two streams," the quotidian and the sensational. This is clearly analogous to what I am calling here an ambivalence between Trollope's realism and his texts' imported romance tropes, but with at least one important distinction: as my analysis is grounded in the foreignness that gives rise to this dilemma, I highlight a particular historical context for this ambivalence.

Redux—as a *Bildungsroman* will reveal the novel(s)[7] to be, alongside Eliot's *Daniel Deronda* (1876), one of the most interesting assimilation narratives among nineteenth-century English novels, if not among English novels writ large. Trollope had already set several of his earlier novels in Ireland: *The Macdermotts of Ballycloran* (1847), *The Kellys and the O'Kellys* (1848), and *Castle Richmond* (1860). Sales had been so dismal that his editor felt prompted to remind him that there was no market in England for fiction about Ireland. However, the relocation to London in *Phineas Finn* represents an important change from Trollope's earlier Irish work, and it was a commercial and critical success. As a *Bildungsroman* featuring an Irish protagonist in England—a protagonist who is also "a formal center for the novel" (Polhemus 150)—*Phineas Finn* becomes a narrative referendum on Irishness, its role in England, and its ability to be represented as a romantic trait within a realist novel.

That Trollope envisioned *Phineas Finn* and *Phineas Redux* as a *Bildungsroman* cannot be doubted. As the novel opens, the reader is repeatedly reminded of "the youth and extreme rawness of the lad" Phineas (1.16). Phineas himself knows simultaneously what is at stake in the story and how it must end, as he answers the questions of his Irish sweetheart, Mary Flood Jones, by saying, "I'll explain it all to you when I come back, after learning my lesson" (1.20). Lady Laura is quickly marked off as Finn's mentor, and the language of socialization, couched in terms of upward mobility, becomes pervasive thanks to the iterated metaphors of ladders (2.44) and stairs (2.293) whose symbolic significance is made clumsily explicit by characters within the novel. Trollope's *Bildungsroman* finally settles into the pattern Moretti traces for all English *Bildungsromane* of aborted upward struggle, lessons learned, and gracious if not heroic final acceptance of failure; thus the narrator ultimately compares Finn with Icarus (2.350). Lady Laura, though, frames the problem in a different way, when she tells the dejected Finn, "You have had your romance and must now put up with reality" (2.293). The language here is important, as Finn's rise and fall are intertwined, in Trollope's novel, with a shifting idea of romance and realism that is inseparable from a shifting position of Irishness.

It would make sense to begin an investigation of Irishness in *Phineas Finn, the Irish Member* with a discussion of the Irishness in Phineas Finn, the Irish Member himself, but this offers immediate challenges. How to mea-

---

7. Trollope, of course, mentions in his *Autobiography* that the two are, in fact, "but one novel, though they were brought out at a considerable interval of time and in different forms," but the structure of each novel is complete on its own, and so it is appropriate to treat them separately, as critics always have done (320). It is equally instructive, though, to see *Redux* as a sequel; Felber has pointed out, in her article on the novel, that "the function of the sequel is to depict change over time," and the Phineas novels certainly do this (120).

sure "Irishness"? Lonergan indignantly quotes at length a 1937 introduction to *Phineas Finn* by Shane Leslie: "The Irish background grows feint despite an occasional 'Bedad' from Laurence Fitzgibbon and Mary Flood Jones, the unconvincing colleen whom Phineas marries.... One thing is certain and that is that Lord Chiltern with his red hair and blackguardly dare-devilling was much more Hibernian than Phineas. He races and gambles and kills a ruffian at Newmarket with his fists" (quoted in Lonergan 148). Lonergan derides such "points of view" as "absurd," but he misses a chance to grapple with an unpleasant truth: according to Victorian conventions of Irishness, Leslie's assessment of Chiltern is absolutely correct, and, furthermore, Trollope's own narrative will support this reading of Chiltern as stereotypically "Irish" and Finn as stereotypically not Irish (Lonergan 149). Maria Bachman has demonstrated, in the historical backdrop she provides for her reading of one of Wilkie Collins's later novels, that Irishness and Irish nationalism were systematically pathologized in later-Victorian England, with nationalists increasingly incarcerated not in prisons but rather in facilities for the mentally ill. The notion that Trollope's view of a romantic Ireland necessarily entails an idealization of Ireland has proven hard to abandon, though. Other critics, like Owen Dudley Edwards, have written perhaps the most comprehensive consideration of Trollope's writerly connection to Ireland, accepting the supposed Irishness of Finn and seeing "preeminently the beautiful savage, straight from the frontier" (16). This sentiment contrasts with that of Dougherty, who claims that "Phineas fulfills none of the Victorian stereotypes of Irishness" (140), or of E.W. Wittig, who asserts that Phineas "is really little different from protagonists of Trollope's British novels" (116). There is a palpable lack of consensus, but it becomes comprehensible when one focuses less on who is Irish and who not, and more on who is Irish when, where, and why. Wittig approaches this line of analysis, claiming that Trollope displaces all of the stereotypical Irish traits onto the lesser character of Laurence Fitzgibbon, but this is only partly true. Irishness, in *Phineas Finn*, is an almost tangible property that signifies roguery or romance and shifts from character to character depending on how and where Trollope's narrative needs it. Because it is equated with romance, and because Irishness is coded in the novel as inversely proportionate to socialization, it bears directly on Trollope's narrative strategy in this novel-length meditation on resignation and more general disenchantment.

Trollope's wavering portrayal of the Irish becomes clear in a brief examination of Laurence Fitzgibbon. Fitzgibbon is a Member for Co. Mayo, but, unlike Finn, he is a member of the upper class. The narrator repeatedly links the two Irishmen early on, referring to them as "countrymen" (1.58, 1.88, 1.111, 1.194). Their differences become more noticeable as the plot progresses, and these differences lend credence to Wittig's reading of Fitzgibbon as the stereotypical Irishman. He is unenthusiastic about working (1.24) or is bluntly "idle" (2.162), and after Finn replaces him at the Colonial Office, Mr. Gresham is overheard saying to Lord Cantrip that Finn is "about the first Irishman we've had that has been worth his salt" (2.144). Most interesting is Fitzgibbon's constantly shifting manner of speech, which flits from English to Irish throughout the novel. When the reader first meets Fitzgibbon, he speaks like a typical English character in a Trollope novel: "I hate all change as a rule, . . . but, upon my word, we ought to alter that" (1.27). This continues until chapter XII, when he slides from a "By George, my dear fellow" to, one page later, the stereotypically Irish speech of "D'ye think," just as he proceeds to ask Finn for a large loan (1.111–12). What is crucial here is not merely the waffling in Trollope's depiction of Fitzgibbon, but the fact that Fitzgibbon consistently speaks with an Irish accent when he is up to no good; the same happens when he serves as Finn's second in the duel at Blankenberg. Fitzgibbon ultimately reneges on his promise to pay back the loan, and this leads to another important moment. Fitzgibbon's sister, Aspasia, who is audibly Irish when the reader first meets her—"Mr. Finn, how d'ye do? I want to say a word to ye" (1.203)—is audibly not Irish when she comes to Phineas to pay back the loan that her brother will not pay, saying to Phineas, "I have just come about a little business, Mr. Finn, and I hope you'll excuse me" (2.295). Trollope's shifts counter the consistent portrayals of the Irish by Brontë, Thackeray and Gaskell. Shane Leslie's observation—that Fitzgibbon's occasional Bedads do not an Irishman make—falls short of engaging the question of when, exactly, Fitzgibbon utters these Bedads. Fitzgibbon's occasional Irishness may serve to appease readerly expectations of Irish portrayal, as partial compensation for what some critics have rightly seen as Phineas Finn's lack of stereotypical Irishness.

The case of Lord Chiltern is yet more complicated. In the comments derided by Lonergan, Leslie points to several traits that make Chiltern "more Hibernian" than Phineas: Chiltern's red hair, his gambling, his dare-devilling. Apart from the red hair, though, these traits are shared by most of Trollope's rogues, from George Vavasor in *Can You Forgive Her?* (1864–65) to Burgo Fitzgerald, the lover from Glencora Palliser's youth who is eternally present in the Palliser series as a symbol of Glencora's own complex experience with having chosen duty over romance; neither Fitzgerald nor Vavasor are coded as Irish in the way that Chiltern is. There is, of course, the red hair, to which Trollope's narrator alludes at every possible chance, but it is important to note that the degree of redness changes depending on the role Chiltern is playing at a given moment in the plot. As with Fitzgibbon, Trollope's narrator modulates the Irish stereotypes of Chiltern. Immediately before the illegal duel fought between Finn and Chiltern (which Chiltern demands and which I discuss at greater length in the next chapter), Chiltern is described thus: "The redness of his complexion had become more ruddy than usual" (1.350). He is found by Phineas "standing there, fiery red," and termed "the fiery-red lord" (1.352; 1.354). Other descriptions dilute this supposed—according to Leslie—Irishness in a discourse of general otherness, as Trollope depicts Chiltern as "half-savage" (2.94) and "wild" (1.96). Chiltern also refers to himself, ironically, as a "gipsy" and "Bohemian" (169). These very traits, though, lead first to assumptions, in others, not of Chiltern's general foreignness but of his supposed Irishness. Trollope dramatizes this logic in an interesting conversation between Lord Fawn and Mr. Bonteen, who says:

> "Those Irish fellows are just the men for that kind of thing [inventing a story about a girl].
>
> "A man, you know, so violent that nobody can hold him," said Lord Fawn, thinking of Chiltern.
>
> "And so absurdly conceited," said Mr. Bonteen, thinking of Phineas.
>
> "A man who has never done anything, with all his advantages in the world,—and never will."
>
> "He won't hold his place long," said Mr. Bonteen.
>
> "Whom do you mean?"
>
> "Phineas Finn."
>
> "Oh, Mr. Finn. I was talking of Lord Chiltern." (2.142)

That Chiltern—a member of the landed English aristocracy—could be simply assumed in conversation to be Irish, and that he could be paired with the Irish Phineas so uncritically, reveals an ease of association on the part of Trollope's narrative and characters that is not corroborated by a closer look at Finn's actual portrayal in the novel.

The astonishing thing about Phineas Finn, the Irish Member, is that he is not dependably or consistently Irish in the novel. I am not referring here to a lack of the stereotypes of Irishness derided by Lonergan and present in the novel via Chiltern and Fitzgibbon, but rather to the narrative's explicitly confused rendering of Finn, who, like Balzac's Vautrin, is always something in between. If Irishness, for Trollope, equals romance, then Trollope's portrayal of Finn, which superficially marks him off as Irish but simultaneously offers him up as unromantic, ushers in some important complexities. Lonergan contends that "Phineas's nationality" is crucial because it "may have made sense of his meteoric rise in *Phineas Finn*, but it also explains his descent in *Phineas Redux*" (148). This misrepresents the troubled relationship between advancement and Irishness in the first novel, though, as much as it overstates the importance of Finn's Irishness to his arraignment on murder charges in the second. Indeed, Dougherty is probably closer to the mark when she contends that "the title of *Phineas Redux* might more accurately have been 'Phineas Reduced,' as Phineas's Irishness becomes ever more closeted" (136). I argue in the next chapter that *Phineas Redux* locates romance elsewhere and thus has less need of Irishness, but the only certainty about Finn's Irishness in *Phineas Finn* is that it appears to *impede* his advancement in English political culture. Finn's Irish identity is finally a necessity of the plot, for it prompts him to support the Irish tenant-rights measure that assures the end of his career in Parliament and thus an end to the novel. Yet this Irishness functions as an aspect of his character that he and the narrator subtly attempt to shed throughout the text. The implications of this authorial strategy—the surface Irishness undercut by Finn's unending attempts at assimilation—disclose a transformation in English culture as its novels consider the human and cultural consequences of the transition from imperialism to globalization, and of the accompanying shrinking of the world.

When the curtain rises on *Phineas Finn*, he is at home in the west of Ireland and, in standard Trollopian fashion, the reader meets him through a brief description of his parentage: a Catholic father, who is a country doctor, and a Protestant mother who married down. From the beginning, Phineas is caught between two poles, and the Irish and English opposition is only part of this. Finn's between-ness is more often expressed as an indefinable mediocrity or an inconstant temperament that mirrors that of Scott's indecisive Waverley. "It soon came to be admitted by all who knew Phineas Finn," writes the narrator, "that he had a peculiar power of making himself agreeable which no one knew how to analyse or define" (1.118). Alongside Finn's agreeability is the absence of the sort of romantic extremes that one might have expected in a hero whose Irishness, according to Trollope, should connote romance. Violet Effingham (the third of Finn's four romantic attractions in the novel) describes him thus: "There is just enough of him, but not too much" (1.201). Phineas cannot even fail spectacularly, as Mr. Monk critiques the young parliamentarian's first speech to the House of Commons with a dismissive "You have done yourself neither good nor harm. . . . [D]o not suppose that you have made an ass of yourself,—that is, in any special degree" (1.247–8). The more curious ambivalence, though, speaks to Finn's apparently shifting nationality. The novel's title announces him as *The Irish Member*, but the Irishness that Dougherty sees as disappearing in *Phineas Redux* is already in jeopardy in the first installment of this novelistic diptych. Despite

Lady Laura's teasing when she calls Finn an "impetuous Irish boy," the more Finn advances the less Irish he becomes in his own eyes[8] and the more Irish he becomes in those of his enemies, primarily Bonteen and Violet's guardian, Lady Baldock (1.75). Lady Baldock opposes Violet's association with Phineas, complaining that he "has come from nobody knows where in the bogs of Ireland" (2.41). This pejorative statement emerges only as Phineas is being considered for an appointment to the Colonial Office, termed as a "Promotion" in the chapter of that name.

While his advancement is framed by an increased attention to his Irishness in the eyes of other characters, though, Finn—and, it seems, the narrator as well—sees himself as increasingly English. At the conclusion of the novel's first volume, the protagonist sits with "great men,—Cabinet Ministers, and beautiful women,—the wives and daughters of some of England's highest nobles. And Phineas Finn, throwing back, now and again, a thought to Killaloe, found himself among them as one of themselves" (1.356). Two snippets of conversation are further revealing, as Phineas talks with Madame Max Goesler, another outsider to England, and he asks her a question about the issue of women's participation in politics:

> "And which side would you take?"
>
> "What, here in England?" said Madame Max Goesler,—from which expression, and from one or two others of a similar nature, Phineas was led into a doubt whether the lady were a countrywoman of his or not. (2.27)

Whereas the term "countryman" has already been used to link Finn and Fitzgibbon in their common Irishness, here it appears to refer to an Englishness in Finn. The narrator, and not Phineas directly, voices this, and so it shows a distancing of Finn from Ireland that cannot be reduced to or wholly explained by his local motives at that particular moment in the narrative. In the next chapter, a second conversation between Phineas Finn and Madame Max witnesses the same slippage. Madame Max claims that "An Englishman hardly ever makes a good servant," to which Finn replies, "Is that a compliment to us Britons?" (2.35). Twice, in quick succession, Finn or the narrator jumps at the notion of Englishness in order to associate himself with it. There are repeated assertions, by other characters as well, that Finn does not behave like an Irishman: Mr. Low praises Phineas for his restraint, for example, by saying, "It was more than I expected from your hot Irish blood" (1.114). Then, on the other hand, there are repeated assertions that Finn is exactly like an Irishman: his skill at riding is attributed to his rural Irish

---

8. Sanders mentions that Finn "thinks of himself as a 'Briton,'" which misses the larger picture of Finn's shifting perception of himself (48).

upbringing, and there are constant references to his hometown and home county, as when Mrs. Flood Jones says, "It is not every day that a man from County Clare gets on as you have done" (2.257). The net effect is a fundamental ambivalence as to Phineas's identity. It is perhaps too much to believe that Trollope set out to destroy Victorian stereotypes of the Irish, especially when those stereotypes are present in abundance in *Phineas Finn*, even if they are not present in Phineas Finn. Trollope's indecision contains traces of a deeper uncertainty endemic to his realist project.

(c) Unrealist History: On Pretending Not to Know

Finn is caught in a delicate balance between Ireland and England and between romance and the real, and on this problematic position rests the importance of Trollope's novel in registering and complicating the very period about which he writes, in which the subjects of imperialism can relocate to and move within the metropolitan centers of imperialism. "Our hero," as the narrator refers to Finn incessantly, hails from a country that Trollope saw as particularly full of romantic potential, but he is imported into a novel whose chief aim is an elaboration of Trollope's political convictions grounded in real-life parliamentary debates and political developments. To this historical end, the narrator will occasionally assume a reader's partial knowledge of political events, as at the novel's conclusion, when the reader is told, "Immediately after the passing of that scrambled Irish Reform Bill, Parliament, *as the reader knows*, was dissolved" (2.354; emphasis mine). Trollope would even, with the characteristic frankness of his autobiography, praise his own realist accomplishments in the Palliser series (*Autobiography* 185). One has the impression that Finn is but the reader's conduit into Parliament, for he all but disappears from the most important scenes of political debate, as the narrative focuses instead and at length on speeches by Members Daubeny, Gresham, and Monk. Trollope may have later confessed his belief that taking his protagonist from Ireland was a "blunder," but it is a blunder that is probably explained by Trollope's own avowed worries over the audience's interest in political novels: "In writing *Phineas Finn*, and also some other novels which follow it, I was conscious that I could not make a tale pleasing chiefly, or perhaps in any part, by politics. If I wrote politics for my own sake, I must put in love and intrigue, social incidents, with perhaps a dash of sport, for the sake of my readers" (317). Taking his hero from Ireland may have been a simple solution to what Trollope perceived as a challenge of inserting romance into what was otherwise a political history of events surrounding the Reform Bill of 1867.

If Finn's Irishness is in part an answer to the challenge of importing intrigue into a historical chronicle, though, it introduces new formal problems, and Trollope seems genuinely challenged by his own protagonist in *Phineas Finn*. The dilemma that the narrative faces revolves around the need to render Phineas simultaneously sympathetic *and* realistic to Victorian readers whose perception of the Irish would not be conducive to sympathy for them—recall Brontë's Hibernice in *Villette*. Trollope was far from oblivious to this hurdle, and especially within the framework of a political plot, admitting "an added difficulty in obtaining sympathy and affection for a politician belonging to a nationality whose politics are not respected in England" (318). The problem is partially resolved early on, because Phineas is presented as modest and unaware of his own skills, "timid" (1.187), and fairly conservative in his politics on the matter of Ireland, at least until the novel's important finale. (Finn explains in 1876's *The Prime Minister* why he is against Irish Home Rule [104].) Trollope leans on a gimmick of emplotment in order to encourage readerly sympathy with Phineas, when he has the Irish Member save the Scottish Member, Sir Robert Kennedy, from being garroted in the street at night. This act of heroism must be kept in perspective as a perhaps cheap narrative means[9] of gaining Finn an unimpeachable aura of heroism. Trollope repeats the trick in *The Prime Minister*, as Ferdinand Lopez's almost identical rescue of Frank Wharton gets him into the good graces of Wharton's father, who soon becomes Lopez's father-in-law; Lopez turns out to be one of the most manipulative and scheming characters in the Palliser series if not in all of Trollope's fiction. Finn is not Lopez, but Trollope still seems to resort to this plot twist in an almost instant bid to secure the audience's—and the other characters'—sympathy with the protagonist of the *Phineas* novels, whom Violet Effingham will then term a "Paladin" (1.285). This one act of heroism serves as a constant reminder of goodness when, later in the novel, others will begin to harbor doubts about Finn, above all after the news breaks of Finn's duel with Chiltern. Even in this episode, though, Trollope paints Phineas in flatteringly decent colors, for it is Chiltern who demands the duel, while Finn resolves not to take full part in it: "Let come what might, he would not aim at his adversary," as if countering Chiltern's red-faced anger (2.2).

The precarious balance that Trollope invokes in *Phineas Finn* is not limited to Phineas's ambivalent portrayal or the manner in which the narrator fobs off onto other characters the stereotypical Irishness that could

---

9. It is noteworthy that these two heroic episodes and the attempted murders they implied are overlooked in P. D. Edwards's catalog of murders and attempted murders in Trollope's fiction (*Anthony Trollope* 4). The omission supports the notion that Trollope's main point in these passages is to quickly portray heroism rather than the crimes that permit the acts of heroism.

Chapter Four: Economies of Romance and History in Phineas Finn ~ 103

have belonged to Finn, had he followed in the pattern of Irish caricature. Ireland itself presents a different problem, because it is not a fictional character, and it has historical traces to which one might expect the narrator of a realist novel to defer, especially when that novel has explicit historicist pretensions. A full discussion of the imaginative geography of the Palliser novels must wait until the next chapter, which examines Trollope's remapping of the British Isles in a reorganization of zones of romance and zones of order. However, Irish history is central to *Phineas Finn*, for the ambivalent attention to it reveals a moment of realist awkwardness when the narrative is confronted with the palpable discrepancies between Ireland as romantic image and Ireland as subjugated British colony. Taking his hero from Ireland afforded Trollope some thematic spice for what he had feared could be a bland political novel, but it also presented the relentless complications of troubled history confronting romance. Ireland in *Phineas Finn* is an island outside of history. This may partially explain, but certainly cannot excuse, the fact that scholarly attention to Trollope's Ireland novels has omitted the *Phineas* novels from consideration.[10] Unlike the four "Irish" novels that Trollope wrote, *Phineas Finn* may begin and end in Ireland but is not set primarily there, and *Phineas Redux* hardly sees the island at all. Yet the depiction of Ireland in *Phineas Finn* is revealing precisely because it differs significantly from the portrait offered in the other novels and because it shows a mobility that brings the Irish into England. Trollope could declare with some confidence that, despite the novel's many shortcomings, the Ireland he had depicted in *The Macdermots of Ballycloran* represented accurately "what Irish life was like before the potato disease, the famine, and the Encumbered Estates Bill" (*Autobiography* 71). This same accuracy cannot be claimed for *Phineas Finn*, and the omissions are especially interesting in the context of realist narrative.

Trollope's stance on the Famine has long been a topic for debate, not because his stance was uncertain—he wholeheartedly supported the British government's policy and even took a Malthusian view of the Famine's damages in Ireland—but because it is so objectionable. Trollope lived in Ireland during the Famine, and his position as postal inspector required him to crisscross the country so regularly that he saw everywhere the ravages of the blight. When Sidney Godolphin Osborne attacked the government's handling of the crisis in a series of letters to London papers, Trollope responded with

---

10. *The Macdermots of Ballycloran*, *The Kellys and the O'Kellys*, *Castle Richmond*, some short pieces like *An Eye for an Eye* (1879) and the unfinished and posthumously published *The Landleaguers* (1883) are all included in most overviews of Trollope's relationship to Ireland, but only Owen Edwards evaluates the importance of *Phineas Finn* and *Phineas Redux* in the equation. Asmundsson, Berol, Johnston, Tracy and Wittig all discuss one or both of the first two Irish novels (*The Macdermots* and *The Kellys*), and *Castle Richmond* has attracted great scrutiny as Trollope's sole fictional approach to the Famine, from Tracy, Matthews-Kane, Nardin, Hennedy, and Fegan.

a defense of those same policies in the *Examiner*, later collected and published as *Six Letters to the Examiner*. Nor was Trollope's assessment of the Famine an uninformed one; on the contrary, he claimed to have witnessed the very scenes of misery that spurred Osborne into editorializing action (Fegan 106). Amongst critics, though, discussions of this episode have invariably exonerated Trollope, claiming, as Fegan does, that his "anxiety about British government policy is submerged in his writing, only to emerge clandestinely, in the subtext of his Irish novels" (107). Tracy is more cautious, allowing only the possibility that, as Lukács argues in defense of Fontane and as Engels argues in defense of Balzac,[11] the work of art counters the objectionable personal politics: "Trollope's whole fictional treatment of the Famine belies [his] position" on it ("Unnatural Ruin" 369). Only Dougherty is slightly more critical of the author. The debate over Trollope's personal political convictions is not within the scope of this project, but the treatment of history in his novels is, because it directly impacts the approach to realist narration that the novels claim. John Halperin has provided an exhaustive account of the parallels between Trollope's parliamentarians and real historical English politicians associated with the Reform Bill of 1867, and his enumeration of the parallels could almost substantiate the reading of *Phineas Finn* as a political *roman à clef*. Given this attention to historical detail, the palpable absence of significant aspects of Irish history from *Phineas Finn* contributes to the idea that Ireland was to serve, in the Pallisers, as a locus of enchantment and idyll in lieu of messier history.

The Famine is not the only, but is certainly the most glaring, of these historical omissions. I have already mentioned above the manner in which Trollope's narrator points to specific historical events and to the reader's assumed familiarity with them; although the Famine of the late 1840s cannot be expected to have a central role in a novel about an Irishman's experiences in English society in England in the mid- to late-1860s, the degree to which it is glossed over is extraordinary. When Lord Chiltern takes Phineas riding, the narrator informs the reader that Phineas "had been riding since he was a child, as is the custom with all boys in Munster, and had an Irishman's natural aptitude for jumping" (1.218). Given the inner chronology of the novel, Finn's childhood would have included the peak years of the Famine, as would a visit to Ireland that Mr. Monk mentions to Phineas: "I thought everybody did

---

11. Of Fontane, Lukács writes, "We repeat: according to his own acknowledged political convictions, Fontane was no democrat. He is one, though, as an author [Gestalter]" (*Deutsche Literatur* 21). Engels's famous letter to Margaret Harkness declares: "That Balzac thus was compelled to go against his own class sympathies and political prejudices, that he saw the necessity of the downfall of his favourite nobles, and described them as people deserving no better fate; and that he saw the real men of the future where, for the time being, they alone were to be found—that I consider one of the greatest triumphs of Realism, and one of the grandest features in old Balzac" (*On Literature and Art* 92).

live in a castle in Ireland," Monk says. "They seemed to do when I was there twenty years ago," a time frame that lands that visit—following the novel's chronology—in 1847 (2.180). Trollope knew Ireland, and so these omissions on the part of the narrator are significant, especially in the story of a man from Killaloe, Co. Clare. Trollope probably chose the town for its added unknown, romantic value, but it was also one of the hardest-hit areas of Ireland during the Famine. Historian Frank Neal writes that "the destruction of the potato crops was not evenly spread out, the worst hit counties being Clare, Cork, Galway, Kerry, Mayo and Roscommon" (4). In addition to this, Ignatius Murphy's *A Starving People: Life and Death in West Clare 1845–1851* details the Famine's deleterious effect on Phineas's home county, while his *The Diocese of Killaloe, 1800–1850* narrows the focus onto Finn's actual hometown, which was absolutely devastated.

Another interesting ellipsis involves the introduction of the Canadian bill Phineas works on for the better part of the second volume of the novel, at his desk in the Colonial Office. The bulk of the narrator's discussion of Canadian history in *Phineas Finn* outlines plans to construct a length of railroad there, the "Inter-colonial Railway line," and Morton Bloomfield has shown how Trollope appears to have culled fairly precise data and facts from contemporaneous newspaper accounts of the project, in order to render it in admirable and accurate detail (68).[12] However, Bloomfield points out that the news from Canada during the period of *Phineas Finn*'s composition and serialization had far less to do with railways and far more to do with Irish rebellion in the New World, the so-called Fenian raids. Three of the most important of of these raids occurred in 1866 at Niagara, Campobello Island and Pigeon Hill, just as Trollope was beginning work on the manuscript of *Phineas Finn*. Trollope had dealt with Irish nationalist aggression before, most notably in *The Macdermots of Ballycloran*, which involves one of its Irish characters in a group of "Ribandmen" carrying out plots against local Royalist constabularies. Fenianism is even mentioned in *Phineas Finn*, but, perhaps predictably, it is located in the past: "It had been all very well to put down Fenianism, and Ribandmen, and Repeal,—and everything that had been put down in Ireland in the way of rebellion for the last seventy-five years" (2.180). Fenianism was far from the past tense, though, both during the narrative present of *Phineas Finn* and during the time of its authoring. Not until *The Eustace Diamonds* (1873) four years later will Trollope situate Fenianism in the present, when his narrator offhandedly remarks of the unsavory character, Lord George de Bruce Carruthers, "young men about

---

12. Gaskell also uses the Canadian railway project a few years earlier than Trollope, in her novella, *Cousin Phillis* (1863). Six years after *Phineas Finn*, in *The Way We Live Now*, this project is still an unfinished political and commercial issue.

London hinted that he was the grand centre of the British Fenians" (1.332). By that time in Trollope's writing, though, as Carruthers' outlandishly English-Norman-Scottish name implies, borders are being constantly redrawn. In *Phineas Finn*, the narrator's curious relocation, into the past, of an ongoing aggression in the present discloses a further effort to minimize the intrusion of history on romance.

The clearest nod to the cold, hard truth in the novel's presentation of Ireland in the mid-nineteenth century is Mary Flood Jones's random remark, in a missive to Phineas, that she never knows whether a letter in the mailbox is a *billet-doux* from him or "an order to go to Botany Bay," a reference to the British practice of deporting Irish petty criminals and nationalist rebels to Australia (2.288). Apart from this, Trollope's Ireland in *Phineas Finn* is a fabulous one, either a romanticization of the Emerald Isle or an attempt to assuage the English reader's colonial conscience. Phineas remarks, late in the novel, that "men in Parliament know less about Ireland than they do of the interior of Africa" (2.178). Wittily meant, to be sure, Finn's comment nevertheless captures the novel's desire to both reflect and amplify the foreignness of Ireland—more foreign, it would seem, than Africa, and more unknown.

To return to considerations with which this chapter opened its inquiry into the ambivalent portrayal of Irishness in *Phineas Finn* and the effects of that ambivalence on the narrative, Lonergan has argued that "the structure of Trollope's Palliser series was thoroughly de-stabilized by his inclusion of an Irish character, just as its realism was compromised. This shows how important Phineas's Irishness is" (157). It is difficult to accept this argument, though, given both the uncertain depiction of Finn's Irishness and the ending of *Phineas Finn*. The novel may find itself challenged by Phineas's Irishness, as Trollope himself felt challenged by it, but it finds its equilibrium in the way that, according to Moretti, every English *Bildungsroman* does; it checks its hero's upward progress and preserves the social order. It is important that Mary Flood Jones's reference to deportation—the novel's closest engagement with the dark side of this period in Irish history—arrives only at the novel's end, once the plot has accepted Finn's Irishness and is prepared to remove him from Parliament for it. John Hynes attributes to Trollope's biographer Michael Sadleir the claim "that Trollope never learned to disentangle Irish individuals from the sorrows and aspirations of their native land" (Hynes 54), but this claim is made first by Phineas Finn, at the novel's end. Defending to Parliament his decision to vote for a doomed Irish Tenant-Rights bill,

Chapter Four: Economies of Romance and History in Phineas Finn ~ 107

Phineas explains that "his Irish birth and Irish connection had brought this misfortune of his country so closely home to him that he had found the task of extricating himself from it to be impossible" (2.340). The finale of *Phineas Finn* ultimately renders him Irish, a decision that facilitates the final adherence to the form of the traditional English *Bildungsroman*, which puts all comers into their proper place. For Finn in England, that proper place is Ireland.

Trollope's resolution here differs greatly from Balzac's in the three novels discussed earlier. Unlike the irremediably foreign and inexplicable object of *La Peau de chagrin*, which vanishes once its damage is done and leaves the narrative mourning the loss; or the criminal of *Père Goriot*, who is forcibly removed by law; or *La Fille aux yeux d'or*, who is brought to a violent end, Phineas removes himself. The precise nature of the geographical removal, though, raises questions of physical space which the next chapter explores in depth. *Phineas Finn*'s clumsy dénouement recalls Pip's end in *Great Expectations* (1861), in which he "quit[s] England" and takes up a clerical position abroad, in the imperial project (474). Phineas finds himself first back in Dublin with the aim of resurrecting an abandoned legal career there, but he is soon whisked further away from the English Pale by a letter from his former Parliament colleagues, inviting him to take up a lowly government position in Cork. "And thus," the narrator concludes, "we will leave our hero an Inspector of Poor Houses in the County of Cork" (2.356). Leaving Dublin (in Leinster) for Munster is significant, in the geography of Ireland that Trollope's novels present: narratologically, it is a cyclical return, as Phineas started in Munster, in Co. Clare; culturally, it represents a final removal from England. In Trollope's first novel, *The Macdermots of Ballycloran*, Dublin is pegged as the central point of reference for his English readers, and the setting is laid only in relation to it, "about 72 miles W.N.W. of Dublin, on the mail-coach road to Sligo" (1). Furthermore, the Irish capital would still long be associated with Englishness. In Roddy Doyle's recent *A Star Called Henry* (2000), an account of the 1916 Easter Uprising,

> Dublin was too close to England; it was where the orders and cruelty came from. And the homespun bollixes in Sinn Féin and the Gaelic League were to blame too; Ireland was everywhere west of Dublin, the real people were west, west, west, as far west as possible, on the islands, the rocks off the islands, speaking Irish and eating wool; the Leaguers lived in Dublin but they went west for their holliers, to the real people. (237)

Here, space—the internal geography of Ireland—determines Irishness. From metropolitan London, Finn returns through metropolitan Dublin to less-metropolitan Ireland, where he weds his Irish beloved. His movements, while finally emphatic of an accepted geographical relationship between England and Ireland, underscore a disenchantment that Trollope only begins to confront in *Phineas Finn* and attempts to undo in *Phineas Redux* (1874) and *The Way We Live Now* (1875).

CHAPTER FIVE

MAPPING AND UNMAPPING
PHINEAS FINN AND *PHINEAS REDUX*

There should be some unknown regions preserved as hunting-grounds for the poetic imagination.
—George Eliot, *Middlemarch*

"I like a descent," said Shirley—"I like to clear it rapidly; and especially I like that romantic Hollow, with all my heart."
"Romantic—with a mill in it?"
"Romantic with a mill in it. The old mill and the white cottage are each admirable in its way."
—Charlotte Brontë, *Shirley*

In *The Realistic Imagination*, George Levine ends his chapter on Trollope's realism by concluding that it "is, then, no more than any other literary method, a precise description of a 'real' world. It is rigorous only in its exclusion of extremes, or in its assimilation of them into the multiplicities and diffusions of the continuing flow of surfaces. Mystery is transformed into the quotidian.... Romantic heights—the rocks and mountains—must be balanced by 'bread and cheese'" (203). Levine here understands Trollope's realism as narrative that disciplines subversive energies or romantic impulses, but what he writes in the following chapter, on "The Landscape of Reality," complicates the polarization of the real and the romantic in Trollope's "exclusion of extremes." Addressing charges against English realism's typical settings, Levine asserts that "The simplest explanation for the absence of the sublime in English realist fiction is the absence of the sublime in English landscape. But the mind is its own place, and the landscape of fiction, as I have been trying to suggest, is no literal transcription of the world as the novelists could see it" (212). Trollope's Palliser novels, and above all the *Phineas* diptych, collude with Levine's claim that the fictional mind "is its own place," and, in so doing, trouble the idea that Trollope's novels consistently quotidianize the mysterious energies that they consistently invoke. The fictional mind in *Phineas Finn* and *Phineas Redux* is actually two places, or, more accurately, two or more versions of the same places. Like the carriage rides of Henri de Marsay in *La Fille aux yeux d'or*, Trollope's shifting portrayal of largely British locations reveals a strategic alternation between disenchantment and reenchantment facilitated by Phineas's mobility as outsider in England.

In this sense, *Phineas Redux* in 1874 functions as an intriguing transitional piece, tethered as it is simultaneously to *Phineas Finn*, its prequel, and to its thematic twin, *The Way We Live Now*. *Phineas Redux* is a radical departure in style and tone, and *The Way We Live Now* is similarly the work of an embittered Trollope who returned to London in April of 1873[1] after a visit to the colonies and was revolted by a lack of decorum in the capital. The last chapter alluded to an economy of romance preserved by the manner in which Trollope seems to code and recode characters as romantic given necessities of the plot at a particular moment. This recoding also impacts space, and it will animate the discussion here of the relationship between four locales which Trollope links through phonological similarity and through the movements of his narrative's hero: Loughshane, Phineas's first and third borough; Loughton, his second; Loughlinter, the Scottish district of Robert Kennedy and his wife, Lady Laura Stanton; and London, the basic center of the action. Following a brief look at the function of various geographical separations in the novels, a more thorough examination of the opposition between Loughlinter and London—the most important geographical axis in the novels—reveals that Trollope uses the two sites to articulate a growing disenchantment in *Phineas Finn* and an apparent confrontation and reversal of it in *Phineas Redux*. First a disenchanted rewriting of, and then a tribute to, Scott and the Gothic, this second half of Trollope's *Bildungsroman* measures the narrative's recovery of romance and simultaneous discomfort at it, and begins the work of implicating the metropolitan imperial center within this loss and recovery.

(a) The Space of Disenchantment

For all the wavering between Irishness and Englishness in the narrator's portrayal of certain characters in *Phineas Finn*, and for all the talk of Ireland as "the colonies next door," there is an equal force invested in preserving the appearance of permanent separation between the two elements. Not coincidentally, this schism emerges through Finn, whose identity, as demonstrated in the last chapter, is uncertain enough to vacillate between Irish

---

1. To a much lesser extent, *Phineas Redux* is also the product of 1873, as debates over Trollope's reworking of the manuscript (the first draft of which he completed before his departure from England) have shown. See Chapman and Tinker.

Chapter Five: Mapping and Unmapping Phineas Finn *and* Phineas Redux

and English through the course of the novel. Early on, the narrator blithely excuses Finn's "lover['s] perjuries" with recourse to distance: "Phineas was a traitor, of course, but he was almost forced to be a traitor, by the simple fact that Lady Laura Standish was in London, and Mary Flood Jones in Killaloe" (1.145). The cleft becomes more emphatic at the end of the first volume, as Finn begins to feel "that he had two identities,—that he was, as it were, two separate persons,—and that he could, without any real faithlessness, be very much in love with Violet Effingham in his position of man of fashion and member of parliament in England, and also warmly attached to dear little Mary Flood Jones as an Irishman of Killaloe," and then becomes final once it is clear that Finn cannot remain in England (1.330). "His Irish life," the narrator tells us at one point, "was a thing quite apart and separate from his life in England" (2.271). At another point, Finn himself admits, "My life in Ireland is to be a new life, and why should I mix two things together that will be so different?" (2.348). At the end of *Phineas Finn*, Finn's marriage to Mary Flood Jones—whom Polhemus has derisively termed "a cute blob of Irish dew bound to fade" (394)—ensures his continued removal from England. The narrator knows that Mary is a distraction from the English portion of Phineas Finn, admitting as much when, briefly returning to her, he writes, "the reader I hope will not quite have forgotten Mary Flood Jones," further stressing the divide between England and the largely forgotten Ireland (1.144). Trollope's solution to this separation was a clumsy but effective one: "As I fully intended to bring my hero again into the world," Trollope writes in his *Autobiography*, "I was wrong to marry him to a simple pretty Irish girl, who could only be felt as an encumbrance on such return. When he did return I had no alternative but to kill the pretty simple Irish girl,—which was an unpleasant and awkward necessity" (318). Dougherty has argued that Mary thus "is imaginatively linked to the Great Famine, functioning as the surplus population of the narrative precisely because of her unhybridized and unassimilable Irishness" (143). There is little in the text to support the Famine association, as the previous chapter demonstrated, but the stability of Mary's Irishness can only be an "encumbrance" to the instability of Finn's nationality as it facilitates his movement in the novels. This movement is ultimately what allows for Trollope's evocation and renegotiation of imaginary borders and spaces.

Moretti's *Atlas of the European Novel* invokes Walter Benjamin's notion of the "phenomenon of the border," from the latter's *Arcades Project*. (Bakhtin's chronotope of the *threshold* could also be included here.) Benjamin imagines the internal divisions of cities as the place where one witnesses this phenomenon at its sharpest, but Moretti broadens it to a "phenomenology of the border" that can encompass his discussion of the rise of the historical novel at the turn of the nineteenth century in Europe (*Atlas* 35). There are "two kinds" of borders, claims Moretti: "external ones, between state and state; and internal ones, within a given state. In the first case, the border is the site of *adventure*" (emphasis in original). Moretti's elaboration of this point and its relevance to one of his main arguments—that the novel created the nation-state and that the nation-state, which cannot be represented visually as a city or village can, found the novel to express it—treats at length Scott's novels of the Lowlands and their relationship to England. *Waverley* in particular is central for Moretti, as it is also central for Trollope. The geographical location of the gothic novel's plots, according to Moretti, had already provided an initial outline for Scott's later drawing of borders; in the handy map Moretti provides, the vast majority of British gothic novels take place in Scotland, well outside of what he calls "Austen's English space" (16). My discussion of Balzac's *La Fille aux yeux d'or* broached the idea of the remoteness and specific properties and function of gothically constructed space in an otherwise urban novel, where it imports an instant aura of mystery and seems to remove the narrative from the urban. Moretti's consideration of the borderlands of the historical novel brings valuable context to Scott, but in order to understand the specific relevance of the border to Trollope's Palliser series, one must examine the manner in which the treatment of it changes over time. Scott's borders are, in Trollope's novels, still very much in play.

Like the British novel over the course of the nineteenth century, Trollope does not simply start in London. Indeed, to some degree his development as a writer mirrors the development and movement of the novel in Britain from Scott onward. If Trollope's earliest fiction is set, like Scott's, at junctures of Englishness and Otherness—and for Trollope, as for Scott, this involves what Michael Hechter has called the "Celtic fringe"—then it moves through its perhaps Austenian period in Barsetshire before it finally settles in Dickensian London (quoted in Moretti, *Atlas* 13). A map of Trollope's settings would square readily with a map of the shifting settings of the nineteenth-century English novel as Moretti describes it. Karen Faulkner has provided a useful look at "Anthony Trollope's Apprenticeship," arguing that "he tries out," in the course of his growth as a writer, "the subjects, voices, and styles of Edgeworth, Carleton, Scott, Austen, Dickens, Fielding, and others" (161). One could also note, though, that in addition to the clear-cut stylistic inheritances from these writers, Trollope also tries on the various spaces they produce and reproduce. The *Phineas* novels are a clear engagement with Scott, but they also mark a shift in Trollope's writing and in the English novel of the nineteenth century. In Trollope's novels, the romantic potential of the border—recall Moretti's "site of *adventure*"—and of what lies across the border can never be taken for granted. Rather, Trollope's narratives alter the specific importance of an area depending on their momentary needs, just as they toy with and constantly alter alterity (Irishness). The unstable political identity of Loughshane and Loughton is a corollary to this process. Moreover, the duel at Blankenberg in *Phineas Finn* and the shady transactions of the Reverend Emilius in *Phineas Redux* adduce the Continent as a source or site of romance, although this, too, will be complicated by a simultaneous domestication of the Continent as England is reenchanted in *Redux*. Finally, the problems of Trollope's portrayal of Loughlinter and London highlight the novelistic remapping of thoroughly disenchanted regions, in order to recuperate or relocate romance.

The political geography of Britain in *Phineas Finn* offers a means of gauging the extent to which the novel openly views the construction of space and what it represents as an arbitrary matter. (The treatment of political "adventurers" in the novel also introduces the abuse of political laxities that will later arise in *Phineas Redux*'s electoral fraud, Melmotte's ascension in *The Way We Live Now*, and Lopez's unsuccessful campaign in 1876's *The Prime Minister*.) The story of Phineas's rise and fall in the first installment is inextricable from the fate of the political districts for which he stands. Parliament only opens for Phineas at the news that the Earl of Tulla, a patient of Phineas's father and a Member for Loughshane, "a little borough in the county Galway," is to step down from his position (1.5). Local differences are, apparently, erased or rendered insignificant, and so the Irish Catholic Phineas succeeds in being elected to a seat vacated by "a fine, high-minded representative of the thorough-going Orange Protestant feeling of Ireland." By the end of the first volume, Finn has lost his seat for Loughshane, only to find himself in the position to stand for a seat in Loughton, in England, which he does successfully. The Anglicizing of Finn discussed in the last chapter seems to begin, predictably, at about this point; Phineas lies "in his bed at the Loughton inn," reflecting on "the great political question on which the political world was engrossed," "the enfranchisement of Englishmen,—of Englishmen down to the rank of artisans and labourers" (1.297). Loughton the district is eventually "doomed," dissolved by an act of redistricting. So, his seat having been politically unmapped out from under him, Finn returns to stand again for Loughshane (2.79). He runs against the very Norman- and English-sounding Lambert St. George and is "returned by a majority of seventeen votes" (2.105). Soon, Loughshane, too, is on the blocks, and it is ultimately dissolved thanks to the very Irish Reform Bill for which Finn himself votes, "the measure which deprived Loughshane forever of its parliamentary honours" (2.342). Phineas's mobility from borough to borough is itself unusual, but it is not nearly as curious as the fact that both of his boroughs are withdrawn from the political map, forcing him first back into an Irish seat and then out of Parliament altogether.

Alongside the political redistrictings, the mapping of the British Isles in *Phineas Finn* simultaneously complicates the pattern of romance and its geographical placement as Moretti describes it. Where it fits Moretti's pattern, one witnesses the lingering traces of traditional recourse to romance on the Continent. The duel between Chiltern and Phineas on the sand dunes at Blankenberg is a throwback to an era that is, by the text's own incessant admission, gone. It is the only duel in the entire Palliser series, with the possible exception of the "high-noon" styled horsewhipping threats between Ferdinand Lopez and Arthur Fletcher in the streets in *The Prime Minister*. Because of its uniqueness, and because the reader is constantly told, through the entirety of the Palliser novels, that duels belong to the past, the meeting on the beach at Blankenberg is crucial. Firearms themselves are out of fashion "in these peaceable days," the narrator of *Can You Forgive Her?* (1864–5) says, and a character later in the novel points out that "men don't fight now-a-days" (1.42; 2.270). Burgo Fitzgerald's hot-headed claim that he would gladly fight Plantagenet Palliser "at two paces' distance" elicits the rebuke that "men do not fight now," and John Grey similarly rebuffs George Vavasor's challenge to a duel, calling it "foolish" (2.81; 2.330).[2] In *Phineas Finn*, too, the narrator repeatedly—and retroactively, only after the duel has actually been fought—insists on the idea that duels are a relic of the past. Even Lady Baldock, who is certainly not inclined to like Phineas Finn, disbelieves Finn's involvement in the duel simply because she disbelieves the possibility of duels in her day and age: "Fought a duel about Violet!" she exclaims, "People don't fight duels now, and I should not believe it. . . . I don't believe a word of it. It is absurd. I dare say that Gustavus invented it at the moment, just to amuse himself" (2.38). Duels are considered, in the narrative present of *Phineas Finn*, part of the past, the stuff of imaginative "invention."

More importantly, though, because of this pastness and rarity, and the surreptitious manner of its execution by Chiltern, Phineas, and their seconds, the episode of the duel is a source of gossip and "mystery" for the London political scene (2.137). Trollope's narrator even renders the scene in the past perfect, rather than the past tense in which Trollope's novels are invariably written. The account begins with the assertion that "the duel did come off on the sly," but as soon as specifics are given, it is pushed further into the grammatical past: Fitzgibbon "had been in Flanders," and "had stood with his friend Phineas on the sands at Blankenberg, a little fishing-town some

---

2. In a sort of narrative amnesia in *Phineas Redux*, Phineas Finn says, "There are times in which one is driven to regret that there has come an end to duelling, and there is left to one no immediate means of resenting an injury" (2.57).

twelve miles distant from Bruges, and had left his friend since that at an hotel at Ostend,—with a wound just under the shoulder, from which a bullet had been extracted" (2.3–4). Even the participants note the pastness of dueling. The narrator points out, as Finn weighs Chiltern's challenge, that "few Englishmen fight duels in these days. They who do so are always reckoned to be fools" (1.353). In the contextual material to his edition of *Phineas Finn*, Jacques Berthoud reminds us that dueling was largely hounded underground by the formation, with royal support, of the Anti-Dueling Association in 1845 (Trollope, *Phineas Finn* 2.370). So, in addition to the pastness of the duel, distance is imperative, and the Continent beckons. Chiltern points out to Phineas, "we can be in Belgium in an hour or two, and back again in a few more hours;—that is, any one of us who may chance to be alive" (1.353). The passage above, which situates the duel in concrete space—"twelve miles distant from Bruges," at Blankenberg—cedes to the slightly more mysterious language of a meeting that remains "quite unobserved amidst the sand-heaps," so that "not a living soul, except the five concerned, was at that time aware that a duel had been fought among the sand-hills" (2.4; 2.5). (The five are Phineas and his second, Fitzgibbon; Chiltern and his second, Captain Colepepper; and Fitzgibbon's doctor, O'Shaughnessy.)

Nor is this the last word on the Continent in the *Phineas* novels, but it changes in *Phineas Redux* as the novel quickly becomes a detective or legal thriller. After the murder of Mr. Bonteen for which Phineas is assumed guilty and tried, Europe is simultaneously the source of the major elements of the crime and of its solution, as it is simultaneously a place of romance and resignation. The Reverend Joseph Emilius, Bonteen's murderer, comes from central Europe, as does the key to Bonteen's apartment that Emilius has made (2.229). The murder weapon "as a certainty . . . was of French,—and probably of Parisian manufacture," and the word "mystery" is used again, as it was in the episode of the duel in *Phineas Finn*, to refer to the character of the weapon and its at first unknown provenance (2.289). And yet, despite the fact that *Phineas Redux* is enabled by objects from the Continent, which inject narrative complications and adventure into London, the Continent is elsewhere coded as disenchanted. After Lady Laura Kennedy has left Robert Kennedy due to his increasing jealousy and fundamentalist religiosity, she and her father settle in Dresden, which is remarkably English to them. Lady Laura tells Phineas in a letter that her father "does—nothing. He reads the English papers, and talks of English parties" (1.58). Not at all confined to *Phineas Redux*, the perceived disenchantment of even the Continent is actually everywhere in the Palliser series: the narrator of *Can You Forgive Her?* complains that "Ludgate Hill is now-a-days more interesting than the Jungfrau" (1.44) and that "almost everybody now does know Lucerne" (2.351), and *The Eustace Diamonds* (1873) says similarly that "Switzerland and the Tyrol, and even Italy, are all redolent of [the tour planner] Mr. Cook" (1.292). Such statements complicate Moretti's argument that the English novel sees only forces of mystery and evil in Europe. In the Pallisers, the Continent is as banal as it is evil.

Of singular importance during Phineas's visit to Dresden is Lady Laura's and Phineas's day-trip to "the fortress of Königstein," perched "on that wonderful rock" and up a "very steep hill" (1.101; 1.107). The narrative's language wants to mark Königstein off as a locus of enchantment, but Lady Laura's conversation with Phineas at Königstein is merely a continuation of their conversation at Loughlinter, a similar exercise in duty over passion. The case of Loughlinter in *Phineas Finn* and the case of Königstein in *Phineas Redux* are clearly analogous, not merely because they construct the expectation of enchantment and then ruthlessly disappoint it, but because of technology's role in the journeys to and from those supposedly remote places. Lady Laura, we are told, "did succeed in carrying him off to the fortress of Königstein," in the vocabulary of an almost mythical abduction, but their return, after the disappointments, is much more mundane: "[T]here they remained till the evening train came from Prague, and took them back to Dresden" (1.101; 1.107). Phineas's first trip to Loughlinter in *Phineas Finn* unfolds in remarkably similar fashion; he and Mr. Ratler approach by coach, slowly, and the narrator describes the romantic landscape: "On the other side of the Lough there rose a mighty mountain to the skies, Ben Linter. At the foot of it, and all round to the left, there ran the woods of Linter, stretching for miles through crags and bogs and mountain lands" (1.119). At Loughlinter, Lady Laura responds to Finn's romantic advances with duty over passion. Only a return trip by train can adequately capture the collapse of romantic potential. Once again, Phineas is taken "to the railway station" for his return voyage to London (1.142).

Königstein in *Phineas Redux* and Loughlinter in *Phineas Finn* (as opposed to Loughlinter in *Redux*, which alters things) both witness a collision of romance and the quotidian that is characteristic of a larger ambivalence. In the evocation of the Continent, there are, of course, the duel, the bludgeon, and the illegal key, but there are also the repeated complaints, in the Palliser series, of a Europe that has become all too known. The indecision here parallels the waffling between romance and its undoing in Balzac's novels, even if Trollope's narratives do not go to Balzacian lengths to interrogate these terms. Violet Effingham and Lord Fawn in *Phineas Finn* voice the dilemma nonetheless, in language that will echo throughout Trollope's rendering of romance and its disappearance and reveal its importance to the Palliser novels: "A mystery is good for nothing if it remains always a mys-

Chapter Five: Mapping and Unmapping *Phineas Finn* and *Phineas Redux* ~ 117

tery," Lord Fawn complains, to which Violet replies, "And it is good for nothing at all when it is found out" (2.34). These are the stakes: the desire for the unraveling of mysteries and the desire for their preservation. Loughlinter's depiction, between *Phineas Finn* and *Phineas Redux*, between disenchantment and reenchantment, mirrors this exchange.

(b) Loughlinter, London, and the Space of Reenchantment

Trollope's narrator, in a brief description of Phineas's leisurely days visiting Loughlinter, emphasizes the importance of certain places to *Phineas Finn* by setting them all in motion around each other in a single paragraph:

> In those days he often wandered up and down the Linter and across the moor to the Linn, and so down to the lake. . . . He was thinking of his life, and trying to calculate whether the wonderful success which he had achieved would ever be of permanent value to him. Would he be nearer to earning his bread when he should be member for Loughton than he had been when he was member for Loughshane? Or was there before him any slightest probability that he would ever earn his bread? And then he thought of Violet Effingham . . . (1.300–1)

Violet, of course, lives in London. Of the four sites specified or alluded to in this paragraph, Loughlinter and London are perhaps the most persistently important to *Phineas Finn* and *Phineas Redux*; however, they function differently in the two novels, and these differences are revealing. Absent from *Can You Forgive Her?*, the first of the Pallisers, Scotland represents disappointed romance in *Phineas Finn* via Lady Laura's decision there for sense over sensibility and via Trollope's equation of Scotland with sense. Four years later, *The Eustace Diamonds* already rethinks this categorization, as if preparing the way for the wholesale attempt to reenchant Scotland to dangerous effect in *Phineas Redux*. The story of these shifts raises questions best answered by attending to their specific narrative purpose. A pattern of enchantment and disenchantment emerges that is at odds with critical renderings of Scotland and the border as consistent sites of otherness and adventure.

Phineas Finn shows Trollope acknowledging a creeping disenchantment that begins by polluting the romantic territories—both literary and geographical—of Scott. Trollope regarded Scott highly, prizing *Ivanhoe* as one of his three favorite English novels (*Autobiography* 41). The clearest debt in *Phineas Finn* is to *Waverley*, a novel informed by events contemporary to its composition but based on events that were, as the novel's subtitle declares, already "Sixty Years" in the past. The historical novel, by definition, constructs the past as its project. Trollope's invocation of *Waverley* is thus doubly ironic; not only does he adduce the perceived romance of Scott's territories in order to subvert it, but this subversion is accomplished partially by means of dragging Scotland into the narrative present. "Loughlinter," the narrator explains, "wanted that graceful beauty of age" (1.119). It "was all of cut stone, but the stones had been cut only yesterday." Odes to the beauty of the rugged landscape and to "waterfall over waterfall" as Phineas arrives, soon give way to the "half natural and half artificial," with a path "arranged so that not a pleasant splashing rush of the waters was lost to the visitor" (1.120). The Highlands have been tamed, the novel posits, and so have the Highlanders of Scott: "these Highlanders, with all that is said of their family pride, have forgotten the Mackenzies[3] already, and are quite proud of their rich landlord," Lady Laura tells Phineas (1.123). The purpose of the half-flattering description of Loughlinter is to taint Robert Kennedy by association. The newness and false character of Loughlinter castle match the newness of Kennedy's money and an upward mobility on which the narrator is quick to cast aspersions as a tired tale and a diminishing of tradition: "He was laird of Linn and laird of Linter, as his people used to say. And yet his father had walked into Glasgow as a little boy,—no doubt with the normal half-crown in his breeches pocket" (1.119). The narrator himself appears bored with Robert Kennedy's story, and the broader depiction of Kennedy emphasizes this by repeatedly categorizing him as dull and unromantic. The text's introduction of him reports that he "seemed to be afflicted with some difficulty in speaking," and Aspasia Fitzgibbon, joking about Mr. Kennedy with Phineas, compares him unflatteringly to a monkey Kennedy gazes on during a visit to the zoo: "Did you ever see such a contrast in your life? . . . Between Mr. Kennedy and a monkey. The monkey has so much to say for himself, and is so delightfully wicked! I don't suppose that Mr. Kennedy ever did anything wrong in his life" (1.40). A later conversation between Lady Laura and Kennedy, after their marriage to each other, reveals to an even greater extent Kennedy's position in the text as the antithesis of romance when he tells his wife, "Passion, Laura, can never be right" (2.115). Kennedy is dull, and his dullness in *Phineas Finn* is depicted by the narrator as powerful enough to have tainted Scott's landscapes. "There is some ballad about the old lairds," the reader is told, "but that belongs to a time when Mr. Kennedy had not been

---

3. The Mackenzies were a highland clan in the upper northwest of Scotland, according to Browne, while the fictional Loughlinter would have fallen into an area of Perthshire marked by astonishing clan mixture. As Scott's *Waverley* is dedicated to Scottish writer Henry Mackenzie, Trollope could also have used the name to amplify the notion that Scott's Scotland is forgotten.

heard of" (1.123).

This idea of a transformation in Scotland, of a shift from the romantic to the dull, is paired with modernization. The Kennedys—Robert and his father—are said to have altered the landscape by vastly increasing the "acres on the property under cultivation" (1.123). Lady Laura, as if in defense of Kennedy, attempts to dismiss the idea of any actual transformation by questioning the picturesque associations of the Highlands; she asserts rather that any romance to the Highlands is the product of imagination, and she blames Scott. After she tells Phineas of the Highlanders' changing allegiance from their clan to their landlord, Phineas remarks, disappointed, "That is unpoetical" (1.124). Veering from history into aesthetics, Lady Laura replies, "Yes;—but then poetry is so usually false. I doubt whether Scotland would not have been as prosaic a country as any under the sun but for Walter Scott;—and I have no doubt that Henry V owes the romance of his character altogether to Shakspeare [sic]." Lady Laura's diatribe is just the most direct shot in Trollope's war on Scott in *Phineas Finn*, and, by extension, on the sort of romance Scott represents. In a later chapter, Kennedy helps Phineas to an appointment with Lady Laura when Phineas is running late and he borrows a pony from a "Donald Bean." Donald Bean is a Highland warrior in Scott's *Waverley*, and Scott's presentation of him is the stuff of adventure. En route to Bean's hideout, Waverley stops to rest and reflect:

> He had now time to give himself up to the full romance of his situation. Here he sate on the banks of an unknown lake, under the guidance of a wild native, whose language was unknown to him, on a visit to the den of some renowned outlaw, a second Robin Hood perhaps, or Adam o'Gordon, and that at deep midnight, through scenes of difficulty and toil, separated from his attendant, left by his guide:—what a fund of circumstances for the exercise of a romantic imagination, and all enhanced by the solemn feeling of uncertainty at least, if not of danger! (78)

Trollope's Donald Bean, on the other hand, is a mere tenant, his pony "not much bigger than a dog" (1.134). Scott's Scotland finds itself brutally reduced and undeniably tamed in Trollope's telling of it.

Indeed, Trollope's taming of Scott creates a locus of destroyed wildness in *Phineas Finn*, a sort of place where romance goes to die. Lady Laura is the first to see this happen, in scenes clearly meant to parallel the fruitless romantic discussions between Flora Mac-Ivor and Waverley in Scott's novel. Flora's passion is to her cause, and so Waverley ultimately marries the safer, less revolutionary Rose Bradwardine. Trollope's narrator makes it clear that Lady Laura's passion is for Phineas, whom she sees as "handsome as a god" (1.136). That she chooses Kennedy over Phineas heightens the sense of damaged romance that pervades Loughlinter, for Lady Laura's decision is based on a fidelity to duty rather than to passion. Of Kennedy, she simply says, "I have thought it wise to accept his offer," hardly a ringing endorsement (1.138). "I have accepted the owner of Loughlinter as my husband," she explains, "because I verily believe that I shall thus do my duty in that sphere of life to which it has pleased God to call me" (1.138–39). The narrator repeatedly frames this resignation to duty as a renunciation of romance, as Laura tells herself that her moment of conference with Finn "would be the alpha and the omega of the romance of her life" and that, "having put aside all romance as unfitted to her life," "life for her must be a matter of business" (1.158; 1.201–2). What is at stake in Laura's choice is clear, and the text actually punishes her for her decision of duty over passion. She confesses to Phineas at the end of the first volume that she has "made a mistake," later specifying to Violet Effingham that she was wrong to "satisfy [her] mind and [her] ambition without caring for [her] heart" (1.302; 2.66). She phrases this even more strongly to Phineas at the close of *Phineas Redux:* "When I was younger I did not understand how strong the heart can be. I should have known it, and I pay for my ignorance with the penalty of my whole life" (2.349). Laura opts for duty, and Trollope's text refuses to see unquestioned virtue in this. Meanwhile, Loughlinter exerts its taming force on still another character: Lord Chiltern, who, unlike Laura, is billed from the outset as wild. I showed, above, the text's portrayal of Chiltern as a savage or wild man, but his marriage to Violet Effingham threatens to socialize him, as he promises to "change for the better" (2.123). Later, in *Phineas Redux*, Phineas asks Lady Laura whether Violet's and Chiltern's marriage has made him "quite tame," and Laura responds in the affirmative (1.98). Bizarrely, the promise of self-control and marriage that Chiltern makes to Violet happens neither where Violet lives nor where Chiltern lives but rather at Loughlinter, where both are visitors. Trollope's narrative seems to require the diminished Scotland as a disenchanted backdrop for the scene of Chiltern's chastening, and it goes out of its way to lure them both there for this scene.

Lady Laura's choice at Loughlinter leads to a disillusionment central to her character in both *Phineas Finn* and *Phineas Redux*. The Königstein episode in the latter summons textual memories of Loughlinter, in its rejection of passion, its spatial construction of disenchantment, and its subjection of romantically inflected territories to a stern quotidianization. These memories of *Phineas Finn* are important, because they highlight the fact that the presence of Loughlinter in *Phineas Redux* will acquire a force blatantly antithetical to its earlier avatar. At Kennedy's request in *Redux*, Phineas travels to Scotland for a visit, but the landscape and its symbolic weight have been

Chapter Five: Mapping and Unmapping Phineas Finn *and* Phineas Redux ~ 121

altered. Loughlinter has been reinvigorated as a site of mystery and romance, and the literary corollaries on which Trollope leans are—not surprisingly, if one recalls Balzac's *La Fille aux yeux d'or*—the Gothic. As Phineas arrives, "The door was opened for him by an old servant in black, who proposed at once to show him to his room. He looked round the vast hall, which, when he had before known it, was ever filled with signs of life, and felt at once that it was empty and deserted. It struck him as intolerably cold, and he saw that the huge fireplace was without a spark of fire" (1.84–5). It is even more significant that the gothic work on which Trollope's narrator appears to be leaning most heavily is one by Scott, *The Bride of Lammermoor* (1819), a debt made clear by allusion to that novel's servant, Caleb Balderstone (1.86). Trollope's resurrection of Scott is concretized by the inclusion of dialect at Loughlinter, as the servant asks Phineas whether he would "visit the laird out o' hand, or would he bide awee?" Not once in *Phineas Finn* was Loughlinter's Scottishness allowed to leach through written speech, but *Phineas Redux* continues in 1874 a process that Trollope began in 1873's *The Eustace Diamonds*, a slow disentangling of Scotland and England that will restore to the Highlands their literary peculiarity and potential as romantic trope. Gowran, who speaks always in dialect in *The Eustace Diamonds*, remarks on differences in riding styles between Scotland and London (1.206); the Londoners are painted as comically ignorant of local Scottish customs (1.222); and, despite the high amount of English tourists to Scotland, the narrator assures us, it is yet unmarred by the tour guides, unlike Europe (1.292). If it were ill-suited for romance in *Phineas Finn*, Trollope's Pallisers have reenchanted Scotland by the time *Phineas Redux* begins.

The significance of this reenchantment extends beyond the local portrayals of a separate Loughlinter, however, because Loughlinter becomes the major source of narrative complication in the first volume of *Phineas Redux*. Finn's meeting with Kennedy there goes badly; Kennedy ultimately threatens Finn with a poker from the fireplace; and the narrator categorizes the Scottish Member, in no uncertain terms, as a "madman" (1.91). This madman soon brings his discontent to London, and Finn is called in to the office of *The People's Banner*, a newspaper edited by Quintus Slide, to peruse a letter that Kennedy hopes the *Banner* will publish. The letter intends to castigate Lady Laura publicly for her decision to separate from Kennedy, and Slide threatens to publish it but agrees to wait until Finn has spoken with Kennedy (1.201–2). If the meeting between the Irish Member and the Scottish Member in Loughlinter goes badly, their meeting in London goes worse, but the narrative's depiction of it redraws some important boundaries. Not only have Loughlinter and Scotland been reenchanted, as it were, in *Phineas Redux*, but the mystery that they represent in the novel now serves to complicate other locations. Finn is told that Kennedy is staying in London at a hotel called "Macpherson's in Judd Street. I suppose he likes to keep among the Scotch" (1.202). And, indeed, Trollope's narrator paints Macpherson's as a dislocated stand-in for Scotland. First, it is *in* London but, apparently, not *of* London: "Judd Street runs into the New Road near the great stations of the Midland and Northern Railways, and is a highly respectable street. But it can hardly be called fashionable, as is Picadilly; or central, as is Charing Cross; or commercial, as is the neighborhood of St. Paul's. Men seeking the shelter of an hotel in Judd Street most probably prefer decent and respectable obscurity to other advantages" (1.203–4). Furthermore, the "landlord [of Macpherson's] had originally come from the neighbourhood of Loughlinter," and the speech of everyone at the hotel is rendered in Scott-like dialect (1.204). The name chosen for the location, in addition, recalls that of James Macpherson, responsible for the Ossian poems hoax in 1765. Trollope uses popular imaginings of Scotland to carve out a section of London in which mystery can exist.

Kennedy, of course, fires a pistol at Phineas during the meeting, and this act has ramifications for the future of *Phineas Redux* even as it simultaneously conjures associations with the past duel between Phineas and Chiltern in *Phineas Finn*. It confirms for Phineas—and for the reader, if there were still any doubt—that Kennedy is insane, "so mad as to be not even aware of the act he had perpetrated" (1.208). Hugh Walpole, writing in 1928, sees the portrayal of Kennedy's madness as praiseworthy because it shows Trollope as a "modern" ("No post-war psycho-analytic realist can teach him anything"), but the larger issue here is the effect of this madness on the novel (108). Because of Finn's mere association with the shot, as its target, and because of the speculation surrounding his friendship with Lady Laura, he is vilified by his political enemies in London. The altercation in Macpherson's hotel is explicitly compared to Phineas's duel with Chiltern in a manner that highlights the difference, that alerts the reader of the Palliser series to some significant changes that must have taken place in Trollope's fictional imagination during the five years between *Phineas Finn* and *Phineas Redux*. One is reminded in *Redux* that Phineas "had once stood up to be fired at in a duel, and had been struck by the ball. But nothing in that encounter had made him feel sick and faint through every muscle as he had felt just now" (1.209). The later encounter, the narrator seems to emphasize, was like a duel but was not a duel; it was something far more nefarious. Furthermore, it happened not on a distant foreign beach, a border site where such activities may be imagined and executed, but in a section of London marked off by the text as a mysterious, foreign place of its own within the larger metropolis. The effects within London society are as those of a boulder heaved into a pond: "A great deal

Chapter Five: Mapping and Unmapping Phineas Finn *and* Phineas Redux ~ 123

was said by very many persons in London as to the murderous attack which had been made by Mr. Kennedy on Phineas Finn in Judd Street, but . . . no public or official inquiry was made into the circumstance. Mr. Kennedy, under the care of his cousin, retreated to Scotland" (1.278). The mysterious lack of closure to the event allows for any amount of speculation public and private, in what the narrator bills as a sort of generator of fiction. The duel gives rise to one "very romantic story" after another regarding Phineas, Lady Laura, and Mr. Kennedy (1.279). The fame attaching itself to Phineas in the wake of the episode is, according to the narrator, what ultimately ushers in the envy of his peers and leads to Finn's downfall: "Fame begets envy, and there were some who said that the member for Tankerville [Phineas's district in *Redux*] had injured his prospects with his party" (1.280). Loughlinter's arrival in London, then, can be seen as a primary determinant in the novel's narrative arc, an incident that will help to dictate Finn's fate hundreds of pages later.

Kennedy and, by extension, Loughlinter are the main source of narrative tension in the first volume of *Phineas Redux*. Despite the shift in Loughlinter's function within the Pallisers, though, Trollope remains true to an economy of romance. At the outset of volume two, of course, the novel's direction changes dramatically when Mr. Bonteen is murdered by another import to London, the Reverend Emilius. Mr. Bonteen's body is discovered in chapter XLVII, and the few chapters immediately thereafter catalogue the social effects, and the effects on parliamentary business, of the murder: Finn and Emilius are arrested, Mrs. Bunce has her say, and then Parliament has its say. But then, apparently no longer needed as a force of mystery in the novel, Kennedy is quickly removed in chapter LII when he dies in his castle at Loughlinter, and with him dies the danger that Loughlinter represents. For the rest of *Phineas Redux*, the trial of Phineas Finn takes center stage. From this point, the multiple references to Loughlinter serve neither to recall Phineas's and Lady Laura's conversation from the beginning of *Phineas Finn*, when she chooses duty over passion, nor to summon the aura of dread surrounding Kennedy in the first half of *Phineas Redux*, but rather to provide a romantic horizon for the future in the form of a sentimental question. With Kennedy hardly in the ground, Lady Laura wonders, "Might it not still be possible that there should be before her a happy evening to her days; and that she might stand once more beside the falls of Linter, contented, hopeful, nay, almost glorious, with her hand in his [Finn's] to whom she had once refused her own on that very spot?" (2.110). Later, again, she asks herself, "How often might they stand there again [at Loughlinter] if only his [Finn's] constancy would equal hers?" (2.223). The novel's portrayal of Loughlinter is extravagantly inconstant. Rather than situate it, à la Scott, as a consistent locus of enchantment on the border between Highlands and Lowlands (it is located, fictionally, in Perthshire, within a short coach trip of Callander), it plays first the part of disillusion in *Phineas Finn* and then that of violent (gothic) Other in *Phineas Redux* before it anchors the sentimentality of Lady Laura's role at the end of the novel. The importing of Loughlinter into the increasingly heterogeneous, late-imperial London, though, opens a fresh channel in Trollope's fiction that will be pursued further in the next chapter, through *Phineas Redux* and *The Way We Live Now*.

(c) On Not Knowing: Detection, Empiricism, and the Verdict on the Evidence

Trollope's shifting borders and his new portrayal of London's openness organize themselves, finally, around two violent crimes in *Phineas Redux*. The first, Kennedy's attempt on Phineas's life, is quickly forgotten when Mr. Bonteen is found bludgeoned to death. Scholarship has, with the exception of Walpole, largely dismissed *Redux*, but the novel's second act contains the most concentrated and self-conscious instance, in Trollope's fiction, of the instability central to my argument, between empiricism and disenchantment and the resistance to them. It is thus especially illuminating as a debate over literary realism's potential and potential complications. Trollope scripts Phineas's trial for the murder of Mr. Bonteen as a clear epistemological duel that occurs in London but is engendered by characters from outside of London, and he does so while simultaneously acknowledging this contest's importance to ideas of fiction and knowledge. The courtroom scenes that preoccupy the second half of *Phineas Redux* continue the negotiation of a narrative epistemology in Trollope's work that begins with *The Eustace Diamonds*—a detective epistemology that is radically empirical, fully rational, and coded as urban. Detection is a subtlety in *The Eustace Diamonds*, but it is made to stand trial in *Phineas Redux*.

Trollope was evidently spurred on by the publication and success of Wilkie Collins's *The Moonstone* in 1868, in which the theft of a gem precipitates Britain's first detective novel. He admits in his *Autobiography* the influence of Collins on *The Eustace Diamonds* but makes an important distinction in authorial method:

> The plot of the diamond necklace is, I think, well arranged, though it produced itself without any forethought. I had had no idea of setting thieves after the bauble till I had got my heroine to bed in the inn at Carlisle; nor of the disappoint-

Chapter Five: *Mapping and Unmapping* Phineas Finn *and* Phineas Redux ~ 125

ment of the thieves, till Lizzie [Eustace] had been wakened in the morning with the news that her door had been broken open. All these things, and many more, Wilkie Collins would have arranged beforehand with infinite labour, preparing things present so that they should fit in with things to come. (344)

As the methods vary, so too have critical appraisals of their success. Robert Polhemus has dismissed the detective thread of *Phineas Redux* as "second-rate Wilkie Collins," and there is indeed sufficient cause to see both stylistic and thematic similarities in *The Eustace Diamonds*, *Phineas Redux*, and *The Moonstone* (179). Both authors present detection and the style of knowledge that underwrites it as profoundly empirical, even scientific. Agents of the police test theories through experiments couched in the language of the laboratory—the hypnosis of Franklin Blake in *The Moonstone*, for example, or the duplication of the murderer's possible pedestrian routes in *Phineas Redux*. Furthermore, crime and detection are foregrounded as urban phenomena. *The Moonstone*'s Sergeant Cuff is called up from London, and his rigorous methodology baffles the rural constabulary, while Major Mackintosh in *The Eustace Diamonds* not only responds to the crime from London but posits that, given the expertise of the theft, the criminals were probably also from London and planned to return the diamonds there in order to fence them (2.76). The metropolis becomes implicated in both the nature of the crime and the solution to it.

Trollope differs from Collins, though, on the status of detective epistemology. D. A. Miller argues that *The Moonstone* "is more fundamentally about the securities of perception and language than about the problems they pose" and that it is "thus perfectly obedient to the imperatives" of monological power (54, 57). *The Eustace Diamonds* appears to toe this line self-consciously and somewhat humorously within its articulation of detection as both absolute and rational. Of Major Mackintosh, the London detective called to the case, the narrator writes that "there was nothing he couldn't find out" (2.70). Another "eminent detective officer," Mr. Bunfit, has the following exchange with Lord George, who asks him:

"Do you believe that I've got [the diamonds]?"
"A man in my situation, my lord, never believes anything. We has to suspect, but we never believes." (2.76)

The remainder of that chapter plays fairly consistently on the "suspicions" of the police and the "beliefs" of the other characters. Compare a similar exchange from *Phineas Redux*, between Lord Chiltern and a detective investigating the murder of Mr. Bonteen: "'You don't mean to say that you believe it?' said Lord Chiltern to the officer. 'We never believe and we never disbelieve anything, my Lord,' replied the man. Nevertheless, the superintendent did most firmly believe that Phineas Finn had murdered Mr. Bonteen" (2.81). The relentless detective epistemology of *The Eustace Diamonds* becomes complicated in *Phineas Redux*. The narrator's sober tone in the second volume of *Redux* even adopts at times the functionality of a police report, as in the startling stylistic shift that occurs at the outset of chapter XLVII, when this detective story is introduced into the novel: "On the next morning at seven o'clock a superintendent of police called at the house of Mr. Gresham and informed the Prime Minister that Mr. Bonteen, the President of the Board of Trade, had been murdered during the night. There was no doubt of the fact. The body had been recognised, and information had been taken to the unfortunate widow" (2.58). Finn is arrested on the strength of empirical evidence—he carried a weapon similar to that used in the murder, was overheard threatening to kill the victim on the night of the murder, is identified by an eyewitness, and has no verifiable alibi—and this evidence is enough to convince even some of his closest friends that he may be guilty.

Even more alarming than the shift to detective fiction in *Phineas Redux*, though, is Trollope's refusal to allow the detective interest to matter to the plot. Where Collins maintains mystery in order to build suspense, Trollope shows his hand immediately:

> The reader need hardly be told that, as regards this great offence, Phineas Finn was as white as snow. The maintenance of any doubt on that matter,—were it even desirable to maintain a doubt,—would be altogether beyond of the power of the present writer. The reader has probably perceived, from the first moment of the discovery of the body on the steps at the end of the passage, that Mr. Bonteen had been killed by that ingenious gentleman, the Rev. Mr. Emilius. . . . (2.77–78)

With Finn's innocence established and Emilius's guilt disclosed to the reader, *Phineas Redux* revolves not around the detectives but rather around the duel between their empirical knowledge and the nonempirical knowledge of others—the love and the character testimonies of Finn's friends—in a court of law. The unasked question of the novel is never "Who done it?" as it is in Collins's novel and, indeed, in most detective fiction. Trollope's work wonders rather which type of knowledge matters more. Coral Lounsbury has argued that legal structure and constant recourse to strictures of the law in Trollope's Pallisers both reveal and satisfy Trollope's personal taste for social order. Yet the legal forum in *Phineas Redux* sees a complex negotia-

Chapter Five: Mapping and Unmapping Phineas Finn and Phineas Redux ~ 127

tion of empirical and emotional knowledge, upsetting the sorts of certainties Miller sees in *The Moonstone*. One might have anticipated Trollope's later ambivalence toward detection. Even as the police enter *The Eustace Diamonds*, their stated goal is "to unravel the mystery" that has already been said, by the narrator, to possess "a certain charm" (2.133; 2.46).

The physical evidence amassed by the police in their investigation of Finn is damning. The trial, though, quietly undercuts this physical evidence through a defense that commences with the decidedly nonempirical values of fiction and friendship. In one of the most perplexing moments in the novel, Mr. Bouncer, a novelist, is called as an expert witness. Bouncer testifies that Finn cannot be guilty because, by having announced his intention to kill Bonteen and then immediately having done it, Finn flouts conventions of literary emplotment as old as Shakespeare and as practiced by Scott (2.193–94). Finn's lawyer, Mr. Chaffanbrass, sums up Bouncer's testimony thus: "If I understand you then, Mr. Bouncer, you would not dare so violate probability in a novel, as to produce a murderer to the public who should contrive a secret hidden murder,—contrive it and execute it, all within a quarter of an hour?" (2.194–95). Bouncer's acknowledgment of this point passes in Finn's favor, and what is improbable first in fiction is *then* held to be improbable in fact. A degradation of empirical knowledge accompanies this glorification of fiction. Lord Chiltern's opinion matches that of Madame Max Goesler and Lady Laura, all of whom believe Finn innocent: "I am quite sure from my knowledge of the man that he could not commit a murder," Chiltern proclaims, "and I don't care what the evidence is" (2.211). While Chiltern carries it to an extreme, there are important examples of the futility of evidence elsewhere in the Victorian novel. In Dorothea Brooke's vindication of Lydgate in Eliot's *Middlemarch*, she claims, "I feel convinced that his conduct has not been guilty. I believe that people are almost always better than their neighbours think they are" (691). The narrator continues by stating that Dorothea prefers to "cautious weighing" "an ardent faith in efforts of justice and mercy, which would conquer by their emotional force." In *The Moonstone*, Mr. Bruff informs Miss Clack that Sergeant Cuff is wrong to suspect Rachel Verinder: "If he had known Rachel's character as I know it, he would have suspected everybody in the house but *her*. . . . If the plainest evidence in the world pointed one way, and if nothing but Rachel's word of honour pointed the other, I would take her word before the evidence, lawyer as I am!" (217)

Trollope reiterates elsewhere in the novel the opposition between "evidence" and "private knowledge or personal affection" (2.280), but his resolution of the opposition in *Phineas Redux* is surprisingly consistent in its anti-empiricism. This belief in Phineas Finn's character, in the face of evidence to the contrary, drives Madame Max to Prague, where she finds opposing evidence that will exonerate him, the mould of the key used to gain entry into the victim's house (2.214). Because the epistemological duel here is between empiricism (evidence) and its opposite (belief), however, the evidence of Madame Max cannot be permitted simply to counter the evidence of the police; were Trollope to do so, the duel between types of knowledge would be over, with empiricism the victor. All that arrives from Prague is a telegram from Madame Max stating what was found there, and as Sir Gregory, the prosecutor, makes clear, a telegram is not evidence and thus "proves nothing" (2.216). Mirroring the language of the police earlier in *Phineas Redux* and in *The Eustace Diamonds*, the prosecutor Sir Gregory goes on to say, of the telegram's report, "I neither believe it nor disbelieve it; but it cannot affect the evidence" (2.217). The jury, however, do believe it. Their belief in Madame Max's *claim of evidence* trumps the solid, *present evidence* offered by the police, and they acquit Phineas Finn. There is no doubt here that the jury's conclusion is correct—as the narrator has already stated, Phineas is not guilty. George Levine has argued that "Trollope's attitude toward meaning and explanation is profoundly secular" and "rational" (*Darwin and the Novelists* 193), yet in the trial of *Phineas Redux* it is non-empirical "belief" in a foreign source—not rational material knowledge—that leads to truth.

Phineas Redux mobilizes many of the same fictional forces on which Trollope first depends in *Phineas Finn*, but an examination of the shifting function of those forces shows a palpable sense of crisis and a commensurate fictional response to it. *Phineas Finn*'s uncertainties as to the location and possibility of romance and mystery, both within England and within a Scotland that we are told is normally dependably romantic, are severely undercut in its sequel. In *Phineas Redux*, the energies that will complicate the plot and drive it forward are neither conveniently contained across the Channel (as the duel at Blankenberg was) nor eviscerated by alleged anachronism (as Scott's Highlands were), as they were in *Phineas Finn*. Rather, romance is at full foreign strength and within striking distance of England's capital, where it occasions serious considerations over the nature of knowledge and its representation in realist fiction. Such transformations are visible through Trollope's confrontation of disenchantment, which sees him simultaneously retreating into the literary and exurban past (the Scottian Gothic) and reinserting borders that had, in *Phineas Finn*, all but lost their relevance. The resurrected borders of England, however, are a failure in the Pallisers if their purpose is the containment and easy localization of mystery and romance, if their aim is a solid and trusty separation of the earth into what McClure calls "zones of order and disorder" in his discussion of empire's imaginative geography (*Late Imperial Romance* 2). *Phineas Redux* imagines the penetrability of London, the heart of the imperium, by foreign energies that are—as they were not in *Phineas Finn*—irremediably and unmistakably and consistently foreign. As in Balzac's *La Fille aux yeux d'or*, the increased mobility of people that Sassen describes in today's "global city" appears here as a cherished opportunity for narrative complication, for romance that will set London abuzz with mysteries to unravel and mysteries to preserve.

It is here, in London, that Trollope differs most significantly from contemporaries who also made the city—and an epistemology coded as urban—a primary focus in their novels. Dickens is, naturally, the exemplary architect of fictional London, and his England is often anchored in a larger, global geography: consider *Martin Chuzzlewit*'s (1844) American journey; *Dombey and Son*'s (1848) shipping concerns and "Native" visitor; *Bleak House*'s "telescopic philanthropy" (1853); the French-Revolutionary preoccupations of *A Tale of Two Cities* (1859); and the transhemispheric movements of Magwitch in *Great Expectations* (1861). However, Dickens's actual foreign incursions into London are largely cosmetic—never major, indispensable players in the manner of Trollope's Phineas Finn, Augustus Melmotte, and Madame Max Goesler. And, for all its variegated social strata, complex inner geography, and position as capital of the world, Dickens's London never feels as dangerously cosmopolitan as Trollope's London is in *Phineas Redux* and *The Way We Live Now* or as Balzac's Paris is in *La Fille aux yeux d'or*. Trollope appears to fully envision, in a way that *The Moonstone* only sensationalistically anticipates,[4] certain results of empire that attend those of the quotidianization of formerly unknown or mysterious corners of the globe: the world's arrival in London, globalization's pivotal role in that arrival, and the broader consequences for fiction and fact. Ashis Nandy's claim, that "the experience of colonizing did not leave the internal culture of Britain untouched," becomes increasingly true (*Intimate Enemy* 32). Having begun to imagine the romantic possibility in the permeability of London by the outside world in *Phineas Finn* and *Phineas Redux*, Trollope's next major work[5] feels like

---

4. Even in *Dombey and Son*'s truly global dealings, and for all of Solomon Gill's acknowledgments of their transformation of London, what lies outside of England is still the stuff of adventure, a vast, foreign expanse in which ships can go down (as Walter Gay's does in Barbados, or as John Harmon's does in *Our Mutual Friend* [1864–65]) and important characters can be presumed missing while others wander the earth looking for them. The world has not yet been disenchanted.

5. After Redux, for which Trollope received $2500 in 1874, he published *Lady Anna* (1874) and *Harry Heathcote of Gangoyl* (1874), both shorter, less substantial and less well-received works, for which he received $450 and $1200, respectively (Trollope, *Autobiography* 364). For *The Way We Live Now* in 1875, Trollope was paid $3000, more than he had received for anything since 1869,

an angry retraction, an elaboration of the dangers of cosmopolitanism. *The Way We Live Now* seeks a refuge of last resort from the battleground of disenchantment and reenchantment that London has become in the *Phineas* novels.

---

when *Phineas Finn* earned him £3200. A debate still rages over the contemporary success of *The Way We Live Now*—cf. Super ("Was *The Way*") and Sutherland ("The Commercial Success")—but that will be treated in the next chapter. More important to the concerns of my argument, though, is the fact that, after *Phineas Redux*, *The Way We Live Now* is Trollope's next novel set in and around London.

CHAPTER SIX

GLOBAL LONDON AND *THE WAY WE LIVE NOW*

Rome, after all, was a special case: an imperial capital, a metropolis. It could have been traced to its sources, in the exploitation of a hundred peoples. But its particular and spectacular corruption becomes very different when it is incorporated into a version of relationship between any urban and any rural order, as a way of ratifying the latter. This, clearly, is the point of ideological transition.
—Raymond Williams, *The Country and the City*

Rome risks losing itself by expatriating itself, by rushing toward foreign lands, toward the non-Roman. Ever since it was founded, Rome has no longer been in Rome.
—Marcel Hénaff, "Of Stones, Angels, & Humans"

... London will break up ...
—Anthony Trollope, *Phineas Redux*

In March of 1873, after moving from Waltham in Hertfordshire to Montague Square in London and signing a contract with Chapman and Hall for the publication of *The Way We Live Now*, Trollope wrote his initial description of the work in progress: "1873. Carbury novel. 20 Numbers. 64 pages each number" (quoted in Sutherland, "Trollope at Work" 474). It seems odd now that Trollope envisioned the Carbury family as the focus of this novel, because they were eclipsed in the writing of it by the character of Augustus Melmotte. One of Trollope's most memorable villains, Melmotte is central to both *The Way We Live Now* and its reception, but the uncertainty surrounding his identity has too often been forgotten by scholars eager to treat the abundant anti-Semitism in the novel. Derek Cohen's quick description of Melmotte as "a Jewish financier" is typical, as critics have constantly bought into the rumors of his Jewishness that fly around the London of *The Way We Live Now* (61). Trollope, though, never settles it so handily, and the final word one gets from the narrator is that "the general opinion seemed to be that [Melmotte's] father had been a noted coiner in New York,—an Irishman of the name of

Melmody" (2.449).[1] Robert Tracy is one of the few to put real pressure on this important revelation, and he relates it to another area of relative silence in scholarship on Melmotte, his possible literary ancestor in Charles Maturin's 1820 gothic novel, *Melmoth the Wanderer* (Tracy, *Trollope's Later Novels* 172). Read together, Melmotte's alleged Irishness and possible gothic roots may represent a surprising fulfillment of what comes undone in *Phineas Finn:* the use of the Irish for romance or narrative complication.

Melmotte encapsulates several concerns central to this project. Like Balzac's and Fontane's imported figures, from the Chinese Mandarin to the Chinese Ghost, Melmotte comes from outside, suggests both romance and its destruction, and defies easy categorization. He is probably Irish but rumored to be Jewish; thought to be from New York but builds his wealth in Vienna and Paris; and held above the law even as he is finally rendered human and culpable. Embodying the worst fears of *The Way We Live Now*—the colonial revenant, the wide world, the dangerous metropolis—Melmotte exemplifies a criminality that takes shape in the inseparable processes of global expansion and global commerce. I argued in the last chapter that the attempted murder (by the Scot, Robert Kennedy) and the murder (by the Hungarian Jew, Josef Emilius) that occur in *Phineas Redux* signal a new direction in Trollope's work by bringing the outside world into London and using it as materiel for fiction, the remapping of the city, and the attempt to define a narrative epistemology. The present chapter probes the manner in which the Carbury novel Trollope planned for *The Way We Live Now* cedes to the international crimes of Melmotte and other foreigners. While crime is already contextualized in *Phineas Redux* as a new collision of empiricism, foreignness, and the city, foreign and colonial figures fill *The Way We Live Now*, providing narrative complications that become overwhelming. Global commerce both anchors and destabilizes England's capital city and its spatial expression in the novel, and Trollope's narrative finally situates this compressed new London within a compressed new world-system. The shift proves catastrophic, and the novel retreats to the countryside.

(a) Business as Unusual: Foreignness, Crime, Commerce

As *The Way We Live Now* is not part of the Palliser series, it may seem an

---

1. Like Cohen, Hertz and Cheyette also rely on the unestablished identification of Melmotte as a Jew. Van rightly highlights the uncertainty but omits the Irishness of Melmotte's father when quoting the line I have just quoted; she thus links him to New York but not to Ireland (76). Her article is illuminating in its charting of anti-Americanism in Trollope, and she too sees *The Way We Live Now* as "a nostalgic response" to advances in speculative commerce (78).

imposition on Trollope to lump it in with *Phineas Finn* and *Phineas Redux*. Trollope must have seen them as somehow related, though; characters first appearing in Palliser novels (Lord Nidderdale, for example) end up in *The Way We Live Now*, and that novel's Beargarden Club later graces *The Duke's Children* (1879), the final in the series. Stephen Wall points out that "Trollope is quite ready to think of its [*The Way We Live Now*'s] personnel as moving in that imaginative continuum on which the Palliser series draws" (53). Abbott Ikeler's contrary assertion that "the lack of parochial setting or a dominant political intrigue makes the novel difficult to wed to either of the chief cycles in the Trollope canon" (the Barsets or the Pallisers) is disingenuous. It forgets both Melmotte's election to Parliament, the peak of his success, and the fact that certain of the Pallisers—*The Eustace Diamonds* (1873) especially— are themselves fairly unpolitical (219). It is important to note that *Phineas Redux* was being proofread (if not substantially revised[2]) immediately before and during the composition of *The Way We Live Now*, and that the London setting of both novels makes them unique among Trollope's vast output between 1869's *Phineas Finn* and 1876's *The Prime Minister*. Despite these cosmetic affinities, though, the most compelling need to read *Phineas Redux* alongside *The Way We Live Now* arises from the manner in which the latter novel continues a proposition begun in the former. If the trial in *Phineas Redux* serves as a venue for interrogating an empirical epistemology associated with detective work, it is no less important toward an understanding of Trollope's patient elaboration of the theme of the foreignness of crime that becomes central to *The Way We Live Now*. In staging a local criminal event with truly transnational sources and solutions, *Phineas Redux* begins envisioning London as a global city. The relationship between crime, the foreign, and the linking together of the world in the novel's articulation of its epistemological quandary sets the stage for the international financial crimes committed by foreigners in the London of *The Way We Live Now*. Initially expressed by violence in *Phineas Redux*, though, globalization is lulled quietly and finally into the monetary terms it will comfortably inhabit in *The Way We Live Now*. It is in *Phineas Redux* that Trollope introduces the single overarching mission of Plantagenet Palliser in the series named for him: the transformation of England's currency to meet world standards. At the end of the novel Palliser, "as all the world knows, is on the very eve of success with the decimal coinage" (2.360).

The Way We Live Now is a deeply uncertain text, despite its reputation amongst critics as a forceful and uncomplicated critique. The source of much of this indeterminacy is the vast cast of foreigners who light on London,

---

2. Scholars disagree on the extent of Trollope's revisions to the manuscript that he locked away in a strong box before leaving for Australia in 1871. See Chapman and Tinker.

bereft of certain origins in a novel that narrates largely uncertain outcomes. Contrast these ex nihilo creations with Trollope's normal strategy of shaping a character through his or her parents or roots, as he does at the outset of every single novel in the Palliser series with the exception of *Phineas Redux*.[3] Any lack of a familial context or pedigree is explained, by the narrator of *The Prime Minister* (published one year after *The Way We Live Now*), as "mysterious, and almost open to suspicion. It begins to be known that nobody knows anything of such a man, and even friends become afraid" (9). The deracinated imports to London in *The Way We Live Now* fit this profile, and as signifiers of mystery and absent origins they both record and produce a changing city. Several critics have referred to a foreign invasion of London in the novel, "a kind of new imperialism by which the mother country is being conquered, occupied, taken over by dark forces from without" (Cohen 68), or "a first impression of the British Isles under siege" (Ikeler 224). This miscategorization is as grave as Raymond Williams's opposite view, in *The Country and the City*, of a one-way flow outward from the British Isles into the wide world—the "way out" that posits "the lands of the Empire" as an "idyllic retreat" for the English but does not really account for immigration into London, "The New Metropolis" (281). What is required, for a reading of Trollope's city and country, is a recognition of circulation. Michael Sadleir offers just that, in his introduction to the first critical biography of Trollope, in 1927. By the 1860s, Sadleir recalls, "the wealth of England was already seeking outlets in distant corners of the globe," but "the 'sixties did not foresee the coming implication of their England with the outer world" (25–26). Trollope recognizes from *Phineas Finn* in 1869 onward the mutual interpenetration of imperial center and colonial periphery. If foreigners are invading London, Trollope balances this with the pat references to colonialism and

3. The first lines of the Pallisers: "Whether or no, she, whom you are to forgive, if you can, did or did not belong to the Upper Ten Thousand of this our English world, I am not prepared to say with any strength of affirmation. By blood she was connected with big people. . . . Her grandfather, Squire Vavasor of Vavasor Hall . . ." (*Can You Forgive Her?* 1.1); "Dr. Finn [Phineas's father], of Killaloe, in county Clare, was as well known in those parts,—the confines, that is, of the counties of Clare, Limerick, Tipperary, and Galway,—as was the bishop himself who lived in the same town, and was as much respected" (*Phineas Finn* 1.1); "It was admitted by all her friends, and also by her enemies,—who were in truth the more numerous and active body of the two,—that Lizzie Greystock had done very well with herself. We will tell the story of Lizzie Greystock from the beginning, but we will not dwell over it at great length, as we might do if we loved her. She was the only child of old Admiral Greystock . . ." (*The Eustace Diamonds* 1.1); "It is certainly of service to a man to know who were his grandfathers and who were his grandmothers if he entertain an ambition to move in the upper circles of society, and also of service to be able to speak of them as of persons who were themselves somebodies in their time" (*The Prime Minister* 9); "No one, probably, ever felt himself to be more alone in the world than our old friend, the Duke of Omnium, when the Duchess died. When this sad event happened he had ceased to be Prime Minister. During the first nine months after he had left office he and the Duchess remained in England. Then they had gone abroad, taking with them their three children" (*The Duke's Children* 1). *Phineas Redux* is the only Palliser novel that does not commence with such a pedigree, but its characters are already known. See also Gilmartin, whose *Ancestry and Narrative in Nineetenth-Century British Literature* organizes itself partly around a split between certain English and uncertain Celtic origins in the novels she analyzes.

colonial travel one expects in a Victorian novel: Roger Carbury's sisters in India and America; Paul Montague's travels in America; and the African travels of an unnamed guest at Melmotte's fête. The governing image here is not of a one-sided assault on Mother England but rather of a new mobility that shrinks the world. The homogenizing effects of this shrinkage peak in *The Duke's Children*, as news of a racehorse's condition spreads not just "about the town," but "to America and the Indies, to Australia and the Chinese cities, ... in Cairo, Calcutta, Melbourne, and San Francisco" (352). One senses this process already in Lady Carbury's requiem for "county feeling" in *The Way We Live Now*, when she complains that "Staffordshire, Warwickshire, Cheshire and Lancashire have become great towns, and have lost all local distinctions" (1.152).

It is perfectly appropriate that *The Way We Live Now*, Trollope's depiction of the London financial world, is underscored by a globalized novelistic scale. In an article on the value of "harriedness" in fictions of globalization—to which this chapter will return in its discussion of the harried, globalizing Melmotte—Bruce Robbins emphasizes that "capitalism's global integration is much more pronounced at the level of finance, for example, than in production or even trade" ("Very Busy" 436–37). Trollope elaborates his discomfort at this integration and at the new primacy of finance by allying finance with crime and by representing it as foreign and, more specifically, American. Trollope's *Autobiography* locates the animus behind *The Way We Live Now* in the author's return from travels through Australia and America to an England whose financial circles had descended into moral decay, and so Trollope's critics have largely repeated this version of events. However, Trollope's disapproval of finance is palpable as early as 1865, when the narrator of *Can You Forgive Her?* tracks the many changes in the professional life of the unsavory George Vavasor. First placed, with the help of his uncle, "in the office of a parliamentary land agent," George leaves to become "a partner in an established firm of wine merchants" (1.35). When he changes jobs yet again, his decision to "become a stockbroker" coincides with the narrator's assurance that George "had gone back greatly in the estimation of men. He had lived in open defiance of decency" (1.37). Trollope already passes judgment here on the core of *The Way We Live Now*, where the movement from the security of land into the flirtation with global commerce ends in the morass of speculation. All that is new about pernicious finance in the later novel is its foreignness.[4]

In *The Way We Live Now*, there is not a single Englishman at the helm

---

4. Cf. Doña Lupe's complaint in Galdós' *Fortunata y Jacinta* (1887), also set in the 1870s, that "everybody's so moral and full of righteousness [rigoristas]. That's why this nation doesn't get ahead [no adelanta] and foreigners [extranjeros] walk off with all our money" (2.290–91).

of the firm organized to "float shares" in an enormous railway scheme to link Salt Lake City with Vera Cruz. The two most important figures in the company are Melmotte and Hamilton K. Fisker, an American from California. Willard Thorp has suggested that Trollope found Americans "useful" in his novels (14), and James Kincaid more specifically asserts that America, in *The Way We Live Now*, "suggests the true hell that England should regard as a warning" (171). Sabine Nathan is more careful; she reads Trollope's somewhat unflattering portrayal of the American Mrs. Hurtle as evidence of "Trollope's prejudiced conception of Americans" but justifies this portrait by arguing that Hurtle's disturbing amorality simply makes her the product of a disturbingly amoral American commercial culture (274). Nathan does not link this culture to Melmotte—his being American is again overlooked—but her view of Trollope's prejudice closes off an important interpretive possibility. The frequent inclusion of Americans in the Pallisers, where they are mostly women who are invariably described as well-read and physically beautiful, belies any notion of a reflexive anti-Americanism. Rather, the normally flattering portrayal of Americans makes Trollope's vilification of them in *The Way We Live Now* all the more pertinent as a sudden re-coding of the value of American-ness that recalls the constant shifting of Irishness in *Phineas Finn*. The foreigners are many in *The Way We Live Now:* the Emperor of China; the Canadian delegation; Herr Vossner, the scheming German attendant at the Beargarden Club; Madame Melmotte, Melmotte's Jewish wife; and Herr Croll, Melmotte's German assistant, for example. The Emperor of China reinforces the global scale of the novel, the Canadian delegates provide added evidence of both Britain's ongoing colonial projects and the importance of railroads to them, and the Continentals end up reflecting Franco Moretti's assertion that the Victorian novel often viewed Europe as a potential source for evil and complication. However, none of these characters is as essential as Fisker, Hurtle, and Melmotte are to the plot of the novel and to Trollope's articulation of increasingly global crime as increasingly global business. Furthermore, the relevance of all of the above parties can ultimately be ascribed to the presence of Melmotte and Fisker in London. *The Way We Live Now* needs the Americans.

(b) "Metropolitan Danger": Melmotte and the (Other) Americans

The novel's two most obviously American characters—Hurtle and Fisker—are treated in two completely different ways by the narrator, but both underscore a complicated picture of Americans as wild yet calculating, fabulous yet historical. Critics point to possible real-life bases for Fisker's character, especially in the person of James Fisk (1834–72), a Gilded Age swindler and smuggler who helped supply the South during the Civil War (a feat attributed to Melmotte in *The Way We Live Now*) and was murdered in New York City in 1872, just as Trollope was about to begin work on the novel. James Fisk's most notorious achievement was a failed attempt to corner the market on gold in 1869. The similarities between Fisk and Fisker are many, but there is another possible template for Trollope's character: Harvey Fisk (1829–90), who co-founded the brokerage firm of Fisk & Hatch with Alfrederick Smith Hatch, a future president of the New York Stock Exchange. Together, Fisk and Hatch supplied the Union during the Civil War and were deeply involved in railroad finance, including peripheral liability in investment panics in 1873, when they briefly suspended business due to troubles at the Central Pacific (the name of which recalls Fisker's "South Central Pacific" in Trollope's novel). As historian Richard White points out, shareholders were lulled into their investments by Fisk & Hatch's assurances of solvency; in a manner reminiscent of the global malfeasance in *The Way We Live Now*, the efforts of Fisk & Hatch were paralleled by those of firms like the Speyer Brothers' of London and Lazard Speyer-Ellissen of Frankfurt (White 27). Adding superficial plausibility to the connection between Fisk & Hatch of New York and Fisker of *The Way We Live Now*, Hatch's wife Theodosia shares her maiden name, Ruggles, with that of the Ruggles family in Trollope's novel. If one then considers Harvey Fisk—and not just James Fisk, for both were in the headlines as Trollope was composing his novel—as a possible source for the character of Fisker, one is forced to reckon with the legitimacy and global reach of the swindling in *The Way We Live Now*. Fisk & Hatch was a major Wall Street firm that prospered and survived through the turn of the century, not merely a colorful smuggler like James Fisk. Trollope's Fisker could thus be read as much more than a comically evil incursion into London economic life.[5]

The drawing of Fisker is admittedly a bit comical, and *The Way We Live Now* positions him, as if against his historical counterpart(s), as a figure of romance and uncertain origins. The reader learns, early on, that Fisker is an associate of Paul Montague's uncle in California, but in a more specific speculation on his history later, we are told that Fisker "had sprung out of some California gully, was perhaps ignorant of his own father and mother, and had

---

[5].. R. H. Super and others have pointed to John Sadleir, George Hudson, and other notorious nineteenth-century swindlers as possible models for either Fisker or Melmotte. See Super, *The Chronicler* 324. Van suggests the fictional figure of "Monroe P. Jones," invented by Trollope in *North America* (1862) to "exemplify frontier spirit and character" (90).

tumbled up in the world on the strength of his own audacity"[6] (1.324). Trollope uses him consistently to illustrate the differences between America and England; after an all-night round of card games at the Beargarden Club, the narrator remarks that "not one there had liked Fisker. His manners were not their manners" (1.93). Lord Nidderdale nationalizes the difference when he says, "He's not a half bad fellow, but he's not a bit like an Englishman" (1.95). Having carefully established the conceptual and cultural distance between England and America, Trollope then shows its troubling dissolution, as English characters, beginning with Sir Felix Carbury, are said to follow Fisker's example in behavior minor and major. Tempted to leave a game that is costing him all of his money, Sir Felix instead, "as he played on, . . . remembered how Fisker had played all night, and how he had gone off from the club to catch the early train" (1.467–68). Fisker is at least competent in financial matters, though, and on his return to London after Melmotte's death he criticizes the English members of the board for their lack of knowledge and discipline in running the company. Ultimately, *The Way We Live Now* manages to shuffle most of the blame for the corruption onto Fisker, claiming that "the work of robbing mankind in gross by magnificently false representations, was not only the duty, but also the delight and the ambition of his life" (2.394–95). We thus have every reason to fear for Marie Melmotte when Fisker proposes marriage to her in terms befitting a global business deal. Marie accepts, and Fisker's response is curious: "'I'm the happiest man on this continent,' he said, forgetting in his ecstasy that he was not in the United States" (2.456). As gratuitous as it is comical, the conflation of geographical distance is symptomatic of what happens to space in *The Way We Live Now*'s representation of the globalizing financial world.

Mrs. Hurtle's function in the novel has little to do with finance and everything to do with romance. She is essential to the development of the love triangle between herself, Paul Montague, and Hetta Carbury, and she has decisive impact also on the triangle between Sir Felix, the country girl Ruby Ruggles, and Ruby's country suitor John Crumb.[7] In short, though, Hurtle is as central to the romantic intrigues of *The Way We Live Now* as Melmotte is to the financial and social ones, although, as with Melmotte, it is impossible to conceive that Trollope envisioned Hurtle as so elemental before actually composing the novel. In his working notes, according to Sutherland's study of the manuscript and sketches, Trollope's first mention of Hurtle is at

---

6. Flabuert's Arnoux, in *L'Éducation sentimentale:* "I'll have to send them to California . . . to the devil!" (2.67).

7. Odden has argued that this "triangulation enables plot complexity," but the triangulation and the accompanying complexity were inevitable necessities in a novel that portrays a shrinking world, in which a greater number of characters from a greater number of places are forced into diminishing novelistic space (140).

best elliptical, as an implied presence in the notes on Paul Montague: "Paul Montague—Hetty's lover. Gets into some scrapes which must be devised" (quoted in Sutherland, "Trollope at Work" 479). "Some scrapes" were indeed devised, as Hurtle, a widow whom Paul promises to marry while in America, turns out to have a long and wild history involving rumors of having shot a man in a duel in Oregon and threatened her first husband in Kansas. "She was regarded," the narrator remarks, "as a mystery," and so she remains for much of the novel, while Paul and the reader are left to speculate on the veracity of the rumors surrounding her (1.243). Trollope goes to great lengths to render Hurtle romantic, a savage import from the frontier. She is repeatedly referred to as a "wild cat," and one character alleges jokingly that "there was a bit of the wild cat in her breeding" (1.355). Fisker may not know his parentage, but Hurtle's is shown in an animalistic light. Capturing this romantic side of Hurtle in a passage that marks her off as Hetta's "rival," the narrator refers to Hurtle as "nasty," in a *style indirect libre* meant to reflect Hetta's thoughts (2.375).

There is, of course, more to Hurtle than the "wild cat," and Trollope emphasizes her dual nature through an almost explicit marriage of Hurtle's two sides in Hetta's eyes. After seeing Hurtle as "nasty," and as a "rival," Hetta adds to her assessment of Hurtle the word, "intriguing," as in "scheming" (rather than merely "interesting") (2.375). The similarity here between Hurtle's dual rational and romantic sides recalls Vautrin's dual portrayal in *Le Père Goriot*. Fittingly, Hurtle does this comparison justice by consistently showing herself capable of Vautrin-like manipulation, and even by parroting his disturbing morality. Hurtle articulates first and most explicitly the increasingly popular paradigm against which the novel rails, most often through the voice of Roger Carbury, whom many critics have read as Trollope's fictional stand-in.[8] In an exchange between Montague and Hurtle regarding Melmotte's alleged dishonesty, Hurtle contends that

> "Such a man rises above honesty . . . as a great general rises above humanity when he sacrifices an army to conquer a nation. Such greatness is incompatible with small scruples. A pigmy man is stopped by a little ditch, but a giant stalks over the rivers."
>
> "I prefer to be stopped by the ditches," said Montague.
>
> "Ah, Paul, you were not born for commerce." (1.245–46)

---

8. Nathan, for example, writes, "Roger Carbury here is clearly Trollope's mouthpiece" (275). R.D. McMaster concurs. Daniel Becquemont disagrees, arguing that "Roger Carbury . . . is not Trollope's spokesman" because Carbury's concept of "rigid social fixity" is far more conservative than Trollope's (142).

When Hurtle goes on, comparing Melmotte to Napoleon and Washington—two men who had fairly recently troubled scrupulous England—several things can be seen happening in this passage. Spoken by an American, and when read in conjunction with the behavior of the Americans Fisker and Melmotte, Hurtle's amorality comes across as a particularly American one. It is, furthermore, explicitly tied to commerce, which is in turn explicitly tied to war. The scripting of the dialogue reminds one of the dilemma of the Mandarin, the allegorical form in which Rastignac packages for Bianchon the question that Vautrin raises, of how far one can go for wealth without jettisoning ethics. Paul's answer here is that of Bianchon's, and he chooses the lowly ditches—the moral choice here, importantly coded as that of the colonized "pigmy"—over the destructiveness of the conquering generals. Hurtle's elaboration of this mindset will be echoed by Melmotte as he gathers admirers, snookers investors, and wins election to Parliament. Her role, as originally planned by Trollope, outgrows the confines of small scrapes and becomes central to the novel as romance partnered with a diabolical logic.

Of the characters associated explicitly or implicitly with America in *The Way We Live Now*, Melmotte of course looms largest. It is not going too far to suggest that he is the center of the entire novel, and the attention to him in both the novel and the reception confirms this. "There was still much to be done in London," the narrator tells us at one point, "in all of which Mr. Melmotte was concerned, and of much of which Mr. Melmotte was the very centre" (1.326). More important, though, Melmotte is also the heart of world commerce, "in company with all the commercial world, for there was no business to which he would refuse his co-operation on certain terms" (1.81). A lengthy list of Melmotte's plans and accomplishments further positions him in the middle of everything, in language that emphasizes the reorganization of global space to accommodate the new aims and means of business:

> He was the head and front of the railway which was to regenerate Mexico. It was presumed that the contemplated line from ocean to ocean across British America would become a fact in his hands. It was he who was to enter into terms with the Emperor of China for farming the tea-fields of that vast country. He was already in treaty with Russia for a railway from Moscow to Khiva. He had a fleet,—or soon would have a fleet of emigrant ships,—ready to carry every discontented Irishman out of Ireland to whatever quarter of the globe the Milesian might choose for the exercise of his political principles. It was known that he had already floated a company for laying down a submarine wire from Penzance to Point de Galle, round the Cape of Good Hope,—so that, in the event of general wars, England need be dependent on no other country for its communications with India. And then there was the philanthropic scheme for buying

the liberty of the Arabian fellahs from the Khedive of Egypt for thirty millions sterling,—the compensation to consist of the concession of a territory about four times as big as Great Britain in the lately annexed country on the great African lakes. It may have been the case that some of these things were as yet only matters of conversation,—speculations as to which Mr. Melmotte's mind and imagination had been at work, rather than his pocket or even his credit; but they were all sufficiently matured to find their way into the public press. (1.412)

Focusing on a much earlier and much quicker enumeration of Melmotte's feats, Annette Van argues that he "allied himself with the wrong sides, sides whose interests run contrary to England's" (81). As this later passage makes clear, though, Melmotte generally serves the ends of empire, including England's, despite his being in some ways a product of the colonies.

The notion of Melmotte's colonial—probably American—identity must be complicated to account for the text's own depiction of the uncertainty surrounding the financier. Melmotte's wife is the object of the novel's initial anti-Semitism, as she is first identified as a "Bohemian Jewess" (1.22, 1.30). The assumption of her Jewishness soon becomes an assumption of Melmotte's Jewishness in the novel (2.71). It is difficult to understand how these rumors have contributed to an acceptance of them in the scholarship on *The Way We Live Now*, though, because the novel clearly vexes them. Georgiana Longestaffe, in a letter to her mother, plainly states that "everybody knows that Madame Melmotte is a Jewess, and nobody knows what Mr. Melmotte is" (2.140). The novel appears to conclude, as mentioned above, that Melmotte is Irish-American, and evidence supporting the American association is given at the outset when Marie Melmotte recalls her earliest memories, "the dirty street in the German portion of New York in which she had been born and had lived for the first four years of her life" (1.106). Marie's later memories, of travels around the European Continent (she mentions specifically Hamburg, Frankfurt, Paris, and Vienna), are much clearer, but it all seems to start in the city from which the novel suggests Melmotte comes. If Hamilton Fisker springs from a gully in California, Melmotte rises from a dangerously cosmopolitan city in the New World, a place of mixture, where he could conceivably learn the flawless German and French that he is said to speak later in the novel. For his part, Melmotte declares himself English on arrival, a notion on which the novel itself vacillates; the narrator reminds the reader that "it had been said repeatedly that Melmotte was not an Englishman" but elsewhere refers to him as "an English merchant" (2.33; 1.297).

Melmotte's being American is clearly not as important to *The Way We Live Now* as the uncertainty is. This uncertainty fuels one of the two essential facets of Melmotte's character and function in the novel, his use as an almost endless source of romance or narrative complication. Tracy has already speculated about Melmotte's possible literary ancestor in Charles Maturin's gothic novel, *Melmoth the Wanderer;* apart from the cosmetic similarity of their names, Trollope's villain shares fundamental character traits with Maturin's Melmoth, who wandered the world and "died as he had lived, in a kind of avaricious delirium" (Maturin 19). A full-fledged comparison of these characters is beyond the scope of this chapter, but the link already intimates the romantic role that Melmotte is to play. Harold James sees the image of the "master magician" as typical among portrayals of financiers in the nineteenth century (251), and Trollope's narrator indeed refers to successful financiers, like Melmotte, as "great conjurors," and proceeds to extend the metaphor of witchcraft—"boiling cauldrons," e.g.—to the field of finance (1.114–15). The irony is thick, but only the narrator seems to realize this, as Mr. Longestaffe is more than content to view Melmotte as a "necromancer" who can help him to prevent the loss of his family's property due to debt and mismanagement. The narrator paints Melmotte several times with an unrepentantly romantic and adventurous brush, and this tone peaks as the thin sheen of respectability dissolves and the financier knows his career is over. Melmotte

> had known that he had to run these risks. He had told himself a thousand times that when the dangers came, dangers alone should never cow him. He had always endeavoured to go as near the wind as he could, to avoid the heavy hand of the criminal law of whatever country he inhabited. He had studied the criminal laws, so that he might be sure in his reckonings; but he had always felt that he might be carried by circumstances into deeper waters than he intended to enter. As the soldier who leads a forlorn hope, or as the diver who goes down for pearls, or as the searcher for wealth on fever-breeding coasts, knows that as his gains may be great, so are his perils, Melmotte had been aware that in his life, as it opened itself out to him, he might come to terrible destruction. He had not always thought, or even hoped, that he would be as he was now, so exalted as to be allowed to entertain the very biggest ones of the earth; but the greatness had grown upon him,—and so had the danger. (2.104)

Melmotte acknowledges here an important paradox of his situation; the very achievements and audacity that give him "greatness" also endanger him. The disequilibrium between earned greatness and its very impossibility reproduces the dilemma of disenchantment and the ambivalence of fiction toward the advances of late-imperial Britain, processes that simultaneously enable and endanger the imagination. Melmotte's more specifically commercial side—the second essential facet of his character—engages the problems more directly, through a redrawing of London that emphasizes its new centrality to the world and the consequences of this new centrality.

(c) Unrealist City: The New Mobility and the Way We Lived Then

In the disenchanted London of *The Way We Live Now*, Melmotte causes a stir no matter what he does. His newly redecorated London house, however, explicitly transports the setting of the novel, if only momentarily, into a place that is both of the past and of an nonurban elsewhere, recalling the unmapping of Paris by Balzac's narrator in *La fille aux yeux d'or*. The Melmotte mansion elicits from Trollope's narrator an uncharacteristically lengthy description of an interior:

> The broad verandah had been turned into a conservatory, had been covered with boards contrived to look like trellis-work, was heated with hot air and filled with exotics at some fabulous price. A covered way had been made from the door, down across the pathway, to the road, and the police had, I fear, been bribed to frighten foot passengers into a belief that they were bound to go round. The house had been so arranged that it was impossible to know where you were, when once in it. The hall was a paradise. The staircase was fairyland. The lobbies were grottoes rich with ferns. Walls had been knocked away and arches had been constructed. The leads behind had been supported and walled in, and covered and carpeted. The ball had possession of the ground floor and first floor, and the house seemed to be endless. (1.34)

The Melmottes' London house appears as a triumph of disorder, misdirection, the exotic, and the infinite, an architecture out of time and place, all of which contribute to Melmotte's romantic purpose. As if in a nod to Scott, Trollope has even the Countess of Mid-Lothian express her admiration at the extravagant décor. The Melmotte house and its London reenchantments, however, are countered by a force that articulates London as a global city and begins to reckon the effects of this change.

In his management of the commercial center of *The Way We Live Now*, Melmotte presides over a compression of the globe on which the novel seems to base its concomitant compression of the English capital. The project of the railroad itself imagines this tampering with distance in several ways.

London society, in the novel, accepts the disenchanting aims of the railways as agents of homogenization and forces for civilizing cultures seen as uncivilized. This aim is presupposed in an article appearing in the "Evening Pulpit" newspaper, which sees "a good deal of praise, but still alloyed by a dash of irony, bestowed on the idea of civilizing Mexico by joining it to California" (1.277). The distances that the railways will destroy are responsible, furthermore, for the entire relationship that springs up between Paul Montague and Mrs. Hurtle (Paul's monumental "scrape"). Detailing the history of their interaction, the narrator recalls that "at this time, the reader will remember, there was no great railway in existence" (1.244). The distance between New York, where they meet, and San Francisco had not yet been abolished by the transcontinental railway, and the increased travel-time and space between the two coasts are adduced as a partial explanation of their relationship. After the relationship unravels, Hurtle refers to the end of a meaningful distance that Paul seems still to take for granted: "Had not the distance between us seemed to have made you safe," she asks Paul, "would you have dared to write that letter [breaking off the engagement]?" (1.443–44). Hurtle's mere presence in London is an assurance that Paul is, in fact, not safe from a woman in America. The effects of facilitated travel on *The Way We Live Now* are profound, as Fisker is able to come and go almost as he pleases between San Francisco, Liverpool, and London. Fisker's trans-Atlantic mobility explains the comical lapse in his confusion of Europe with America, as he forgets which continent he is on. Melmotte's confusions are likewise global. In a similar slip to Paul Montague, whom Melmotte would send to investigate the progress of the railroad (a cheap excuse to be rid of Paul, who is asking too many questions), the great financier says:

"I was proposing that you should go to Pekin?"
"To Mexico."
"Yes, yes;—to Mexico." (1.427)

Twice, Trollope employs these humorous errors that nevertheless testify to diminishing distance and geographical difference, and to Fisker's and Melmotte's role in the process.

The lengthy citation, above, that lists Melmotte's alleged achievements, underscores his global reach and intimacy with political and colonial processes in diverse places. He is simultaneously in India, Ireland, South Africa, Egypt, and, by implication, everywhere. Yet Trollope's novel is careful also to provide a solid, site-specific origin for the current diffusion of Melmotte's global commercial power: London. The *global city* is sociologist Saskia Sassen's term for the localization of the apparently ubiquitous forces behind globalization, the place that organizes—even if it cannot fully contain—these broader, more diffuse networks (her exemplars in *The Global City* are London, New York, and Tokyo).[9] Such cities only become possible in the wake of advances in telecommunications technology; for Sassen, this implies the onset of the internet, as she argues in an essay on "Electronic Space," but her observations can be fruitfully applied to the projections of Trollope's London and to Melmotte himself. Indeed, communications capabilities are central in the novel and are articulated as allies of both the police and the railroad, the forces of disenchantment and the destruction of distance. The narrator refers to Fisker's and Melmotte's railway as "means of communication," and the increased effectiveness of the telegraph arises as a tool for detection (1.82). Already in *The Eustace Diamonds*, Trollope has a character express the sentiment that it is futile to flee the police, "now we has the wires" (2.217). The wires, one recalls, are explicitly linked in *The Way We Live Now* to Melmotte (just as they will be explicitly linked to Gordon in Fontane's *Cécile*), who plans to lay down enough of them to bring India into instantaneous contact with London. Elsewhere, the narrator asserts that "Melmotte had the telegraph at his command, and had been able to make as close inquiries as though San Francisco and Salt Lake City had been suburbs of London" (1.84).[10] The telegraph's effects are palpable in Melmotte's worry that "he could reach no place so distant but that he would be known and traced," and in Cohenlupe's attempts to "remember what happy country still was left in which an order from the British police would have no power to interfere with the comfort of a retired gentleman such as himself" (2.116; 2.182).

The importance of Melmotte to Trollope's portrayal of London can be enriched by Sassen's notion of time in the global city and by the "harriedness" that Robbins explores as an aspect of globalization. *The Way We Live Now* is easily categorized as a "London novel," according to Michael Cotsell, who declares it the only "major Victorian novel to deal with the subject of London" between Dickens's *Our Mutual Friend* (1865) and George Gissing's novels in the 1880s (ix). Trollope makes it clear that Melmotte is, to a certain extent, London's heart. When a parliamentary seat for Westminster is vacated, the narrator reveals that "it was considered indispensable to the country that

9. Sassen writes that "The global city is a function of the global grid of transactions, one site for processes which are global because they have multiple locations in multiple countries" (213). The financial transactions of Melmotte are precisely transnational, involving banks and investors from at least North America and the European Continent, and truly global projects.

10. "To no one's surprise, it was an American who found a way to put electricity in the service of communication and, in doing so, eliminated the problem of space once and for all. I refer, of course, to Samuel Finley Breese Morse, America's first true 'spaceman.' His telegraph erased state lines, collapsed regions, and, by wrapping the continent in an information grid, created the possibility of a unified American discourse.

"But at considerable cost. For telegraphy did something that Morse did not foresee when he prophesied that telegraphy would make 'one neighborhood of the whole country'" (Postman 64–65).

Mr. Melmotte should go into Parliament, and what constituency could such a man as Melmotte so fitly represent as one combining as Westminster does all the essences of the metropolis?" (1.326). It goes deeper than this, though, because London soon begins openly accommodating the presence of Melmotte, and noblemen like Lord Alfred suddenly feel "no aristocratic twinges" when "called by [their] Christian name" (1.340). Melmotte represents, moreover, the sort of time compression that Sassen relates to the development of the global city, in which time accrues more value in the changing economy. "As the market becomes a key site for new opportunities for profit," Sassen argues, "speed is of the essence," increasingly (209). Robbins's attention to harriedness as a symptom of globalization is especially useful here, because it examines what is ultimately a personal expression of global shifts in public dealings. Robbins remarks that "this time pressure *reflects* global capital, of course, but that is not the only relation between the two terms," and he goes on to posit the transfer of harriedness from the workplace into the home (429). Trollope's novel conditions this reflection in one more way, for Melmotte's harriedness is presented, in *The Way We Live Now*, not merely as a symptom of his global dealings but rather as the condition of their possibility; the world shrinks, in other words, because people like Melmotte remain constantly busy. Excusing himself from a meeting with Paul Montague, during which Montague wishes to air his concerns for the company's methods and aims, Melmotte acknowledges that the meeting "was quite necessary,—only you see I am a little busy" (1.427). To Dolly Longestaffe, he claims, "I have so many things on my brain, that I hardly know how to get along with them" (2.28). Melmotte, the "essence of the metropolis," openly identifies himself and his commercial dealings with the value of harriedness: "A man with my business on his hands," he states, "is bound to be quick" (1.428).

The compression of time and space bleeds into the city that Melmotte is said to embody, drastically affecting its perceived geography. A contemporary reviewer noted the novel's hurry, as Tony Tanner has pointed out, and this same reviewer explicitly ascribed this hurry to Trollope's change of venue, his movement to London (257–58). Philip Collins has claimed that Trollope's aim in *The Way We Live Now* was "to explore and relate to one another a series of London worlds," but this implies too concrete a conceptual separation between these worlds (23). The example of Islington alone demonstrates a change in Trollope's mapping of London from *Phineas Redux* as discussed in the last chapter. Through the madness of Robert Kennedy, one recalls, Trollope renders a quadrant of the city foreign and dangerous. Islington appears to perform a similar function in *The Way We Live Now*. The country girl Ruby Ruggles, who has easy access to London from her country origins, thanks to the regular train service, and the American Mrs. Hurtle take rooms in the same house. Mrs. Hurtle comes to metonymize Islington, and Paul's visits to her are even referred to, by the narrator, as trips "to Islington" (1.371, e.g.). But Trollope emphasizes the nearness to—rather than the distance from—Islington and the other worlds of London. Paul's first visit to Hurtle calls attention to the nearness, as Paul

> threw himself into a Hansom cab, and ordered the man to drive to Islington.
> How quick that cab went! . . . Paul was lodging in Suffolk Street, close to Pall Mall—whence the way to Islington, across Oxford Street, across Tottenham Court Road, across numerous squares north-east of the Museum, seems to be long. The end of Goswell Road is the outside of the world in that direction, and Islington is beyond the end of Goswell Road. And yet that Hansom cab was there before Paul Montague had been able to arrange the words with which he would begin the interview. (1.371)

The effect here is the opposite of that in Balzac's *La Fille aux yeux d'or*, where the speed of de Marsay's carriage ride renders Paris foreign to him. Paul's conception of distance in the passage is first excused by the narrator—"the way to Islington . . . seems to be long"—but then viciously undercut. Islington, it appears, "the outside of the world in that direction," is in truth not at all far away. Moretti relates, in *Atlas of the European Novel*, the manner in which Dickens first transforms the binary city—East London, West London—of *Oliver Twist* into the interwoven complexity that one sees at its peak in *Our Mutual Friend*, with its long and twisting coach ride from the neighborhood of gentlemen to the neighborhood of watermen (86). By contrast, Trollope's coach rides finally disenchant London by abbreviating it. Hetta Carbury's later visit to Hurtle is less eventful than Paul Montague's but similarly stresses the compactness of the city. Abetted by the new Underground and a solid knowledge of London's layout, "Hetta trusted herself all alone to the mysteries of the Marylebone underground railway, and emerged with accuracy at King's Cross. She had studied her geography, and she walked from thence to Islington" (2.385). The mysteries of the new railway cannot detract from the easy navigability of the city. Only a drunken Felix Carbury gets lost in London in *The Way We Live Now*, and a policeman (of course) helps him find his way home.

The compression of urban space, which shortens the narrative rendering of carriage rides in a city that seems to host the world in *The Way We Live Now*, arises as well in the actual act of narration in the novel. Despite his modesty when comparing himself to the thorough designs of Wilkie Collins, as we saw in the last chapter, Trollope's emplotment is usually careful; his novels were, almost without exception, completed well before their serialization began, so that Trollope could avoid scurrying around under deadline pressure. The structure of *The Way We Live Now* is thus striking in its nonlinearity, especially for Trollope. The narrator repeatedly backtracks, often with an explicit admission: "But we must go back a little" we are told in one place, and in another we hear of "Fisker,—whose subsequent doings have been recorded somewhat out of their turn" (1.77; 2.410). Trollope's narrator seems incapable of managing the compression, within its own pages, of so many characters and so little time.[11] As Tanner has observed, "it is a crowded book, but that very crowdedness is part of its meaning" (263). Another stylistic upheaval in the novel, the drifting attention of individual chapters, similarly testifies to its compression of London life. The most pertinent example is chapter XLV, "Mr. Melmotte Is Pressed For Time" (1.421–29). Trollope's chapters in the Palliser series and elsewhere normally focus on the development of one character or situation; divergences from this are rare enough that they are explicitly acknowledged. In the first chapter of *Barchester Towers* (1857), for example, "Mr. Harding went out and sent the message, and it may be as well that we should follow it to its destination" (7–8). In *The Way We Live Now*, however, "Mr. Melmotte Is Pressed For Time" floats from a conversation between Dolly Longestaffe and Melmotte to one between Dolly and his father, returns to Melmotte in order to show him speaking with Sir Felix Carbury, who upon leaving bumps into Paul Montague. Paul and Felix converse until Paul is let in to see Mr. Melmotte, at which point the scene shifts to a board meeting the following day, and concludes with Melmotte leaving another meeting. The point of the chapter is clear: Melmotte is very, very busy. The execution, though, by involving multiple characters and floating between them as they come and go from Melmotte's office, simultaneously incarnates the harriedness of Melmotte and compresses the city and its characters around him. Another chapter, "Melmotte in Parliament," goes

---

11. David Harvey accuses "realist narrative structure" of being so linear as to ignore "a reality in which two events in quite different spaces occurring at the same time could so intersect as to change how the world worked" (265). Ramponi's work on globalization in German realism confronts Harvey's argument but neglects to answer the charge in terms of "narrative structure"; Ramponi offers instead remarks made by characters in Freytag's *Soll und Haben* on the interconnectedness of the world. Trollope's *The Way We Live Now* actually addresses Harvey's accusations more directly, because in Trollope we see not just the content but that actual structure of the book change in order to accommodate this complex reality. See also Hamer, who examines the particular challenges of complexity in the realm of serialization, and Tracy's chapter on "Multiple Structure" in *Trollope's Later Novels*. Hornback argues, in an article matching the chronology of *The Way We Live Now* to the actual calendar of 1872, that the complexity of the novel required faithful adherence to a realistic chronology: "The novel is very dependent upon its chronological structure because of the method Trollope uses in presenting his characters: first one is set in motion, then the narrator turns back to pick up another" (456). P. D. Edwards disputes Hornback's claims, concluding that no amount of interpretive juggling of dates can show that Trollope used one chronology consistently ("The Chronology" 216). Sutherland diplomatically sides with Edwards but acknowledges "the salience of time markers in the novel" ("Introduction" xxxv). Grawe has similarly argued that precise historical dates for events in Fontane's *Effi Briest* can be calculated (51–53). See also Riechel.

to even greater lengths in this same way. Trollope's form in *The Way We Live Now* is frequently prey to a harried content.

If Paul's journey to Islington emphasizes minimized distance within the city, another journey strives to preserve the divide between country and city. In a last effort to win his cousin Hetta Carbury's affections, Roger Carbury "determined that he would again go up to London. He would have the vacant hours of the journey in which to think of it all again" (2.405–6). The slow lapse of time in the train is performed by Trollope's text, as the narrator spends half a page elaborating on the fact that "those vacant hours" did not "serve him much" (2.406). Roger Carbury stands in opposition to the zero-sum commercial ethos embodied by Melmotte, articulated by Hurtle, and enacted within the city. Roger is, through the course of the novel, "manly" (1.51), "good" (1.362), "true" (1.72), and a "rock" (1.361). Rather than merely *represent* the rural, though, Roger *is* the country; his family's roots stretch back so far in Suffolk that parts of it bear the name of Carbury, a fact that sets Roger at odds with the new global mobility that Trollope's novel thematizes (1.50). Trollope's brief description of Suffolk architecture relies on English history: Carbury Manor is "a Tudor building," while the Longestaffes' Caversham was "built in the early part of George III.'s reign," for example (1.128–30). Roger is also the most vocal opponent of the Melmottes when he says of their stay with the Longestaffes, "I don't approve of them in London, you know; but I think they are very much worse in the country" (1.136). At once setting city against country and the Melmottes against all, Roger's sentiment is soon parroted by Georgiana Longstaffe, albeit hypocritically: "What makes me most angry," Georgiana says, "is that we should have condescended to be civil to the Melmottes down in the country. In London one does those things, but to have them here was terrible!" (1.197) The opposition is made clear.

It is important that Trollope ends *The Way We Live Now*, as the last chapter's title has it, "Down in Suffolk," at Carbury Manor, where Roger magnanimously invites Hetta and Paul—the man who bested Roger in the contest for Hetta's affections—to live with him. The only three characters in the novel whom one can claim as uncomplicatedly sympathetic, Hetta, Paul, and Roger choose country over city. The choice is not surprising; we learn early on that Paul "found that he could not wake up on these London mornings with thoughts as satisfactory as those which attended his pillow at the old Manor House" (1.88). Contrast, with this, the unsympathetic Sir Felix's complaint that Carbury Manor is "like a prison ... with that moat round it" (1.163). The moat around Carbury Manor, an earnestly reiterated symbol of both the age of the Manor and its function as a place of defense, recalls Wemmick's Castle in Dickens's *Great Expectations*.[12] Its "chasm about four feet wide and two deep" is meant to, Wemmick tells Pip, "cut off the communication" (204). Moretti produces this as an example of the "two lives" one must lead in Dickens's vision of middle class London (*Atlas* 120), Brooks sees it as a consolidation of and safe haven for Wemmick's "portable property" (*Realist Vision* 15), and Robbins reads this "archaic fantasy of suburban self-containment" as a "vision of domestic self-reliance" emblematic of the concerns of upward mobility in *Great Expectations* (*Upward Mobility* 78). It also represents the notion of defense against—and an alternative to—the encroachment of the urban, but in *The Way We Live Now*, suburbia will not suffice. If Islington ("the outside of the world in that direction") can be so quickly reached by cab, then Wemmick's Walworth is also imperiled. Trollope's Carbury Manor, accessible only via "a short, private road," is in another place and time (1.128). Fittingly, one of the last images in the novel is of Roger, "walk[ing] up and down the walk by the moat" that separates his bit of country from the shrinking, compacting world (2.468).[13]

The phrase "Metropolitan Danger" comes not from *The Way We Live Now* but from *Phineas Finn*, where my discussion of Trollope began. Miss Boreham bemoans her over-protective guardians and their penchant for travel: "Fancy going to Brighton! And then they have proposed Switzerland. If you could only hear Augusta talking in rapture of a month among the glaciers! And I feel so ungrateful. I believe they would spend three months with me at any horrible place that I could suggest,—at Hong Kong if I were to ask it,—so intent are they on taking me away from metropolitan danger" (2.63). *Phineas Finn*, in all its domestic disenchantment, does not really envision the metropolis as a site of danger; duels, for example, are meant for the Continent. Yet by importing danger from the north and murder from the south, its sequel begins the reconstruction of London that culminates in *The Way We Live Now*. *Phineas Redux* moreover commences, on a much smaller scale with its Channel crossings and detective efforts, a version of the mobility and communication that *The Way We Live Now* will make entirely global and entirely perilous for England's stability. "The movement of men," Eric Hobsbawm has noted, acquires "the momentum of a landslide" (*Revolution*

---

12. Fontane, too, will employ this pre-modern motif in *Irrungen, Wirrungen*'s "'castle' [Schloß] with its green-and-red-painted turret" located right in the middle of Berlin (I.2.341).
13. Cf. Flaubert, *L'Éducation sentimentale*:
"A better solution would be to decentralize, to spread the surplus population of the towns [villes] over the countryside."
"But the towns are rotten to the core [gangrenées]!" exclaimed a Catholic. (2.190)

171–72). As in *Phineas Redux*, the constant trafficking in people across national borders underscores new possibilities for both good and ill. Trollope, whom A. O. J. Cockshut pegged as a pessimist in 1955, chose to see mixture as debilitating.[14] The long list of Melmotte's fictional achievements includes the brokering of peace between warring nations and the solution of long-standing political squabbles, including that between Britain and Ireland in which Trollope was so emotionally invested. *The Way We Live Now*, though, tempers these possible goods with its own angry version of the probable bad.

The novel requires the new mobility and communication that it ultimately comes to fear. Trollope's deployment of a fraudulent railroad investment scheme captures perfectly the intersection of transportation, communication, and an increasingly global financial world reducible, according to Trollope, to crime and foreignness.[15] All of these concerns converge in the figure of Melmotte. *The Way We Live Now* apparently breaks down in the face of too much complexity, too much intrigue, too many foreign incursions for Trollope and his narrative to tolerate. The controlled recodings and bursts of complication in *Phineas Finn* and *Phineas Redux* are all over London in *The Way We Live Now*, changing it in ways that the novel cannot stomach. In the final Palliser novel, *The Duke's Children*, Lord Silverbridge laments, "I hear men say that it isn't quite what it used to be" (282). Wistfully, another character replies, "Nothing will ever be quite what it used to be." These are first Roger Carbury's words, though, as the Melmottes invade the countryside on their weekend visit: "Things aren't as they were, of course, and never will be again" (1.136). The last refuge of *The Way We Live Now* from the threats of compressed time and shrunken space, is a deliberately located nostalgia. In resisting foreign amorality and the future, the novel's closing pages recall the final images of Balzac's *La Peau de chagrin*, and Pauline's desperate, losing battle against the upriver steamer, the onslaught of modernity. *The Way We Live Now*'s retreat to Carbury Manor, in the good old English countryside, realizes a desire to be where things, according to the novel's understanding of them, still recall the way we lived then.

---

14. On the pessimistic Trollope, see also Brantlinger 6–8.
15. Perera's discussion of Dickens's *Edwin Drood* offers opium rather than railroads: "If *Edwin Drood* suggests that the increasing savagery of English domestic life is a product of the imperial connection, the register of that guilty relation is opium, a commodity made globally available only through the workings of the imperial system, while that system depends for its viability on promoting opium consumption anywhere *outside* its own metropolis" (108).

Part III

Fontane and the Problem of Familiarity

CHAPTER SEVEN

"BERLIN WIRD WELTSTADT"
Nation, City, and World in Cécile

> The ultimate decisions ... lie in totally different places today, and it's only a few of those newspapers of yours that never weary of assuring the world to the contrary. All nothing but dying echoes. Our modern age is mercilessly ridding itself of all that's been handed down. Whether they succeed in erecting an empire on the Nile, whether Japan becomes the England of the Pacific, whether China with its four hundred million souls wakes up from its slumbers and raises its hand to call out to us and the rest of the world, "Here I am" ... all of that is of far greater weight.
> —Theodor Fontane, *Der Stechlin*

That Germany was only belatedly a colonialist nation is not disputed. In 1899, one year after the passing of Theodor Fontane, a young English scholar of history and future Member of Parliament made an intellectual pilgrimage to Berlin to study under Theodor Mommsen. L. S. Amery recalls his brush with academic celebrity in the preface to his book *The German Colonial Claim* (1940), and he paints a pithy picture of certain conditions surrounding the period during which Fontane was active as a writer of prose fiction:

> I remember a visit to Mommsen, the great historian, then well in his eighties and a stately and magnificent presence. I had come, still fresh from my own historical studies, full of eagerness to sit at his feet and to learn more of the government of Imperial Rome. Instead I was treated to a diatribe on England's wickedness: how we had filched an empire while Germany was weakened by the Thirty Years' War and subsequently engrossed, for nearly two centuries, in the long and costly struggles between Prussia and Austria or against France. Now the time had come to change all that. . . . It was all stuff that I had heard and read many times before in current publications. . . . It was only a little later that I read Treitschke, and realised that for twenty years already the doctrine of the wrong done to Germany by our existence as a world Power, and of the necessity of

displacing us by force, had been systematically preached in those professional and pedagogic circles which have always exercised so great an influence on German policy. (11–12)

Amery wrote this recollection as German colonial sentiment was being rabidly revived in the mid- to late-1930s,[1] and he stakes out the area around 1879 (implied by the phrase "for twenty years already") as the origin of militant German expansionism. Not coincidentally, in that same year Friedrich Fabri published *Bedarf Deutschland der Colonien?* [*Does Germany Need Colonies?*], which would ultimately become, according to Russell Berman, "the most influential manifesto of the colonialist movement" (*Enlightenment* 136).[2]

Like the German proponents of imperialism, who discovered after unification in 1871 that other European powers had long outpaced them in conquering the globe, fiction in German was somewhat slower to take on—and take in—the world. Recent scholarly attention to imperialism in German literature has foregrounded this notion of belatedness, both in German literature's delayed self-implication in the world and *Germanistik*'s delayed analysis of it. Fontane, whom Heidenreich and Kroll have called the *Poet of German Unification*, chronicled as perhaps no other author this period of German history and was himself a late arrival, publishing his first novel in 1878, when he was fifty-nine. Unlike Balzac's France and Trollope's England, Fontane's culture was only beginning its imperial days when he commenced his twenty-year career as a novelist. Because his case and the case of German imperialism in the nineteenth century are unique, it may be useful first to chart the gradual and simultaneous arrival, in Fontane's earlier works, of two inextricable and important aspects of his later novels: the world and the city. As Berlin's rise parallels the increasing interconnectedness of the globe, the enchantment once represented by distant places is drastically transformed, as is the perception of rural Prussia from Fontane's early novels. While Fontane's sweeping novelistic debut, the historical *Vor dem Sturm*, focuses

---

1. Amery joined an international chorus of scholars in responding to defenses of German imperial claims. In 1936, for example, Johannsen and Kraft published their stern report on what they call *Das Kolonialproblem Deutschlands* (1936), translated with little delay into English as *Germany's Colonial Problem* (1937). They laud "Herr Hitler, the Leader and Chancellor," in the preface, and appeal to the issue of "the unequal distribution of the earth's surface" (6–7). The slew of rebuttals in subsequent publications include Amery's book (1940); *Germany's Claim to Colonies*, the Royal Institute of International Affairs' official and critical 1938 response to expressions of "Germany's right to share in the work of world colonization" (3); Taylor (1938); and Bullock (1939), who debunks the German need for *Raum*. Bullock recalls that Germany was only the fourth most densely populated European country, with roughly half the density of the Netherlands, the most populous (270).

2. Hansen's study of German colonialism traces the German imperial impulse to around or before 1815, as Said also does, citing Taylor (*Culture and Imperialism* 58–59). Kwame sets the date much later, at 1884 (97). Brunschwig locates fifteenth-century commercial expansion by (largely Hanseatic) German interests as the root of later imperial expansion.

on an emergent Prussia within a traumatized Europe, his fiction over the next eight years depicts a unified Germany that becomes increasingly open to and enmeshed in the wide world. This process culminates in the depiction of greater mobility in 1886's underestimated *Cécile*, and the moment at which, in that novel's words, "Berlin becomes a metropolis" [Berlin wird Weltstadt] (I.2.250).[3]

(a) Nation and World in Fontane's Early Fiction

"German cultural studies comes belatedly to the investigation of colonialism and postcoloniality"—so begins the introduction to the groundbreaking collection of essays on the German *Imperialist Imagination* edited by Sara Friedrichsmeyer, Sara Lennox, and the late Susanne Zantop (1). They resist, though, the notion of belatedness in German imperialism itself, because "the term implies . . . that there was a proper moment for colonialism" (19). Yet others, like Todd Kontje and Nina Berman, have readily accepted what the historical facts bear out: that German colonial projects on any national level began well after those of other European nations. This delay is a direct result of what Russell Berman calls "Germany's ambivalent situation within Europe," which gives rise, in his opinion, to a "German colonial discourse" that is "interesting because it is different from the more emphatically universalizing claims of British and French colonial discourses" (10). The above sections on Balzac and Trollope have argued that what Berman sees as "emphatically universalizing" in British and French colonial discourse is actually more complex, especially in the literary evocations of this discourse. Yet Berman's attempts to separate Germany from Britain and France are indicative of a few larger problems in attempts by Germanists to engage in the ongoing examination of imperialism from the perspective of cultural studies.[4] As Berman himself makes clear, the imperial project was not a strictly nationalized one; Germans participated in important voyages like those of Cook, whose cartographer, Johann Reinhold Forster, Berman profiles at length. Adhering to a rigidly national view of imperialism encourages one to ignore imperialism writ large. One of the most intriguing chapters in Fontane's *Vor dem Sturm*, in which a tale from Greenland with openly

---

3. Translators invariably render *Weltstadt* as *metropolis*, and so has Radcliffe in his translation of *Cécile*, but it is important to keep in mind the idea of the *Welt* or *world* in the German word.

4. Berman has expressed discomfort at the trend toward "cultural studies" and away from more traditional historiography. He asks, "How does one verify, for example, observations about historical fantasies?" ("Der ewige Zweite" 22). He explains the rise of such approaches in *Germanistik* circles by pointing out that "German colonialism [is], because of its brevity, relatively poor in empirical material," implying that scholars have had to make more out of less evidence (23).

colonial importance is told at length, relates to multinational religious imperialism in a Danish colony. Moreover, *Cécile*'s Herr von Gordon, an avowed participant in various British colonial projects and in the construction of the technological infrastructure responsible for the shrinking of the world, is obviously pertinent to any reading of Fontane invested in empire, despite the fact that Gordon does not serve as a stand-in for a specifically German imperialism.

Germanists interested in confronting imperialism in German literature have tended toward one of two strategies, both of which help to explain the reception of certain of Fontane's works. These two approaches choose between the analysis of colonialist fantasy and colonialist history, a problematic dichotomy that neglects the mutually reinforcing nature of the two terms. Edward Said, one recalls, sees both history and fantasy in the Orientalist mindset. Susanne Zantop's important study of *Colonial Fantasies: Conquest, Family, and Nation in Precolonial Germany, 1770–1870* focuses, as the title implies, on the structures of knowledge that contributed to the desire to obtain colonies. Zantop specifies that she is "less concerned with the colonial reality of the late nineteenth century than with the formation of a sense of German difference" (3) and of "exclusivity and moral superiority ... constructed in the writings of eighteenth- and nineteenth-century authors" (8).[5] Consider, then, on the other hand, the work of Nina Berman and John Noyes, who both focus on literature specifically of or about the German colonies or on orientalist travel fantasies like Karl May's *Orientzyklus* (1881–1888).[6] The result of this methodological split—between attention to *either* domestic colonial fantasies *or* distant colonial realities—is a lack of scholarship on domestic realities (and thus the entire realist canon) in the burgeoning German empire. We thus lose the opportunity to investigate the subtle but important ways in which the imperialist shrinking of the world brings colonial difference into the domestic sphere and allows it to complicate the act of representation. For this reason, Judith Ryan's essay on "The Chinese Ghost" in *Effi Briest* and Claudius Sittig's article on Gieshübler's servant, Mirambo, in that same novel, represent an interesting development in such readings of Fontane, because they attempt to reconcile the two

---

5. In this sense, Zantop's work seems only peripherally to address colonialism as a unique phenomenon separable from more general racism with colonialist inflections. This is equally true of Kontje's central chapter on Herder. Such methodologies are similar to those of Holocaust studies and the manner in which a culture of German superiority may have provided the underlying potential for catastrophic action. Nina Berman's and John Noyes's work relies on a methodology organized specifically around colonial concerns, rather than more abstract notions of otherness, and yet their work simultaneously relies on texts set only in the colonies. Russell Berman's essay, "Der ewige Zweite," offers a nice, cogent documenting of general means of grappling with colonialism in German cultural and literary studies.

6. Claudius Sittig's definition of *Kolonialliteratur* adds the element of propagandism: "By 'Kolonialliteratur,' I understand any literature whose setting [Schauplatz] is the German colonies and which makes a propagandistic contribution to political agitation for colonialism" (546–47).

Chapter Seven: Berlin Wird Weltstadt ~ 159

strategies. Ryan aims to subject German novels to the sort of analyses she claims already exist in studies of English literature, showing that a novel like *Effi Briest* is "in some sense 'about' empire even though it does not always make this explicit" (367). It is important that she chooses, as exemplars from the English canon, *Great Expectations* and *Jane Eyre*. Ryan considers the manner in which empire is coded and written into German domestic life and German realism not necessarily as pure fantasy, but as an increasingly palpable presence and socioeconomic reality. This sort of approach permits us to chart, within Fontane's early fiction, the increased fictional profile of the notions of both empire and the imperial city. Both are central to the fate of disenchantment as it is portrayed in and troubled by nineteenth-century realist fiction.

Vor dem Sturm is a fitting debut for Fontane's novelistic output, because it introduces certain narrative habits and thematic game that remain important throughout his œuvre. A story of the first stirrings of Prussian nationalism against Napoleon's troops in the winter of 1812–13, the novel is set in and around the fictional Hohen-Vietz, located in Brandenburg, just north of Frankfurt on the banks of the Oder. The centripetal importance of Berlin is already palpable, if muted, in the novel; Fontane sets several important scenes there, and the city's role as a sort of national indicator is implied by the quick manner in which Lewin, just arrived from Berlin, is immediately asked how "the mood" [die Stimmung] there is (I.3.33). The empirical narrative epistemology of *Vor dem Sturm* is recognizable from Fontane's extensive earlier travel writings, as observations are laid out in detail and then followed by insights into them, the same strategy we saw in the novels of Balzac discussed above. Proceeding by vision and deduction, this approach sits well with the occasional detective elements in Fontane's fiction: the investigation of the burglary at Hohen-Vietz in *Vor dem Sturm*'s chapter called "The Search," for example, or the "half-detective novel" Ernst Bloch saw in Fontane's *Unterm Birnbaum* (*Under the Pear Tree*, 1885) (Bloch 261). At one point in *Vor dem Sturm*, in what amounts to a metacommentary on poetic language by the pastor Seidentopf, poetry is praised not for its sentiment but for its optics and acoustics: after reciting a stanza describing a wedding party in great detail, Seidentopf exclaims, "That is what I call language. I can *see* the bridegroom in his worsted waistcoat and *hear* them all clicking their heels together as they dance" (I.3.111; my emphases). Following this empirical predilection, all events of questionable veracity—that is, events with supernatural implications—are offered only framed within stories told by characters, so that the narrator's and the novel's empirical sympathies are never tested. This strategy has its precedents in German fiction in the nineteenth century, extending back at least to Jeremias Gotthelf's *Die schwarze Spinne* (*The Black Spider*,

1842) and Annette von Droste-Hülshoff's *Die Judenbuche* (*The Jews' Beech Tree*, 1842). Empirically dubious events are embedded within characters' tales and gossip, safely isolated from a determinedly objective and empiricist narrator. Fontane's narrator is well aware of what gets termed "the romantic need for the spectral [Spukhaft] and dreadful" or, later, the "need for specters and ghosts" [Spuk- und Gespensterbedürfnis] (I.3.22; I.3.77). Such "romantic" needs are contained outside of Berlin in *Vor dem Sturm*, but they already foreshadow Effi Briest's longing for the Chinese ghost.

A point of contact and contrast between *Vor dem Sturm* and Balzac's *Peau de chagrin* illustrates to what extent Fontane's early fiction seems uninterested in questions of the larger world into which Germany will "belatedly" venture. The hobby of collecting in *Vor dem Sturm* certainly owes more to Scott's *Antiquary* than to Balzac, but reading it against the collection in *La Peau de chagrin* is illuminating. I argued above that the international make-up of the items in Balzac's antiquities shop attests to the function of Paris as a sort of nexus of imperial undertakings, as artifacts from the Americas mingle with those from Asia, Africa, and Europe. The whole world, objectified, is in Balzac's Paris, but Fontane's collections in *Vor dem Sturm* are almost entirely composed of ancient German finds, especially the archaeological remains of the Wends assembled by Pastor Seidentopf, "a passionate collector" (I.3.84). Major-General von Bamme, too, collects "Germanic" [Urgermanisch] artifacts (I.3.151), as does Chamberlain von Medewitz (I.3.153–54). Fontane's novel remains largely in the same confines as the architect's collection in Goethe's *Die Wahlverwandschaften* (1809), whose narrator states that "Most of these objects were German in origin [Ursprung]" (6.367). In fact, the artifacts from furthest afield in the *Vor dem Sturm*'s collections were "excavated at Herculanum and Pompeii" (I.3.573). Fontane's fiction still has not left Europe. These collections, with their archaeological devotion to the prehistory of Germany, can be read in conjunction with a larger, unstated purpose of the text as a novelistic construction of a German nation.

Saree Makdisi argues, in *Romantic Imperialism*'s persuasive reading of Scott's *Waverley*, that Scott essentially uses a past episode (the novel's subtitle, of course, is *'Tis Sixty Years Since*) to build Scotland as against England in the novel, by creating a history and a geography on which a nation might stand, independent.[7] Heide Grieve, Hans Vilmar Geppert, and Lambert Shears have probed the debt that Fontane's novel owes to Scott's novels—and especially to *Waverley*—and so one could suggest that *Vor dem Sturm*'s apparent European insularity and intensely Prussian focus imply a

---

7. See also Trumpener's chapter "National Character, Nationalist Plots: National Tale and Historical Novel in the Age of *Waverley*, 1806–1830," in *Bardic Nationalism* (128–57).

project akin to the one Makdisi sees at work in *Waverley*. Indeed, Fontane's novel explicitly knits Germany together at times, as if mapping out a coherent national space. Space is crucial to the novel's conception of history and narrative; this much is clear at the outset of Aunt Schorlemmer's tale from Greenland. She asks, "Well, what shall we begin with?" [Nun, womit beginnen wir?] and Renate, eager to hear the story, answers, "With the beginning, naturally; that is, with the land itself [mit dem Lande selbst]" (I.3.254). The most significant instance of this land-based approach introduces the climactic battle near the end of the novel, which is preceded by a reconnoitring tour that shows the characters and the narrator piecing the region together into a continuity: "The next village was Clessin," one paragraph begins, and the next paragraph continues the progression, "And then Cliestow too lay behind them" (I.3.600). The idea of national unification is further alluded to in the collapsing foreignness of other Germans in the build-up to battle. Bamme asks Bernd von Vitzewitz about the standard being flown by Revenue Officer Mollhausen of Lietzen, who has come to join the fight: "The standard that the old guy is carrying?" Bamme asks, "Red and white. I've never seen it before in all my life" (I.3.595). The notion of foreignness *within* Germany is bundled alongside national unity in this image; Bamme may not have seen that particular flag before, being flown by his soon-to-be comrade in arms, but the red in it looks beyond an isolated Prussia to the red of the German imperial flag. Fontane might also refer to this imperial red later in *Der Stechlin* (1897), when a character considers (and finally rejects) the idea of repairing a tattered black-and-white Prussian flag with a bit of "red" [was Rotes] (I.5.15).[8]

This brief discussion of the quite long *Vor dem Sturm* highlights two important things. First, Fontane's fiction does not start out in the globally cosmopolitan territory it will inhabit from approximately 1886 (in the form of *Cécile*) on, with agile plotlines that can carry mobile characters all over the world and back or, at the very least, with characters who can claim to have traveled all over the world and back. Second, despite what appears, on close examination, to be a gradual if not belated insertion of Germany into the world between *Vor dem Sturm* and *Cécile*, Fontane's primary interests and narrative strategies remain constant, even if he consistently develops more sophisticated means of elaborating them. Space is of persistent importance in his fiction, and the anecdotal elements of colonialism in Aunt Schorlemmer's story of Kaiarnak hint in 1878 at an imperial theme that will become less anecdotal as Fontane's fiction progresses. (Some Danish writers—Peter Høeg, for example—have even begun reckoning in their novels the lingering

---

8. The revolutionary associations of the color red are, to be sure, another means of reading this passage in *Der Stechlin*. Without arguing for a sort of deliberate narrative construction of nationhood in *Vor dem Sturm*, Osinski and Vom Hofe both nevertheless read the novel as an exercise in patriotism.

postcolonial relationship between Denmark and Greenland.) Similarly, the theme of empire begins to refuse the Romantic shade it possesses in Kaiarnak's story, which reads like Chateaubriand's *Atala* (1801) or *René* (1802), or Longfellow, perhaps even Cooper.[9] This is not to suggest that there are only Germans in the Germany of *Vor dem Sturm*. Indeed, Berlin is home to a host of Europeans from France, Russia, and Poland, for example, the result of Napoleonic upheavals and resettlements. But with the exception of the Greenland interlude, which segues into a triumph of religious imperialism and ultimately becomes a stock conversion story, one never leaves Europe in *Vor dem Sturm*.

Increased mobility becomes explicit in *L'Adultera* (1882), Fontane's fourth work of fiction and the first to be set in his contemporary Berlin.[10] Fontane's fiction begins consistently to see outside of Germany. Ebenezer Rubehn returns to Berlin after time abroad in New York, and the novella sends its protagonists, Rubehn and Melanie van der Straaten, on a makeshift honeymoon to Italy. Planning a similar honeymoon itinerary in *Schach von Wuthenow* (1883), Schach and his betrothed, Victoire von Carayon, consider going even further, as they plan

> to cross over to Sicily and sail past the islands of the Sirens, "whether unfettered or tied to the mast he would leave up to Victoire and her trust." And then they would want to go on to Malta. Not because of Malta, no, certainly not. But on the way to it there would be the site where the mysterious Black Continent would for the very first time hold discourse in reflections and mirages with the Hyperborean native of fog and snow. (I.1.672)

Schach von Wuthenow postulates a mixture of north and south, of Europe and Africa unexpressed in Fontane's previous fiction. The broader gaze and the more widely imagined mobility are, admittedly, largely cosmetic in that novella and in *L'Adultera*. However, they become crucial to *Cécile*'s presentation of Berlin and of Herr von Gordon, who comes to stand for the wider world, its immanent reduction, and the consequences of this reduction for Berlin as it enters the global stage and becomes a *Weltstadt*.

---

9. Chateaubriand's *René* was published in the same year as his essay *Génie du christianisme*, in which he spells out the parable of the Mandarin that Balzac finds so useful in *Goriot*. If the Kaiarnak episode in *Vor dem Sturm* betrays the possible influence of these writers, Hayens suggests that Fontane made similar stylistic borrowings—from Cooper and Harte in particular—in the writing of the American half of *Quitt* in 1891 (101).

10. *Grete Minde* (1880) and *Ellernklipp* (1881) are both set in the rural past, in the seventeenth and eighteenth centuries, respectively, in Tangermünde and in "one of the northern valleys of the Harz," the future destination of *Cécile* (I.1.103).

(b) Region, Romance, and the Rails

Cécile is the exception amongst the fiction Fontane produced in the early- or mid-1880s, which has not received as much scholarly attention as his major, later works, like *Irrungen, Wirrungen* (*Delusions, Confusions*, 1888), *Unwiederbringlich* (*Beyond Recall*, 1892), *Effi Briest*, or *Der Stechlin*. Yet it has often been read as an introduction to themes—adultery especially, or general decadence—that pervade Fontane's other novels and novellas. Friedrich writes, for example, that *Cécile* "is valid above all as a preliminary stage [Vorstufe] for Fontane's great Berlin novels at the end of the eighties and in the nineties. Fontane takes the first step, here, into a new area: the representation of contemporary Prussian nobility" (520). *Cécile* has more value in and of itself than Friedrich might allow, yet this novel is indeed useful toward an exploration of Fontane's development of Berlin as a fictional site. As Henry Garland notes, in the introduction to his *The Berlin Novels of Theodor Fontane*,

> Most of the "Berlin novels" are not concentrated solely on the capital. *Vor dem Sturm* alternates between Berlin and the New March. The scene of *L'Adultera* shifts for a time to Italy; *Cécile* begins in the Harz mountains. *Effi Briest* includes the Old March and Pomerania. *Die Poggenpuhls* has an interlude in Silesia, Der *Stechlin* commutes between the Middle March and Berlin, and the posthumous *Mathilde Möhring* moves briefly to West Prussia. In all of these novels Berlin is the focus and pivot, and its centripetal pull is constantly evident. (vii)

Cécile stands out in this group as a novel that, according to Garland, begins elsewhere and moves surely and irrefutably into Berlin; moreover, the novel highlights this movement, just as it seems to underscore movement in general. The new mobility in *Cécile* demonstrates the novel's substantial investment in concerns of colonialism and globalizing commerce, and their effect on the city that Garland rightly singles out as "focus and pivot." The undercurrents that critics have seen in *Effi Briest*—adultery, duels, empire—are already present in *Cécile*, and their negotiation in the novel offers a useful context for the next chapter's discussion of *Effi Briest*.

Cécile, as a novel, is actually born in motion, on a northbound train. Garland's claim that it begins in the Harz mountains, only later moving to Berlin, misses this. The novel's first word, "Thale," is spoken on the train platform in Berlin by Colonel Pierre St. Arnaud, Cécile's husband, as he gives their destination to the porter (I.2.141). Once St. Arnaud and Cécile are seated on board and the train has started to move, St. Arnaud begins "to study a map marked with thick lines which showed the railway network in the immediate vicinity of Berlin. He did not get far with his orientation [Orientierung], however, and it was only when they skirted the edge of the Zoological Gardens that he seemed to get his bearings" (I.2.142). Already in the opening salvos of the novel, Fontane's narrator introduces Berlin, the railways, the newness of the railways—St. Arnaud, for one, appears unfamiliar with their route—and the maps meant to render them navigable. The entire first chapter is devoted to this journey, the narration of which positions Thale far from Berlin, but not too far; it is, after all, within a day's journey by train. Yet the narrator's lingering on this journey simultaneously allows for the introduction of tension into the relationship between St. Arnaud and Cécile—it is clear from the reaction to them on the train that there is some mystery in their past—and the spatial articulation of the distance between Thale and Berlin as we leave the urban:

> Soon one passed this congestion of streets [Straßenenge] . . . and the journey continued over the Havel bridges, first Potsdam Bridge, then Werder. . . . After an interval [Cécile] opened her eyes once more and looked out at the landscape, which was constantly changing: cornfields and orchards and then again broad expanses of heath. . . . And now the conversation came to a stop again, and faster and faster they sped on, first past Brandenburg with its St Godehard Church and then past Magdeburg and its cathedral. At Oschersleben they were joined by the Leipzig train, and at somewhat slower speed because the ascent was beginning to make itself felt, they travelled on towards Quedlinburg, behind whose abbey church the heights of the Brocken already rose up. (I.2.142–44)

The narrative makes the most out of the distance to the final destination, the Ten Pounds Hotel, positioning it at quite a fictional distance from Berlin, the story's origin.

Heinrich Heine's essay *Die Harzreise*, which was first published in 1826, lends dependably romantic shadings to the region portrayed in the first half of *Cécile*. Fontane clearly has a literary precedent and tradition from which to draw, but, as the recodings of romantic space in Trollope's novels demonstrate, nothing can be taken for granted later in the nineteenth century. The deliberate performance of the distance between the city and the Harz as a rural tourist site is just one important factor in *Cécile*'s rendering of the Harz in romantic, mysterious, nonurban light. The distance is necessary, if Fontane's narrator is to re-secure the rural Harz as a site of potential romance in the face of the very unromantic means of journeying there. Paul Youngman has argued that the rails in *Cécile* are a marriage of myth and technology, but their effect on the novel's geography is complex.

Youngman (95) and Helen Chambers (106) both emphasize the so-called *Hexentanzplatz*, "Witches' Dance Floor," and a scene in which the narrator claims that "it almost sounded as though a constant succession of trains was coming" down from this mystically named place (I.2.207). Heine's *Harzreise* mentions a hill called *der Hexenaltar* (60), and, bearing this in mind, Gordon makes it clear that the romance is in the region and not the rails, that it is the land if anything that is bewitched: "Wherever one stays one is under some obligation to acquaint oneself with the characteristic features of the region, in Samarkand the temple doors and their guards, in the desert the king of the desert, and in the Harz the witches. For the witches here are a local product [Landesprodukt]" (I.2.165). Cécile herself repeats the regional ties later, saying that Gordon was right (I.2.259). Trains are momentarily linked, in the Harz, with talk of the supernatural, but they eventually become again a call back to reality and the urban. The narrator explicitly opposes the railways to the realm of dreams and fantasies, in a manner that also links this new technology to the city. Leaning against her husband, Cécile "remained in this reverie [Träumen] until suddenly the signals were changed along the railway line and the sharp sound of the departure bell rang out from Thale. And not a minute later the whistle of the locomotive was heard, followed immediately by a coughing and snorting and now the train was steaming scarcely a hundred paces away past the Lindenberg" (I.2.207). After the train passes, St. Arnaud points out that it is headed for Berlin, and Cécile, the romantic, turns away from it.

While the rails are an interruption to dreams and are linked to the urban, Thale and its environs are portrayed quite differently. The painter Fräulein Rosa complains to Gordon that Thale is being ruined by "too much dust and too many Sunday trippers" (I.2.220), but the novel itself undercuts this claim. One of the first descriptions of the local color in Thale is Gordon's of an abandoned "villa densely overgrown with wild vines" (I.2.157). Cécile calls it "magical" [zauberhaft] and remarks that it "is indeed the enchanted castle of fairy-tale" [ist ja das ›verwunschene Schloß‹ im Märchen]. Gordon quickly removes the villa into a darker Gothic: "A dark spirit [finsterer Geist] goes through this house and its last occupant shot himself here, by that window (the second-to-last one on the left), and when I look at it, it is as though he is still looking out and seeking the happiness that he could not find. Places with blood on them fill me with dread [Plätze, daran Blut klebt, erfüllen mich mit Grauen]." Later, a guesthouse is likened to "a medieval Rodenstein castle" as even the infrastructure of tourism is made over to fit an image of the rural past (I.2.227). Despite his skepticism, St. Arnaud plays on the relationship of the rural and the Romantic toward the end of their stay in Thale; gently ridiculing Cécile for seeing a blackbird as "unheimlich," St. Arnaud tells her,

"Those are feelings one gets when lost in the woods. But we shall be spared that little bit of romanticism [dies Stück Romantik]" (I.2.236). St. Arnaud frames the rural in the very romantic terms in which the novel in general appears to view it.

St. Arnaud's recourse to an idea of being lost, though, merits closer attention, for the act of losing oneself speaks to an unaccomplished navigation, a failure of familiarization, and thus the sort of shaky new ground of uncertainty and complication. I argued above that becoming lost serves, in Balzac's *La Fille aux yeux d'or*, to render a familiar Paris foreign, in essence reenchanting it, and that the impossibility of becoming lost in Trollope's London—except for Felix Carbury when drunk—reveals the extent to which the English capital has been rendered all too compact, knowable, and navigable. St. Arnaud, in *Cécile*, rehearses these same questions. While he casually relates being lost to *Romantik*, Cécile herself pairs being lost—in spatial terms—both with romanticism and adultery, in a revealing conversation with her husband. Following a brief discussion of Gordon, St. Arnaud says,

> "I should be curious to know what you might be inclined not to find trivial."
>
> "Well, the Regensteiner[11], for instance. He is so much more romantic. And if it can't be the Regensteiner, well then, adventures, tiger-hunting, the desert, getting lost . . . "
>
> "Geographically or morally?"
>
> "Both." (I.2.193)

Under the larger umbrella of the romantic, Cécile links a lack of geographical orientation to a lack of moral orientation, speaking favorably of both, and this particular evocation of the spatial possibility of adultery becomes central to *Effi Briest*, as does the idea of "lostness." More important, this entire exchange occurs as a result of Cécile's denigrating Gordon's professional work, his involvement in international projects laying telegraph wires. Cécile is unimpressed by such labor, and, as one might expect, she specifically opposes it to romance. The opposition is essential, for it complicates the overall picture of Gordon, whom one is tempted to read as a mysterious if not exotic energy in the text.

---

11. Most likely an allusion to the exploits of Prince Albrecht II of Regenstein (1310–1349), which had recently been recounted in Julius Wolff's *Der Raubgraf: Eine Geschichte aus dem Harzgau* (1884). The ruins of the Regenstein castle are nearby, in the Harz.

(c) Business as Usual: Berlin and the Banality of the Foreign

> What excites the traveler is the new; when the foreign [das Fremde] has become the everyday, it looks completely different.
>
> —Freytag, *Soll und Haben*

Herr Robert von Gordon-Leslie, a civil engineer, is not quite an analogue to other narrative complications from outside domestic space, like the Magic Skin or the Girl With the Golden Eyes in Balzac's novels, or Augustus Melmotte in Trollope's *The Way We Live Now*. He considers Germany his "Heimat," and Cécile too seems to accept this. Yet much is made in *Cécile* of Gordon's Scottish roots and ancestry, mostly by St. Arnaud, and this Celtic background accounts for a distinctly romantic side to his character. On a day trip while at Thale, St. Arnaud hands Cécile a plaid travel rug, joking to her, "Herr von Gordon will drape it artistically about you; he owes that to his Gordon clan. And then we shall have you as a Highland apparition between us. Lady Macbeth or something of the sort" (I.2.237). Later, St. Arnaud warns Cécile of his fear "that once [Gordon] has got something into his head then he'll charge at things head foremost [so will er auch mit dem Kopf durch die Wand]. The Scottish still haunts [spukt] through him. All Scots are headstrong [hartköpfig]" (I.2.258). The use of the verb *spuken* is curious but further highlights a fantastic romanticism in Gordon and in the value of Scottishness. To Cécile and St. Arnaud, Gordon's romantic aura has precise literary associations. Gordon gives Cécile "the impression of being a born guide and scout [Pfadfinder]," and St. Arnaud instantly associates Cécile's word "Pfadfinder" with the Cooper novel of that name, *The Pathfinder* (1840), first translated into and published in German in 1841 (I.2.157). Continuing his wife's thought, St. Arnaud sees in Gordon "an echo of [Cooper's] *Leatherstocking*" [Reminiszenz aus ›Lederstrumpf‹]. A closer examination of Gordon's name, however—an examination which the narrator openly invites—stresses the complications in Gordon's romance. His position between enchantment and disenchantment is a deeply ambivalent one.

Gordon's name is not actually "Gordon." When St. Arnaud asks him if he is related to the infamous British General Charles George Gordon, he replies, "No, my dear colonel, hardly even related, for I am actually a Leslie. The name Gordon only came into our family by adoption [durch Adoption]" (I.2.154). Nowhere does the novel explain precisely why or how the name was "adopted" into Gordon's family, but it proves very convenient for the novel, as a means of rendering Gordon simultaneously mysterious and indefinable *and* suggestive of a concrete historical association. The other characters' reactions capitalize on these multiple possibilities. The Berliners—so the narrator calls the two unnamed members of the tourist party at the Ten Pounds Hotel—envision him as "straight out of *Wallenstein's Death*" [der reine ›Wallensteins Tod‹] (I.2.156). Encouraged by the romantic possibilities inherent in the presence of a Schiller character at the hotel, they wryly comment on the beginnings of tension between Gordon and St. Arnaud, knowing that St. Arnaud has already allegedly killed one rival in a duel.[12] Hungry for excitement at the prospect of such tension, they relish the thought that "we really could see something at the end" [da könnt man am Ende noch was erleben], clumsily foreshadowing the novel's fatal conclusion. It is St. Arnaud, though, the military man, who adduces the less literary, more historical namesake for the novel's Gordon, and in so doing he ushers in the first of many allusions in the novel to British imperialism. As Fontane was writing *Cécile*, which he began in June of 1884, British General Charles George Gordon was fighting to retain command of Khartoum, to which Mahdists under the command of the Sudanese Muhammad Ahmad laid siege for ten months between March 13, 1884, and January 26, 1885. The siege concluded with the death of Gordon and the British loss of the city. The name of *Cécile*'s Gordon may only be an "adoption," but it constructs him as a self-consciously complex character, weighted on one side by heroic literary associations, and on the other by British colonialist projects of which Fontane was a savage critic,[13] that Cécile herself labels "trivial," and that the novel will equate with disenchantment.

This second, disenchanted, "trivial" side of Gordon is elaborated in a lengthy description of his accomplishments by St. Arnaud:

[H]is career as chevalier errant begins as trivially as you could imagine. He was stationed at first with the pioneers in Magdeburg, then with the railway battalion under Golz, a unit that is usually much too clever and shrewd to distinguish

12. On duels in Fontane, see Radecke.
13. Roch, in his study of Fontane's Berlin, describes the circumstances surrounding Fontane's most strident and prescient outburst on British colonialism, in a letter to an English friend:

In 1897, at the outbreak of the worst uprising that the English had yet had to defeat there, Fontane wrote to [the London doctor James] Morris:

English rule in India *must* fall apart, and it is a wonder that it has held to the present day. It is failing, not because of mistakes or crimes—all of that counts for little in politics. No, it is failing because the clock has run out. . . . The time of the conquistadors, where twenty thieves could drive much more civilized people apart and burn alive the kings of these better peoples, just because those thieves had muskets—this brutal time is past, and juster days are upon us. The whole politics of colonization is lunacy. . . . With a shudder I read now daily of the dubious measures England wants to take in order to preserve the old way [den alten Zustand] at any price. Up to now one could think, looking at England, that there was at least *one* people in Europe who still believed in another ideal than a "million soldiers." If England willingly abandons this colossal preference, which is inseparable from human understanding [Menschenverstand], and begins forcing a rifle into everyone's hands, then England will fall from the heights that she has held until today. (281)

itself by falling into debt. But every rule has its exceptions. In short, he could not maintain his position and emigrated, if one can speak of emigration in such a situation, to England, where he hoped to put his scientific knowledge to use in a practical way. And he succeeded in doing this and went to Suez in the mid-seventies to lay a cable through the Red Sea and Persian Gulf in the service of a big English company. You won't be familiar with the geography but I can show you on the map [Du wirst nicht orientiert sein, aber ich zeige dir's auf der Karte]. . . . Later he entered Persian service and then, after completion under his overall direction of a telegraphic link between the two main cities of the country, Russian service. . . . He is now managing director of the same English firm in whose service he started his career and is at the moment engaged in plans to lay a new cable in the North Sea. (I.2.192)

The geographical range of Gordon's activities compares favorably with Melmotte's in *The Way We Live Now*, but the focus on telegraphy and the military is almost absolute in Gordon's professional life, which seems to alternate comfortably between military service and the laying of cable. Fontane does not make as much of this as Trollope does toward a thematization of the telegraph's contribution to the shrinking of the wide world—recall the moment at which Melmotte turns the western United States into "suburbs of London" through the use of the telegraph. But Gordon's travels on behalf of the telegraph manage a similar feat. St. Arnaud mentions Russia, Persia, the Suez, the Red Sea, and the North Sea, but Gordon can also casually refer to having seen the Himalayas, for example, and come back somewhat unimpressed (I.2.210, I.2.215). A dinner in Berlin, to which Gordon is invited by a business colleague, sums up for Gordon an idea that *Effi Briest* expresses even more drastically, the idea that the world has become small. "The evening in Charlottenburg," the narrator reports, "had been delightful and Gordon had once again convinced himself 'how small the world was.' Mutual friends had been discovered, in Bremen, England, New York and last of all in Berlin itself" (I.2.249).

It is surely not a coincidence that the novel reinforces Gordon's perception of the smallness of the world in introducing the very passage during which he will declare Berlin a metropolis, a world-city. Fontane's narrative raises, within this same passage, the possibility of Berlin's value as a site of disenchantment and of Gordon's contribution to this disenchantment. Gordon, the Civil Engineer, has already been linked to science by St. Arnaud, who claims that Gordon moved "to England, where he hoped to put his scientific knowledge to use in a practical way" [nach England, woselbst er seine wissenschaftlichen Kenntnisse praktisch zu verwerten hoffte] (I.2.192). The rationalization and exploitation of science are marked here, because the German *verwerten* denotes *to put to use*, as Radcliffe's translation has it, but carries the etymological traces of *worth* or *value;* Gordon goes to England in order to give value to his scientific knowledge, to make it worth something by using it for commercial ends. Gordon himself reinforces his ordered and rational side when, surveying the scattered objects in his newly acquired room in Berlin, he says, in what feels scripted as a sort of declaration, "And now, . . . I suppose I ought to create order out of this chaos" [Und nun sollt' ich wohl . . . in diesem Chaos Ordnung stiften] (I.2.249). Gordon's presence seems set consistently to invoke and yet frustrate enchantment once in Berlin, until the duel at the end. When he surprises Cécile and her guest, Privy Councillor Hedemeyer, in her box at the opera, the narrator's *style indirect libre* reveals Hedemeyer's view of Gordon as "the 'Canadian' who in the great world outside had broken free from 'Europe's whitewashed politeness'" [de[r] draußen in der Welt von »Europens übertünchter Höflichkeit« frei gewordenen »Kanadier«] (I.2.300). Like Cécile's and St. Arnaud's earlier associations of Gordon with the frontiers of Cooper, the reference here is also a literary one, to the first lines of Johann Gottfried Seume's "The Hospitality of the Huron" ("Die Gastfreundschaft des Huronen," 1801) and its "Canadian, who did not yet know Europe's whitewashed politeness" [Kanadier, der noch Europens / übertünchte Höflichkeit nicht kannte]. Fontane's narrator has changed the Huron from one who "did not know" European politeness to one who "had broken free" from it. The change is significant, because it parallels the novel's careful reversal of Gordon's alleged ignorance and savagery, with all their romantic connotations. St. Arnaud, incensed at Gordon's treatment of Cécile, tells her that "Gordon is a man of breeding [von Familie], of polite society [*Welt*] and of discrimination, and such a man does not operate with *undetermined* purpose [handelt nicht ins Unbestimmte hinein]. He assesses the situation" (I.2.308; emphases mine). St. Arnaud's language returns Gordon to the reality of exchange (*einhandeln*), science, and order, far from contingencies (*das Unbestimmte*), and this is all linked to Gordon's embodiment of the *world* and his knowledge of its rules.

Gordon is, as St. Arnaud pronounces him to be, a man of the world. His arrival in Berlin coincides with its transformation to a declared *Weltstadt* in *Cécile*, and the novel frames this within a process of disenchantment and a progress expressed in terms of the foreign rendered accessible and familiar. Gordon's labors on behalf of telegraphy are just one example of this, and they depict a tightly bound globe in 1886 to which Gustav Freytag's *Soll und Haben* was yet unprepared to submit in 1855. Freytag's hero Anton Wohlfart revels at length in the romance and poetry he sees in global trade, but trade is only made romantic because the novel rejects the historical present. The narrator confesses early on to preferring and depicting the older arrangements of distance, a world "rare nowadays, when railroads and telegraphs unite sea and inland [See und Inland verbinden]. . . . Back then [Damals], the sea was far off" (47). The nostalgia of Freytag's setting[14] describes a business in which commerce is more difficult, subject to complication, and thus more poetic and heroic. Gordon undoes the distance in *Cécile*, however. His very anti-romantic notions of travel—an area in which one would have to consider him an expert of sorts—foreshadow the jaded view of the exotic in Wilhelm Raabe's *Stopfkuchen* (1890) or in Fontane's own *Effi Briest*, whose La Tripelli claims that, even in the middle of Africa, one is now bound to bump into an acquaintance. In a letter to his sister, Clothilde, Gordon writes, "I love journeys around the world and wouldn't want to miss them in the future, although I feel the passion diminishing, but on the other hand I am no friend of ordeals as such, and the more comfortably I can travel up and down the Congo, so much the better. Economy of forces [Ökonomie der Kräfte]. But enough of the Congo!" (I.2.186). Gordon would gladly trade romance for comfort, erasing the difference of distant, even exotic, places in exchange for ease and familiarity. Even his moments of fantasy in pursuit of Cécile are scripted as disenchantments. Thinking, en route to visit Cécile at home, that he can tell from the address which house the St. Arnauds occupy, Gordon says to himself

> They will be living in the Diebitsch house. A touch of the Alhambra, that is most appropriate for my beautiful Cécile. To be sure, she does have the almond eyes and the deeply melancholic strain of a Zoë or a Zuleika. Only the colonel, with all due respect, does not stem from the Aben Ceras, least of all does he represent the poetic end of their line. If I am to fit him into those Moorish regions à tout prix, then he is either the rebel leader Abdel Kader or a Riff pirate from the Moroccan coast. (I.2.252)

The reality is a slight disappointment, as it turns out; the St. Arnauds' house is "not the house with the Alhambra dome." Contrasting Berlin with Delhi, where he apparently had an affair, Gordon imagines that the sheer size of a metropolis like Berlin should make erotic dalliance easy: "What was possible

---

14. This nostalgia for an era before rails and wires is too often omitted from readings of Freytag's *Soll und Haben* in the light of globalization; most focus on a speech later in the book in which Anton sings the poetic praises of trade in goods as a sign that all beings are linked by "countless threads" (186). (See, for example, Ramponi 37–39.) Anton sees this linkage as poetic precisely because it is still only *metaphorical*, as objects "connect" people by moving from one to another. The earlier passage, which I cite, clearly opposes this with the newer *actual* linkage brought on by technology: railroads and the telegraph. It is this newer condition that the novel wishes to forget.

in an Indian garrison town must be much more so amidst the distraction of a capital city [innerhalb der Zerstreuungen einer großen Residenz]" (I.2.246). The plot of the novel proves him wrong, in a fierce and fatal rebuke. Berlin, it seems, is in fact too crowded for romantic affairs.[15]

A chance meeting in Fontane's crowded Berlin offers one of *Cécile*'s most striking pronouncements on the relationship of the disenchanted city to what is outside it, to what is, in the novel's words, simply *draußen*. The two tourists mentioned above, the natives of Berlin who relished the thought of romantic complications between St. Arnaud and Gordon in Thale, represent, according to Gordon, a stereotype of Berlin eccentricity that the novel will ultimately disappoint. When Gordon meets the two again, at random, in the metropolis, they are less than friendly, and less than interested in complication. Their behavior in the glass-covered pavilion at the Hôtel du Parc is marked by "pretended dignity" [gekünstelte Würde] and "ostentation" [Pomphaftigkeit] (I.2.253). Gordon remarks on the difference between the Berliners on tour and the Berliners at home, and voices his thoughts on the stereotype in a conversation with the proprietor of the establishment: "They were very different [ganz anders] there," Gordon claims, "rather loud, somewhat eccentric [sonderbar], so very Berlin-style [so berlinisch]." The proprietor laughs, responding, "It's always like that. True Berliners only really exist outside [draußen] and on journeys. At home [zu Hause] they are quite reasonable." The dampening effect of the city and the rationality of the domestic (the *zu Hause*) belie even entrenched cultural assumptions about the eccentricity of Berlin's inhabitants.

Fontane's later works often continue the description of Berlin and Germany as part of a larger, global system. There is constant talk of America and the ease of traveling there in *Irrungen, Wirrungen*, the work that followed *Cécile*, and both of these novels linger on the elephant cages in the Zoological Gardens in Berlin (I.2.343; I.2.142), convenient symbols of the domesticated exotic.[16] The opening lines of *Der Stechlin* even allegorize global intercon-

---

15. One year later, a character in Galdós's *Fortunata y Jacinta* gives stronger airing to this new urban claustrophobia in a warning against extra-marital impropriety: "Madrid may seem big, but it's very small—it's a village" (2.79).

16. In this light, *Quitt* (1891) distinguishes itself as an almost romantic throwback, as its protagonist flees the murder he commits in Germany by emigrating to America. As Christine Brieger has pointed out, though, while Fontane's America was culled partly from adventure stories by Cooper and Harte, Fontane's most significant source was the travel writings of his acquaintance Paul Lindau, published in 1885 as *Aus der neuen Welt* (301). The similarities to Dickens's *Martin Chuzzlewit* are also worth noting.

nectedness in a fundamentally geological manner, as the waterspouts of Lake Stechlin are said to be linked to the volcanic activity of Iceland, Java, and Hawaii (I.5.7). What *Der Stechlin* positions as a mysterious subterranean linkage, though, *Effi Briest*, with its constant references to the outer world and essential incorporation of figures from the supposed margins of that world, renders as the result of a shrinking and increasingly traversable global space. Critics have largely ignored the coding and construction of certain spaces and certain types of space in *Cécile*, focusing instead on the themes that stand out most explicitly; hence Hohendahl's verdict on the "cult of honor" in the novel (400), and Jung's attention to the historical contexts of militarism (202). Stephan, who notices a key difference between Thale and Berlin—there are witches in the Harz, one character claims—writes off these allusions to romance and the supernatural as "Männerphantasie" (135). Friedrich correctly notes the duality of the novel's setting, "between Harz and Berlin, between 'Spree and Havel,'" but the ramifications of this comparison in the narrative extend beyond an opposition of town and country or of crowded capital and open rural roads (535). Thale in the Harz expresses, for the narrator and the Berliners portrayed in *Cécile*, an area of possibility contrasted with Berlin's populous rationality. The world traveler and civil engineer Herr von Gordon-Leslie seems to oversee and announce Berlin's fictional transition to *Weltstadt* in the novel, and he exemplifies the ambivalence of enchantment. Partly painted as a savage Canadian or a savage Celt, yet partly rendered as the embodiment of technology and disillusion, Gordon emphasizes the worldliness of Berlin as it further integrates itself—both in Fontane's fiction and in historical fact—into the same increasingly interconnected global economy that destabilizes Trollope's *The Way We Live Now*.

In *Colonial Fantasies*, Susanne Zantop cites Sara Lennox's assertion that "the lack of a metropolis" in German imperial culture has, along with many other factors, "obscured the significance of colonial fantasies in the formation of German national identity and of race relations within Germany" (3). The notion of the city's centrality here is telling. However, while "the lack of a metropolis" may pertain to Germany's postcolonial period, with its national split and literally fractured capital, certainly Fontane's era and its novels not only conceived of Berlin as a metropolis, but actively wrote it as a metropolis. There is an obvious difficulty in envisioning a global scale within the more condensed narrative confines of the novella, and one might argue, given the popularity of the novella over the novel in much of the German nineteenth century, that this reduced narrative scope offers at least a partial explanation for the belated arrival of the world in nineteenth-century German prose fiction. As slim a work as it is, however, *Cécile* goes a long way toward articulating the Berlin that peoples much of Fontane's later fiction and often serves as geographical center. And *Cécile* does so through a cast of largely imported—although, admittedly, largely European—characters: St. Arnaud from France, Cécile from Silesia, and Gordon from everywhere. The narration of their coming to rest in one place suggests a consolidation of sorts. Long ago, Lukács recognized precisely this notion of urbanization when, in a brief discussion of Fontane in his essay on *German Literature in the Age of Imperialism*, he refers to the "poetry of the German metropolis that was just then coming into being" [Poesie der damals entstehenden deutschen Großstadt] (19).

CHAPTER EIGHT

THE IMAGINATIVE GEOGRAPHY OF *EFFI BRIEST*

It's the maps that are always dangerous.
—Theodor Fontane, *Effi Briest*

No, I merely mentioned his name. But a Chinese man is already a story in and of himself....
—Theodor Fontane, *Effi Briest*

One image in particular from Fontane's *Effi Briest* has readily facilitated recent critical attemps to implicate the novel in the discourse of imperialism: the Chinese ghost. Critics who focus on the colonial resonance of *Effi Briest* do so in deference to the ethnicity of the Chinese ghost, but these same readings tend to ignore the "ghost-ness" of the ghost. Colonial-minded exgeses shy away from the potential of quasi-spiritual matters in discussion of this quasi-spiritual matter, and the supernatural properties of the Chinese ghost remain largely unarticulated.[1] In a manner reminiscent of Said's "secular criticism" or J. P. Stern's absolutely empiricist realism, most critics have followed the example of Fontane's Baron von Innstetten and simply rationalized the ghost away. The apparition that haunts Effi has been explained in several different ways, all of which rigorously diminish its theoretically supernatural possibilities either as a psychic projection of Effi's repressed longings,[2] as a strictly pedagogical tool,[3] as the return of the oppressed colo-

---

1. Scholars who *do* focus on the ghost-ness of the ghost, like Chambers and Reichelt, tend to be uninterested in its ethnicity, or link it, like Hirsch and Guidry do, to classical mythology divorced from its spiritual origins.
2. See Subiotto, for example, who promises to fill the void left by readings that deal "with the Chinaman rather than his ghost, a sociological rather than a supernatural phenomenon" (137), only to admit later a preoccupation more "existential" than spiritual (148). Ingrid Schuster claims that "the Chinese man... represents young, passionate (that is, unconventional) love" (117). For Swales, the ghost is "the uncanny that derives from repressed psychic areas" (123), and Avery sees the ghost as "a symbol for a Chinese Wall of dissimulation and intolerance, an artificial barrier erected by reserve and guilt" (34). Müller-Seidel psychologizes the ghost as an "artificially introduced 'Symbol' of a psychologically motivated angst" ("Fontanes »Effi Briest«" 47).
3. See Gault and Jamison.

nial or female Other,[4] as a penchant for the exotic,[5] or as a systematically thematized allusion to political and social history during the period of the novel's production.[6] If the wealth of scholarly scrutiny of the Chinese ghost seems academic overkill, it must be remembered that virtually all critics emphasize the ghost's pivotal role as an enabler of the novel's plot, just as Fontane himself did when he famously labeled the apparition "a fulcrum for the whole story" [ein Drehpunkt für die ganze Geschichte] (*Fontanes Briefe* 386).[7]

I consider here *both* components of the Chinese ghost, because it functions as indicator of, simultaneously, the colonial and the supernatural. This more inclusive reading might contribute to the construction of a framework for reading problematically "realist" works whose fiction seems to generate itself out of figures imported from the cultural margins. Fontane's novel and its reception both highlight the cautious resistance to treatment of the supernatural and the implications that this resistance has for our critical capacity to account for certain aspects of the imperial imagination and of realist novels. As I demonstrated in the introduction, numerous critics and major novelists have theorized a deeply disenchanting backdrop to imperial ambitions, which they tether to the historical narrative of secularization. The work of these critics, and especially of Edward Said, helps to show how Fontane's novel mobilizes the contradictions of its particular historical moment. The spectral and colonial Chinese ghost has a decisive and decisively troubled impact on the novel's arrangement of rationalism and enchantment, and it blurs both the comfortable imperial divisions between zones of domestic

---

4. See Ryan, discussed more substantially later; and Evans, who argues that the ghost plays the role of "threatening 'chao[tic]'" force normally allotted to "female characters . . . in Fontane's novels" (38–39).

5. Guthke constructs an exotic/domestic binary that becomes so central that the reading begins to claim larger and larger areas, as long as they are non-Prussian, for the exotic in a way that elides crucial cultural asymmetries (103). Rainer holds that "The Chinese man is only the most extreme example of not-belonging in the novel. He serves as a variable for all outsiders, as well as a foil to all others: in contrast to them, he never made compromises with convention" (553). Her final assertion that Effi as "nature-child [Naturkind] is, in Kessin, a sight as foreign and exotic as the man from the Far East" forgets harsh realities of colonial history (561). Finally, see also Andermatt and Ingrid Schuster.

6. See Bernd, who draws very useful Bismarck connections (esp. 68–71); Müller-Seidel; Parr; Storch; and Utz, who provides illuminating information on Germany's perception of China (esp. 214). Utz is the first critic to tangle explicitly with *Effi Briest* as a critique of empire, arguing that the novel does not become "critical of imperialism" through the numerous trivial allusions to empire but rather "through the Chinese man" (223). Sittig asserts against Utz that *Effi Briest* is *not* critical of imperialism, that it "follows . . . in central passages the rules of contemporary colonial discourse" (544).

7. In a letter to Joseph Viktor Widmann dated 19 November, 1895, Fontane writes: "You are the first to point to the haunted house and the Chinese; I don't understand how people can see past them, since this ghost is, first of all, at least as I picture it, interesting in and of itself, and second, as you've pointed out, not placed there for fun, but rather as a fulcrum for the whole story [ein Drehpunkt für die ganze Geschichte]" (*Fontanes Briefe* 386).

Chapter Eight: The Imaginative Geography of Effi Briest ~ 177

order and zones of mystery, and the hierarchies of city and country. Upsetting distinctions that are both acknowledged and reproduced in *Effi Briest*, Fontane articulates the tension between the spiritual imagination and the secular rationalizations of geographical expansionism. It attempts to envision, in the carefully attempted but ultimately failed recuperation of the mysterious, a means of unmapping the mapped and ordered world and restoring uncertainty to a text that both craves and fears it.

(a) Unreal Realism: Imperial Knowledge and Space

Judith Ryan's essay on *Effi Briest* anticipates a measurable resistance to recent theoretical trends in the description of literary evocations of empire. This resistance pertains especially to the field of German cultural studies, according to Friedrichsmeyer, Lennox, and Zantop. One could postulate a variety of reasons for the supposed disciplinary insularity, but, even if it does show signs of its own demise,[8] it is certainly at play in Ryan's appeal to Germanists everywhere to hoist German realism "out of the purdah into which" it "has been relegated on the international scene," so that *Effi* can take her "place with the great English novels of the Victorian era" (383). It is worth examining exactly why the novel's Chinese ghost is so crucial to an imperial reading of *Effi Briest* (recalling that, in Fontane's opinion, it was crucial to *any* reading of *Effi Briest*). In 1984, Peter Utz became the first to attend to the colonial implications of the Chinese ghost in *Effi Briest*, in an article to which all ensuing analyses acknowledge their debt. Utz's case is built on traditional historical and comparative scholarship rather than on the postcolonial theory that informs the most recent contributions to this discussion. He details Germany's involvement in and perception of China around the turn of the twentieth century, arguing that Wilhelm II's and Bismarck's overt military incursions both represent the "culminat[ion of] a half-century of German policy toward China" and corroborate contemporary literary evocations of the Far East (215). Utz briefly mentions Karl May's "China novel," *Der blaurote Methusalem* (1892), which was first published as *Kong-Kheou, das Ehrenwort* (1888–89), alongside Jules Verne's *Les Tribulations d'un*

---

8. Ryan; Kontje; Lennox, Friedrichsmeyer, and Zantop; Noyes; and Nina Berman are just a few scholars engaging imperialism in German literature and culture from within the discourse of what one might call cultural studies (as opposed to the more traditionally historical study ably and importantly represented by scholars like Utz and Müller-Seidel). See also Russell Berman's *Enlightenment or Empire*, which explicitly opposes the use of the sort of contemporary theory to which Ryan and the others have turned. Berman derides what he terms "deconstructive antilogocentrism" as "a fraudulent basis for a critique of empire" (7). His views of imperialist conceptions of space, however, come very close to those of Said (3).

Chinois en Chine (1879) and Kipling's travel writings from China, "which appeared in English newspapers between 1887 and 1889" (217). While Fontane composed *Effi Briest*, Utz recalls, a German flotilla stood off China's shores to safeguard what had by then become "the prime example of a German commercial empire." In addition to the discovery of Chinoiserie in dinnerware referenced by Innstetten in the novel, Ryan's attention to the long history of Prussian and German missionarization and diplomacy in China in the mid-nineteenth century bolsters the connections Utz draws between Germany and China. In *Effi Briest* as in *Cécile*, the notion of empire-building and global expansion is a recurring, if often subtle, preoccupation. Beyond the often remarked Chinese associations of *Effi Briest*, critics have touched also on Fontane's glance toward Africa (with the character of Gieshübler's servant Mirambo, for example), another locus of German imperial interest.[9] The historical specifics of Fontane's gestures to colonialism through the Chinese ghost have, by now, been convincingly established. What has not been addressed, though, is the manner in which the novel's construction of space is deeply affected by the marginal figure of the Chinese ghost.

The Chinese ghost's impact on the negotiation and spatial organization of enchantment in *Effi Briest* is profound. Yet critics who emphasize the Chinese half of the ghost largely ignore its spiritual or supernatural component. This hybridized colonial-supernatural symbiosis forces to the forefront a preoccupation with disenchantment, which Fontane's novels register acutely. A return to Brontë's *Jane Eyre*—to which Spivak, Ryan and *Effi Briest* all gesture—illustrates the point.[10] One can footnote *Jane Eyre*, along with Dickens's *Great Expectations*, as a perfect example of a great English novel that "implicitly involves an exploration of empire," as Ryan puts it (367). This is too modest, though, for Brontë's exploration of empire is entirely explicit, represented powerfully in the character of Bertha Mason, the madwoman in the attic. Bertha Mason is, as Spivak reminds us, a "white Jamaican Creole" animalized by Brontë's narrative; through her very physical and violent pres-

---

9. Friedrichsmeyer, Lennox, and Zantop offer a cogent summary: "By 1885, then, Germany had acquired its entire, not unsubstantial, colonial empire: four African territories (Southwest Africa, Togo, Cameroon, and German East Africa) and several territories in the Pacific (northeastern New Guinea, part of Samoa, the Bismarck, Marshall, Caroline, and Mariana Islands, and Kiaochow on the Shantung Peninsula in China)" (10). Sittig rightly disputes this, pointing out that Kiaochow does not become an official colony until 1898 (551); ties to Kiaochow were well established by 1885, however, in the form of commerce and missionarization. Overly dismissive of the China connections and of all preceding critical attention to them, Sittig instead grounds his article on very close readings of the few passages in the novel that involve Gieshübler's African servant, Mirambo, whom he treats in noteworthy depth (555–59).

10. *Jane Eyre* is ignored in the reception of *Effi Briest*, which has primarily linked Fontane's novel with Flaubert's *Madame Bovary* and Tolstoy's *Anna Karenina*. Ibsen's Nora Helmer, from *A Doll House*, is also occasionally factored in. See Stern's "*Effi Briest: Madame Bovary: Anna Karenina*"; Rollins; Bonwit; Seiler; and Warning's chapter "Flaubert und Fontane" (185–239). Furst's essay gives a useful history of comparative work on Flaubert and Fontane (124–25).

ence in *Jane Eyre*, she articulates an anger sparked by a colonial background story central to the development of Rochester's character (Spivak 247). Despite the striking but unremarked symbolic affinities between the very real madwoman in Jane Eyre's attic and the ontologically dubious Chinese ghost that haunts Effi in Kessin, there is a vast difference between the *physical* and *spiritual* presence of these two colonial Others. If one considers Bertha Mason a prototypical figure for the exploration of empire in *Jane Eyre*—as Spivak does—then an examination or mobilization of empire in *Effi Briest* needs to confront the crucial distinction between the colonial Other who physically hunts Jane Eyre, and the colonial Other who metphysically haunts Effi Briest.

Partly at issue in allying empire with realist narrative—in *Effi Briest* as in any novel of the age of empire—is the notion that the imperial endeavor was indispensible to the mimetic project. Imperialism, Spivak contends, was a vital frame of reference in order for English readers to recognize themselves in a novel. In the passage from *Orientalism* that has already borne some analysis, however, Said specifically derides the very realism so common in novels of the period, and at which Spivak's notion of readerly identification hints. Said asserts that "Orientalism very generally is a form of radical realism," and whoever practices it strives to "designate, name, point to, fix what he is talking or thinking about with a word or phrase, which then is considered either to have acquired, or more simply to be, reality" (72). While Orientalism is "absolutely anatomical and enumerative," however, it is also paradoxically "a form of paranoia, knowledge of another kind, say, from ordinary historical knowledge." Said's diagnosis of Orientalism as paranoia is useful for a reading of *Effi Briest*'s Chinese ghost, just as it opens the collision of empiricism and enchantment so central to Balzac's *La Peau de chagrin* and *La Fille aux yeux d'or*. The Orientalist mindest as Said describes it can be more broadly considered as just one aspect of a general ideology that grounds any colonial project. Central to such projects is what Said calls "imaginative geography" (71). This capacity to envision the ordering of space has been discussed already, above, and several prominent scholars have taken concerns of space very much to heart in their work on German imperialism. Russell Berman, for example, claims that colonialist "progress . . . entails an ongoing conquest of space. That is, colonial discourse is implicated in some underlying epistemological questions relating to the construction of time and, especially, space, and these issues are prior to any specific or crude program of domination or ideologies of a civilizing mission. For the analysis of colonial discourse, then, the key question is one of space, not race" (3). Said similarly holds that "The geographical sense makes projections—imaginary, cartographic, military, economic, historical, or in a general sense cultural. It also makes possible the construction of knowledge" (*Culture* 78).[11] Said does not elaborate here or, to my knowledge, elsewhere, on the capacity of geography to structure knowledge. He shares common ground, however, with Fontane's Briest, and Briest's repeated allusions to the "too wide a field" [zu weites Feld], a quite spatial image for what can and cannot be known with certainty.

If the run-up to the climactic battle scene in *Vor dem Sturm* turns a reconnaissance mission into a narrated cartography in miniature, geography is also deployed early on in *Effi Briest* in a way that must shape any reading of Effi's relationship to the colonial-era project of mapping the known world and the effects of this undertaking on the possibility of knowledge. During the garden scene at the novel's outset, Effi reminds Hulda Niemeyer that unfaithful wives in Constantinople are drowned in punishment. Both are quick to underscore the difference between the domestic and the foreign:

"But not here."

"No, not here," laughed Effi. "Here things like that don't happen. But in Constantinople—and you must know about this as well as I do, since you were right there when Mr. Holzapfel spoke of it in Geography class."

"Yes," said Hulda, "he always talked about such things. But one forgets them again."

"I don't. I remember them." (I.4.15)

Effi seems to emphasize the conceptual cleft between the homely and the exotic rather than the actual geographical separation, and Innstetten later casts aspersions on the extent of Effi's actual geographical knowledge. Jokingly contrasting Gieshübler's African servant Mirambo with the latter's more notorious namesake, he teases, "The real Mirambo is the head of a band of thieves in Africa, Lake Tanganyika, if your geography reaches that far [wenn deine Geographie so weit reicht]" (I.4.82). Men with maps are apparently a running theme in the nineteenth-century novel. St. Arnaud remarks to Cécile, as he describes the transnational movements of Gordon in *Cécile*, "You won't be oriented, but I can show you on the map" (I.2.192). Flaubert's *L'Éducation sentimentale* contains a similar scenario: "Rosanette thought that Lebanon was in China; she laughed at her own ignorance and asked Frédéric to give her some lessons in geography" (2.234). In casually asserting the authority

---

11. Berman does not engage Said's elaboration of space in the imperialist project, and the declaration that the "key question" in colonialism is one of "space, not race" is problematic. Clearly, colonial discourse is animated by questions of *both* space *and* race, and it is difficult to see removing all considerations of ethnicity from an examination of empire.

of his geographic learning, Innstetten situates himself as the rationalistic European geographer in *Effi Briest*. Moreover, Frau Briest insinuates that he would be incapable of visiting the "Walhalla" on his honeymoon without in essence numbering its "art treasures" (I.4.37) and cataloguing the contents of every gallery (I.4.42). If Innstetten is not himself a collector, he is nevertheless described as having a collector's aura of order. Effi's father includes the Baron among the forces of bureaucracy, in a telling bit of dialogue; after raging against all manner of officialdom ("Antibeamtliches"), Briest quickly adds, "Pardon, Innstetten" (I.4.21). Innstetten then "nodded mechanically [mechanisch] in agreement." And it is Innstetten who, when pondering the later move to Berlin, expressly prefers a home situated between conveniently ordered and tamed exotic spaces, "between the Tiergarten and the Zoo" (I.4.191).

Innstetten's rationalizing impulse, most visible in his reaction to the ghost, colors his interaction with everything. One instance, though, almost comically links concerns of cultural otherness (within an imperial context[12]) to their rationalized control and to their role in the production of literature. The "Maschinen- und Baggermeister Macpherson," a veritable Highland Scot and Kessin resident, is trotted out by Innstetten as an example of a clearly domesticated, even modernized, savage. When Effi asks whether Macpherson actually exhibits the bearing of a true Highlander, Geert replies, "No, thank God, no, because he's a wizened little man, of whom neither his clan nor Walter Scott would be particularly proud" (I.4.46). Macpherson earns his keep creating order in Innstetten's garden, and yet Fontane may have chosen the name for its romantic associations with the name of the author of the Ossian hoax (Trollope may have done the same in *Phineas Redux*, as I argued above). Innstetten similarly makes Macpherson antithetical to the romances of Scott, just as Trollope's *Phineas* novels attempt to unwrite Scott's Highlands. Fontane's scripting of this exchange between Effi and Innstetten reveals intolerance of the stuff of romance, and does so with distinctly civilizing undertones. Innstetten's chosen alliance in this equation seems fairly clear, even if Fontane complicates it later in the novel—but Effi's relationship to the tension between disenchantment and enchantment stands at the center of the novel, alongside the Chinese ghost.

---

12. Fontane viewed England's relations with Scotland as indisputably colonial, perhaps a reverberation of his long admiration of the works of Scott. The Scottish character Armstrong in *Irrungen, Wirrungen* tells his hosts in Berlin stories of the Scots' stealing horses from the English as retaliation for the English practice of "stealing countries" [Länderraub] (I.2.468). Compare Andrew in Scott's *Rob Roy* (1817), who defends his smuggling in similar terms: "It's a mere spoiling o' the Egyptians... puir auld Scotland suffers eneugh by thae blackguard loons o'excisemen and gaugers, that hae come down upon her like locusts since the sad and sorrowfu' [Act of] Union [in 1707]" (231).

(b) Secularization and the Place of Enchantment

There is a certain affinity between the reception's constant "naturalization" or "rationalization" of *Effi Briest*'s Chinese ghost, and the problems associated with a potentially overly secularizing approach to investigations of imperialism. Dipesh Chakrabarty's warning in *Provincializing Europe* against an overly secular mindset is appropriate here. Such paradigms, he contends, set troubling "limits to the ways the past can be narrated," and "one has to take these limits seriously" (89). *Effi Briest* has always stood as an exemplar of German realism, and yet Fontane's Chinese ghost, if read as both disembodied spirit and historical substance, creates problems for the traditionally absolutist secularization of realist narrative. Such absolutism has the potential to generate hermeneutic inadequacies like those at work in, for example, J. P. Stern's verdict on *Effi Briest:* "The only blemish in the novel—the imagery of a mysterious Chinaman which Effi discovers on a set of chairs in Kessin, symbolical of her longing for freedoms far away—is a very minor one, a piece of bric-à-brac left over by 'poetic realism'" (*Re-interpretations* 319). Radcliffe likewise demeans the "motif" of the Chinese ghost as a mere leftover from the "'Gothic' or trivial novel" (39). Such readings are better at dismissing the ghost than interpreting it. Besides, as Christian Grawe points out, "That the ghost really exists is asserted nowhere in *Effi Briest*" (112). Stern and Radcliffe are stating their case against, apparently, a novel's *mere mention* of a supernatural being, even where that mention is a point of conversation for the characters that is not substantiated by the supposedly objective and authoritative realist narrator. The worries these critics betray are analogous to the reading practices of "secular criticism" as Said describes it; in *The World, the Text, and the Critic*, Said even relates "secular criticism" to his definition of "realism" in *Orientalism* (*The World* 290). This relationship might be especially fraught in the German context, because German literary realism, more so than its French or English counterparts, often enmeshes itself in religious concerns and yet is still read by some critics as a straightforward exercise in secularization. Russell Berman's "*Effi Briest* and the End of Realism," for example, explicitly opposes the religious to realism (343), bluntly claiming that "literary realism participated in the larger movement of nineteenth-century culture toward secularization" (359).[13] It is worth

---

13. Berman's essay offers the most holistic recent view of *Effi Briest*, but he consciously operates with the same modernist stereotypes of realism that Levine, Marshall Brown, and others have problematized. Berman writes of "the naïve epistemology of realism, the notion that its literary language provides a transparent window on the world" (345), bolstering both his earlier claim that realist novels "prohibit speculative speech and, in particular, philosophical discourse" (340) and his later claim that "realist referentiality" needs "to assume and assert an unproblematic presence of things" (355). Philosophical debates and arguments over representation are precisely *not* absent from realist novels, as Levine has recently shown in a reading of the "new epistemology" of Eliot's

asking how, exactly, the impulses of realism and secularization operate in Fontane's novel.

Effi Briest, for one, posits the process of secularization as somehow bound to that of imperial and commercial expansion. In an irreverent rhyme written on a Christmas card attached to a gift from Gieshübler redolent of *japonisme*, Effi reads:

> Three kings did come to the blessed Christ,
> One was a Moorish king;
> A Moorish chemist
> Appears today with dainty things,
> Instead of incense and myrrh, they wouldn't do,
> He brings pistachio and almonds
>
> [Drei Könige kamen zum Heiligenchrist,
> Mohrenkönig einer gewesen ist; —
> Ein Mohrenapothekerlein
> Erscheint heute mit Spezerein,
> Doch statt Weihrauch und Myrrhen, die nicht zur Stelle,
> Bringt er Pistazien- und Mandel-Morselle] (I.4.97)

Gieshübler's little poem radically modifies the Christian rendering of the Three Kings, first by inserting Mirambo, his African assistant, and then by substituting kitschy imported gifts for the traditional frankincense and myrrh. Trade and empire, in this otherwise superfluous poem, displace Christian tradition, just as critics have assumed literary realism does. The more important questions, though, go to how the text reacts to such displacements, and what effect they have on the form of the novel.

It may be useful at this point to briefly characterize Said's sponsorship of secular criticism and its potential drawbacks, for Said's work and its influence have made its advantages abundantly clear. How can this sort of criticism read texts that deploy figures—Chinese ghosts, for example, or Magic Skins—of an existential status at best questionable, according to empirical standards of truth? Bruce Robbins has written of "the messiness of the word *secular*" itself, a messiness that is perhaps "a necessary antidote to [the] invocation of world capitalism, which might be described as overtidy or even theological" (*Feeling Global* 123). For Said, as for others, Robbins argues, "the word *secular* has usually served as a figure for the authority

---

Daniel Deronda, which, Levine claims, "is explicitly about knowledge" (*Dying to Know* 171). Such debates instead, and fittingly, take the shape of narrative, where they are sustained, enacted, and tested by the plots and characters.

of a putatively universal reason or (narratively speaking) as the ideal end point of progress in the intellectual domain" (117). Might secularism also be conceived of as an endpoint, "narratively speaking," to the supposedly disenchanting teleology of realism and of realist emplotment, or to that of technological progress? Said's insistence on secularism in the conclusion of *The World, the Text, and the Critic* can itself almost be seen as theological; religion of any stripe is partnered with authoritarianism and "closure," and Said advocates instead "a purely secular view of reality" (290–91). McClure notes that if Said's articulation of secularism relies on "familiar binary equations" like "secular/religious," as it does, then it "can also serve as an agent of closure" (*Partial Faiths* 101). In addition to McClure's concerns, Said here reduces or runs afoul of his stance in *Orientalism* discussed above, where he phrases the damaging Orientalist mindset not just as "a form of paranoia, knowledge of another kind, say, from ordinary historical knowledge" but also as a "radical realism" (72). Said's paradox of Orientalism challenges any notion of a binarized colonialism driven only *either* by colonial fantasy *or* a colonial reality of domination and bureaucracy. *Orientalism* acknowledges both those drives in the imperial imagination, and it thus exposes potential shortcomings of the "secular criticism" Said later sponsors. Similarly, the intersection of disenchantment, literary realism, and otherness in *Effi Briest* challenges the most absolute definitions of realist narrative. Fontane's novel embraces these complications and even organizes itself around them.

Critics who shy away from dealing with the ghost as a spiritual phenomenon defer to the same modes of rationalization that form the backbone of Effi's society, according to Fontane's novel. Sidonie von Grasenabb, for example, unwittingly highlights the problematic constraints of rationality and normative Christianity, telling Effi, who believes she is hearing things in her new house, "Those are deceptions of the senses [Sinnestäuschungen]. . . . You're neurotic. You're hearing voices. Pray God that you're also hearing the right voice" (I.4.157). Sidonie's responses begin in a blunt vernacular, shift quickly into a pseudoscientific psychological vocabulary, and finally rest on a religious injunction that, in its speculation over the *origin* of the alleged hallucinations, contradicts the initial doubt over their actual existence. Fontane structures this conversation in a way that troubles Sidonie's efforts to dispense with the spirit and reveals an ambiguity mirrored in Innstetten's changing reaction to the ghost over the course of the novel. Like Sidonie von Grasenabb, Innstetten is nonplussed by the initial allegation that a specter is haunting his Kessin house, in the telling exchange between him and the maid Johanna after the ghost's first appearance:

"My lady ... just had a dream, but perhaps it was also the other."
"What other?"
"Milord knows, I'm sure."
"I know nothing. ... And what did she dream, or for all I care, what did she hear or see? [Und was hatte sie geträumt oder meinetwegen auch, was hatte sie gehört oder gesehen?] What did she say?"
"It crept up on her, right past her."
"What? Who?
"Him, upstairs. Him from the room or from the small chamber."
"Nonsense [Unsinn], I say." (I.4.77)

Innstetten gives the same rational response to Johanna that he gives later to Effi, even if his exchange with Effi is a bit more diplomatic. Repeating the words of Sidonie von Grasenabb, the Baron says, "You see, a dream, a deception of the senses" [Siehst du, Traum, Sinnestäuschung] (I.4.79). This does not, however, dispel the puzzling ambiguities of his conversation with Johanna. When Johanna points to "Him from the room or from the small chamber," Innstetten quickly interjects, "Nonsense," without asking to whom or to what Joanna is referring; clearly, this is not the first time he has heard a ghost story involving his Kessin house. But his denial of the truth of the tale is only with difficulty reconciled with his earlier question: "What did she dream, or for all I care, what did she hear or see?" Like the arc of Sidonie's conversation with Effi, Innstetten's question begins by relegating the ghost to the status of dream, but then introduces other possibilities, among which the reader must include the Baron's openness to the notion of his wife's actual sensory experience of this apparition: *gehört (heard), gesehen (seen)*. Despite the novel's general portrayal of Innstetten as imminently rational, these are not the protestations of a man cloaked entirely in the mantle of rationalized doubt.

Innstetten's final assessment of the ghost in this exchange, though, in his concluding dismissal of it, is likely indistinguishable from the reaction of anyone else of his rational intellect and class position. *Effi Briest* thus clarifies the secular environs of the novel. Innstetten later explains to Effi that they cannot switch houses for the sake of untenable superstitions: "I can't have people in the city saying that Baron Innstetten is selling his house because his wife took a drawing of a Chinese man for a ghost in her bed. I'd be lost, Effi [Dann bin ich verloren, Effi]. One never recovers from such ridicule" (I.4.80). Ingrid Schuster ascribes Innstetten's nervousness on this point to his fear of the "ridicule of too tender a bond of love" for which the Chinese ghost is "emblem" [Sinnbild], but Fontane's concerns here seem more entangled in the disenchantment of the supernatural than in romantic passion (120). Innstetten's worry over embarrassment stems not from his fear of public displays of tenderness, but rather from his certain knowledge that public avowal of belief in ghosts is simply not acceptable; it is, rather, ridiculous, *lächerlich*.[14] For the same reason, he tells Effi in Berlin, after she has decided to bring along a picture of a saint in order to protect herself from the picture of the Chinese man, which Roswitha carries with her in her purse, "Oh, do what you like. But don't tell anybody" (I.4.208). (This is almost too convenient a dramatization of Jameson's notion of "smuggling" enchantment in *The Political Unconscious*—the ghost's image has to be imported from the geographical margins, from a port city linked to the outside world.) In such secularized environs, any revelation of susceptibility to superstition would be fatal, Innstetten's reaction affirms, be it in Kessin or in Berlin. Although the Baron's penchant for ghost stories during his active military service complicates this, the seriousness of his fear of public humiliation in the Kessin conversation cited above cannot be underestimated, and Fontane's narrative underscores this by creating a point of contact with another crucial textual moment. If word of the superstition gets out, Innstetten swears to Effi, "I'd be lost" [Dann bin ich verloren] (I.4.80). One must at this point bear in mind Effi's soliloquy before her mirror, certainly a dramatic climax of sorts, where she says to herself, "Effi, you are lost" [Effi du bist verloren] (I.4.169). We recall the metaphor of "lostness" from the previous chapter's discussion of *Cécile*, and these moments of congruence (the twin *verlorens*) are not the only effort Fontane makes in *Effi Briest* to bind the ghost to the adultery. Consider the similarities between the narrator's description of Effi after her first "encounter" with the ghost, when she is presented as "totally pale" [ganz blaß] and Innstetten's look after he discovers the hidden Crampas letters revealing the affair; he, too, is "ganz blaß" (I.4.78; I.4.232). Fontane's parallels place Innstetten's stigmatization of superstition right alongside Effi's social ruination caused by adultery, a comparison that paints the embarrassment of public belief in a quite serious light.[15] That the shame of adultery is only social and not religious, as Effi decides in Berlin towards the novel's end, amplifies the secular environs of the novel (I.4.219).

Innstetten's resistance to metaphysical matters is undercut by the novel's spatial organization of them, and much separates Berlin from Kessin. John McClure's notion of the "basic imperial division of the world (metropolis and

---

14. Chambers argues that this view is Fontane's, that there is "no place in the reality of the modern world" for such "mystification" (188). This may be true, but the novel nevertheless subjects such views to major complications.

15. Mittenzwei ascribes equal narrative importance to Effi's admission of belief in the ghost—and fear of it—to Crampas: "This conversation is decisive [entscheidend]; it determines all to come" (141).

colonies or potential colonies)" is helpful here, because it employs "a familiar romance division, with the West represented as a zone of relative order, security and secularity, the non-Western world as a zone of magic, mystery, and disorder" (7). A closer look at the inner geography of *Effi Briest* problematizes any idea of a uniform domestic level of disenchantment. Fontane's novel, rather than merely reproduce the familiar imperial divisions to which McClure refers, instead reveals the manner in which increased mobility and changing spatial relationships have altered the terrain. Berlin as metropolis may not be completely impervious to reenchantment—apparently, one can smuggle it in, in a purse—but Kessin seems to see it flourish. Effi and her friends already see Kessin well divided from the civic center that is Berlin: Bertha hasn't even heard of it (I.4.13), Effi's imagination positions it halfway to Siberia (I.4.28), and Roswitha simply states, "Kessin, well, yes . . . but it's not Berlin" (I.4.187). It may be just this distanciation of the town from the metropolis—a distance both real and conceptual—that grants the former a certain status as a locus of openness to magic and mystery. Immediately prior to the move to Kessin, Effi goes so far as to place the town's remoteness from the comforts of the metropolitan in terms befitting a colonial imagination. Kessin is "a whole new world" [eine ganz neue Welt], she says twice (I.4.45). The colonial shadings are reinforced later, when we learn that the Kessin home is adjacent an area referred to by the townspeople as "the plantation" [die »Plantage«] (I.4.48–49). The phrasing is no accident, as Fontane repeats it twice later and keeps it usually within quotation marks (I.4.59–60). Russell Berman has pointed out that *Effi Briest* "unfolds primarily in Hohen-Cremmen, Kessin, and Berlin—distinct locales, to be sure, but all in the Prussian northeast," but Fontane goes well beyond what Berman terms "the semiotics of local particularity" in his scripting of Kessin (*"Effi Briest"* 348–49). The language of the novel sets Kessin up as a sort of imperial outpost, adding to its removal from the metropolitan space of Berlin. Effi explicitly notices the internationalism of Kessin, which, despite its size, contains people and things from all over the world, thanks to its thriving port. Innstetten explains to Effi the significance of the mixture of people that occurs in "commercial towns" [Handelsstädten]: "Their interests lie in the areas where they trade and as they trade with the whole world and have connections with everybody, you'll find people among them from every corner and end of the world" [Worauf sie angewiesen sind, das sind die Gegenden, mit denen sie Handel treiben, und da sie das mit aller Welt tun und mit aller Welt in Verbindung stehen, so findest du zwischen ihnen auch Menschen aus aller Welt Ecken und Enden] (I.4.45). Though no metropolis of global renown, the port town and its commercial undertakings nevertheless organize links between disparate places and people.

Innstetten himself divorces the town from the essence of rationalist certainty, complaining, "everything is uncertain [unsicher] here" (I.4.44). Much later in the novel, when their sleighs are caught during the fateful homeward journey from a dinner party, a narrated *style indirect libre* clearly meant to reflect the thoughts of Innstetten allows that, "People here were superstitious, even fearful, while it actually didn't mean much [wenig zu bedeuten habe]" (I.4.160). With its air of mystery, uncertainty, and foreignness (to which Effi and Innstetten repeatedly allude), Kessin is a site of porous boundaries, of nascent cosmopolitanism, where one sees perhaps some of the mapped-out magic imported to the mainland. We are reminded by Innstetten, after all, that nobody in Berlin lives in a haunted house: "There's one good thing about Berlin: there aren't any haunted houses there [Spukhäuser gibt es da nicht]. Where would they come from?" (I.4.183). It is in Kessin that the ghost makes its appearances. The divisions between metropolitan and rural space in *Effi Briest* recall those between Berlin and the Harz in *Cécile*, but an important distinction must be made: Kessin's mysteries and foreignness are largely imported from faraway lands by international shipping concerns, while the Harz is enchanted by a uniquely Germanic past. Innstetten himself affirms this difference in his dismissal of the Chinese ghost, disparaging the idea of a foreign haunting by virtue of its being "made" [gemacht] rather than "natural" [natürlich] to the house or the land (I.4.207).

(c) Dueling Epistemologies and the Chinese Ghost

The Chinese ghost, which Fontane claimed as the novel's center, anchors in many ways the text's portrayal of the other key characters. Chambers points out that the ghost appears first in a terrifyingly banal capacity, as an excuse for Effi to sleep in late (197). On the occasion of Effi's first morning in Kessin, she tells Innstetten, "For a whole hour, when I awoke in the night, it seemed to me as if shoes slid across the earth and as if dancing and almost music could be heard. But all very lightly. And then I told Joanna all about it this morning, just to excuse myself for sleeping in so late" (I.4.58). So, the ghost arises first as an excuse before it ever emerges as, depending on whom one asks, an actual apparition or a hallucination. Oddly, the novel later gives a certain material form to the ghost, or at least explains its invention as inspired by a material object, as Innstetten shows Effi around the attic in the Kessin home:

> In one of them [the rooms in the attic] only were three rush-seated chairs, whose seats had collapsed, and on the back of one of these there had been stuck a tiny

picture, only half an inch or so high, depicting a Chinaman in a blue tunic and baggy yellow breeches with a broad flat hat on his head. Effi saw it and asked: "What's the Chinaman doing there?" Innstetten seemed surprised himself by the little picture, and replied that he did not know what it was. "Christel must have stuck it there, or Johanna, for fun. You can see that it's been cut out of a spelling book." Effi thought so, too, and was only perplexed that Innstetten took it all so seriously, as if it did have some importance [Effi fand es auch und war nur verwundert, daß Innstetten alles so ernsthaft nahm, als ob es doch etwas sei]. (I.4.61)

The material basis of the ghost is simultaneously trivialized and made a matter of concern to Innstetten, but it is precisely this little picture that frightens Effi when Roswitha later brings it with her to Berlin.

The triviality of the ghost's picture and of the manner in which the ghost is first used as an excuse does not diminish its terrifying effect on Effi, however, and she remains under the spell of her fear until it is rationalized away from her. The dismissive rationalization first comes, not from the reasonable Innstetten, but from his rival Crampas. Crampas builds up carefully to his speculation on Innstetten's motives for using the ghost. He apprises Effi of Innstetten's penchant, during his service in the military, for telling ghost stories in order to secure his advancement, a pure instrumentalization of the public experience or transmission of supernatural belief. From there it is an easy step to the point at which Crampas accuses Innstetten in absentia of cultivating Effi's fear of the ghost in an effort to keep her faithful to him: "Education through a ghost" [Erziehen durch Spuk] (I.4.133). Innstetten, Crampas declares, is a born pedagogue, and a zealous one, but the word Crampas selects to pinpoint the nature of Innstetten's zeal is not *religiös* but rather *kirchlich* (*churchly*), a word that highlights rationalistic organization rather than spirituality in Innstetten. The notion of a rational Innsetten is also at work in the narrator's description of his alleged "calculated means of inspiring fear" [Angstapparat aus Kalkül] (I.4.134). Crampas's rational explanation prompts Effi, it seems, to cease believing so fervently in the truth of the Chinese ghost. The next time it is referred to, albeit obliquely, Innstetten is the one broaching the topic: "And don't worry . . . it won't come back . . . you know, him upstairs" (I.4.172). No longer prey to her fear, "Effi laughed to herself, and it faded somewhat into melancholy." The dreaded magic and mystery that is thus leached out of her life in Kessin comes to be missed when Effi openly wishes the ghost back in, later. To her mother, Effi writes from Kessin, "If everything is quiet, then I'm almost disappointed and say to myself, 'If only it would come back'" (I.4.104). Finally, after she has been banished to Berlin, Effi remembers the days in Kessin as "happy times, ... back when the Chinaman was haunting us [spukte]" (I.4.262). Crampas first dispels her fear of the ghost, enabling these later moments of nostalgia for it.

It is difficult to chart the status of Crampas in romance's beleaguered negotiation in *Effi Briest*. Jamison problematizes the strict confinement of the Major to the realm of the rational, pointing out that "Fontane may have intended a subtle identification of the ghost and Crampas, for Crampas's name is reminiscent of *Krampus*, a demon-figure common in Austrian folklore" (32). He is, moreover, linked to the horrors Effi encounters while traveling with Innstetten in the north of Germany. Near a town called "Crampas," Effi is terrified by vestiges of a barbaric Germanic past, in sacrificial stones engineered for better bleeding of their victims (I.4.211). Such sites also frame important scenes in George Eliot's *Daniel Deronda* (1876) and Thomas Hardy's *Tess of the D'Urbervilles* (1891).[16] Crampas is essential to the romantic possibilities inherent in the act of adultery, the duel, and the dunes toward the end of the novel; yet, still, it is he who attempts to dismiss the supernaturality of the ghost-image. Between Crampas's rational explanation of the Chinese ghost and Effi's much later longing for its return, the ghost's only function is to cover for a sudden outburst from Effi. This outburst, as Evans, Rainer, Ingrid Schuster, and Avery have pointed out, gives Effi a rare opportunity to manipulate her husband, but it also again instrumentalizes the supernatural. Otherwise, the burden of preserving the ghost's symbolic weight in and relevance to the narrative is shouldered by the maid Roswitha, who consults Frau Kruse in an effort to get the whole story behind the ghost. The frequent invocation of this background story, and of the desire of a few of the novel's characters to hear it, recalls Innstetten's remark, in a quote that has already served as an epigraph above, that narrative can easily be generated by a character so foreign in the novel's domestic space: "a Chinese man is already a story in and of himself" [ein Chinese ist schon an und für sich eine Geschichte] (I.4.48). Innstetten's language recalls Fontane's statement that the ghost is "interesting in and of itself" [an und für sich interessant] in the same letter in which he declares it the *Drehpunkt* of the novel (*Fontanes Briefe* 386). If the raw materials of adventure and mystery are in short supply in the culture Fontane describes, then strange and exciting stories like that of the Chinese man represent a tantalizing possibility. In an era in which the thorough exploration of the world and its attendant mapping have striven

---

16. In Eliot's novel, "The roving had been lasting nearly an hour before the arrival at the Whispering Stones, two tall conical blocks that leaned towards each other like gigantic grey-mantled figures. They were soon surveyed and passed by with the remark that they would be good ghosts on a starlit night" (127). As the party moves on, Gwendolen doubles back to the site and meets Lydia Glasher, the mother of Grandcourt's secret children. Hardy's *Tess*, of course, ends with the title character's arrest at Stonehenge, "the heathen temple" (411).

to eradicate what Jameson calls "magical content," it is possible that Effi's Chinese ghost is "smuggled" into the narrative "in order to find symbolic appeasement," in order to generate fiction (*Political Unconscious* 134). The word "smuggled" is especially apposite here, given the opinion of so many critics that the ghost is merely an unwanted addition to an otherwise exemplary realist novel.

Certainly, though, while the culture depicted by Fontane in *Effi Briest* perceives itself as bled dry of romance, glimmers of enchantment emerge in Kessin. On arrival, as Innstetten describes some of the town's inhabitants, Effi exclaims, "This is marvelous, Geert. It's like six novels" (I.4.47).[17] Innstetten later remarks, similarly, that Kessin was "rich with characters" [reich an Figuren] (I.4.222). Kessin sparks Effi's imagination, and "all sorts of thoughts" [allerhand Gedanken] come to her just by looking around (I.4.56). After touring the house for the first time, while it is still uncharted territory for her, "Effi felt none of this loneliness, for her imagination was still with the wondrous things that she had seen just before, during her look around the house" (I.4.59–60). At the end of that very chapter, however, a prescient narrative moment affords us, in the person of the town pharmacist Gieshübler, a look at the disenchantment that has already taken up residence, as the narrator describes Gieshübler's momentary impulsiveness at first meeting Effi: "Gieshübler would have preferred to make a declaration of love to Effi, begging to be her Cid or Campeador, to fight for her and die. But since that didn't happen and his heart couldn't bear it any longer, he stood up" to leave (I.4.65). The point is driven home again, toward the novel's close, in Berlin, through Frau Zwicker's assertion that "the actual Don Juans always end up disappointing [erweisen sich jedesmal als eine Enttäuschung]" (I.4.257). In this she rephrases a conversation from 1891's *Unwiederbringlich* during which a group of characters discusses mythical heroism. The narrator tells us that Westergaard and Lundbye "chimed in together to point out that, where the most important form of heroism, the heroism of passion [Heldenmut der Leidenschaft], was concerned, times never changed and that they personally would guarantee that love could still perform the same wonders [Wunder] as in former days" (I.2.756). Ebba retorts, "The same wonders.... That is impossible, because such wonders were the product of something that has been lost [Produkte dessen, was der Welt verloren gegangen ist]." Frau Zwicker, like Ebba in *Unwiederbringlich*, maintains that the classic models of adventure and romance are out of place.

---

17. Herr von Gordon in *Cécile* makes a similar observation regarding the twenty-year age difference between St. Arnaud and Cécile: "There's a novel in all this [Dahinter steckt ein Roman]. He is more than twenty years older than she" (I.2.149). Apparently, in the arithmetic of Fontane's characters, while an unusual marriage is worth one novel, a Chinese man in Germany is worth six.

The duel between the opposed terms of disenchantment and romance supports a durable tension in *Effi Briest*. Crampas may not be anything but a disappointment, finally, but there *is* nevertheless something of the Don Juan in him, bravely at first and somewhat shamefacedly at last.[18] He wants his romantic "soldier's death" [Soldatentod], as he tells Innstetten, a declaration that elicits sarcasm: "That will be difficult, Crampas, unless you take up service with the King of Turkey or under the Chinese dragon. There, they're still killing each other off. Here, that whole story—believe you me—is thirty years gone [Hier ist die Geschichte, glauben Sie mir, auf dreißig Jahre vorbei]" (I.4.124). Heroism and war are relegated to foreign space, and so is grand history, if Innstetten's use of the word *Geschichte* is any indication. The past is elsewhere, according to him, and Germany stands poised for a future that outpaces the past. Crampas still manages to find his death in Germany, but it is most assuredly not that of a soldier in battle, and instead of explosive glory Crampas accepts it with a "melancholy resignation" [wehmütige Resignation] not unlike that of the disillusioned Effi (I.4.239). In staging a duel between Innstetten and Crampas on the dunes of Kessin, Fontane injects into the novel a trope of romance that one might be tempted to pass over as a thoroughly quotidianized literary mannerism. The narrative, however, resists this interpretation.

Even if Fontane does not send his duelists across the Channel to a foreign beach, as Trollope does in *Phineas Finn*, or up into the mountains, as Balzac does in *La Peau de chagrin*, *Effi Briest*'s narrative goes to great lengths to thematize the liminality of the act within the domestic space of the novel. Prior to the duel, Innstetten's conversation with Wüllersdorf, his faithful second, highlights the extreme nature of dueling, and Fontane details Innstetten's journey via rail and steamer in a manner that makes the ultimate destination seem quite distant from rational Berlin. This outbound journey is accomplished much in the same way as St. Arnaud's and Cécile's departure from Berlin in *Cécile*. Innstetten's return trip, by contrast, fits into one sentence—"On the night of the same day, Innstetten stepped again into Berlin"—before the prose elaborates on his avoidance of Kessin, where he leaves to "the two seconds the task of notifying the authorities" (I.4.242). This stark difference between the outbound and homebound legs of Innstetten's journey recalls the difference between similar legs of journeys in Trollope's fiction: the journeys to Loughlinter and Königstein, for example, which begin excitingly but end with a quotidian rail journey back home. Fontane lingers on this outbound journey to Kessin for a long paragraph full of reflections

---

18. Herbert Josephs contends that, beginning in the Enlightenment, the cradle of Weberian *Entzauberung*, Don Juan's status and the erotic in general are mythologized, their import transferred to the realm of the magical.

on earlier moments in the novel. En route to the duel, Innstetten even opens himself to sentiments of which he was imminently wary earlier. As he passes by the old Kessin house, "the feeling of the uncanny [des Unheimlichen], over which Innstetten had so often argued with or ridiculed [belächelt] Effi, now it overcame even him, and he was happy once they were past it [als sie dran vorüber waren]" (I.4.241). Still more could have been made of the legal or social marginality of the duel, perhaps, had Fontane clung more tightly to the Ardenne case on which *Effi Briest* is rudimentarily based. As Jean Leventhal reminds us, the real Ardenne served actual prison time for his adherence to an officer's code and duelling (183). But the stand-off in the dunes is billed by *Effi Briest*'s narrator as the stuff of romance, and not least because of where it takes place.

(d) Effi's End: Disenchanting Enchantment

In the imaginative geography of *Effi Briest* and the distribution of what enchantment remains, Kessin looms large, but the dunes at its outskirts are even more significant. They are, first and foremost, the location of the grave of the Chinese man, as Innstetten points out to Effi during their first tour through Kessin (I.4.45). In addition to the drawing of the Chinese man in the attic, there is this spatial reference for the Chinese ghost as the story is spun out through a series of interrupted segments. Innstetten relates in chapter 10 that a Chinese man came to Kessin with a sea captain named Thomsen and a woman said to be either Thomsen's niece or granddaughter (I.4.85). It is strongly implied by Frau Kruse later that the Chinese man and the niece/granddaughter became romantically involved until she married another man (I.4.174-75). The siting of the grave thus becomes a convenient shorthand for all of the related ideas that the story of the Chinese ghost represents—the foreign, the supernatural, the idea of forbidden love—and Fontane puts it to frequent use, allowing the implied presence of the ghost to haunt the narrative. When Effi first meets Roswitha, their gaze ultimately leads to the resting place: "Over there lay the enclosure where the white stone glittered and shone in the afternoon sun" (I.4.114). Not much later, after the first walk in the dunes with Crampas, "Effi looked towards the stone and the fir tree where the Chinaman lay" (I.4.133). These moments serve as the ending of chapters 13 and 16, respectively, allowing the narrator to let the weight of the allusion sink in as each chapter comes to a dark close.

It is in the dunes during this first recreational ride that Crampas, in one of his earliest and most provocative conversations with Effi, discourses on "das Romantische" and on New World deities like the Mexican god "Vitzliputzli" from Heinrich Heine's poem (I.4.138). Zantop, too, references this poem in her book *Colonial Fantasies,* even quoting a whole stanza as an epigraph to her final chapter:

> To my enemy's own homeland,
> Which goes by the name of Europe,
> Will I flee to take my refuge
> And begin a new career there.
>
> [Nach der Heimat meiner Feinde,
> Die Europa ist geheissen,
> Will ich flüchten, dort beginn ich
> Eine neue Carrière.] (qtd. on 202)

If Heine's poem is an example of Romanticism, however, it is scripted specifically as against modern disenchantment associated with empire. "Vitzliputzli" is only able to achieve its romantic tones by explicitly forgetting the disenchanted present in favor of the pre-Encounter past, as its first lines make clear. The "Präludium" begins:

> This is America!
> This is the new world!
> Not today's, which already
> Withers away Europeanized.—
>
> This is the new world!
> As Christopher Columbus
> Pulled it out of the ocean.
>
> [Dieses ist Amerika!
> Dieses ist die neue Welt!
> Nicht die heutige, die schon
> Europäisieret abwelkt. —
>
> Dieses ist die neue Welt!
> Wie sie Christoval Kolumbus
> Aus dem Ozean hervorzog.]

"Vitzliputzli" is as much a poem of disenchantment as it is an instance of Romanticism; it is thus especially appropriate here, for disenchantment pervades Effi's and Crampas's attempted romance, although they do not seem aware of it. In addition to Heine, Effi and Crampas delve into the poetry of Brentano, bolstering a distinctly Romantic link to the open nature of the seafront. The reader later learns, as Innstetten peruses the long-concealed correspondence between Effi and Crampas, that the dunes were the focal point of the affair. In one of Crampas's letters to Effi, Innstetten reads, "Be in the dunes again this afternoon," and in another, "Be in the usual place [an der alten Stelle] again today" (I.4.232–33). The interaction of Crampas and Effi in the dunes, from their early conversations there to their later use of the location as a meeting place, seems to—or at the very least seems to *want* to—fashion the area into a zone of romantic permissiveness and romantic indiscretions, a field of possibilities outside the strictures of bourgeois marriage morality. Crampas is ultimately a let-down on these very sands, just as Frau Zwicker claims all Don Juans are, but the dunes emblematize more powerfully not only the edge of Kessin but the frontier of the domestic and thus the instance of its commingling with what is not domestic, what may not yet have been fully rationalized.

Fontane's mapping of adultery, a recurring theme in his novels and one that periodically marked him as a controversial writer in his day, reveals an intriguing pattern that has consequences for our understanding of the place of disenchantment. The three novels in which adultery figures most prominently—*L'Adultera* (1882), *Cécile* (1887), and *Effi Briest* (1895)—all involve complications within marriages between older men and younger, teenaged women, the very twenty-year age difference that prompts Gordon in *Cécile* to see possibilities for the generation of fiction: "There's a novel in all this [Dahinter steckt ein Roman]. He is more than twenty years older than she" (I.2.149). The plots of all three texts also hover unmistakably around the city of Berlin, and this is no coincidence.[19] Berlin is essential to the mapping of adultery in these three works, not as a condition of its possibility but rather because it becomes, in a complex way, an apparent location of its impossibility. Moretti briefly refers to *Effi Briest* as one in a cluster of "novels that arrive from the center, with provincial malaise as one of their favorite themes," but *malaise* hardly captures Fontane's Kessin (*Atlas* 166). When one recalls that the abortive adultery of *Cécile* begins in the rural Harz and ends as the scene shifts to Berlin, and that *Effi Briest*'s clandestine meetings

---

19. Because of this thematic confluence, Friedrich has asserted of *L'Adultera*, just as he has of *Cécile*, that the work is most often read as mere "Vorstufe" to Fontane's later fiction ("Das Glück" 359). Tebben has argued that Fontane found the theme of adultery so appealing because, arising as it does in his novels from a forced marriage, it served as a convenient metaphor for his own personal attempts to reconcile his chosen career as writer with his "forced" role as father and husband.

occur on the dunes at the outskirts not just of a port town but of the new Germany itself, then the case of *L'Adultera* sheds interesting light on the development of this theme. This earlier novella is organized entirely around adultery, and, although the spatial situation of it is quite different, the key difference is revealing. While the liaison between Melanie van der Straaten and Ebenezer Rubehn, recently arrived from America, does indeed begin in Berlin before moving to Italy, Fontane's narrative goes to great pains to remove it from the rational metropolis. The unmapping or remapping is not as broad and deliberate here as it is in Balzac's *La Fille aux yeux d'or* or in Trollope's *Phineas* novels or *The Way We Live Now*. Yet Fontane carefully constructs links between the extramarital relationship and a domestic space suddenly recoded as nonurban and tropical.

From the outset, Melanie's husband, the cynical Berlin native, Commercial Councillor van der Straaten, envisions the novella's adultery as an inevitability. He shows his wife the copy he has had made of Tintoretto's *L'Adultera*, referring to it as a sort of "memento mori" (I.2.15). The effect of this painting as a pronouncement on the fate of the novel feels almost oracular. What begins with the certainty of mythologized fate does not come to fruition, though, until Rubehn's visit to the van der Straaten residence in Berlin. As he peruses part of van der Straaten's collection of tropical plants in the private garden of the Berlin home, Rubehn is overcome: "Oh, Frau van der Straaten, what an enchanted garden [Zaubergarten] you live in! A peacock sunning itself, and so many and such tame doves ... as though this veranda were Saint Mark's Square or the island of Cyprus itself!" (I.2.48). In a Berlin garden that seems not to be in Berlin, the flirtation begins. The association between potential adultery and an urban space rendered exotic is emboldened in a chapter called "Beneath the Palm Tress." After a picnic in the park, they walk toward "the center of the whole layout," toward "a couple of palm houses with high glass domes ... after the manner of the famous English Gardens at Kew. One of them was joined to an old-fashioned greenhouse [Treibhaus]" (I.2.76). As they walk through the palm house, Melanie and Ebenezer finally come to the threshold of the greenhouse: "A few more steps brought them to what seemed like the entrance to a tropical forest, with the huge glass structure arching above them. This was where the finest specimens of the van der Straaten collection were to be found: palms, drakea, and giant ferns" [Wenige Schritte noch, und sie befanden sich wie am Eingang eines Tropenwaldes, und der mächtige Glasbau wölbte sich über ihnen. Hier standen die Prachtexemplare der van der Straatenschen Sammlung: Palmen, Drakäen, Riesenfarren] (I.2.81). The language even evokes the yielding to temptation alluded to in the notion of the *Schritt*, or *step;* Fontane's *L'Adultera* and *Effi Briest* both repeatedly adduce Ernst Wichert's 1873 play about adultery, *Ein*

Schritt vom Wege [*A Step Off the Path*].[20]

Heide Eilert has read the greenhouse (*Treibhaus*) as an allusion to styles of decadence in European culture in the late-nineteenth century, but it has particular resonance in relation to adultery in *L'Adultera*. The passion between Melanie and Rubehn becomes explicit in the greenhouse and coheres with an earlier scene in the novella through a weak phonological similarity. In the chapter, "Wohin Treiben Wir?" [Whither Are We Drifting?], Rubehn and Melanie float down the Spree and ask each other—in a clumsily repeated leitmotif—in which direction they are drifting. Probably indebted to George Eliot's *Mill on the Floss* (1860) and Maggie Tulliver's accidental but scandalous river journey with Stephen Guest, Fontane's scene likewise pairs lack of navigational control (being "lost," again) with a temporary freedom from social strictures. The scene, in *L'Adultera*, is already rampant with allusive speculation as to their impending affair, but when the *treiben* of the drifting is paired with the *Treibhaus* of the later chapter, even these earlier allusions to adultery are brought under the umbrella of the collected exotic and tropical. In *Effi Briest*, Effi will similarly be said twice to let herself *treiben*, linking her perhaps to the drift of adultery in the earlier novella: "She likes to let herself drift" [Sie läßt sich gern treiben], Roswitha says of Effi, and the narrator similarly asserts that, under the influence of Berlin, Effi has a tendency "to let herself drift to the left" [sich nach links hin treiben zu lassen] (I.4.216; I.4.225). Fontane's narrative carves out a reenchanted space, within a rationalized Berlin ably represented by Melanie's husband, for an adultery offered up as an alternative to domesticated and rationalized European culture. The happy ending to the adultery story in *L'Adultera* clashes with the conclusive later tragedies of *Cécile* and *Effi Briest*, both of which end not with an extramarital harmony and declaration of feminine independence, but rather with dead rivals and either disillusionment (*Effi Briest*) or inexplicable, sudden religious fervor (*Cécile*). Yet the careful mapping of adultery in *L'Adultera* corroborates *Cécile*'s inability to imagine it within the city as such, and it hints as well at *Effi Briest*'s location of adultery in the dunes at the periphery of novel, land, and nation.

In their role as site of the impermissible and the peripheral, the shifting dunes also recall Innstetten's telling of ghost stories during his military service. Crampas tells Effi of her husband's reputation as teller of ghost stories among his men in the army, but the episode, tinged with both mysticism and the simultaneous exploitation of it, is ambiguous. Innstetten had, Crampas says to Effi,

---

20. The play is performed in the town in *Effi Briest*, and so when Innstetten discovers the correspondence between Crampas and Effi, he finds as well a series of photos taken of her around the time of the play's performance (I.4.232).

a predilection for telling us ghost stories [Spukgeschichten]. And when he'd gotten us all worked up and even worried some of us, he would suddenly make it seem as if he had only been amusing himself at the expense of all those who had been so gullible [Leichtgläubigen]. To cut a long story short, once I responded, "For goodness' sake, Innstetten, that's just a performance [Komödie]. You're not deceiving me. You don't really believe that any more than we do, but you want to appear interesting and you've the idea that eccentricity is a better recommendation. They don't want ordinary people [Alltagsmenschen] in the upper ranks. (I.4.131)

If Crampas is to be believed, the upwardly mobile Innstetten tells the ghost stories for the purely strategic reasons of career advancement, and neither Crampas nor Innstetten nor the men really believe in the tales. Even if Crampas is right, though, the tales get told, and the supernatural exerts an explicit pull on the group. That such stories are repeated at all, within the very forces charged with shoring up and defending the porous frontiers of the *imperium*, speaks to their lingering cultural resonance.

Part of *Effi Briest*'s realist project is a depiction of the rationalizations and disenchantments that accompany the shrinking of the world in an era of imperial and commercial expansion. In much of Fontane's later fiction, the world is known, and what is known is mapped, and what is mapped is rendered familiar. La Trippelli's benign and touristic worldliness emerges early in the text as a positively valorized alternative to disenchantment, as a mindset whose cosmopolitanism renders it capacious enough to allow for even the mystical. Yet she is later quoted by Effi in a manner reminiscent of the English writers at the turn of the century to whom McClure refers in *Late Imperial Romance*, writers who bemoan the loss of the uncharted, the shrinking of the world and the disappearance of its secret corners. Effi remembers that La Trippelli "once said that the world was so small, and that in Central Africa one could be sure that one would suddenly run into an old acquaintance" (I.4.267). The language here repeats that of Gordon in *Cécile*, when a dinner party in Charlottenburg confirms for him "how small the world is." It is odd that these jaded words are attributed to Trippelli, because, as Evans has suggested, she represents a continuing openness to the irrational (40). Reflecting Innstetten's fear of shame at the public avowal of belief in ghosts and Effi's parallel shame of being unfaithful, Subiotto echoes Evans's thought: "Any belief in spiritualism" on the part of Trippelli, Subiotto writes, "is firmly underpinned by a healthy respect for the social rejection she must suffer because of her status as a Russian prince's mistress" (140). So, what is most interesting about her character's relationship to both the world outside and the otherworldly may not be that her cosmopolitanism passively permits openness to enchantment, but rather that it is adduced as the sole cause of it. "My dear lady," she says to Effi, "when you're as old as I am and have been moved all over the place and have lived in Russia and half a year in Romania, you realize anything's possible [da hält man alles für möglich]" (I.4.94). Departure from the comforts of the domestic, she implies early on, breeds broader understandings of the possible. The text's portrayal of Trippelli first complicates this notion when her performance of even passionate romantic songs is said to be bored and mechanical. And it finally overturns it completely in her dictum on the smallness of the world.

Immediately after Effi recalls this verdict on the shrinking of the world— actually, *precisely because* she recalls it—Effi is reunited briefly with her daughter Annie. The reunion leaves much to be desired, and Effi's dissatisfaction is evident at the close of her subsequent prayer, where she complains of Innstetten, "Before he sends our child, he trains her like a parrot" (I.4.275). The image of the parrot resounds in *Effi Briest*, if one recalls Innstetten's wish for exotic birds safely tucked away in the ordered and domesticated space of a zoo, within earshot of his Berlin home. One should also read into the exoticism of the parrot yet another brief gesture toward the colonies, just as it is in Flaubert's *Un cœur simple* (1877). In referring to her daughter as a parrot, Effi implies that her husband has reproduced within domestic space, as a child-rearing strategy, the sort of domestication of the exotic at work in the projects of public zoos. As she realizes this during an important prayer scene, Effi ceases praying to the *du* of God. Instead, she turns herself to more immanent targets, declaiming against "*your* (plural) virtue. Away with *you* (plural)" [*eure* Tugend. Weg mit *euch*] (I.4.275; emphases mine). No immediate referent is provided for these second-person-plural pronouns, and they can only be assumed to refer to Innstetten and Annie, unless they refer to everybody. The secular turn of Effi's prayer—its slide from dialogue with the transcendent to diatribe against the immanent—endows it with obvious importance for any examination of spiritual matters in Fontane's novel. It is doubly interesting, though, in its relation to two other textual moments late in *Effi Briest*, moments at which the prose is lulled toward transcendence before being yanked back earthward.

These two moments—Effi's seemingly romantic communions with the night air through her window—occur at her parents' home at Hohen-Cremmen. Effi's final return to Hohen-Cremmen, although a revisiting of where she was wild and younger, is staged by Fontane rather as an embedding within an ordered space: "Here is my place," she says, "The sunflowers down on the round, encircling the sundial, are dearer to me than Mentone" (I.4.283). The total symbolic weight of Effi's childhood home cannot be said completely to invoke rationalism and imperialism, although it specifically bears these marks. It also represents the comforts of home, to Innstetten, who chides Effi for her occasional degradation of Hohen-Cremmen: "I know well how much you love Hohen-Cremmen and still cling to it, but you make fun of it so often and really have no idea what silent days, like those in Hohen-Cremmen, mean" (I.4.87). However, in contrast to these testimonials of hermeticism—a hermeticism that in itself contrasts with the open Hanseatism of Kessin[21]—that arise when Effi is or has been away from Hohen-Cremmen, there is the introductory image of her, painted in far more adventurous relief. It is one thing to read Effi's blue and white dress as a typological rendering of her virginity and purity (in the colors of the Virgin Mary), as Peter-Klaus Schuster has done. Blue and white are also colors stereotypical of sailor dress, however; Fontane's narrative itself invites this connection in referring to Effi's "sailor-collar" [Matrosenkragen] and comparing Effi to a "cabin-boy" [Schiffsjunge] (I.4.8; I.4.15). This rendering of Effi as sailor situates her simultaneously as one bound for adventure and as a representative of the physical apparatus of empire-building, the pragmatic, maritime forces ultimately responsible for the eradication of the raw materials of romance. In this tension, one recalls the problematic dual-coding of Balzac's disenchanting adventurers, who are equal parts romance and business, at the end of the opening portion of *La Fille aux yeux d'or*.

Hohen-Cremmen is thus an ambiguous place, simultaneously coded as wild and domestic, neither port nor metropolis, and Effi's days end there. She gazes out the open window at the heavens until the very activity lays her into her sick bed, and the narrator describes this act twice, in detail. In the first instance,

> Time passed. A voice rang out from across the village street: it was the old nightwatchman Kulicke calling out the time, and when he stopped, she could hear, half a mile away, the clatter of the train [das Rasseln des Zuges] passing through Hohen-Cremmen. Then the noise grew fainter and died away completely and only the rustle of the plane-trees remained, like the sound of gentle rain.
>
> But it was only the night breeze passing. (I.4.220)

This last sentence is an uncharacteristically reductive intrusion by the narrator, who breaks the spell of the prose and shrinks the moment down in almost spiteful fashion. Any effort at a divine moment—the narrator will later say Effi gazes at the "wonders of the heavens" [Himmelwundern]—is consciously attenuated by the narrative's reminder that it is, after all, just the

---

21. Brunschwig points out that, of sixty-four German firms known to have had commercial ties to China in the late nineteenth century, fifty-seven were German Hanseatic companies, located primarily in Hamburg and Bremen (66).

night air. However, the next such episode allows the shadings of a Romantic communion with nature. Perhaps not coincidentally, it is also the beginning of Effi's end. Rising from the bed, Effi "sat down by the open window to breathe in once again the cool night air. The stars were twinkling and, in the park, not a leaf stirred. But the longer she listened, the more clearly she could hear once more that a gentle drizzle [ein feines Rieseln] fell on the plane trees. A feeling of release [Befreiung] came over her. 'Peace, peace' ['Ruhe, Ruhe']" (I.4.294). Fontane is clearly evoking here a moment of potentially spiritual if not religious enchantment, one that recalls the earlier scene but softens its sounds: the technology in the *Rasseln des Zuges*, the clattering of the train, in the first passage gives way to the *feines Rieseln*, or gentle drizzle, of the second. It is tempting to read the congruence of these two moments as a movement or development, as a progression *from* a secular containment of the religious moment *toward* a moment that is truly spiritualized. To do so only further accentuates the problematic position of enchantment in the novel, though, because this later scene occurs precisely as a death. The narrator specifically names Effi's skyward gaze as the cause of her end, in the only moment in the entire novel at which the narrator addresses a character: "Poor Effi, you had looked too long up to the wonders of the heavens and thought about them, and the end was, that the night air and the fog rising up from the pond threw her again onto her sick bed" [Arme Effi, du hattest zu den Himmelwundern zu lange hinaufgesehen und darüber nachgedacht, und das Ende war, daß die Nachtluft und die Nebel, die vom Teich her aufstiegen, sie wieder aufs krankenbett warfen] (I.4.292). First addressing Effi directly, the narrator, as if self-consciously, retreats from the second-person singular into the comfortable third person. The pronouncement of Effi's end, though ("das Ende war"), is as much a rational and scientized end to the attempted communion with nature, as it is a narratological declaration that is then made final. The doctor has the last word in this paragraph, and he tells the reader and Effi's parents: "There's no more; prepare yourselves for a sudden end." The end that follows is indeed sudden. The novel closes soon thereafter on Briest's repetition of the "weites Feld," his familiar spatial metaphor for subjects too large to be contained or known.

In an examination of the sudden ending of *Effi Briest*, Ernst Nef puts a new face on an old reading of the novel as *Sozialroman*, concluding that, "It deals with a wholly secular totality [eine ganz sekuläre Totalität]" (75). Nef does not elaborate on his inclusion of secularization in the list of ills confronted thematically by Fontane, but he does connect it loosely to the "wholly domesticated world" [ganz domestizierte Welt] of the novel (76). This turn in his critique is potentially productive but finally left unelaborated. The status of secularization in *Effi Briest*, where it is intimately related to a broader disenchantment, is similarly nebulous, however, just as it is in the novels of Balzac and Trollope. Russell Berman has clearly shown that there are aspects of Fontane's work altogether troubling, if not irreconcilable, to a reading of the novel as a hermetically sealed secular totality, protected and immuzined against spiritual or supernatural contagion, as Stern and Radcliffe would perhaps have it.[22] Michael Minden reminds us of "Fontane's often declared programmatic commitment to reality," which Fontane spoke of as "the 'quarry' from which the raw material of art must come" (22). Hans-Heinrich Reuter likewise recalls that "Fontane was—in his own words—'colossally empirical [kolossal empirisch]' and a lifelong virtuoso lover of all 'details'" (631). Fontane's "reality," which included conversations about and fears of an alleged Chinese ghost, has proven difficult for some prominent critics to accept at face value. Yet what Stern and Radcliffe call a blemish and a leftover, Fontane calls his fulcrum or *Drehpunkt*, and authorial declarations like this always end up sounding prescriptive. Thanks to Fontane's high opinion of the Chinese ghost, it has a prominent place in the reception of *Effi Briest;* thanks to its prominent place in the reception, this spectral figuration of the colonial is probably now the *Drehpunkt*, not just of the novel, but of the critical conversations surrounding it.

As critics have long noted, *Effi Briest* is a novel invested in the discourse of empire, but its particular engagement with empire becomes an engagement as well with the possibilities of realism. Readings of the novel that pass over the Chinese ghost as a supernatural blemish on an otherwise exemplary empirical realism, as well as readings of the novel that see the ghost only as a superficial signpost for colonialism, can find new possibilities. In the paradoxical simultaneity of a secular realism and a nonsecular paranoia in the imperial imagination, the ghost fulfills its role as centerpoint to the novel. The Chinese ghost is twice marginal, in the dual form of an ethnicity minor in nineteenth-century Germany, and a supernaturality that is antithetical to the forces of rationalization represented in the novel. In reading *Effi Briest*, one cannot divorce the symbolic content of the colonial from that of the spiritual, because they are, as the ghost makes clear, intimately related. Because of this, *Effi Briest* might further complicate rigidly empiricist notions of realism

---

22. Berman convincingly argues that "the landscape of *Effi Briest* is as much religious as it is natural, despite the secularizing predisposition of the realist program," and he refers to the importance of religion in the novel (360–61). Religion and the *Kulturkampf* are indeed important, but placing them within the larger discourse of disenchantment allows for a reading that incorporates the central image of the Chinese ghost and the importance of lingering and coveted Romantic tropes in the novel.

that have largely dominated the critical landscape, just as Balzac's and Trollope's approaches to realism trouble the idea that it is always and unremittingly secular or empirical. Such one-sided notions of the realist novel have proven themselves unable to account for the idea of disenchantment, which was both entirely immeasurable and yet deeply felt in the era's fictions.

CONCLUSION

THE LIMITS OF "REALISM"

(a) Realism and Romance, Reconsidered

> Knowledge has transformed the world from a system of well-marked moral domains into a complicated geography, period. And yet, this very difficulty seems to have induced the novel to its most ambitious wager: to be the bridge between the old and the new, forging a symbolic compromise between the indifferent world of modern knowledge, and the enchanted topography of magic story-telling. Between a new geography, that we cannot ignore—and an old narrative matrix, that we cannot forget.
> —Moretti, *Atlas of the European Novel 1800–1900*

Four linked problems are implied by the idea of the limits of realism, and we could label them problems of geography, epistemology, aesthetic terminology, and periodization. These problems are related enough that one could imagine them as causes and effects of each other—as mutually reinforcing, even—and they hover around the historical narrative of empire, with its warring core concepts of empiricism and enchantment. They have all arisen and been discussed in the preceding chapters, to varying degrees, because they are provoked by the novels on which I have focused and the disproportionate importance they accord to foreign figures within European metropolitan settings. Four of the eight novels analyzed in depth here are even named for these figures (Balzac's *Peau de chagrin* and *La Fille aux yeux d'or*, and Trollope's *Phineas* diptych), and this is not to mention Trollope's Melmotte, said to be the center of London, or Fontane's Chinese Ghost, the author's pivot (*Drehpunkt*) in *Effi Briest*. I have tried to show what can happen to the form of the realist novel and to its articulation of space when these marginal figures become so central. There are additional consequences, though, and some larger conclusions can be teased out through a brief look at the various problems implied by the limits of realism.

The marginal characters themselves represent, on one level, geographical limits of realism. They embody the faraway places from which they are said to come, but, because of their presence in metropolitan centers of Europe, they also stand paradoxically for the collapse of the distances between those faraway places and the domestic settings in which realism encounters them. Accompanying that collapse of distance is the chaotic intermingling of foreign and familiar, which results in the rationalization of the exotic foreign and the abortive reenchantment of the domestic. Internal limits, such as those between city and country, also come into play in new ways, and there follows a frustration of boundaries between zones of order and zones of disorder. This geographical valence is, moreover, inextricable from the frustration of the dueling epistemologies linked to domestic order and colonial disorder—realist, secular, European reason and the nonrealist, nonsecular, irrational world beyond Europe. This is, at least, how so many postcolonial critics have described imperialism's schismatic view of types of knowledge, and the novels adopt this view as well. Yet attending to realism as an epistemology—or as a narrative mode organized by a certain epistemology—creates new limits and ushers in a different set of problems, because it goes right to issues of aesthetics and periodization. In other words, it goes to the two main ways in which we normally employ the term "realism": to designate a method/mode, and to designate a period. As I demonstrated in the introduction, and as critics like Raymond Tallis and George Levine have shown, realism's epistemology invariably gets pigeonholed or stereotyped as rigidly secular, empirical, scientific, rational, and so on. Even if it is true that the epistemology which we call "realist" fits those stereotypes, however, it is not so simply true of the narratives that we call "realist" or of the literary-historical period we call that of "realism." As the preceding chapters have shown, these canonically realist authors regularly amplify their texts' own claims to empiricism and secularism while simultaneously—and often explicitly and self-consciously—troubling those very claims. When some of the most famous and successful realist texts or authors of realist texts consistently evoke energies at odds with supposedly realist epistemology, and when those energies are not always neatly wrapped up or unambiguously disciplined, then what we are calling realist narrative cannot easily be reduced to narrative that deploys a realist epistemology. Nor can any so-called era or epoch of realism.

One recent historical overview of realism and naturalism underscores some of the difficulties in these last two limits of "realism" (our use of it as a way of describing a transhistorical aesthetic mode and as a period-specific literary-historical designation). In the preface and introduction to *Realism and Naturalism: The Novel in an Age of Transition* (2005), Richard Lehan continues a critical tradition that pits romance and realism against each other as mutually exclusive terms in a Darwinian fight for survival.[1] "Writers in the early nineteenth century," Lehan writes, believed "that the romantic view of nature was inadequate to the new city with its commercial and industrial institutions. Realism/naturalism was the first corrective to this anachronistic view. As a result, subject matter and narrative technique were drastically changed. The romance did not do justice to the new reality" (xii). Later, "Realism/naturalism challenged a false idealism" and thus "gradually eliminated the fantasy elements it shared with the romance from its plots and began depicting a more ordinary reality. Rider Haggard gave way to Rudyard Kipling, Kipling to Jack London, London to Joseph Conrad, Conrad to Ernest Hemingway, Hemingway to the noir reality of a James M. Cain—each new form of the mode moving it further away from forms of the romance" (xxi–xxii). There is an unspoken tension, in this assessment, between romance as a type of content (the "nature" of the romantics) and romance as a form or structure; the genealogy of imperial and late-imperial romances chosen are not examples of Wordsworth's domestic natural landscapes (static *content*) but rather of narrative *structures* driven by adventure and exploration.[2] In any case, though, this understanding of the development has realism slaying the falsely ideal and "anachronistic" dragon of romance, and Lehan turns to Balzac as the writer who begins evacuating romance from the novel (44–48). One can trace this view through René Wellek, who claims in the early 1960s that "realism definitely breaks with the romantic" (253), and at least as far back as Lukács's *Studies in European Realism*, in 1948, where he claims that Balzac "overcame" romanticism (64). Yet Lukács quickly produces a paradox analogous to Said's paradox in *Orientalism*, and such paradoxes might finally be endemic to realism. According to Lukács, romanticism was just "one feature of Balzac's total conception, a feature which he overcame *and developed further*" (my emphases). Lukács does not elaborate on the role of romanticism in Balzac's realist attempt at "an active and objective presentation of things in themselves." But this dialectical model offers an alternative to the zero-sum configuration, in which realism appears as a necessary answer to new realities, and romantic modes are discarded as hopelessly out

---

1. Moretti's recent *Graphs Maps Trees* offers a different Darwinian model of literary-historical development, one that emphasizes evolutionary theory's ability to account for the inheritance and diversity of literary forms in addition to their emergence and extinction. See esp. 67–92.
2. There are probably very romantic roots to the idea of common or ordinary reality often linked to realism. It was one of the main drives of Wordsworth's and Coleridge's *Lyrical Ballads* (1798) and is advanced repeatedly in their famous 1800 Preface. Knoepflmacher explicitly links the Preface's concern with common, ordinary reality to the development of George Eliot's realism (12).

of step with a modern knowledge that will not accommodate them.

The monological view of realism that has persisted presents clear limitations for describing an aesthetic mode or a literary-historical period. It either abominates realism as a stereotype that any close examination of realist narrative belies, or it elevates realism as an absolute ideal that the works we call realist cannot and do not really meet. Most often, the critical reaction to this incongruity amongst scholars of realism has been to eliminate from consideration what does not fit the model of "ordinary," empirical reality. We see such exclusions at work in, for example, the dismissal of the Chinese ghost by prominent critics of *Effi Briest*. Fontane's novel, moreover, appears very late in the game, at a time when one would expect realism to have already been crowned the victor in its struggle against superfluous romance. So, it is undoubtedly true that romantic conceptions of the world were "anachronistic" in the era of industrialization and urbanization which Lehan describes and which critics situate as the historical frame of realism. Authors generally allied with realism, including the ones discussed above, openly concede this, beginning with Balzac's *La Peau de chagrin:* Paris and the nineteenth century are "times and places where magic should be impossible" (10.79). It is equally true that the "romantic view of nature" was "inadequate" to this new and disenchanted reality, and Trollope obligingly unwrites the romance of Scott's Highlands for us in *Phineas Finn*, as if to prove their obsolescence. As all of these authors openly admit, the false, romantic values dying along the trail in the nineteenth century's march toward progress, were not of a piece with what their century knew and lived.

And yet that was precisely their appeal. To Balzac, Trollope, Fontane, and many others, anachronism, idealism (however false), and mystery were necessary counterweights to the insistent presence of the present and to technology that hustled society toward the future and actively diminished distance. Thus, Balzac proffers an object that resists modern scientific explanation; Trollope reverses his own disenchantment of Scott, pushing his prose back into the enchanted Gothic; and Fontane defers to Heine's older version of the Harz as a region of romance, offsetting the disenchantment of Berlin. Consistently, realist novels and characters in realist novels turn to these very outmoded and perhaps falsely ideal paradigms, contrasting them with new reality and allowing them to challenge and occasionally even undo that new reality. Romance rarely wins, as these novels make clear. But its intensified and foregrounded presence in the texts troubles the notion that it is there simply in order to be abandoned or mocked. In this fact, our conception of realism confronts an internal paradox that sees its assumed mission—to represent reality—challenged by what Jameson calls a "longing for magic and providential mystery" (*Political Unconscious* 152). Critics of realism have largely equated a teleology of disenchantment with an uncomplicatedly heroic narrative of progress. We cannot say the same of realist authors.

(b) Epilogue

These particular tensions in nineteenth-century realism survive into the twentieth century and beyond, as does the theme of the central foreigner which focalizes them. However, the sociohistorical contexts become so altered that neither the form nor the exact function of these tensions and themes in the narrative remains the same. In a world knit even more tightly together by technology than the one offered in Fontane's *Cécile* or Trollope's *The Way We Live Now*, can distance and foreignness still have any currency as markers of enchantment or narrative complication? In a globally integrated economy, can foreign figures still serve as emblems of the collision between empiricism and enchantment, between the familiar and the unfamiliar? There is not space here for a thorough answer, but a few examples might offer a partial one. Through the twentieth and into the twenty-first century, certain novelists make use of either realist narrative strategies or foreignness in a manner not wholly dissimilar to the tactics of Balzac, Trollope, and Fontane. Because the material and historically specific world which realists depict is so essential to conditioning the form and content of their works, as I argued in the introduction, and because the perceived realities of the nineteenth century are no more, this particular realism has its historical moment and then can no longer be imaginable in that form. And if changing realities alter the realism that depicts them, they must also alter the values that counter those changing realities, including the foreign figure that was so useful to nineteenth-century novels.

It is nevertheless interesting to look at the changes in the thematic terrain, because in some prominent works of modernist fiction, foreignness is still very important. It becomes, however, central to the plot and to a protagonist's self-discovery without being central to the depiction of domestic space. This much is summed up by the title and plot of Virginia Woolf's first novel, *The Voyage Out* (1915). Urban domestic space, moreover, is itself a locus of alienation in works like Alfred Döblin's *Berlin Alexanderplatz* (1929) and Joyce's *Ulysses* (1922), but a number of works in the wake of the nineteenth century exploit foreign settings as backdrops for a battle against the perceived claustrophobia of middle-class morality in northern Europe. Against the dark adventure narratives of Conrad, Haggard, May, and Anatole France and the tradition of imperial romance, there is another tradition of touristic or even commercial travel that permits contact with the foreign without straying totally from domestic concerns. If this is already visible in Fontane's Gordon, one sees it as well in Thomas Mann's *Buddenbrooks*[3] (1900), which sends the restless son Christian "out there [drüben]" to South America to satisfy his "adventure-lust [Abenteuerlust]" (237). He returns full of stories of "Chilean stabbings [chilenische Messerabenteuer]," reassurances that there is still a different world out there (448). But Christian is also said, at this same moment, to be "speaking in tongues," and if there is a different epistemology in the novel it is that of western religious belief within an unbelieving narrative, and not a knowledge attributed to foreign spaces. Missionaries belonging to Madame Buddenbrook's "Jerusalem Evenings" are described with "parrot heads [Papageiköpfe]," "enigmatic brown eyes," and hearts "full of marvelous and mysterious knowledge [wunderbaren und geheimnisvollen Kenntnissen]" (280). Their exoticized looks are paired with their mystical knowledge. And it is the *Prophetin* Sesame Weichbrodt who, in a manner reminiscent of Pauline's war against "modern invasions" in Balzac's *Peau de chagrin*, stands at the novel's end "victorious in the good fight she had waged all her life against the onslaughts [Anfechtungen] of reason" (759). For Christian Buddenbrook, as for later characters in Mann's own *Tod in Venedig* (*Death in Venice*, 1912), André Gide's *L'immoraliste* (1902), E. M. Forster's *A Room with a View* (1908), and even perhaps Lawrence Durrell's later *Alexandria Quartet* (1957–60), these foreign locales hold a value of difference despite their accessibility. The banal continent that Trollope's and Fontane's characters complain about can be reenchanted, anyway, if needed—in Forster's novel, simply losing one's guidebook will do, as in the chapter "In Santa Croce with No Baedeker."

In an illuminating conversation with the *Paris Review* in 1959, midway through the publication of the four novels in the *Alexandria Quartet*, Durrell highlights both what these later evocations of the foreign in fiction share with their nineteenth-century predecessors and what makes them part of a wholly different paradigm. He begins by expressing it not as a duel of epistemologies but rather an attempt to marry them:

> The ideas behind this thing [the *Quartet*], which have nothing whatsoever to do with the fun of it as reading matter, are roughly these. Eastern and Western metaphysics are coming to a point of confluence in the most interesting way. It seems unlikely in a way, but nevertheless the two major architects of this breakthrough have been Einstein and Freud. Einstein torpedoed the old Victorian material universe—in other words, the view of matter—and Freud torpe-

---

3. The name is Mann's tribute to Fontane, drawn from a minor character in *Effi Briest* named Buddenbrook.

doed the idea of the stable ego so that personality began to diffuse. Thus in the concept of the space-time continuum you've got an absolutely new concept of what reality might be, do you see? Well, this novel is a four-dimensional dance, a relativity poem. (26–27)

At great length, Durrell expounds on the relationship his novels bear to both theoretical physics and Freudian and Jungian psychology. His scientific leanings here recall Balzac's general preface to the *Comédie humaine*, where Balzac names natural historians as his real inspirations. Yet these very influences Durrell claims emphasize the vast differences between Balzac's nineteenth-century natural history, which fuses disparate events or objects into coherent narrative, and what Durrell calls his diffuse "stereoscopic narrative with stereophonic personality" (26). The cosmopolitan cast of characters in a foreign city emphasizes this gesture, and it is clear to Durrell that the supposed epistemology of nineteenth-century realism no longer exists as it did. It has become intellectual history, lost out to relativity.

This picture of Durrell's tetralogy—of its celebration of the epistemological marriage of East and West—is incomplete, though, without a mention of another series of novels from Egypt published at the same time as Durrell's. Naguib Mahfouz' *Cairo Trilogy* (1956–57) is palpably influenced by European realism in both its domestic content and narrative method. While Durrell's multi-novel project seeks to combine its two spatially-coded paradigms of East and West, Mahfouz captures instead the idea of invading forms of knowledge. My introduction discussed the postcolonial theorization of this invasion in the works of Ashis Nandy and others, and Mahfouz clearly narrativizes the process. As Rasheed El-Enany has argued, the trilogy's depiction of "social progress" pits the forces of Islam against those of "science and socialism" (73). El-Enany reads the second novel in the series, *Palace of Desire*, as a staged battle between the creationism of Islam and the evolutionary theories of Darwin, which enter the novel (and thus the novel's Cairo) through a newspaper article. The clash between Arabic tradition and European modernity is cast in generational terms (father against son) that amplify the difference on which the novel is based. In this sense, Mahfouz' trilogy stands out against the current of twentieth-century European writers I listed above, as he engages epistemological questions much as Balzac did, but from vastly different perspectives.

The mobility implied by the novels of the twentieth century already animates the work of Balzac, Trollope, and Fontane. Mobility and life in the foreign for authors and their plots ultimately becomes a new norm in the twentieth century, but it barely alters the idea of foreignness in the twentieth-

and twenty-first-century novel.[4] Foreignness retains the specific weight that it brought to nineteenth-century realist works, and it can still instill a sense of other regions and other types of knowledge. In narrative melting-pots like the London of Salman Rushdie, Zadie Smith, or Hanif Kureishi, for example—that is, in today's truly global city—foreign figures arise more often with a fully historicized biography than with the comically uncertain origins of Trollope's adventurers in *The Way We Live Now*. Epistemological differences are still linked to cultural differences in these later works, but those differences are often negotiated *within* rather than *between* cultures and spaces, just as they are in Mahfouz' *Cairo Trilogy*. The conflicts are also frequently mapped onto generational misunderstandings: between immigrants seen clinging to their home culture and their children, who were born and raised in England; or between immigrants seduced by Western culture and a second generation seeking to reestablish contact with the culture of their parents' homeland or with identities founded on extremism (e.g., Kureishi's "My Son the Fanatic" or the KEVIN faction of extremist Muslims in Smith's *White Teeth* [390]). This is not even to mention the formal shifts at work in the magical realism of Rushdie[5] and in Smith's foregrounded fascination with the interconnectedness of the various plots in *White Teeth*, which finally converge at the climactic ending: "And all these people are heading for the same room," the narrator declares (428). This sort of interconnectedness, this confluence of differences in a major city, was prime material for Balzac's fiction, a source of deep concern for Trollope's sense of tradition, and a sign for Fontane that the earth was shrinking steadily. What is new and thus a formal challenge for Trollope, though, is cultivated and handled authoritatively by Smith's narrator. Because it is no longer new, such connectedness has to be foregrounded as exceptional rather than banal, the small world once again made into a source of possibility rather than pessimism.

The epistemological and cultural conflicts also take the shape of an internal struggle within the development of one character, as they do in Peter Høeg's *Frøken Smillas fornemmelse for sne* (*Smilla's Sense of Snow* [US] or *Miss Smilla's Feeling for Snow* [UK], 1992). Høeg's novel matches some of the narrative strategies of nineteenth-century realism with the complication of them by a bi-cultural first-person narrator who is torn between the fierce independence of her mother (a native of Greenland), and the Danish ration-

---

4. Consider the number of major European novelists who either were born outside of Europe (Rudyard Kipling, George Orwell, Doris Lessing, Albert Camus, Marguerite Duras, Lawrence Durrell, J.G. Ballard, William Boyd) or who, born in Europe, either emigrated or spent significant time abroad (Knut Hamsun, Hermann Hesse, James Joyce, Thomas Mann, Samuel Beckett, Karen Blixen, Graham Greene, Anthony Burgess).

5. Magical realism itself is constituted by colliding epistemologies, as numerous critics have pointed out. See especially Faris.

ality of her father (a surgeon). Smilla Jaspersen is self-consciously poised between the nineteenth-century roots of the detective novel and a more introspective modernist search for identity. She is also very explicitly made the center of a war between the scientific epistemology of rational Europe and the mythical epistemology of Greenland. At the burial of a murdered young Greenlander named Isaiah (Esajas), the novel's first paragraphs evoke a stable, realist sense of a particular setting, from the precise temperature ("0° Fahrenheit") to the time of year ("December"), to the location: Vestre Cemetery, Copenhagen (11). Yet Smilla simultaneously ushers in the idea of unstable cultural identity that will permeate the book; stating that, "in the language that is no longer mine, the snow is *qanik*" (a Greenlandic word for the type of snow she is describing), she goes on to distinguish "outsider[s]" from those who have "grown up in Greenland" (12). Difference is constructed here immediately in terms of language and space, but it quickly expands to include competing interpretations of natural phenomena, from the explanatory science of the hexagonal shape of ice crystals to an explanatory myth that "the heavens are weeping for Isaiah, and the tears are turning into frosty down that is covering him up" (12). Like the novels of Balzac, Trollope and Fontane discussed above, Høeg's is set into motion by the presence of Isaiah, a colonial character in a post-imperial European metropolis. Smilla's presence, too, is key to the maintenance of tension between spaces, cultures, languages, and types of knowledge. Her narration repeatedly refers to the Danish imperial project in Greenland, which she sees as motivated simultaneously by commercial and scientific concerns.

The novel structures itself, and its understanding of the competing Arctic and European epistemologies, in terms of absolute spatial divisions that are also narrative divisions, sections of the book: the City (*Byen*), the in-between zone of the Sea (*Havet*) and the othered zone of the Ice (*Isen*).[6] These divisions are then repeatedly troubled. The relationship is clearly hierarchical and indicative of a slow attrition: the first section of the novel, "The City," consists of three parts, "The Sea" then of two, and "The Ice," finally, of just one. There are also correspondingly different units of time-measurement, as Smilla explains the gap between absolute, measured European time, and North Greenland's more relative idea of the *sinik*, "the number of overnights that a journey requires": "*Sinik* is not a distance, not a number of days or hours. It is both a spatial and a temporal phenomenon... that is taken for granted [selvfølgelig] by Inuits but that cannot be captured by

---

6. Stounbjerg, who urges the novel's depiction of space towards a compelling reading of Høeg as critic of the "instrumental logic" inherent in the project of "the domination of nature" (388), claims that "culture, the subject and western reason meet their limit" in the novel (389), but the novel's ending suggests a more durable tension. On imperialism more generally in the novel, see Poddar and Mealor.

ordinary speech in any European language" (299). The novel straddles the line between Smilla's "feeling" for ice and snow—which, she claims, "is incomprehensible [uforståelig] to those who were not born to it"—and the empirical data-collection endemic to the detective project (398). The ending bluntly defies the closure one associates with detection, though. As the scientist/imperialist Tørk takes off on foot into the Arctic cold, Smilla tells us in the novel's last words that "There will be no resolution [afgørelse]" (435). The final word, *afgørelse*, has legal connotations of "verdict" or "settlement" that speak directly to Høeg's frustration of the detective project. The narratological implications are no less important, and the many oppositions on which the novel is based will remain undecided. Høeg's novel combines a realist mode of external observation and description, complete with a deep respect for the function of the archive; a self-consciously irresolvable ending; and a first-person interiority that moves fluidly between memory and present, between waking and dreaming, and between emotion and enumeration. In this sense, *Smilla's Sense of Snow* offers us an instructive view of how the theme of the central foreigner negotiates several major narrative trends since Balzac. This is at least one compelling version of what happens in the late twentieth century when a (partially) colonial figure is imported into a metropolitan novel whose aims and claims are (partially) realist ones.

WORKS CITED

Adorno, Theodor. "Extorted Reconciliation: On Georg Lukács' *Realism In Our Time.*" *Notes to Literature*. Trans. Shierry Weber Nicholsen. Vol. 2. New York: Columbia University Press, 1991. 216–40.

———. "Letters to Walter Benjamin." Trans. Harry Zohn. *Aesthetics and Politics*. Ernst Bloch, Georg Lukács, Bertolt Brecht, Walter Benjamin, and Theodor Adorno. New York: Verso, 1980. 110–33.

Allen, James Smith. "Obedience, Struggle, and Revolt: The Historical Vision of Balzac's *Father Goriot*." *CLIO* 16.2 (1987): 103–19.

Alpers, Svetlana. "The Museum as a Way of Seeing." *Exhibiting Cultures: The Poetics and Politics of Museum Display*. Ed. Ivan Karp and Steven D. Lavine. Washington, DC: Smithsonian Institution Press, 1991. 25–32.

Altick, Richard D. *The Presence of the Present: Topics of the Day in the Victorian Novel*. Columbus: The Ohio State University Press, 1991.

Amery, L. S. *The German Colonial Claim*. New York: Longmans, Green and Co., 1940.

Andermatt, Michael. "'Es rauscht und rauscht immer, aber es ist kein richtiges Leben': Zur Topographie des Fremden in Fontanes *Effi Briest*." *Theodor Fontane: Am Ende des Jahrhunderts*. Ed. Hanna Delf von Wolzogen and Helmut Nürnberger. Vol. 3. Würzburg: Königshausen & Neumann, 2000. 189–99.

Anderson, Benedict. *Imagined Communities: Reflections on the Origin and Spread of Nationalism*. London: Verso, 1983.

Asmundsson, Doris R. "Trollope's First Novel: A Re-examination." *Éire-Ireland: A Journal of Irish Studies* 6.3 (1971): 83–91.

Auerbach, Erich. *Mimesis: The Representation of Reality in Western Literature*. Trans. Willard R. Trask. Princeton: Princeton University Press, 1953.

Austen, Jane. *Pride and Prejudice*. 1813. Oxford: Oxford University Press, 2004.

Avery, George C. "The Chinese Wall: Fontane's Psychograph of Effi Briest." *Views and Reviews of Modern German Literature: Festschrift for Adolf D. Klarmann*. Ed. Karl S. Weimar. München: Delp, 1974. 18–38.

Azim, Firdous. *The Colonial Rise of the Novel*. London: Routledge, 1993.

Bachman, Maria K. "'Furious Passions of the Celtic Race': Ireland, Madness and Wilkie Collins's *Blind Love*." *Victorian Crime, Madness and Sensation*. Ed. Andrew Maunder and Grace Moore. Aldershot: Ashgate, 2004. 179–94.

Bal, Mieke. "Telling Objects: A Narrative Perspective on Collecting." *The Cultures of Collecting*. Ed. John Elsner and Roger Cardinal. Cambridge, MA: Harvard University Press, 1994. 97–115.

Baldensperger, Fernand. *Orientations étrangères chez Honoré de Balzac*. Paris: Honoré Champion, 1927.

Balzac, Honoré de. *La Comédie humaine*. Ed. Pierre Citron. 12 vols. Paris: Gallimard, 1976.

Bang, Herman. *Realisme og Realister: Portrætstudier og Aforismer*. 1879. København: Gyldendals, 1966.

Bann, Stephen. "Poetics of the Museum: Lenoir and Du Sommerard." *Grasping the World: The Idea of the Museum*. Ed. Donald Preziosi and Claire Farago. Burlington: Ashgate, 2003. 65–83.

Bardèche, Maurice. *Balzac, romancier: La formation de l'Art du Roman chez Balzac jusqu'à la publication du "Père Goriot" (1820–1835)*. 1944. Geneva: Slatkin Reprints, 1967.

Barthes, Roland. "L'effet de réel." *Littérature et réalité*. R. Barthes, L. Bersani, Ph. Hamon, M. Riffaterre, and I. Watt. Paris: Seuil, 1982. 81–90.

Beckett, Samuel. *Molloy*. *Three Novels: Molloy, Malone Dies, The Unnamable*. Trans. Patrick Bowles and Samuel Beckett. New York: Grove, 1991.

Becquemont, Daniel. "Politics in Literature, 1874–1875: *The Way We Live Now* and *Beauchamp's Career*." *Politics in Literature in the Nineteenth Century*. Ed. Janie Teissedou et al. Lille: PU de Lille, 1974. 137–51.

Bell, David F. "Balzac and the Modern City: Mapping Paris in *Old Goriot*." *Approaches to Teaching Balzac's Old Goriot*." Ed. Michael Peled Ginsburg. New York: The Modern Language Association of America, 2000. 81–89.

———. *Circumstances: Chance in the Literary Text*. Lincoln: University of Nebraska Press, 1993.

———. *Real Time: Accelerating Narrative from Balzac to Zola*. Urbana: University of Illinois Press, 2004.

Bennett, Tony. *The Birth of the Museum: History, Theory, Politics*. New York: Routledge, 1995.

Berman, Nina. "K.u.K. Colonialism: Hofmannsthal in North Africa." *New German Critique* 75 (Fall 1998): 3–27.

———. *Orientalismus, Kolonialismus und Moderne: zum Bild des Orient in der deutschsprachigen Kultur um 1900*. Stuttgart: M und P, 1997.

Berman, Russell A. "*Effi Briest* and the End of Realism." *A Companion to German Realism, 1848–1900*. Ed. Todd Kontje. London: Camden House, 2002. 339–64.

———. *Enlightenment or Empire: Colonial Discourse in German Culture*. Lincoln: University of Nebraska Press, 1998.

———. "Der ewige Zweite: Deutschlands sekundärer Kolonialismus." *Phantasiereiche: Zur Kulturgeschichte des deutschen Kolonialismus*. Ed. Birthe Kundrus. Frankfurt: Campus, 2003. 19–32.

Bernd, Clifford Albrecht. "Die Politik als tragendes Strukturelement in Fontanes Effi Briest." *Wahrheit und Wort*. Ed. Gabriela Scherer and Beatrice Wehrli. Bern: Peter

Lang, 1996. 61–71.
Berol, Laura M. "The Anglo-Irish Threat in Thackeray's and Trollope's Writings of the 1840s." *Victorian Literature and Culture* 32.1 (2004): 103–16.
Bersani, Leo. *A Future for Astyanax: Character and Desire in Literature*. New York: Columbia University Press, 1984.
Bhabha, Homi K. "DissemiNation: Time, Narrative, and the Margins of the Modern Nation." *Nation and Narration*. Ed. Homi K. Bhabha. London: Routledge, 1990. 291–322.
———. *The Location of Culture*. London: Routledge, 1994.
Bisztray, George. *Marxist Models of Literary Realism*. New York: Columbia University Press, 1978.
Bloch, Ernst. *The Utopian Function of Art and Literature: Selected Essays*. Trans. Jack Zipes and Frank Mecklenburg. Cambridge, MA: MIT Press, 1989.
Bloomfield, Morton W. "Trollope's Use of Canadian History in 'Phineas Finn' (1867–1869)." *Nineteenth-Century Fiction* 5.1 (June 1950): 67–74.
Bock, Henning. "Fürstliche und öffentliche Kunstsammlungen im 18. und frühen 19. Jahrhundert in Deutschland." *The Genesis of the Art Museum in the 18th Century*. Ed. Per Bjurström. Stockholm: Nationalmuseum, 1993. 112–30.
Bonwit, Marianne. "Effi Briest und Ihre Vorgängerinnen Emma Bovary und Nora Helmer." *Monatshefte* 20.1 (January 1948): 445–46.
Bordas, Eric. "La composition balzacienne dans *Ferragus* et *La Fille aux yeux d'or*: de la négligence à l'ambivalence." *Orbis Literarium* 49 (1994): 338–47.
Brantlinger, Patrick. *Rule of Darkness: British Literature and Imperialism, 1830–1914*. Ithaca: Cornell University Press, 1988.
Brewer, Kenneth L., Jr. "Colonial Discourse and William Makepeace Thackeray's *Irish Sketch Book*." *Papers on Language & Literature* 29.3 (Summer 1993): 259–83.
Brontë, Charlotte. *Jane Eyre*. 1847. Oxford: Oxford University Press, 2000.
———. *Shirley*. 1849. Oxford: Oxford University Press, 1998.
———. *Villette*. 1853. Harmondsworth: Penguin Classics, 1985.
Brooks, Peter. *Reading for the Plot: Design and Intention in Narrative*. New York: Vintage, 1985.
———. *Realist Vision*. New Haven: Yale University Press, 2005.
Brown, Bill. *A Sense of Things: The Object Matter of American Literature*. Chicago: University of Chicago Press, 2004.
Brown, Marshall. "The Logic of Realism: A Hegelian Approach." *PMLA* 96.2 (March 1981): 224–41.
Browne, James. *A History of the Highlands and of the Highland Clans*. Glasgow: Fullarton, 1835–38.
Brunschwig, Henri. *L'expansion allemande outre-mer du XVe siècle à nos jours*. Paris: PU de France, 1957.
Buchanan, Alexandrina. "Science and Sensibility: Architectural Antiquarianism in the Early Nineteenth Century." *Producing the Past: Aspects of Antiquarian Culture and Practice 1700–1850*. Ed. Martin Myrone and Lucy Peltz. Brookfield: Ashgate, 1999.
Bullock, A. L. C. *Germany's Colonial Demands*. London: Humphrey Milford, 1939.
Burke, Edmund. *Reflections on the Revolution in France*. 1790. Oxford: Oxford University Press, 1999.

Byron, Lord. *The Major Works*. Ed. Jerome J. McGann. Oxford: Oxford University Press, 2000. 274–315.
Cailliet, Émile. *The Themes of Magic in Nineteenth Century French Fiction*. 1932. Philadelphia: Porcupine Press, 1980.
Carofiglio, Vito. "Mondi, immondi e mondani nel «*Père Goriot*»." *Athanor* 6 (1995): 151–58.
Cazauran, Nicole. "Le «Tableau» du magasin d'antiquités dans *La Peau de chagrin*." *Mélanges de langue et de littérature française offerts à Pierre Larthomas*. Ed. Jean-Pierre Seguin. Paris: École Normale Supérieure de Jeunes Filles, 1985. 87–98.
Chakrabarty, Dipesh. *Provincializing Europe: Postcolonial Thought and Historical Difference*. Princeton: Princeton University Press, 2000.
Chambers, Helen Elizabeth. *Supernatural and Irrational Elements in the Works of Theodor Fontane*. Stuttgart: Akademischer Verlag Hans-Dieter Heinz, 1980.
Chapman, R. W., and C. B.Tinker. "The Text of Trollope's *Phineas Redux*." *The Review of English Studies: A Quarterly Journal of English Literature and the English Language* 18.1 (January 1942): 86–92.
Chasles, Philarète. "Introduction: 1831–1833." *La Comédie Humaine*. Honoré de Balzac. Vol. 4. Paris: Gallimard, 1979. 1185–97.
Chatterjee, Partha. *The Nation and Its Fragments: Colonial and Postcolonial Histories*. Princeton: Princeton University Press, 1993.
Cheyette, Bryan. *Constructions of 'The Jew' in English Literature and Society: Racial Representations, 1875–1945*. Cambridge: Cambridge University Press 1993.
Clifford, James. *The Predicament of Culture: Twentieth-Century Ethnography, Literature, and Art*. Cambridge, MA: Harvard University Press, 1988.
Cockshut, A. O. J. *Anthony Trollope: A Critical Study*. London: Collins, 1955.
Cohen, Derek. "Constructing the Contradiction: Anthony Trollope's *The Way We Live Now*." *Jewish Presences in English Literature*. Ed. Derek Cohen and Deborah Heller. Montreal: McGill-Queen's University Press, 1990. 61–75.
Cohn, Bernard S. *Colonialism and Its Forms of Knowledge: The British in India*. Princeton: Princeton University Press, 1996.
Colby, Robert A. "*Barry Lyndon* and the Irish Hero." *Nineteenth-Century Fiction* 21.2 (September 1966): 109–30.
Colley, Linda. *Britons: Forging the Nation 1707–1837*. New Haven: Yale University Press, 1992.
Collins, Philip. *Trollope's London*. Leicester: Victorian Studies Centre, 1982.
Collins, Wilkie. *The Moonstone*. 1868. Oxford: Oxford University Press, 1999.
Conrad, Joseph. *Heart of Darkness*. 1899. New York: Dover, 1990.
Cotsell, Michael. "Introduction." Charles Dickens. *Our Mutual Friend*. Oxford: Oxford University Press, 1998. ix–xxi.
Crane, Susan A. "Curious Cabinets and Imaginary Museums." *Museums and Memory*. Ed. Susan A. Crane. Stanford: Stanford University Press, 2000. 60–80.
———. "Story, History and the Passionate Collector." *Producing the Past: Aspects of Antiquarian Culture and Practice*. Ed. Martin Monroe and Lucy Peltz. Brookfield: Ashgate, 1999. 187–203.
Curtis, L. Perry, Jr. *Apes and Angels: The Irishman in Victorian Caricature*. 1971. Rev. ed. Washington, DC: Smithsonian Institution Press, 1997.

Dali, Shen. "Une Chine à la Balzac." *L'Année balzacienne* 2 (2001): 317–24.
Dällenbach, Lucien. *La canne de Balzac.* Paris: José Corti, 1996.
Dargan, E. Preston. "Balzac's General Method; An Analysis of His Realism." *Studies in Balzac's Realism.* Ed. E. Preston Dargan. New York: Russell & Russell, 1967. 1–32.
de Cervantes Saavedra, Miguel. *The Adventures of Don Quixote.* Trans. J. M. Cohen. Harmondsworth: Penguin, 1950.
———. *Don Quijote de la Mancha.* 1605, 1615. 2 vols. Ed. Martín de Riquer. Barcelona: Editorial Juventud, 1995.
de la Motte, Dean. "Balzacorama: Mass Culture in *Old Goriot.*" *Approaches to Teaching Balzac's* Old Goriot. Ed. Michal Peled Ginzburg. New York: MLA, 2000. 54–61.
Debreuille, Jean-Yves. "Horizontalité et verticalité: Inscriptions idéologiques dans *La Fille aux yeux d'or.*" *La femme au XIXe siècle: Littérature et idéologie.* Ed. R. Bellet. Lyon: PU de Lyon, 1985. 151–65.
Defoe, Daniel. *Robinson Crusoe.* 1719. Harmondsworth: Penguin, 1965.
Diamond, Marie Josephine. "The Monstrous Other: The Chimera of Speculation in Balzac's *The Girl with the Golden Eyes.*" *Nineteenth-Century Contexts* 18 (1994): 249–62.
Dickens, Charles. *Bleak House.* 1853. Harmondsworth: Penguin, 1997.
———. *David Copperfield.* 1850. London: Penguin Classics, 1996.
———. *Dombey and Son.* 1848. Oxford: Oxford University Press, 2001.
———. *Great Expectations.* 1861. Oxford: Oxford University Press, 1998.
———. *The Old Curiosity Shop.* 1841. Oxford: Oxford University Press, 1998.
Doody, Margaret Anne. *The True Story of the Novel.* New Brunswick: Rutgers University Press, 1996.
Dougherty, Jane Elizabeth. "An Angel in the House: The Act of Union and Anthony Trollope's Irish Hero." *Victorian Literature and Culture* 32.1 (2004): 133–45.
Douglas, Roy, Liam Harte, and Jim O'Hara. *Drawing Conclusions: A Cartoon History of Anglo-Irish Relations 1798–1998.* Belfast: Blackstaff Press, 1998.
Downing, Eric. *Double Exposures: Repetition and Realism in Nineteenth-Century German Fiction.* Stanford: Stanford University Press, 2000.
Doyle, Roddy. *A Star Called Henry.* Harmondsworth: Penguin, 2000.
Drent, Janke. "Balzac et le nom de Paquita Valdès." *L'Année balzacienne* 1974: 325–27.
Dubois, Jacques. *Les Romanciers du réel: De Balzac à Simenon.* Paris: Seuil, 2000.
Durrell, Lawrence. "The Art of Fiction No. 23: Interviewed by Gene Andrewski & Julian Mitchell." *Paris Review* 22 (Autumn–Winter 1959–1960): 1–30.
Eagleton, Terry. *Heathcliff and the Great Hunger: Studies in Irish Culture.* London: Verso, 1995.
Edwards, Owen Dudley. "Anthony Trollope, the Irish Writer." *Nineteenth-Century Fiction* 38.1 (June 1983): 1–42.
Edwards, P. D. *Anthony Trollope: His Art and Scope.* Brisbane: University of Queensland Press, 1977.
———. "The Chronology of 'The Way We Live Now.'" *Notes and Queries* 214.6 (June 1969): 214–16.
Eilert, Heide. "Im Treibhaus: Motive der europäischen Décadence in Theodor Fontanes Roman »L'Adultera«." *Jahrbuch der deutschen Schillergesellschaft* 22 (1978): 494–517.

El-Enany, Rasheed. "The Dichotomy of Islam and Modernity in the Fiction of Naguib Mahfouz." *The Postcolonial Crescent: Islam's Impact on Contemporary Literature.* Ed. John C. Hawley. New York: Peter Lang, 1998. 71–83.

Eliot, George. *Adam Bede.* 1859. Oxford: Oxford University Press, 1998.

———. *Middlemarch.* 1871. Oxford: Oxford University Press, 1998.

Ellison, David R. "Moral Complexity in *Le Père Goriot:* Balzac Between Kant and Nietzsche." *Approaches to Teaching Balzac's* Old Goriot. Ed. Michal Peled Ginzburg. New York: MLA, 2000. 72–80.

Evans, Christine Ann. "New Wine in Old Bottles: On Appropriating Male Speech in Effi Briest." *Germanic Notes & Reviews* 19.3 (1988): 38–41.

Faris, Wendy B. *Ordinary Enchantments: Magical Realism and the Remystification of Narrative.* Nashville: Vanderbilt University Press, 2004.

Faulkner, Karen. "Anthony Trollope's Apprenticeship." *Nineteenth-Century Fiction* 38.2 (September 1983): 161–88.

Fegan, Melissa. *Literature and the Irish Famine 1845–1919.* Oxford: Oxford University Press, 2002.

Felber, Lynette. "Trollope's Phineas Diptych as Sequel and Sequence Novel." *Part Two: Reflections on the Sequel.* Ed. Paul Budra and Betty A. Schellenberg. Toronto: University of Toronto Press, 1998. 118–30.

Felman, Shoshana. "Re-reading Femininity." *Yale French Studies* 62 (1981): 19–44.

Fernandez, Ramon. *Balzac: ou l'envers de la création romanesque.* Paris: Grasset, 1980.

———. "La Méthode de Balzac: Le Récit et l'esthétique du roman." *Messages.* Paris: Bernard Grasset, 1981. 54–69.

Findlen, Paula. "Inventing Nature: Commerce, Art, and Science in the Early Modern Cabinet of Curiosities." *Merchants and Marvels: Commerce, Science, and Art in Early Modern Europe.* Ed. Pamela H. Smith and Paula Findlen. New York: Routledge, 2002. 297–323.

Fischler, Alexander. "Rastignac-Télémaque: The Epic Scale in 'Le Père Goriot.'" *Modern Language Review* 63 (1968): 840–48.

Flaubert, Gustave. *Œuvres.* Ed. A Thibaudet and R. Dumesnil. 2 vols. Paris: Gallimard, 1936.

———. *Sentimental Education.* Trans. Geoffrey Wall. Harmondsworth: Penguin, 2004.

Fontane, Theodor. *Fontanes Briefe.* Ed. Gotthard Erler. Berlin and Weimar: Aufbau Verlag, 1968.

———. *Werke, Schriften und Briefe.* 20 vols in 4 sections. Ed. Walter Keitel and Helmuth Nürnberger. Munich: Hanser, 1974.

Foster, R. F. *Paddy and Mr. Punch: Connections in Irish and English History.* Harmondsworth: Penguin, 1993.

Foucault, Michel. *The Order of Things: An Archaeology of the Human Sciences.* 1966. No trans. New York: Vintage, 1994.

Freytag, Gustav. *Soll und Haben.* 1855. Kehl: SWAN Buch-Vertrieb, 1993.

Friedrich, Gerhard. "Das Glück der Melanie van der Straaten: Zur Interpretation von Theodor Fontanes »L'Adultera«." *Jahrbuch der deutschen Schillergesellschaft* 12 (1968): 359–82.

———. "Die Schuldfrage in Fontanes »Cécile«." *Jahrbuch der deutschen Schillergesellschaft* 14 (1970): 520–45.

Friedrichsmeyer, Sara, Sara Lennox, and Susanne Zantop. "Introduction." *The Imperialist*

Imagination: German Colonialism and Its Legacy. Ed. Sara Friedrichsmeyer, Sara Lennox, and Susanne Zantop. Ann Arbor: University of Michigan Press, 1998. 1–29.

Frølich, Juliette. *Des hommes, des femmes et des choses: Langages de l'Objet dans le roman de Balzac à Proust.* Saint-Denis: PU de Vincennes, 1997.

Furst, Lilian R. *All Is True: The Claims and Strategies of Realist Fiction.* Durham: Duke University Press, 1995.

——— "Madame Bovary and *Effi Briest:* An Essay in Comparison." *Romantisches Jahrbuch* 41 (1961): 124–35.

Garland, Henry. *The Berlin Novels of Theodor Fontane.* Oxford: Clarendon, 1980.

Gärtner, Martine. *Balzac et l'Allemagne.* Paris: L'Harmattan, 2000.

Gault, Rebecca S. "Education by the Use of Ghosts: Strategies of Repetition in *Effi Briest.*" *Repetition in Discourse: Interdisciplinary Perspectives.* Ed. Barbara Johnstone and Roy O. Freedle. Vol 1. Norwood, NJ: Ablex, 1994. 139–51.

Geppert, Hans Vilmar. "Ein Feld von Differenzierungen: Zur kritisch-produktiven Scott-Rezeption von Arnim bis Fontane." *Beitrage zur Rezeption der britischen und irischen des 19. Jahrhunderts im deutschsprachigen Raum.* Ed. Norbert Bachleitner. Atlanta: Rodopi, 2000. 479–500.

Gilmartin, Sophie. *Ancestry and Narrative In Nineteenth-Century British Literature: Blood Relations from Edgeworth to Hardy.* Cambridge: Cambridge University Press, 1998.

Ginzburg, Carlo. "To Kill a Chinese Mandarin: The Moral Implications of Distance." *Wooden Eyes: Nine Reflections on Distance.* Trans. Martin Ryle and Kate Soper. New York: Columbia University Press, 2001. 157–72.

Glauser, Alfred. "Balzac/Vautrin." *Romanic Review* 79.4 (November 1988): 585–610.

Goethe, Johann Wolfgang von. *Werke: Hamburger Ausgabe.* 14 vols. München: C.H. Beck, 1996.

Gould, Cecil. *Trophy of Conquest: The Musée Napoléon and the Creation of the Louvre.* London, 1965.

Grawe, Christian. *Theodor Fontane: Effi Briest.* Frankfurt/Main: Verlag Moritz Diesterweg, 1985.

Grieve, Heide. "Fontane und Scott: Die *Waverley-Romane* und *Vor dem Sturm.*" *Fontane Blätter* 3 (1974): 300–12.

Guha, Ranajit. "The Prose of Counter-Insurgency." *Selected Subaltern Studies.* Ed. Ranajit Guha and Gayatri Chakravorty Spivak. Oxford: Oxford University Press, 1988. 45–86.

Guichardet, Jeannine. *Balzac: «Archéologue de Paris».* Paris: SEDES, 1986.

Guidry, Glenn A. "Myth and Ritual in Fontane's *Effi Briest.*" *Germanic Review* 59.1 (Winter 1984): 19–25.

Guthke, Karl S. "'Jott, Frau Rätin, Palme paßt immer': Aspekte des Exotischen in Fontanes Erzählwerk." *Fontane Blätter* 55 (1993): 91–111.

Hall, N. John. *Trollope and His Illustrators.* New York: St. Martin's Press, 1980.

Halperin, John. "Trollope's *Phineas Finn* and History." *English Studies* 59 (1978): 121–37.

Hamer, Mary. *Writing by Numbers: Trollope's Serial Fiction.* Cambridge: Cambridge University Press, 1987.

Handke, Peter. *Repetition.* Trans. Ralph Manheim. New York: Farrar, Straus and Giroux, 1988.

Hansen, Marcus L. *German Schemes of Colonialization before 1860. Smith College Studies in History* 9.1–2 (October 1923–January 1924).
Hardy, Thomas. *Tess of the D'Urbervilles.* 1891. New York: Signet, 1980.
Harrer, Heinrich. *Seven Years in Tibet.* 1953. Trans. Richard Graves. London: Harper Collins, 1994.
Harvey, David. *The Condition of Postmodernity: An Enquiry into the Origins of Cultural Change.* Oxford: Blackwell, 1990.
Hayens, Kenneth. *Theodor Fontane: A Critical Study.* London: Collins, 1920.
Heathcote, Owen N. "The Engendering of Violence and the Violation of Gender in Honoré de Balzac's *La Fille aux yeux d'or.*" *Romance Studies* 22 (Autumn 1993): 99–112.
Heidenreich, Bernd, and Frank-Lothar Kroll, eds. *Theodor Fontane: Dichter der Deutschen Einheit.* Berlin: BWU, 2003.
Heine, Heinrich. *Die Harzreise.* 1826. Leipzig: Reclam, no date.
———. *Sämtliche Gedichte in zeitlicher Folge.* Frankfurt/Main: Insel, 2001.
Hennedy, Hugh L. "Love and Famine, Family and Country in Trollope's *Castle Richmond.*" *Éire-Ireland: A Journal of Irish Studies* 7.4 (1972): 48–66.
Hirsch, Marianne. "Spiritual *Bildung:* The Beautiful Soul as Paradigm." *The Voyage In: Fictions of Female Development.* Ed. Elizabeth Adel, Elizabeth Langland, and Marianne Hirsch. Hanover: University Press of New England, 1983. 23–48.
Hobsbawm, Eric. *The Age of Capital: 1848–1875.* 1975. New York: Vintage, 1996.
———. *The Age of Revolution: 1789–1848.* 1962. New York: Vintage, 1996.
Hoefnagel, Dick. "Irish Conspiracy and Sir Walter Scott's Marriage." *Wordsworth Circle* 16.3 (1985): 149–50.
Hohendahl, Peter Uwe. "Theodor Fontane: Cécile: Zum Problem der Mehrdeutigkeit." *Germanisch-Romansich Monatsschrift* 18.4 (October 1968): 381–405.
Holub, Robert C. *Reflections of Realism: Paradox, Norm, and Ideology in Nineteenth-Century German Prose.* Detroit: Wayne State University Press, 1991.
Hooper-Greenhill, Eilean. *Museums and the Interpretation of Visual Culture.* New York: Routledge, 2000.
Horkheimer, Max, and Theodor W. Adorno. *Dialektik der Aufklärung.* Frankfurt/Main: Fischer, 1998.
Hornback, Bert G. "Anthony Trollope and the Calendar of 1872: The Chronology of 'The Way We Live Now.'" *Notes and Queries* 208.12 (December 1963): 454–58.
Howells, William Dean. *Criticism and Fiction and Other Essays.* Ed. Clara Marburg Kirk and Rudolf Kirk. New York: NYU Press, 1959.
Hugo, Victor. *Les Orientales/Les Feuilles d'Automne.* Paris: Livres de Poche, 2000.
Husson-Casta, Isabelle. "Hyper-réel fictionnel et récit policier." *Roman, réalités, réalismes.* Ed. Jean Bessière. Paris: PU de France, 1989. 113–19.
Hynes, John G. "An Eye for an Eye: Anthony Trollope's Irish Masterpiece." *The Journal of Irish Literature* 16.2 (May 1987): 54–58.
Høeg, Peter. *Frøken Smillas fornemmelse for sne.* Copenhagen: Rosinante, 1992.
———. *Smilla's Sense of Snow.* Trans. Tina Nunnally. New York: Dell, 1995.
Ikeler, A. Abbott. "That Peculiar Book: Critics, Common Readers and *The Way We Live Now.*" *CLA Journal* 30.2 (December 1986): 219–40.
James, Harold. "The Literary Financier." *The American Scholar* 60.2 (Spring 1991): 251–57.

James, Henry. *Literary Criticism, Volume Two*. New York: Library of America, 1984.
Jameson, Fredric. "Cognitive Mapping." *Marxism and the Interpretation of Culture*. Ed. Cary Nelson and Lawrence Grossberg. Urbana: University of Illinois Press, 1988. 347–57.
———. *The Political Unconscious: Narrative as a Socially Symbolic Act*. Ithaca: Cornell University Press, 1981.
Jamison, Robert L. "The Fearful Education of Effi Briest." *Monatshefte*. 74.1 (Spring 1982): 20–32.
Johannsen, G. Kurt, and H. H. Kraft. *Germany's Colonial Problem*. 1937. London: Kennikat Press, 1970.
Johnston, Conor. *"The Macdermots of Ballycloran:* Trollope as Conservative-Liberal." *Éire-Ireland: A Journal of Irish Studies* 16.2 (1981): 71–92.
Jordanova, Ludmilla. "Museums: Representing the Real?" *Realism and Representation: Essays on the Problem of Realism in Relation to Science, Literature, and Culture*. Ed. George Levine. Madison: University of Wisconsin Press, 1993. 255–78.
Josephs, Herbert. "Don Juan in the Enlightenment: The Twilight of the Erotic as Myth." *Degré second* 6 (July 1982): 89–100.
Jourda, Pierre. *L'Exotisme dans la littérature française depuis Chateaubriand*. Paris: Boivin, 1938.
Jung, Winfried. "'Bilder, und immer wieder Bilder . . .': Bildern als Merkmale kritischen Erzählens in Theodor Fontanes 'Cécile.'" *Wirkendes Wort* 40.2 (July–August 1990): 197–208.
Kadish, Doris Y. "Hybrids in Balzac's *La Fille aux yeux d'or.*" *Nineteenth-Century French Studies* 16.3–4 (Spring–Summer 1988): 270–78.
Kearns, Katherine. *Nineteenth-Century Realism: Through the Looking-Glass*. Cambridge: Cambridge University Pres, 1996.
Kemp, Martin. *The Science of Art: Optical Themes in Western Art from Brunelleschi to Seurat*. New Haven: Yale University Press, 1992.
Kincaid, James R. *The Novels of Anthony Trollope*. Oxford: Clarendon, 1977.
Kipling, Rudyard. "The Mutiny of the Mavericks." *War Stories and Poems*. Oxford: Oxford University Press, 1990. 70–88.
Klotz, Günther. *Thackeray's Ireland: Image and Attitude in the* Irish Sketch Book *and* Barry Lyndon. Tübingen: Narr, 1987.
Knoepflmacher, U. C. *George Eliot's Early Novels: The Limits of Realism*. Berkeley: University of California Press, 1968.
Kontje, Todd. *German Orientalisms*. Ann Arbor: University of Michigan Press, 2004.
Krakauer, Jon. *Into the Wild*. New York: Anchor, 1996.
Kwame, Ahyi. "Le Roman colonial allemand entre les deux guerres mondiales." *Peuples noirs/peuples africains* 43 (January–February 1985): 97–109.
Leathers, Victor L. *L'Espagne et les Espagnols dans l'œuvre d'Honoré de Balzac*. Paris: Honoré Champion, 1931.
Lehan, Richard. *Realism and Naturalism: The Novel in an Age of Transition*. Madison: University of Wisconsin Press, 2005.
Lenin, V. I. *Imperialism: The Highest Stage of Capitalism*. 1917. New York: International Publishers, 1997.
Leventhal, Jean H. "Fact into Fiction: Effi Briest and the Ardenne Case." *Colloquia Germanica* 24.3 (1991): 181–93.

Lévi-Strauss, Claude. *Structural Anthropology*. 1958. Trans. Claire Jacobson and Brooke Grundfest Schoepf. New York: Basic Books, 1963.

Levin, Harry. *The Gates of Horn: A Study of Five French Realists*. New York: Oxford University Press, 1963.

Levine, George. *Darwin and the Novelists: Patterns of Science in Victorian Fiction*. Cambridge, MA: Harvard University Press, 1988.

———. *Dying to Know: Scientific Epistemology and Narrative in Victorian England*. Chicago: University of Chicago Press, 2002.

———. *The Realistic Imagination: English Fiction from Frankenstein to Lady Chatterley*. Chicago: University of Chicago Press, 1981.

Lonergan, Patrick. "The Representation of Phineas Finn: Anthony Trollope's Palliser Series and Victorian Ireland." *Victorian Literature and Culture* 32.1 (2004): 147–58.

Lounsbury, Coral. *The Reasonable Man: Trollope's Legal Fiction*. Princeton: Princeton University Press, 1981.

Luckhurst, Roger. "Knowledge, Belief and the Supernatural at the Imperial Margin." *The Victorian Supernatural*. Ed. Nicola Brown, Carolyn Burdett, and Pamela Thurschwell. Cambridge: Cambridge University Press, 2004. 197–216.

Lukács, Georg. *Balzac und der französische Realismus*. Berlin: Aufbau, 1952.

———. *Deutsche Literatur im Zeitalter des Imperialismus*. Berlin: Aufbau, 1950.

———. *The Meaning of Contemporary Realism*. Trans. John and Necke Mander. London: Merlin Press, 1963.

———. *Studies in European Realism*. New York: Grosset & Dunlap, 1964.

———. *The Theory of the Novel: A Historico-Philosophical Essay on the Forms of Great Epic Literature*. Trans. Anna Bostock. Cambridge: MIT Press, 1996.

MacRaild, Donald M. "'Principle, party and protest': the language of Victorian Orangeism in the north of England." *The Victorians and Race*. Ed. Shearer West. Hants: Scolar Press, 1996.

Makdisi, Saree. *Romantic Imperialism: Universal Empire and the Culture of Modernity*. Cambridge: Cambridge University Press, 1998.

Mann, Thomas. *Buddenbrooks*. 1900. Frankfurt/Main: Fischer, 2001.

Marx, Karl. *Capital: Volume 1*. Trans. Ben Fowkes. Harmondsworth: Penguin, 1990.

Marx, Karl, and Friedrich Engels. *On Literature and Art*. Moscow: Progress Publishers, 1984.

Massol-Bedoin, Chantal. "La charade et la chimère: Du récit énigmatique dans *La Fille aux yeux d'or*." *Poétique* 89.23 (February 1992): 31–45.

Matthews-Kane, Bridget. "Love's Labour's Lost: Romantic Allegory in Trollope's *Castle Richmond*." *Victorian Literature and Culture* 32.1 (2004): 117–31.

Maturin, Charles. *Melmoth the Wanderer*. 1820. Oxford: Oxford University Press, 1989.

McClure, John. *Late Imperial Romance*. London: Verso, 1994.

———. *Partial Faiths: Postsecular Fiction in the Age of Pynchon and Morrison*. Athens: University of Georgia Press, 2007.

McKeon, Michael. *The Origins of the English Novel*. Baltimore: Johns Hopkins University Press, 2002.

McMaster, R. D. "Women in *The Way We Live Now*." *English Studies in Canada* 7.1 (Spring 1981): 68–80.

Michel, Arlette. *Le Réel et la Beauté dans le roman balzacien*. Paris: Honoré Champion, 2001.

Miller, D. A. *The Novel and the Police*. Berkeley: University of California Press, 1988.
Millott, H. H. "*La Peau de Chagrin:* Method in Madness." *Studies in Balzac's Realism*. Ed. E. Preston Dargan. New York: Russell & Russell, 1967. 68–90.
Minden, Michael. "Realism versus Poetry: Theodor Fontane, 'Effi Briest.'" *The German Novel in the Twentieth Century: Beyond Realism*. Ed. David Midgley. Edinburgh: Edinburgh University Press, 1993. 18–29.
Mitchell, W. J. T. "Romanticism and the Life of Things: Fossils, Totems, and Images." *Critical Inquiry* 28.1 (Autumn 2001): 167–84.
Mittenzwei, Ingrid. *Die Sprache als Thema: Untersuchungen zu Fontanes Gesellschaftsromanen*. Bad Hamburg: Gehlen, 1970.
Mitterand, Henri. *L'illusion réaliste: De Balzac à Aragon*. Paris: PU de France, 1994.
Montaigne, Michel de. *Essais*. 1580. 3 vols. Paris: Flammarion, 1979.
Moretti, Franco. *Atlas of the European Novel 1800–1900*. London: Verso, 1999.
―――. *Graphs Maps Trees: Abstract Models for Literary History*. London: Verso, 2005.
―――. *The Way of the World: The* Bildungsroman *in European Culture*. Trans. Albert Sbragia. London: Verso, 2000.
Mortimer, Armine Kotine. *Writing Realism: Representations in French Fiction*. Baltimore: The Johns Hopkins University Press, 2000.
Mozet, Nicole. *La Ville de Province dans l'œuvre de Balzac*. Paris: SEDES, 1982.
Müller-Seidel, Walter. "Fontanes »Effi Briest«." *Wissenschaft als Dialog: Studien zur Literatur und Kunst seit der Jahrhundertwende*. Ed. Renate von Heydebrand and Klaus Günther Just. Stuttgart: Metzler, 1969. 30–58.
Murphy, Andrew. *But the Irish Sea Betwixt Us: Ireland, Colonialism, and Renaissance Literature*. Lexington: University Press of Kentucky, 1999.
Murphy, Ignatius. *The Diocese of Killaloe, 1800–1850*. Dublin: Irish Academic Press, no date.
―――. *A Starving People: Life and Death in West Clare, 1845–1851*. Dublin: Irish Academic Press, 1996.
Nabokov, Vladimir. *The Annotated Lolita*. Ed. Alfred Appel, Jr. New York: McGraw, 1970.
Nandy, Ashis. *The Illegitimacy of Nationalism: Rabindranath Tagore and the Politics of Self*. Delhi: Oxford University Press, 1994.
―――. *The Intimate Enemy: Loss and Recovery of Self under Colonialism*. New Delhi: Oxford University Press, 1983.
―――. "The Savage Freud: The First Non-Western Psychoanalyst and the Politics of Secret Selves in Colonial India." *The Savage Freud and Other Essays on Possible and Retrievable Selves*. Oxford: Oxford University Press, 1995. 81–144.
―――. "Shamans, Savages and the Wilderness: On the Audibility of Dissent and the Future of Civilizations." *Alternatives* 14.3 (July 1989): 263–77.
Nardin, Jane. "*Castle Richmond*, the Famine, and the Critics." *Cahiers victoriens et édouardiens* 58 (2003): 81–90.
Nathan, Sabine. "Anthony Trollope's Perception of the Way We Live Now." *Zeitschrift für Anglistik und Amerikanistik* 10.3 (1962): 259–78.
Neal, Frank. *Black '47: Britain and the Famine Irish*. New York: St. Martin's, 1998.
Nef, Ernst. "Notizen zum Schluss von Effi Briest." *Der gesunde Gelehrte: Literatur-, Sprach- und Rezeptionsanalysen*. Ed. Arnold Armin and C. Stephen Jaeger. Heri-

sau: Schlapfer, 1987. 70–77.

Noakes, Richard. "Spiritualism, Science and the Supernatural in Mid-Victorian Britain." *The Victorian Supernatural*. Ed. Nicola Brown, Carolyn Burdett, and Pamela Thurschwell. Cambridge: Cambridge University Press, 2004. 23–43.

Noyes, John K. "Wide Open Spaces and the Hunger for Land: Production of Space in the German Colonial Novel." *Faultline: Interdisciplinary Approaches to German Studies* 1 (1992): 103–17.

Nykl, Alois Richard. "The Talisman in La Peau de chagrin." *Modern Language Notes* 34 (1919): 479–81.

O'Connor, Kevin. *The Irish in Britain*. London: Sidgwick & Jackson, 1972.

Odden, Karen. "Puffed Papers and Broken Promises: White-Collar Crime and Literary Justice in *The Way We Live Now*." *Victorian Crime, Madness and Sensation*. Ed. Andrew Maunder and Grace Moore. Aldershot: Ashgate, 2004. 135–46.

Orlando, Francesco. *Obsolete Objects in the Literary Imagination: Ruins, Relics, Rarities, Rubbish, Uninhabited Places, and Hidden Treasures*. 1993. Trans. Gabriel Pihas and Daniel Seidel. New Haven: Yale University Press, 2006.

Osinski, Jutta. "Romantikbilder und patriotische Gesinnung in Fontanes 'Vor dem Sturm.'" *Zeitschrift für Deutsche Philologie* 123 [supplement] (2004): 142–52.

Parr, Rolf. "Kongobecken, Lombok und der Chinese im Hause Briest: Das ‚Wissen um die Kolonien' und das ‚Wissen aus den Kolonien' bei Theodor Fontane." *Fontane und die Fremde, Fontane und Europa*. Ed. Konrad Ehlich. Würzburg: Königshausen & Neumann, 2002. 212–28.

Payne, David. *The Reenchantment of Nineteenth-Century Fiction: Dickens, Thackeray, George Eliot and Serialization*. New York: Palgrave, 2005.

Pecora, Vincent P. *Households of the Soul*. Baltimore: Johns Hopkins University Press, 1997.

Perera, Suvendrini. *Reaches of Empire: The English Novel from Edgeworth to Dickens*. New York: Columbia University Press, 1991.

Pérez Galdós, Benito. *Fortunata and Jacinta: Two Stories of Married Women*. Trans. Agnes Gullón. Harmondsworth: Penguin, 1988.

———. *Fortunata y Jacinta: Dos historias de casadas*. 1887. Ed. Francisco Caudet. 2 vols. Madrid: Cátedra, 1999.

Petrey, Sandy. *Realism and Revolution: Balzac, Stendhal, Zola, and the Performances of History*. Ithaca: Cornell University Press, 1988.

Pimentel-Anduiza, Luz Aurora. "El espacio en el disurso narrativo: Modos de proyección y significación." *Morphe: Ciencias del Lenguaje* 1.1 (1986): 115–28.

Poddar, Prem, and Cheralyn Mealor. "Danish Imperial Fantasies: Peter Hoeg's *Miss Smilla's Feeling for Snow*." *Translating Nations*. Ed. Dominic Rainsford. Aarhus: Aarhus University Press, 2000. 161–202.

Podmore, Frank. *The Naturalisation of the Supernatural*. New York and London: G. P. Putnam's Sons, 1908.

Pold, Søren. "Panoramic Realism: An Early and Illustrative Passage from Urban Space to Media Space in Honoré de Balzac's Parisian Novels, *Ferragus* and *Le Père Goriot*." *Nineteenth-Century French Studies* 29.1–2 (Fall–Winter 2000–2001): 47–63.

Polhemus, Robert M. *The Changing World of Anthony Trollope*. Berkeley: University of California Press, 1968.

Pomian, Krzysztof. "De la collection particulière au musée d'art." *The Genesis of the*

Art Museum in the 18th Century. Ed. Per Bjurström. Stockholm: Nationalmuseum, 1993. 9–27.

———. *Collectors and Curiosities: Paris and Venice, 1500–1800.* Trans. Elizabeth Wiles-Portier. Cambridge: Polity, 1990.

Poncin-Bar, Geneviève. "Aspects fantastiques de Paris dans les romans réalistes de Balzac." *L'Année balzacienne* 1974: 227–44.

Postman, Neil. *Amusing Ourselves to Death: Public Discourse in the Age of Show Business.* Harmondsworth: Penguin, 1985.

Prendergast, Christopher. *Paris and the Nineteenth Century.* Oxford: Blackwell, 1992.

Proust, Marcel. *Contre Sainte-Beuve (suivi de Nouveaux mélanges).* Paris: Gallimard, 1954.

Pugh, Anthony R. "The Complexity of *Le Père Goriot*." *L'Esprit créateur* 7.1 (Spring 1967): 25–35.

Radcliffe, Stanley. *Fontane: Effi Briest.* London: Grant & Cutler, 1986.

Radecke, Gabriele. "Das Motiv des Duells bei Theodor Fontane und Eduard von Keyserling." *»Die Dekadenz ist da«: Theodor Fontane und die Literatur der Jahrhundertwende.* Ed. Gabriele Radecke. Würzburg: Königshausen & Neumann, 2002. 61–78.

Rainer, Ulrike. "Effi Briest und das Motiv des Chinesen: Rolle und Darstellung in Fontanes Roman." *Zeitschrift für Deutsche Philologie* 101.4 (1982): 545–61.

Ramponi, Patrick. "Orte des Globalen: Zur Poetik der Globalisierung in der Literatur des deutschsprachigen Realismus." *Poetische Ordnungen: Zur Erzählprosa des deutschen Realismus.* Ed. Ulrich Kittstein and Stefani Kugler. Würzburg: Königshausen & Neumann, 2007. 17–59.

Reichelt, Gregor. *Fantastik im Realismus: Literarische und gesellschaftliche Einbildungskraft bei Keller, Storm und Fontane.* Stuttgart: Metzler, 2001.

Reid, James H. "Reading Social and Historical Space in *Le Père Goriot*'s Descriptions." *Approaches to Teaching Balzac's Old Goriot.* Ed. Michal Peled Ginzburg. New York: MLA, 2000. 62–71.

Reuter, Hans-Heinrich. "Theodor Fontane." *Deutsche Dichter des 19. Jahrhunderts: Ihr Leben und Werk.* Ed. Benno von Wiese. Berlin: Schmidt, 1979.

Riechel, Donald C. "*Effi Briest* and the Calendar of Fate." *Germanic Review* 48.3 (May 1973): 189–211.

Rivers, Christopher. *Face Value: Physiognomical Thought and the Legible Body in Marivaux, Lavater, Balzac, Gautier, and Zola.* Madison: University of Wisconsin Press, 1994.

Robb, Graham. *Balzac: A Biography.* London: Picador, 1994.

Robbins, Bruce. *Feeling Global: Internationalism in Distress.* New York: New York University Press, 1999.

———. *Upward Mobility and the Common Good: Toward a Literary History of the Welfare State.* Princeton: Princeton University Press, 2007.

———. "Very Busy Just Now: Globalization and Harriedness in Ishiguro's *The Unconsoled*." *Comparative Literature* 53.4 (Fall 2001): 426–41.

Roch, Herbert. *Fontane, Berlin und das 19. Jahrhundert.* Düsseldorf: Droste, 1985.

Rollins, Yvonne B. "*Madame Bovary* et *Effi Briest:* Du symbole au mythe." *Stanford French Review* 5.1 (Spring 1981): 107–19.

Ronaï, P. "Tuer le mandarin." *Revue de littérature comparée* 10.3 (1930): 520–23.

Royal Institute of International Affairs, London. *Germany's Claim to Colonies.* New

York: Oxford University Press, 1938.
Ryan, Judith. "The Chinese Ghost: Colonialism and Subaltern Speech in Fontane's *Effi Briest*." *History and Literature: Essays in Honor of Karl S. Guthke*. Ed. William Collins Donahue and Scott D. Denham. Tübingen: Stauffenburg, 2000. 367–84.
Sadleir, Michael. *Trollope: A Commentary*. 1927. New York: Farrar, Strauss, 1947.
Said, Edward W. *Culture and Imperialism*. New York: Vintage, 1993.
———. *Orientalism*. New York: Vintage, 1979.
———. *The World, the Text, and the Critic*. Cambridge: Harvard University Press, 1983.
———. "Yeats and Decolonization." *Nationalism, Colonialism, and Literature*. Ed. Seamus Deane. Minneapolis: University of Minnesota Press, 1990. 69–95.
Sainte-Beuve, Charles Augustin. *Correspondance générale*. Ed. Jean Bonnerot. Paris: Stock, 1935.
Saisselin, Rémy G. *The Bourgeois and the Bibelot*. New Brunswick: Rutgers University Press, 1984.
Salih, Tayeb. *The Wedding of Zein and Other Stories*. Trans. Denys Johnson-Davies. Boulder: Lynne Rienner, 1999.
Sanders, Andrew. *Anthony Trollope*. Plymouth: Northcote House, 1998.
Sassen, Saskia. *Globalization and Its Discontents: Essays on the New Mobility of People and Money*. New York: New Press, 1998.
Savage, Catherine H. "The Romantic *Père Goriot*." *Studies in Romanticism* 5.1 (Autumn 1963): 104–12.
Schuster, Ingrid. "Exotik als Chiffre: Zum Chinesen in *Effi Briest*." *Wirkendes Wort* 2 (1983): 115–25.
Schuster, Peter-Klaus. *Theodor Fontane: Effi Briest—Ein Leben nach christlichen Bildern*. Tübingen: Niemeyer, 1978.
Scott, Sarah. *A Description of Millenium Hall*. 1762. Peterborough: Broadview Press, 1995.
Scott, Sir Walter. *Rob Roy*. 1817. Oxford: Oxford University Press, 1998.
———. 1814. *Waverley; or, 'Tis Sixty Years Since*. Oxford: Oxford University Press, 1998.
Seiler, Christine. "Representations of the Loving, Hateful and Fearful Wife in Flaubert's *Madame Bovary*, Fontane's *Effi Briest*, and Tolstoy's *Anna Karenina*." *Germanic Notes and Reviews* 25.2 (Fall 1994): 3–7.
Sharpley-Whiting, T. Denean. "'The Other Woman': Reading a Body of Difference in Balzac's *La Fille aux yeux d'or*." *Symposium* 51.1 (Spring 1997): 43–50.
Shears, Lambert Armour. *The Influence of Walter Scott on the Novels of Theodor Fontane*. New York: Columbia University Press, 1922.
Shklovsky, Viktor. *Theory of Prose*. 1929. Trans. Benjamin Sher. Normal: Dalkey Archive Press, 1990.
Sittig, Claudius. "Gieshüblers Kohlenprovisor: Der Kolonialdiskurs und das Hirngespinst vom spukenden Chinesen in Theodor Fontanes ‚Effi Briest.'" *Zeitschrift für Deutsche Philologie* 122.4 (2003): 544–63.
Smith, Pamela H., and Paula Findlen. "Introduction: Commerce and the Representation of Nature in Art and Science." *Merchants and Marvels: Commerce, Science, and Art in Early Modern Europe*. Ed. Pamela H. Smith and Paula Findlen. New York: Routledge, 2002. 1–25.

Soelberg, Nils. "La narration de «La Fille aux yeux d'or»: une omniscience encombrante." *Revue Romane* 25.2 (1990): 454–65.
Spivak, Gayatri Chakravorty. "Three Women's Texts and a Critique of Imperialism." *Critical Inquiry* 12 (Autumn 1985): 243–61.
Sprenger, Scott. "Balzac as Anthropologist." *Anthropoetics* 6.1 (Spring–Summer 2000): 1–9.
Stephan, Inge. "'Das Natürliche hat es mir seit langem angetan': Zum Verhältnis von Frau und Natur in Fontanes *Cécile*." *Natur und Natürlichkeit: Stationen des Grünen in der deutschen Literatur*. Ed. Reinhold Grimm and Jost Hermand. Königstein: Athenäum, 1981. 118–49.
Stern, J. P. "*Effi Briest: Madame Bovary: Anna Karenina*." *Modern Language Review* 52.3 (1957): 363–75.
———. *Re-interpretations: Seven Studies in Nineteenth-Century German Literature*. London: Thames and Hudson, 1964.
Stewart, Susan. *On Longing: Narratives of the Miniature, the Gigantic, the Souvenir, the Collection*. Baltimore: Jonhs Hopkins University Press, 1984.
Storch, Dietmar. ",... unterm chinesischen Drachen ... Da schlägt man sich jetzt herum': Fontane, der Ferne Osten und die Anfänge der deutschen Weltpolitik." *Theodor Fontane: Am Ende des Jahrhunderts*. Ed. Hanna Delf von Wolzogen and Helmuth Nürnberger. Vol. 1. Würzburg: Königshausen & Neumann, 2000. 113–28.
Stounbjerg, Per. "Byen og isen: Det urbane og dets grænser i *Frøken Smillas fornemmelse for sne*." *Københavner romaner*. Ed. Marianne Barlyng and Søren Schou. Copenhagen: Borgen, 1996. 387–401.
Subiotto, Frances M. "The Ghost in Effi Briest." *Forum for Modern Language Studies* 21.2 (1985): 137–50.
Suck, Titus T. "The Paternal Signifier: The Monetary Metaphor in Balzac's *Le Père Goriot*." *Romanic Review* 81.1 (January 1990): 25–44.
Sue, Eugène. *Les Mystères de Paris*. Paris: Laffont, 1989.
Super, R. H. *The Chronicler of Barsetshire: A Life of Anthony Trollope*. Ann Arbor: University of Michigan Press, 1988.
———. "Was *The Way We Live Now* a Commercial Success?" *Nineteenth-Century Fiction* 39.2 (September 1984): 202–10.
Sutherland, John A. "The Commercial Success of *The Way We Live Now*: Some New Evidence." *Nineteenth-Century Fiction* 40.4 (March 1986): 460–67.
———. "Introduction." Anthony Trollope. *The Way We Live Now*. Oxford: Oxford University Press, 1999. vii–xli.
———. "Trollope at Work on *The Way We Live Now*." *Nineteenth-Century Fiction* 37.3 (December 1982): 472–93.
Swales, Erica. "Private Mythologies and Public Unease: On Fontane's *Effi Briest*." *Modern Language Review* 75 (1980): 114–23.
Swenson, James. *On Jean-Jacques Rousseau: Considered as One of the First Authors of the Revolution*. Stanford, CA: Stanford University Press, 2000.
Taine, Hippolyte Adolphe. *Nouveaux essais de critique et d'histoire*. Paris: Librairie de la Hachette, 1865.
Tallis, Raymond. *In Defence of Realism*. 1988. Lincoln: University of Nebraska Press, 1998.
Tanner, Tony. "Trollope's *The Way We Live Now*: Its Modern Significance." *The Critical*

Quarterly 9.3 (Autumn 1967): 256–71.
Taylor, A. J. P. *Germany's First Bid for Colonies 1884–1885: A Move in Bismarck's European Policy.* 1938. Hamden, CT: Archon Books, 1967.
Tebben, Karin. "'Der Roman dahinter': Zum autobiographischen Hintergrund von Theodor Fontanes *L'Adultera.*'" *German Life and Letters* 55.4 (October 2002): 348–62.
Thompson, E. P. *The Making of the English Working Class.* New York: Vintage, 1966.
Tintner, Adeline R. "James and Balzac: *The Bostonians* and 'La Fille aux yeux d'or.'" *Comparative Literature* 29.3 (Summer 1977): 241–54.
Todorov, Tzvetan. *The Fantastic: A Structural Approach to a Literary Genre.* Trans. Richard Howard. Ithaca: Cornell University Press, 1975.
Tracy, Robert. *Trollope's Later Novels.* Berkeley: University of California Press, 1978.
———. "'The Unnatural Ruin': Trollope and Nineteenth-Century Irish Fiction." *Nineteenth-Century Fiction* 37.3 (December 1982): 358–82.
Trollope, Anthony. *An Autobiography.* 1883. Oxford: Oxford University Press, 1999.
———. *Barchester Towers.* 1857. Oxford: Oxford University Press, 1998.
———. *Can You Forgive Her?* 1864. Oxford: Oxford University Press, 1999.
———. *The Duke's Children.* 1879. Oxford: Oxford University Press, 1991.
———. *The Eustace Diamonds.* 1873. Oxford: Oxford University Press, 1998.
———. "Father Giles of Ballymoy." *The Complete Shorter Fiction.* Ed. Julian Thompson. New York: Carroll & Graf, 1992. 437–51.
———. *The Letters of Anthony Trollope.* Ed. Bradford Allen Booth. London: Oxford University Press, 1951.
———. *The Macdermots of Ballycloran.* 1847. Mineola: Dover, 1988.
———. *Phineas Finn: The Irish Member.* 1869. Oxford: Oxford University Press, 1991.
———. *Phineas Redux.* 1874. Oxford: Oxford University Press, 1991.
———. *The Prime Minister.* 1876. Harmondsworth: Penguin, 2004.
———. *The Way We Live Now.* 1875. Oxford: Oxford University Press, 1999.
Trumpener, Katie. *Bardic Nationalism: The Romantic Novel and the British Empire.* Princeton: Princeton University Press, 1997.
Turner, David. "Theodor Fontane: *Effi Briest* (1895)." *The Monster in the Mirror: Studies in Nineteenth-Century Realism.* Ed. D. A. Williams. Oxford: Oxford University Press, 1978. 234–56.
Utz, Peter. "Effi Briest, der Chinese und der Imperialismus: Eine 'Geschichte' im geschichtlichen Kontext." *Zeitschrift für Deutsche Philologie* 103.2 (1984): 212–225.
Van, Annette. "Ambivalent Speculations: America as England's Future in *The Way We Live Now.*" *Novel* 39.1 (Fall 2005): 75–96.
Vanoncini, André. "La dissémination de l'objet fantastique." *Balzac et* La Peau de chagrin. Ed. Claude Duchet. Paris: SEDES. 61–77.
Viswanathan, Gauri. "The Ordinary Business of Occultism." *Critical Inquiry* 27 (2000): 1–20.
Vom Hofe, Gerhard. "Das Eintreten einer großen Idee: Zum Thema des Patriotismus in Fontanes Preußenroman *Vor dem Sturm.*" *"Was hat nicht alles Platz in eines Menschen Herzen . . .": Theodor Fontane und seine Zeit.* Ed. Evangelische Akademie Baden. Karlsruhe: Evangelischer Presseverband für Baden, 1993. 32–61.
von Hofmannsthal, Hugo. "Balzac [1908]." *Gesammelte Werke in Einzelausgaben: Prosa*

II. Ed. Herbert Steiner. Frankfurt/Main: Fischer, 1951. 378–98.
Wall, Stephen. "Trollope, Satire, and *The Way We Live Now.*" *Essays in Criticism* 37.1 (January 1987): 43–61.
Walpole, Hugh. *Anthony Trollope.* New York: Macmillan, 1928.
Warning, Rainer. *Die Phantasie der Realisten.* München: Fink, 1999.
Watson, Janell. *Literature and Material Culture from Balzac to Proust: The Collection and Consumption of Curiosities.* Cambridge: Cambridge University Press, 1999.
Watt, Ian. *The Rise of the Novel: Studies in Defoe, Richardson and Fielding.* Berkeley: University of California Press, 1957.
Weber, Max. "Science as a Vocation." *From Max Weber: Essays in Sociology.* Ed. and trans. H. H. Gerth and C. Wright Mills. New York: Oxford University Press, 1958. 129–56.
Weber, Samuel. *Unwrapping Balzac: A Reading of* La Peau de Chagrin. Toronto: University of Toronto Press, 1979.
Wellek, René. "The Concept of Realism in Literary Scholarship." *Concepts of Criticism.* Ed. Stephen J. Nichols, Jr. New Haven: Yale University Press, 1963. 222–55.
White, Hayden. *Figural Realism: Studies in the Mimesis Effect.* Baltimore: Johns Hopkins University Press, 2000.
White, Richard. "Information, Markets, and Corruption: Transcontinental Railroads in the Gilded Age." *The Journal of American History* 90.1 (June 2003): 19–43.
Williams, Raymond. *The Country and the City.* New York: Oxford University Press, 1973.
———. *Marxism and Literature.* Oxford: Oxford University Press, 1977.
Wittig, E. W. "Trollope's Irish Fiction." *Éire-Ireland: A Journal of Irish Studies* 9.3 (1974): 97–118.
Woloch, Alex. *The One vs. the Many: Minor Characters and the Space of the Protagonist in the Novel.* Princeton: Princeton University Press, 2003.
Wrigley, Richard. "The Class of 89?: Cultural Aspects of Bourgeois Identity in France in the Aftermath of the French Revolution." *Art in Bourgeois Society.* Ed. Andrew Hemingway and William Vaughan. Cambridge: Cambridge University Press, 1998. 130–53.
Youngman, Paul A. *Black Devil & Iron Angel: The Railway in Nineteenth-Century German Realism.* Washington, DC: The Catholic University of America Press, 2005.
Zantop, Susanne. *Colonial Fantasies: Conquest, Family, and Nation in Precolonial Germany, 1770–1870.* Durham: Duke University Press, 1997.

INDEX

Adorno, Theodor W., 15*n*16, 29, 44–46, 90
adultery: in *Cécile* , 163, 166; in
    Effi Briest, 22, 186, 190, 195, 195*n*,
    197; in *L'Adultera*, 196–97
Africa, vanishing mystery of, 7
The Age of Capital (Hobsbawm), 12
ahistorical societies, 12
Alexandria Quartet (Durrell), 210–11
Allen, James Smith, 57
Altick, Richard, 18
Americans, in *The Way We Live Now*,
    136–43
Amery, L. S., 155–56, 156*n*1
Anderson, Benedict, 4, 29–30, 32
Andreas-Salomé, Lou, 12
Anna Karenina (Tolstoy), 178*n*10
Annette et le criminel (Balzac), 52*n*
Anti-Dueling Association, 114
antiquarianism, 41, 45, 47. *See also* antiquities; collections; museums
The Antiquary (Scott), 41, 45, 160
antiquities, 32–34, 38–40, 160. *See also*
    antiquarianism; collections; museums
anti-Semitism, 131, 141
Asmundsson, Doris R., 103*n*
Atala (Chateaubriand), 162
Atlas of the European Novel 1800–1900
    (Moretti), 3, 5, 6, 71, 77, 90, 94, 111
Au Bonheur des Dames (Zola), 46*n*, 84

Auerbach, Erich, 15
Austen, Jane, 3, 5–6, 6*n*5, 32, 112
An Autobiography (Trollope), 93, 95*n*,
    101, 111, 124, 135
Avery, George C., 175*n*2, 190

Bachman, Maria K., 96
Bakhtin, Mikhail, 111
Bal, Mieke, 28
Baldensperger, Fernand, 67, 69
Balzac (Fernandez), 37*n*10
Balzac, Honoré de, 27–46, 47–64, 65–84;
    Buffon and, 11; cartography and, 32,
    69–70; collections in, 28–35; empiricism and, 18; interest in science of,
    46; on public transportation, 72;
    scientific progress and, 19. *See also*
    La Fille aux yeux d'or; *La Peau de
    chagrin*; *Le Père Goriot*; other specific works
Bang, Herman, 45*n*15
Bann, Stephen, 33
Barchester Towers (Trollope), 148
Bardèche, Maurice, 49
Barry Lyndon (Thackeray), 92, 92*n*4
Barthes, Roland, 16
Beckett, Samuel, 16, 16*n*17
Becquemont, Daniel, 139*n*
Bedarf Deutschland der Colonien?

233

(Fabri), 156
Bell, David F., 39, 64n, 71–72, 72n3
Benjamin, Walter, 111
Bennett, Tony, 31, 33
Berlin: in *Cécile*, 155–74; in *Effi Briest*, 181, 186–89, 191–92, 195–97, 199; in *L'Adultera*, 162; metamorphosis of museums in, 30, 33, 35; in *Vor dem Sturm*, 159, 160
Berlin Alexanderplatz (Döblin), 209
Berman, Nina, 157–58, 158n5, 177n
Berman, Russell, 15, 34n3, 156–57, 158n5, 177n, 179, 180n, 182, 187, 202
Bernd, Clifford Albrecht, 176n6
Berol, Laura M., 103n
Bersani, Leo, 39
Bhabha, Homi, 14n14, 20
Bildungsroman, 88, 90–91, 94–95, 106–7, 110
Bisztray, George, 44n
Bleak House (Dickens), 129
Bloomfield, Morton W., 105
Bock, Henning, 30
Boileau, 15
Bonard, Olivier, 66
Bonwit, Marianne, 178n10
borders: in *Phineas Finn*, 111–13, 128–29; in *Phineas Redux*, 117, 124; in *The Way We Live Now*, 151
Brantlinger, Patrick, 29
bricabracologie, 45
The Bride of Lammermoor (Scott), 121
Brieger, Christine, 172n16
British colonialism, 168, 168n13
British Family Antiquity: Containing the Baronetage of Ireland (Playfair), 12
British imperialism, 6, 168, 168n13
Brontë, Charlotte, 92, 97, 102
Brontë, Emily, 90
Brooks, Peter, 5n, 13, 37n9, 59
Brown, Bill, 17n20
Brown, Marshall, 15n16, 16, 17, 19
Brunschwig, Henri, 156n2
Buchanan, Alexandrina, 41
Buddenbrooks (Mann), 210
Buffon, Georges-Louis Leclerc de, 11

Bullock, A. L. C., 156n1
Burke, Edmund, 57
Byron, Lord, 80

Cabinet des antiques (Balzac), 45
Cailliet, Emile, 44n
Cain, James M., 207
Cairo Trilogy (Mahfouz), 211
Can You Forgive Her? (Trollope), 97, 114, 117, 135
Capital (Marx), 59
capitalism, 7n, 14
Carofiglio, Vito, 57
cartography: Balzac and, 32, 69–70; Fontane and, 180; impact on fiction of, 3–9. *See also* mapping; unmapping
Castle Richmond (Trollope), 95
Cazauran, Nicole, 39
Cécile (Fontane), 67, 155–74; adultery in, 163; Berlin and the foreign in, 166–72; colonialism in, 163–66, 166–74; disenchantment in, 167–71; dueling in, 168, 170; enchantment in, 156, 167, 170, 173; familiarity in, 155–74; foreigner-in-Europe motif in, 173–74; Friedrich on, 195n; globalization in, 22, 163; imperialism in, 156–58, 162; importance of world in, 162; lostness in, 166; magic in, 165; mystery in, 164; romance in, 163–66, 167, 171; scientific progress and, 19; shrinking of world in, 22, 158, 169, 173; supernatural in, 165, 173, 175; telegraphy in, 19, 166, 169–70, 171n
Cervantes, 14, 18
Chakrabarty, Dipesh, 13, 19, 30, 32, 182
Chambers, Helen Elizabeth, 164–65, 175n1, 186n14
Champfleury, 15n15
Chasles, Philarète, 36
Chateaubriand, François-René de, 162, 162n9
Chatterjee, Kaylan, 11n11
Chatterjee, Partha, 11, 11n10, 17
Cheyette, Bryan, 132n
Chinese ghost, 22–23, 132, 158, 160, 175–81, 182–88, 188–93, 202, 205, 208

Citron, Pierre, 36
city, global. *See* global city
Clifford, James, 28, 34*n*4
Cockshut, A. O. J., 151
Cohen, Derek, 131, 132*n*
Cohn, Bernard, 29, 46
collection-as-history, 33
collections: in *La Peau de chagrin*, 28–35, 36–41, 44–46, 160; in *Vor dem Sturm*, 160
Colley, Linda, 90
Collins, Philip, 146
Collins, Wilkie, 42, 46, 68, 96, 124, 148
colonial imagination, 187
colonialism: British, 168, 168*n*13; in *Cécile*, 163–66, 166–74; in *Effi Briest*, 53, 175–80; fiction and, 2–9, 10–14; in Fontane's early fiction, 157–62; German, 53, 155–57, 157–63, 163–66, 166–74, 175–80; in *La Fille aux yeux d'or*, 71; in *Le Père Goriot*, 48–53; Moretti on, 71; in *Phineas Finn*, 89–94, 94–101; Said on, 89, 89*n*, 156*n*; in *The Way We Live Now*, 53
colonial knowledge, 9–13. *See also* historiography
Comédie humaine (Balzac), 11, 67, 71
conflict, novelistic, 9, 28, 79–80, 212
conjuring, 142
Conrad, Joseph, 7, 45*n*14, 55, 207, 209
content, narrative, 6–7, 17–18, 17*n*19
Cook, James, 34*n*3, 157
Cooper, James Fenimore, 162, 167, 172*n*16
Cotsell, Michael, 145
The Country and the City (Williams), 134
The Country of the Pointed Firs (Jewett), 34*n*5
Cousin Phillis (Gaskell), 105*n*
Crane, Susan, 32
criminal underworld, 48–53
Curtis, L. Perry, Jr., 89
Cuvier, Georges, 33, 34*n*5, 41

Dällenbach, Lucien, 41

Daniel Deronda (Eliot), 95, 182*n*, 190
Dante, 81
Dargan, E. Preston, 37*n*10, 41
Das Amulett (Meyer), 46
Das Kolonialproblem Deutschlands (Johannsen and Kraft), 156*n*1
David Copperfield (Dickens), 92–93
Death in Venice (Mann), 210
Debreuille, Jean-Yves, 66
de Duras, Claire, 2
Defoe, Daniel, 1–2
de la Motte, Dean, 48, 57–58
demystification, 5, 13–14, 21
department stores, 46*n*, 84
Der blaurote Methusalem (May), 177
Der Raubgraf: Eine Geschichte aus dem Harzgau (Wolff), 166*n*
Der Stechlin (Fontane), 161, 172
desacralization, 5, 14
"Des Cannibales" (Montaigne), 1–2
Description de l'Égypte (Fourier), 32
A Description of Millenium Hall (Scott), 6*n*
detective novels, 59–60, 115, 124–26, 133, 150, 159, 213–14
Dialectic of Enlightenment (Horkheimer and Adorno), 29
Diamond, Marie Josephine, 67
Dickens, Charles, 45, 53, 72, 92, 129, 145, 150, 151*n*15, 172*n*16, 178
Die Harzreise (Heine), 164
Die Judenbuche (von Droste-Hülshoff), 160
Die schwarze Spinne (Gotthelf), 159–60
Die Wahlverwandschaften (Goethe), 160
difference, narrative, 9–13
Diocese of Killaloe (Murphy), 105
disenchantment: in *Cécile*, 167–71; in *Effi Briest*, 178, 181, 184, 186–87, 188–93, 193–203; in Fontane's early fiction, 159; *in La Fille aux yeux d'or*, 65, 67, 70*n*, 71–77, 78–84; in *La Peau de chagrin*, 29, 35, 36–45, 60–64; in *Le Père Goriot*, 48, 53, 58–60, 60–64; overview, 4, 7–9, 10*n*, 14, 19–22, 208–9; in *Phineas Finn* and *Phineas Redux*, 96, 108, 110–17, 120, 124, 128, 130; in *The Way We*

Live Now, 143, 145, 150. *See also Entzauberung*
disorder, zones of, 10
distance, narrative, 1–9, 209
Divine Comedy (Dante), 81
Döblin, Alfred, 209
Does Germany Need Colonies? (Fabri), 156
A Doll House (Ibsen), 178n10
Dombey and Son (Dickens), 129, 129n
domestic center, national, 3–5
domestic space, 23, 42, 167, 190, 192, 196, 199, 207
Don Quixote (Cervantes), 14, 18
Doody, Margaret Anne, 37n10
Dougherty, Elizabeth Jane, 88, 94, 96, 99, 111
Douglas, Roy, 90
"The Doum Tree of Wad Hamid" (Salih), 45n14
Downing, Eric, 14–15
Doyle, Arthur Conan, 7
Doyle, Roddy, 107
Dreiser, Theodore, 8
Drent, Janke, 83
du Camp, Maxime, 71
dueling: in *Cécile*, 168, 170; in *Effi Briest*, 163, 192–93; in *Phineas Finn*, 114–15, 122–23, 150; in *The Way We Live Now*, 139
The Duke's Children (Trollope), 72n4, 133, 135, 151
Duranty, Louis Edmond, 15n15
Durrell, Lawrence, 210–11
Du Sommerard, Alexandre, 33–34

Eagleton, Terry, 89–90
Eça de Queirós, José Maria, 46
Éducation sentimentale (Flaubert), 84
Edwards, Owen Dudley, 96, 103n
Edwards, P. D., 94, 148
Effi Briest (Fontane), 175–203; adultery in, 22, 186, 190, 195, 195n, 197; Berlin in, 186–89, 191–92, 195–97, 199; Chinese ghost in, 22–23, 132, 158, 160, 175–81, 182–88, 188–93, 202, 205, 208; colonialism in, 53, 175–80; critics on, 175–76, 202; disenchanting enchantment in, 193–203; disenchantment in, 178, 181, 184, 186–87, 188–93, 193–203; dueling in, 163, 192–93; empire in, 159; empiricism in, 179; enchantment in, 23, 176, 178–79, 181, 182–88, 191, 193–203; ethnicity in, 22, 175, 175n1, 180, 180n, 202; imaginative geography in, 175–203; imperialism in, 175, 176n6, 177n, 179, 182; lostness in, 166; magic in, 187–91, 192n; mystery in, 177, 187–90; otherness in, 181, 184; parrot image in, 199; reenchantment in, 187; romance in, 181, 187, 188–93, 195, 200; scientific progress and, 19; secularization and enchantment in, 182–88; sensory impact of nature in, 78; shrinking of world in, 198–99; supernatural in, 22, 42, 175–203
Eilert, Heide, 197
Ein Schritt vom Wege (Wichert), 196–97
El-Enany, Rasheed, 211
Eliot, George, 8, 95, 182n, 190
Ellernklipp (Fontane), 162n10
Ellison, David, 54
empire: in *Effi Briest*, 159, 179; empiricism and, 27–46; in *La Fille aux yeux d'or*, 65; in *La Peau de chagrin*, 27–46; in *Le Père Goriot*, 48–53; objects of, 29–36; orientalist paradox and, 29–36; remapping realism and, 1–23; subjects of, 48–53. *See also* imperialism
empirical science, 11
empiricism: in *Effi Briest*, 179; empire and, 27–46; in *La Fille aux yeux d'or*, 179; in *La Peau de chagrin*, 27–46, 179; overview, 14, 17–19, 205–6, 209; in *Phineas Redux*, 124–30, 132
enchantment: in *Cécile*, 156, 167, 170, 173; in *Effi Briest*, 23, 176, 178–79, 181, 182–88, 191, 193–203; in *La Fille aux yeux d'or*, 64–66, 70–78, 82–83; in *La Peau de chagrin*, 27–46; in *Le Père Goriot*, 53–54, 57–58; in *Phineas Finn* and *Phineas*

Redux, 104, 116–17, 124
Encyclopédie, 2
Engels, Friedrich, 71, 104, 104*n*
England's relations with Scotland, 181*n*
Enlightenment, 14, 29, 41, 192*n*
Entzauberung, 19, 29, 35, 55, 73, 78, 192*n*. *See also* disenchantment
epistemology: detective, 124–26; empirical, 28, 40, 46, 49; empirical, scientific, 79; of enumerative empiricism, 44; of imaginative mysticism, 44; materialist, 34*n*5; narrative, 45, 124, 132, 159; optical, 58, 67; overview, 12, 17; realist, 205–6; transhistorical, 29; urban, 129
espionage, 7, 54
Essais (Montaigne), 1–2
ethnicity: in *Effi Briest*, 22, 175, 175*n*1, 180, 180*n*, 202; in *Phineas Finn*, 89–94, 94–101
Eugénie Grandet (Balzac), 51
The Eustace Diamonds (Trollope), 105, 116, 117, 121, 124–28, 145
Evans, Christine Anne, 176*n*4, 190, 198

Fabri, Friedrich, 156
Famine, Irish, 90, 92, 103–5, 111
The Fantastic (Todorov), 37
"Father Giles of Ballymoy" (Trollope), 93
Faulkner, Karen, 112
Faulkner, William, 91
Faust (Goethe), 80
Fegan, Melissa, 103*n*, 104
Felber, Lynette, 95*n*
Felman, Shoshana, 67
Fernandez, Ramon, 37*n*10
feudalism, 8
Findlen, Paula, 35, 41
Fischler, Alexander, 57, 61
Fisk, Harvey, 137
Fisk, James, 137
Flaubert, Gustave, 45*n*14, 57, 84, 138*n*6, 150*n*13, 178*n*10, 180, 199
Fontane, Theodor, 155–74, 175–203; cartography and, 180; early fiction of, 157–62; on England's relations with Scotland, 181*n*; foreigner-in-Europe motif, 67, 70; importance of space in, 161; scientific progress and, 19. *See also Cécile*; *Effi Briest*; *other specific works*
foreigner-in-Europe motif: in *Cécile*, 173–74; Fontane, Theodor and, 67, 70; in *La Fille aux yeux d'or*, 205; in *La Peau de chagrin*, 205; Lukács, Georg on, 174; overview, 1–5, 8, 10, 16, 19, 205–6; in *Phineas Finn*, 205; in *Phineas Redux*, 205; Trollope, Anthony and, 67, 70; in *The Way We Live Now*, 67, 132–36. *See also* otherness
foreignness in modernist fiction, 209–14
form, narrative, 2–3, 6, 13, 17–18, 17*n*19
Forster, E. M., 210
Forster, Johann Reinhold, 157
Fortunata y Jacinta (Galdós), 135, 172*n*16
fossils, 34*n*5
Foster, Georg, 34*n*3
Foster, Roy, 89
Foucault, Michel, 34*n*5, 89
Fourier, Jean-Baptiste-Joseph, 32
France, Anatole, 209
Freud, Sigmund, 12
Freytag, Gustav, 171–72, 171*n*
Friedrich, Gerhard, 163, 173, 195*n*
Friedrichsmeyer, Sara, 157, 177, 177*n*, 178*n*9
Frøken Smillas fornemmelse for sne (Høeg), 212–13
Furst, Lilian R., 16*n*18

Galdós, Benito Pérez, 135, 172*n*16
Gärtner, Martine, 67
Gaskell, Elizabeth, 92, 97, 105
geography, 205; imaginative, 3, 27, 103, 129, 175–203; novels and, 3–9; political, 113
Geppert, Hans Vilmar, 160
The German Colonial Claim (Amery), 155–56
German colonialism, 53, 155–57, 157–63, 163–66, 166–74, 175–80

German imperialism. *See* German colonialism
German Literature in the Age of Imperialism (Lukács), 174
Germany's Claim to Colonies (Amery), 156n1
Germany's Colonial Problem (Johannsen and Kraft), 156n1
ghost, Chinese. *See* Chinese ghost
ghost stories, 197–98
Gide, André, 210
Gilmartin, Sophie, 134
Ginzburg, Carlo, 52–53, 63–64
Gissing, George, 145
Glauser, Alfred, 57
global city, 64, 129, 133, 143, 145–46, 145n, 212
globalization: in *Cécile*, 22, 163; in *Phineas Finn*, 99, 129; in *Phineas Redux*, 133; Ramponi on, 148n; in *Stopfkuchen*, 171n; in *The Way We Live Now*, 22, 135, 145–46, 173
Goethe, Johann Wolfgang von, 8, 32–33, 35, 80, 80n, 160
Gordon, Charles George, 167
Graffigny, Madame de, 2
Grawe, Christian, 148, 182
Great Expectations (Dickens), 53, 107, 129, 150, 159, 178
Grieve, Heide, 160
Guha, Ranajit, 12, 13, 17
Guichardet, Jeannine, 64n, 71
Guidry, Glenn A., 175n1
Gulliver's Travels (Swift), 9
Guthke, Karl S., 176n5

Haggard, H. Rider, 7, 207, 209
Halperin, John, 104
Hansen, Marcus L., 156n2
Hardy, Thomas, 190, 190n
harriedness, 135, 145–46, 149
Harte, Bret, 172n16
Harte, Liam, 90
Harvey, David, 72n3, 148
Hatch, Alfrederick Smith, 137
Haussmann, Georges-Eugène, 71
Hayens, Kenneth, 162n9

Heart of Darkness (Conrad), 45n14
Heidenreich, Bernd, 156
Heine, Heinrich, 164, 194
Hemingway, Ernest, 207
Hennedy, Hugh L., 103n
Hertz, Bertha Keveson, 132n
Hinsley, Curtis, 34n5
Hirsch, Marianne, 175n1
historical societies, 12
historiography, 12–14, 17–20, 30, 39, 41, 157n4
history: realism and, 10, 12–13; as source for deed, 18; as source for plot, 18
Hobsbawm, Eric, 12, 19n, 151
Hoefnagel, Dick, 91
Høeg, Peter, 161, 212–13
Hohendahl, Peter Uwe, 173
Holub, Robert, 15, 16, 19
home, vs. away, 4
The Home and the World (Tagore), 11n10
Hooper-Greenhill, Eilean, 31–32, 35
Horkheimer, Max, 29
Hornback, Bert E., 148
Howells, William Dean, 17n19
Hudson, George, 137n
Hugo, Victor, 81
Hynes, John, 106

Ibsen, Henrik, 178n10
imagination: colonial, 187; enchantment and, 82; fate of, 7–8; imperial, 143, 176, 184, 202; science vs., 35–36, 41; senses vs., 36–45; spiritual, 177
imaginative geography, 3, 27, 103, 129, 175–203
imperial centers, 10, 64
imperial imagination, 143, 176, 184, 202
imperialism: British, 6, 168, 168n13; in *Cécile*, 156–58, 162; in *Effi Briest*, 175, 176n6, 177n, 179, 182; in *La Fille aux yeux d'or*, 84; in *La Peau de chagrin*, 28–29, 43; in *Le Père Goriot*, 54; overview, 5–6, 11–12, 11n10, 206; in *Phineas Finn*, 89, 99, 101; in *The Way We Live Now*, 134
imperialism, German. *See* German colo-

nialism
Imperialism: The Highest Stage of Capitalism (Lenin), 7n
Imperialist Imagination (Friedrichsmeyer, Lennox, and Zantop), 157–62
imperial knowledge, 9–13
imported foreigners. *See* foreigner-in-Europe motif
Irishness, 89–94, 94–101
Irish Reform Bill, 101, 104
Irrungen, Wirrungen (Fontane), 150n12, 172, 181n
Ivanhoe (Scott), 117

Jakobson, Roman, 16
James, Harold, 142
James, Henry, 45–46
Jameson, Fredric, 8–10, 13–14, 186, 191, 208, 209–10
Jamison, Robert L., 190
Jane Eyre (Brontë), 9, 159, 178, 178n10
Jewett, Sarah Orne, 34n5
Jewishness, 131, 141
The Jews' Beech Tree (von Droste-Hülshoff), 160
Johannsen, G. Kurt, 156n1
Johnston, Conor, 103n
Josephs, Herbert, 192n
Jourda, Pierre, 67
Joyce, James, 15, 209

Kafka, Franz, 15
Kearney, Richard, 89
Kearns, Katherine, 15, 16n18, 17n19
The Kellys and the O'Kellys (Trollope), 95
Kemp, Martin, 41
Kincaid, James, 136
Kipling, Rudyard, 55, 178, 207
Knoepflmacher, U. C., 41n, 207n2
knowledge, imperial, 9–13
Kolonialliteratur, 158n6
Kong-Kheou, das Ehrenwort (May), 177
Kontje, Todd, 157, 158n5, 177n
Kraft, H. H., 156n1

Kroll, Frank-Lothar, 156
Kunstkammer, 30
Kureishi, Hanif, 212
Kwame, Ahyi, 156n2

La Comédie humaine (Balzac), 18
L'Adultera (Fontane), 22, 162–63, 195–97, 195n, 196–97
La Fille aux yeux d'or (Balzac), 65–84; alternating styles in, 66–67, 79; colonialism in, 71; crisis of knowledge and narrative in, 84; critics on, 66–67, 71, 78; disenchantment in, 65, 67, 70n, 71–77, 78–84; empire in, 65; empiricism in, 179; enchantment in, 64–66, 70–78, 82–83; foreigner-in-Europe motif in, 205; imperialism in, 84; *La Peau de chagrin* vs., 69, 82–83; *Le Père Goriot* vs., 49; lesbianism in, 83; London in, 69, 72; lostness in, 166; mystery in, 70–72, 76–77, 112; otherness in, 65–67, 69, 76, 78; overview, 65–66; Paris and disenchantment in, 78–84; Paris and enchantment in, 70–78; Paris in, 21, 65, 66–70; *Phineas Finn* vs., 107; realism and romance in, 65–84; reenchantment in, 65, 70, 75–76; romance in, 73, 75, 80, 82; sensory impact of nature in, 78; stylistic and thematic imbalance of, 66; supernatural in, 81; violence against the feminine in, 83; vision and disenchantment in, 78–84; *The Way We Live Now* vs., 147
La Muse du départment (Balzac), 33
L'Antiquaire, 33
La Peau de chagrin (Balzac), 27–46; collections in, 28–35, 36–41, 44–46, 160; crisis of knowledge and narrative in, 84; disenchantment and realism in, 36–45; disenchantment in, 29, 35, 60–64; empire in, 27–46; empiricism vs. enchantment in, 27–46, 179; enchantment in, 28, 30, 35–37, 39, 45–46; foreigner-in-Europe motif in, 205; imperialism in, 28–29, 43;

240 ~ Index

Le Père Goriot vs., 49–50; magic in, 42, 44, 44n, 49, 208; museums and, 28–35, 34n5, 40; mystery in, 42, 44; orientalist paradox in, 29–36; overview, 27–28; Paris in, 28–29, 33, 37, 42, 46, 48–49; *Phineas Finn* vs., 107; supernatural in, 43, 45; vision vs. knowledge in, 36–45; *Vor dem Sturm* vs., 160; *The Way We Live Now* vs., 151
La Recherche de l'Absolu (Balzac), 46
La Vendée (Trollope), 91n2
Leathers, Victor, 67
Leatherstocking Tales (Cooper), 167
Le Cabinet des antiques (Balzac), 46
Le Colonel Chabert (Balzac), 51
Le Cousin Pons (Balzac), 33, 46
L'Éducation sentimentale (Flaubert), 45n14, 57, 138n6, 150n13, 180
"L'effet de réel" (Barthes), 16
Lehan, Richard, 209
Lenin, Vladimir Ilyich, 7n
Lennox, Sara, 157, 173, 177
Le Père Goriot (Balzac), 47–64; colonialism in, 48–53; criminal underworld in, 53–60; crisis of knowledge and narrative in, 84; as detective novel, 59–60; disenchantment in, 48, 53, 58–60, 60–64; empire in, 48–53; enchantment in, 53–54, 57–58; imperialism in, 54; marginal realism in, 47–64; mystery in, 59; overview, 47–48; Paris in, 21, 47–55, 59, 61, 63–64, 63n; *Phineas Finn* vs., 107; romance in, 54, 56–67
Le Réalisme (Duranty), 15n15
lesbianism, 83
"Les Djinns" (Hugo), 81
Les Illusions perdues (Balzac), 46, 49, 60, 77
Leslie, Shane, 96
Les Mystères de Paris (Sue), 55
Les Tribulations d'un Chinois en Chine (Verne), 177–78
Lettres d'une Péruvienne (de Graffigny), 2
Lettres persanes (Montesquieu), 2
Levin, Harry, 40

Levine, George, 10, 15, 16, 45, 109, 182n, 207
Lévi-Strauss, Claude, 12n
L'Histoire des Treize (Balzac), 49, 65
L'Immoraliste (Gide), 210
Lindau, Paul, 172n16
L'Ingénu (Voltaire), 2
Linnaeus, Carolus, 11
literary realism, 88
Lodge, David, 92n5
Lolita (Nabokov), 15
London: in *La Fille aux yeux d'or*, 69, 72; Makdisi on, 35n7; in *Phineas Finn*, 88, 93, 107, 110–17, 117–24; in *Phineas Redux*, 117, 121–24, 129; in *The Way We Live Now*, 131–36, 137–40, 143–51
London, Jack, 207
Lonergan, Patrick, 88, 92, 96–98, 106
Longfellow, Henry Wadsworth, 162
The Lost World (Doyle), 7
Louis Lambert (Balzac), 36n, 46
Lounsbury, Coral, 126–27
Lukács, Georg: on Balzac and romanticism, 37n, 207; on birth of the novel, 5, 13; Bisztray on, 44n; on Fontane, 104, 104n; on foreigner-in-Europe motif, 174; on *The Home and the World*, 11n; on *La Fille aux yeux d'or*, 71; on *Le Père Goriot*, 59, 60; on modernism and realism, 15, 15n; on *Waverley*, 91

Macdermotts of Ballycloran (Trollope), 95, 103, 105, 107
Macherey, Pierre, 16
MacRaild, Donald M., 90
Madame Bovary (Flaubert), 178n10
magic: in *Cécile*, 165; in *Effi Briest*, 187–91, 192n; Jameson on, 8–10, 14; in *La Peau de chagrin*, 42, 44, 44n, 49, 208; otherness and, 8–10
Mahfouz, Naguib, 211
Makdisi, Saree, 35n7, 91, 160–61
The Making of the English Working Class (Thompson), 90
Manfred (Byron), 80

Mann, Thomas, 15, 210
Mansfield Park (Austen), 3, 5–6, 32
mapping: in *Phineas Finn* and *Phineas Redux*, 109–30; of the world, 3–9, 32, 180. *See also* remapping
Martin Chuzzlewit (Dickens), 129, 172*n*16
Marx, Karl, 59
Massol-Bedoin, Chantal, 77
Mathews-Kane, Bridget, 103*n*
Maturin, Charles, 132, 142
May, Karl, 158, 209
McClure, John, 7–10, 54, 66, 72*n*, 72*n*3, 129, 184, 185, 186–87, 198
McKeon, Michael, 13
McMaster, R. D., 139*n*
The Meaning of Contemporary Realism (Lukács), 15
Melmoth the Wanderer (Maturin), 132, 142
metropolitan center, 4, 70–71, 101, 206
Meyer, Conrad Ferdinand, 46
Michel, Arlette, 39*n*, 49
Middlemarch (Eliot), 8
Millais, John Everett, 91*n*3
Millott, H. H., 39*n*
Mimesis (Auerbach), 15
Miss Smilla's Feeling for Snow (Høeg), 212–13
Mitchell, W. J. T., 34*n*5
Mittenzwei, Ingrid, 186*n*15
Mitterand, Henri, 6, 20, 37–39, 44
modernism, 15
modernist fiction, foreignness in, 205–14
Modeste Mignon (Balzac), 51–52, 54–55
Molloy (Beckett), 16*n*17
Mommsen, Theodor, 155
monological realism, 16
Montaigne, Michel de, 1–2
Montesquieu, 2
The Moonstone (Collins), 42, 46, 68, 124–25, 127, 129
Moretti, Franco: on borders, 111–13; on colonialism, 71; on conservative narratives in English novels, 94–95; on Dickens and London, 147, 150; on *Effi Briest*, 195; on evil and mystery in English novels, 116; on France in 19th-century English novels, 90–91; on literary-historical development, 207*n*; on novelistic space, 3–8, 8*n*, 17, 20; on *Phineas Finn*, 106; Said on, 32; on space and style in *La Fille aux yeux d'or*, 77–78; on Victorian novels, 136
Morse, Samuel, 145*n*
Mortimer, Armine Kotine, 15*n*15
Mozet, Nicole, 64*n*, 71
Müller-Seidel, Walter, 175*n*2, 177*n*
Murphy, Andrew, 89, 94
Murphy, Ignatius, 105
museums, 28–35, 34*n*5, 40, 46, 46*n*. *See also* collections
"The Mutiny of the Mavericks" (Kipling), 55
"My Son the Fanatic" (Kureishi), 212
mystery: in *Cécile*, 164; disappearance of, 3, 7, 19, 35; in *Effi Briest*, 177, 187–90; imported foreigners and, 5; Jameson on, 10, 14, 208–9; in *La Fille aux yeux d'or*, 70–72, 76–77, 112; in *La Peau de chagrin*, 42, 44; in *Le Père Goriot*, 59; Moretti on, 116; in *Phineas Finn*, 114, 117, 128–29; in *Phineas Redux*, 115, 121–23; Trollope and, 109; in *The Way We Live Now*, 134, 139
The Mystery of Edwin Drood (Dickens), 151*n*15

Nabokov, Vladimir, 15
Nandy, Ashis, 11–12, 11*n*11, 17, 30, 129, 211
Napoleon, 32, 42, 48, 57–58, 90–91, 94, 140, 159, 162
Nardin, Jane, 103*n*
Nathan, Sabine, 136, 139*n*
national domestic center, 3–5
nationalism, master narrative of, 5. *See also* mapping
natural history, 31, 34–35, 34*n*5, 35*n*7, 41, 46
The Naturalisation of the Supernatural (Podmore), 11*n*10
naturalism, 44, 45*n*15, 206–7

Neal, Frank, 105
Nef, Ernst, 201
Noakes, Richard, 11n10
North America (Trollope), 137n
North and South (Gaskell), 92
nostalgia, 151
novelistic conflict, 9, 28, 79–80, 212
novelistic style, 4, 6, 17
Noyes, John K., 158, 158n5, 177n
Nykl, Alois Richard, 43

objects of empire, 29–36. *See also* antiquities; collections; museums
occult, 11n10
Odden, Karen, 138n7
O'Hara, Jim, 90
The Old Curiosity Shop (Dickens), 45
Oliver Twist (Dickens), 72, 147
opium, 151n15
order, zones of, 10
The Order of Things (Foucault), 34n5
Orientalism, 14, 27–30, 179
Orientalism (Said), 4, 11, 14, 27, 182, 207
orientalist paradox, 14, 27–29, 29–36, 44, 46, 184, 207
Orientzyklus (May), 158
Orlando, Francesco, 39n
Osinski, Jutta, 161n
otherness: Berman and Noyes on, 158n5; in *Effi Briest*, 181, 184; Holub and Berman on, 15; in *La Fille aux yeux d'or*, 65–67, 69, 76, 78; magic and, 8–10; in *Phineas Finn*, 89, 98, 112; in *Phineas Redux*, 117. *See also* foreigner-in-Europe motif
Ourika (de Duras), 2
Our Mutual Friend (Dickens), 145, 147

Palace of Desire (Mahfouz), 211
paranoia, 14
Paris: in *La Fille aux yeux d'or*, 21, 65, 66–70, 70–78, 78–84; in *La Peau de chagrin*, 28–29, 33, 37, 42, 46, 48–49, 52–55; in *Le Père Goriot*, 21,

47–55, 59, 61, 63–64, 63n
The Pathfinder (Cooper), 167
Payne, David, 14n13
Pecora, Vincent, 46
Perera, Suvendrini, 151n15
periodization, 205–6
Phineas Finn (Trollope), 87–108, 109–30; as *Bildungsroman*, 88, 90–91, 94–95, 106–7, 110; borders in, 111–13, 128–29; Canadian history in, 105–6; colonialism in, 89–94, 94–101; critics on, 96, 104; disenchantment in, 96, 108, 110–17; dueling in, 114–15, 122–23, 150; enchantment in, 104; ethnicity in, 88, 94; *The Eustace Diamonds* and, 105; Famine in, 90, 92, 103–5, 111; foreigner-in-Europe motif in, 205; globalization in, 99, 129; *Great Expectations* vs., 107; historical detail in, 101–8; imperialism in, 89, 99, 101; importance of space in, 114–24; Irishness as realist fact, 89–94; Irishness as realist problem, 94–101; *La Fille aux yeux d'or* vs., 107; *La Peau de chagrin* vs., 107; *Le Père Goriot* vs., 107; London in, 88, 93, 107, 110–17, 117–24; mapping and unmapping, 109–30; mystery in, 114, 117, 128–29; otherness in, 89, 98, 112; overview, 87–88, 109–10; reenchantment in, 110, 117–24, 130; remapping in, 103, 113; romance in, 87–88, 93–99, 101, 103, 106, 110, 128–29, 132; shrinking of world in, 87, 94, 99
Phineas Redux (Trollope), 109–30; borders in, 117, 124; as detective novel, 115–17, 124–26; disenchantment in, 108, 110–17, 120, 124, 128, 130; empiricism in, 124–30, 132; enchantment in, 116–17, 124; *The Eustace Diamonds* and, 116, 117, 121, 124–28; foreigner-in-Europe motif in, 205; globalization in, 133; importance of space in, 114–24; London in, 117, 121–24, 129; mapping and unmapping, 109–30; *The Moonstone* and, 124–25, 127, 129; mystery

in, 115, 121–23; otherness in, 117; overview, 109–10; reenchantment in, 110, 117–24, 130; romance in, 113–23; transformation of English currency in, 133; *The Way We Live Now* and, 133
physical space, 4
Pick, Franz, 32
Pimentel-Anduiza, Luz-Aurora, 64*n*
Playfair, William, 12
plot, history as source for, 18
Podmore, Frank, 11*n*10
Pold, Søren, 64*n*
Polhemus, Robert M., 111, 125
political geography, 113
Pomian, Krzysztof, 30–31
Poncin-Bar, Geneviève, 55
Prendergast, Christopher, 71, 81–82
The Prime Minister (Trollope), 102, 113–14
progress, and fate of 13-20
Proust, Marcel, 36, 41
Provincializing Europe (Chakrabarty), 30, 182
psychoanalysis, 12
public transportation, 72
Pugh, Anthony, 62

Quitt (Fontane), 162n9, 172*n*16

Raabe, Wilhelm, 171-72
race. *See* ethnicity
Radcliffe, Stanley, 157*n*3, 169, 182, 202
radical realism, 27
railways, 144–45; in *Cécile*, 163–65, 168, 170; in *La Fille aux yeux d'or*, 72
Rainer, Ulrike, 176*n*5, 190
Ramponi, Patrick, 148
rationalization, 10
realism: disenchantment and, in *La Peau de chagrin*, 36–45; limits of, 205–14; literary, 88; marginal, in *Le Père Goriot*, 47–64; monological, 16; overview, 10, 14–15; radical, 27; remapping, 1–23; romance and, reconsidered, 205–9; romance in

La Fille aux yeux d'or and, 65–84; secularism and, 13
realisms of content, 17
realisms of form, 17
realistic *détaillisme*, 18
reenchantment: in *Effi Briest*, 187; in *La Fille aux yeux d'or*, 65, 70, 75–76, 78; overview, 14, 14*n*, 206; in *Phineas Finn*, 110, 117–24, 130; in *Phineas Redux*, 110, 117–24, 130; in *The Way We Live Now*, 143
Reflections on the Revolution in France (Burke), 57
Reichelt, Gregor, 175*n*1
Reid, James H., 54, 64*n*
religion, master narrative of, 5
A Relíquia (Eça de Queirós), 46
remapping: in *L'Adultera*, 196; of narrative space, 3, 9; in *Phineas Finn*, 103, 113; of realism, 1–23. *See also* mapping
René (Chateaubriand), 162, 162n9
Renoux, Charles Caius, 33
Reuter, Hans-Heinrich, 202
Revolutionaries, 57
Robb, Graham, 72
Robbins, Bruce, 53, 146, 150, 183–84
Robinson Crusoe (Defoe), 1–2, 5
Roch, Herbert, 168*n*13
Rollins, Yvonne, 178*n*10
romance: in *Cécile* , 167, 171; disappearance in fiction of, 7–10; in *Effi Briest*, 181, 187, 195; in *Effi Briest*, 200; in *La Fille aux yeux d'or*, 73, 75, 80, 82; in *La Vendée*, 91*n*2; in *Le Père Goriot*, 54, 56–67; in *Phineas Finn*, 87–88, 93–99, 101, 103, 106, 110, 128–29, 132; in *Phineas Redux*, 113–23; realism and, reconsidered, 205–9; in *The Way We Live Now*, 137–38, 140, 142
Ronaï, P., 52*n*
A Room with a View (Forster), 210
Rushdie, Salman, 212
Ryan, Judith, 158–59, 176*n*4, 177*n*, 178

Sadleir, John, 137

Sadleir, Michael, 106, 134
Said, Edward W.: *Effi Briest* and, 175–76; on empire and space, 65; on German colonialism, 156*n*; on historiography, 14, 17; imaginative geography and, 179–80, 180*n*; imperialist conceptions of space and, 177*n*; on imperialist organization of space, 22; Irish colonialism and, 89, 89*n*; on narrative space, 3–7, 9; on Orientalist mindset, 158; orientalist paradox and, 14, 27–29, 29–30, 32, 35, 37, 44, 46, 184, 207; on science and imperialism, 11; on secular criticism, 182–84
Sainte-Beuve, Charles Augustin, 36
Saisselin, Remy G., 46*n*
Salih, Tayeb, 45*n*14
Sassen, Saskia, 64, 145–46
Savage, Catherine, 57
Schach von Wuthenow (Fontane), 162
Schuster, Ingrid, 175*n*2, 185, 190
Schuster, Peter-Klaus, 200
scientific progress, 13–20
Scotland, England's relations with, 181*n*
Scott, Sarah, 6*n*
Scott, Sir Walter, 33, 41, 45, 90–91, 99, 112, 117–19, 121, 160
secular criticism, 182–84
secularism, 13, 30, 184, 206
secularization, 5*n*, 7–8, 15, 29, 74, 81, 176, 182–88
Seller, Christine, 178*n*10
semi-historical cultures, 12
senses vs. imagination, *La Peau de chagrin*, 36–45
shamanism, 30
Shears, Lambert, 160
Shirley (Brontë), 92
Shklovsky, Viktor, 6
shrinking of world: in *Cécile*, 22, 158, 169, 173; in *Effi Briest*, 198–99; in *Phineas Finn*, 87, 94, 99; in *The Way We Live Now*, 18, 22, 135, 138*n*7, 146, 150
Sidney, Philip, 15
Sittig, Claudius, 158, 158*n*6, 176*n*6, 178*n*9

Smilla's Sense of Snow (Høeg), 212–13
Smith, Pamela H., 41
Smith, Zadie, 212
social spaces, 4
Soelberg, Nils, 67
Sozialroman, 201
space: domestic, 23, 42, 167, 190, 192, 196, 199, 207; novelistic, 2–4, 6–7, 9, 13, 17, 21–23, 65; physical, 4
spaces, hierarchy of, 4
spiritual domain, 11
spiritual imagination, 177
spiritualism, 198
Spivak, Gayatri Chakravorty, 178–79
Splendeurs et misères des courtisanes (Balzac), 33
Sprenger, Scott, 36*n*
A Star Called Henry (Doyle), 107
Stephan, Inge, 173
A Step Off the Path (Wichert), 196–97
Stern, J. P., 175, 178*n*10, 182, 202
Stopfkuchen (Raabe), 171–72
Before the Storm (Fontane), 45
Stounbjerg, Per, 213
Structural Anthropology (Lévi-Strauss), 12*n*
Studies in European Realism (Lukács), 207
style, novelistic, 4, 6, 17
Subiotto, Frances M., 175*n*2, 198
Suck, Titus S., 57
Sue, Eugène, 55
Super, R. H., 137
supernatural: in *Cécile*, 165, 173, 175; in *Effi Briest*, 22, 42, 175–203; in *La Fille aux yeux d'or*, 81; in *La Peau de chagrin*, 43, 45
Sutherland, John A., 139, 148
Swales, Erica, 175*n*2
Swift, Jonathan, 9

Tagore, Rabindranath, 11*n*10
Taine, Hippolyte Adolphe, 14, 37*n*10, 45*n*15
A Tale of Two Cities (Dickens), 129
Tallis, Raymond, 16*n*17, 206
Tanner, Tony, 146, 148

Taylor, A. J. P., 156n1, 156n2
Tebben, Karin, 195n
telegraphy: in *Cécile*, 19, 166, 169–70, 171n; in *The Way We Live Now*, 145–46, 145n
tension, epistemological, 10
tension, narrative, 6
Tess of the D'Urbervilles (Hardy), 190, 190n
Thackeray, William Makepeace, 68, 92–94, 97
Theory of Prose (Shklovsky), 6
Thérèse Raquin (Zola), 45n15
Thompson, E. P., 90
thresholds, 111
Tod in Venedig (Mann), 210
Todorov, Tzvetan, 37–38, 43–44
Toelken, E. H., 33
Tolstoy, Leo, 178n10
totems, 34n5
Tracy, Robert, 103n, 104, 132, 148
Trollope, Anthony, 87–108, 109–30, 131–51; challenges to form and, 18; foreigner-in-Europe motif in, 67, 70; scientific progress and, 19. See also *Phineas Finn*; *Phineas Redux*; *The Way We Live Now*; other specific works
Trumpener, Katie, 160

Ulysses (Joyce), 209
the uncharted, 11
Un cœur simple (Flaubert), 199
Under the Pear Tree (Fontane), 159
underworld, criminal, 53–60
unhistorical cultures, 12
United Irishmen's Rebellion of 1798, 89–91
unmapping: in *La Fille aux yeux d'or*, 70–78, 78–79; of narrative space, 3, 9, 66, 77; in *Phineas Finn* and *Phineas Redux*, 109–30
Unterm Birnbaum (Fontane), 159
Utz, Peter, 176n6, 177n, 178

Van, Annette, 137n, 141

Vanity Fair (Thackeray), 68, 92
Vanoncini, André, 49
Verne, Jules, 177–78
Vigny, Alfred de, 71
Villette (Brontë), 92, 102
violence against the feminine, 83
vision: in *La Fille aux yeux d'or*, 78–84; in *La Peau de chagrin*, 36–45
Voltaire, 2
Vom Hofe, Gerhard, 161n
von Droste-Hülshoff, Annette, 160
von Hofmannsthal, Hugo, 49
von Humboldt, Wilhelm, 8, 30, 35, 44
Vor dem Sturm (Fontane), 45, 156–57, 159–63, 180
The Voyage Out (Woolf), 7, 209

Wall, Stephen, 133
Wallraf, Ferdinand Franz, 32
Warning, Rainer, 64n, 70n, 178n10
Watson, Janell, 39n
Watt, Ian, 13, 18
Waverley (Scott), 118–19, 160–61
The Way of the World (Moretti), 90, 94
The Way We Live Now (Trollope), 131–51; Americans in, 136–43; challenges to form of, 18; colonialism in, 53; commerce in, 132–36; crime in, 132–36, 137–38; critics on, 131–32, 134, 137; disenchantment in, 143, 145, 150; dueling in, 139; foreigner-in-Europe motif in, 67, 132–36; globalization in, 22, 135, 145–46, 173; harriedness in, 135, 145–46, 149; imperialism in, 134; *La Fille aux yeux d'or* vs., 147; *La Peau de chagrin* vs., 151; *Le Père Goriot* vs., 52, 139; London in, 131–36, 137–40, 143–51; mystery in, 134, 139; nonlinearity of structure, 148; overview, 131–32; *Phineas Redux* and, 133; romance in, 137–38, 140, 142; scientific progress and, 19; shrinking of world in, 18, 22, 135, 138n7, 146, 150; telegraphy in, 145–46, 145n
Weber, Max, 19, 35, 39n
Weber, Samuel, 39

Wellek, René, 207
White, Richard, 137
White Teeth (Smith), 212
Wichert, Ernst, 196
Widman, Joseph Viktor, 176n6
Williams, Raymond, 134
witchcraft, 142
Wittig, E. W., 96–97, 103n
Wolff, Julius, 166n
Woloch, Alex, 62n

Woolf, Virginia, 7, 15, 209
Wordsworth, William, 35n7, 207
Wuthering Heights (Brontë), 90

Youngman, Paul, 164–65

Zantop, Susanne, 157–58, 158n5, 173, 177, 177n, 194
Zola, Émile, 45n15, 46n, 84

www.ingramcontent.com/pod-product-compliance
Lightning Source LLC
Chambersburg PA
CBHW021838220426
43663CB00005B/300